Optimistic Parenting

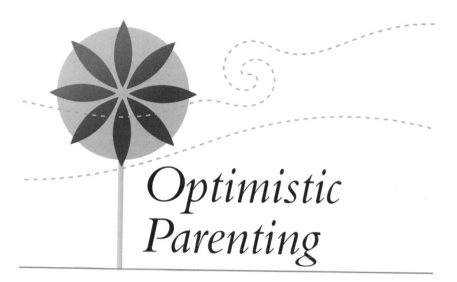

Optimistic Parenting

Hope and Help for You and Your Challenging Child

by

V. Mark Durand, Ph.D.
University of South Florida St. Petersburg

·P A U L·H·
BROOKES
PUBLISHING CO.®

Baltimore • London • Sydney

Paul H. Brookes Publishing Co.
Post Office Box 10624
Baltimore, Maryland 21285-0624
USA

www.brookespublishing.com

Typeset by Spearhead Global, Inc., Bear, Delaware.
Manufactured in the United States of America by
Versa Press, Inc., East Peoria, Illinois.

Library of Congress Cataloging-in-Publication Data

Durand, Vincent Mark.
   Optimistic parenting : hope and help for you and your challenging child / by V. Mark Durand.
     p.   cm.
   Includes bibliographical references and index.
   ISBN-13: 978-1-59857-052-6 (pbk.)
   ISBN-10: 1-59857-052-8 (pbk.)
    1. Behavior disorders in children—Treatment.   2. Problem children—Behavior modification.
  3. Parenting.   I. Title.
  RJ506.B44D895 2011
  618.92'89—dc22
                                      2011001802

British Library Cataloguing in Publication data are available from the British Library.

2015   2014   2013   2012   2011

10   9   8   7   6   5   4   3   2   1

Contents

About the Author

V. Mark Durand, Ph.D., is known worldwide as an authority in the area of autism spectrum disorders. He is a professor of psychology at the University of South Florida St. Petersburg, where he was the founding Dean of Arts & Sciences and Vice Chancellor for Academic Affairs. Dr. Durand is a fellow of the American Psychological Association. He has received more than $4 million in federal funding since the beginning of his career to study the nature, assessment, and treatment of behavior problems in children with autism spectrum disorders. Before moving to Florida, he served in a variety of leadership positions at the University at Albany–State University of New York (SUNY–Albany), including Associate Director for Clinical Training for the doctoral psychology program from 1987 to 1990, Chair of the Psychology Department from 1995 to 1998, and Interim Dean of Arts and Sciences from 2001 to 2002. There he established the Center for Autism and Related Disabilities at SUNY–Albany. He received his B.A., M.A., and Ph.D. degrees—all in psychology—at Stony Brook University.

Dr. Durand was awarded the University Award for Excellence in Teaching at SUNY–Albany in 1991 and in 2007 received the Chancellor's Award for Excellence in Research and Creative Scholarship at the University of South Florida St. Petersburg. Dr. Durand is currently Co-editor of the *Journal of Positive Behavior Interventions*, is a member of the Professional Advisory Board for the Autism Society of America, and is on the Board of Directors of the international Association of Positive Behavioral Support. He serves on a number of editorial boards, has reviewed for dozens of journals, and has more than 100 publications on functional communication, educational programming, and behavior therapy. His books include several best-selling textbooks on abnormal psychology, *Severe Behavior Problems: A Functional Communication Training Approach* (Guilford Press, 1990), *Sleep Better! A Guide to Improving Sleep for Children with Special Needs* (Paul H. Brookes Publishing Co., 1998), and *When Children Don't Sleep Well: Interventions for Pediatric Sleep Disorders, Therapist Guide* (Oxford University Press, 2008). In his leisure time, he enjoys long-distance running and just completed his third marathon.

Preface

This book chronicles a lifetime of experience aimed at helping people with special needs. For more than 3 decades I have been interested in why these individuals behave in ways that can be devastating to them and those around them. At the same time, I have tried to use what has been learned about behaviors such as self-injury, aggression, tantrums, and other challenging behaviors to develop and evaluate strategies to improve their lives. Within these pages are many of the lessons I have learned from working with countless children, youth, and adults with many different diagnoses, along with their families and other professionals. In particular, I describe a unique approach for aiding families in not only helping their children but also helping themselves as well. This is important—the book is as much about helping parents with their own personal struggles as it is about how to help their children. One cannot be a truly successful parent without coming to terms with one's own challenges. Although this book is intended for parents or other caregivers, I believe that those who work with these families will also benefit from what my colleagues and I learned through our research.

I designed the book to be a true self-help guide, one that provides enough examples and specific steps for many families to read through these pages and find good, solid strategies for their child and for themselves. The goal is of course to help reduce the problem behaviors families face each day with their challenging child. At the same time, my colleagues and I found through our work that we can help caregivers improve their own lives. The strategies that I outline can lead to better insight into one's own thoughts and behaviors. Many of the parents who completed our program found that they felt better about themselves as a result and that their lives improved independent of their child's improvements. In other words, many were happier in the truest sense of this word.

When writing a book that includes so many personal stories such as this one, you obviously change the names and the identifying information so as not to subject the families to any potential embarrassment. The family members who participated in our projects over the years shared a tremendous amount of personal information about themselves and their loved ones to further their efforts to help their children. I am deeply indebted to them for their trust, candor, and faith in our ability to help them. In a previous book on helping parents with their child's sleep problems, I wrote about the travails of the families in our sleep studies. I also described my own son's many difficulties with sleep and the challenges my wife and I had in common with these families until we were able to settle on a strategy that continues to help our son.

In this book, I carry on the style of including some of my own stories because many readers have told me this helps to personalize the sometimes technical sections. My family is intricately woven throughout the book, but I've disguised us enough to avoid embarrassing my wife and son any more than I already do! I decided to share stories about my own childhood and my parents but have not clearly identified situations involving my own child-rearing challenges with my son. In case there is any doubt, we are not a perfect family and I am not a perfect father. I could very clearly relate to many of the difficulties facing the families in our studies, and this motivated me to find answers to help them with their urgent needs.

The audience for this book is a broad one because my colleagues and I have evidence from so many families and so many different types of children. The families who participated in our studies are quite diverse and come from all walks of life. We found that regardless of financial circumstances, many families still need the advice found in this book. The approaches to changing difficult child behavior are similar whether you have a child with significant cognitive and social problems (e.g., autism) or a child who can do well in school but continues to be distracted or oppositional at home. I include many masked examples from these courageous families to help illustrate their struggles and successes.

Throughout the decades, I have been fortunate to learn from and work with many remarkable people. These collaborations provided the foundation for the rich experiences I have enjoyed with so many different families who have children with difficult clinical diagnoses. Perhaps the first major influences on my view of behavior were Sue and Dan O'Leary, both professors of psychology at Stony Brook University, where I received all of my academic degrees. Sue O'Leary in particular introduced me both to children with behavioral challenges (through her pioneering work at the Point of Woods School for children with attention-deficit/hyperactivity disorder, or ADHD) and to a scientific view of these types of problems. Later I was privileged to work with Ray Romanczyk (Professor of Psychology at Binghamton University), where I worked with children in his learning disorders clinic and in his program for students with autism spectrum disorders (ASDs). A long and winding road eventually brought me back to Stony Brook University to do my dissertation research with the late Ted Carr. Ted was my mentor and later a friend. We had a 25-year collaboration that resulted in important approaches for people with severe behavioral challenges (including the development of a new treatment for behavior problems—functional communication training). My internship under the guidance of Dennis Dubey at the Sagamore Children's Psychiatric Center greatly expanded my experience with different types of children and adolescents and their varied diagnoses (e.g., schizophrenia spectrum disorders, bipolar disorder, conduct disorder, anxiety and mood disorders). My social conscience during my early career was Luanna Meyer (Professor of Education [Research] at Victoria University of Wellington), and her influence on my work continues today. Through her help, I conducted research in inner-city neighborhoods with children having dual sensory impairments (deaf-blind), and this strengthened my view that anyone can make meaningful changes in their lives. I would be remiss if I did not also mention my long-term collaboration with Dave Barlow (Professor of Psychology, Boston University). Dave is an internationally known researcher in the area of anxiety disorders. Although our research areas have yet to overlap, our work together on abnormal psychology textbooks over the last 20 years has had a profound influence on how I view children and families.

I have also been lucky to have many outstanding doctoral students who have worked with me on a range of research projects related to the work described in this book, including Jodi Mindell, Susan Sprich Buckminster, Denise Berotti, Cindy Alterson, Arleen Lanci, Kristin Christodulu, Christie Tanner, Adam Haim, Eileen Merges, and Carolyn Kessler. All have gone on to important careers of their own. Finally, many colleagues have contributed to the success of the federally funded Positive Family Intervention Project, which created the data on which Optimistic Parenting is based. This 5-year research project was conducted in both Florida (through the University of South Florida St. Petersburg) and New York (through the University at Albany—State University of New York) and could not have been completed without the dedicated efforts of Meme Hieneman. Meme was the project coordinator, served as the clinical director, and co-authored the protocols for this new approach. I am deeply indebted to her for all of her hard work and insights. The therapists who worked with the families are talented professionals, and I would like to thank the groups from New York (Kristin Knapp-Ines, Suzanne Milnes, and Melissa Rinaldi) and Florida (Shelley Clarke, Laura Casper, Bobbie Vaughn, Kim Crosland) for their many hours of work. The following research assistants collected and analyzed countless hours of data and visited families' homes to assess their progress, and I am in their debt: Clarisse Barbier, Brandy Benson, Brian Constantine, Renee Elosge, Viviana Gonzales, Salima Lakhani, Robin Lane, Angie Lascano, Jessica Morgan, Josh Nadeau, Sarah Pigott, Jacqueline Thompson, Claudia Villari, Lindsay Washington, and Katie Wrolson. The Advisory Board members for our project (Lise Fox, Connie Hayden-McPeak, Cindy Bania, Flora Howie, Millie Pou, and Rich Labelle) were extremely supportive throughout the years and I thank them as well.

The staff at Paul H. Brookes Publishing Co. were extremely supportive of this effort. Rebecca Lazo's encouragement and extraordinary patience were essential for producing this book. In addition, the editorial support from Johanna Cantler, Nicole Schmidl, and Steve Plocher made this a much better book. Finally, I thank my research support specialist Marly Sadou at the University of South Florida St. Petersburg for her help and quiet professionalism. I could not have completed this project without her.

To Wendy, the love of my life

Introduction

Parenting a child with special needs can be a joy. Parents love to tell us the everyday humorous stories that are unique to raising a child with extreme challenges—for example, the time their son inexplicably laughed directly in the face of the pediatrician, which started the doctor and the nurse laughing uncontrollably, or the time their child helped a stranger with directions, providing seemingly endless exact and intricate turn by turn instructions for a far away destination. Of course, there are also the stories that were not funny at the time—for example, how their daughter "fixed" the DVD player with peanut butter or how their apparently runaway child was found sitting on the floor of a closet after frantic hours searching the neighborhood. Unfortunately, the challenges faced by parents, especially when their child is very disruptive, can also lead to significantly decreased life satisfaction. Marriages are threatened and parents talk of feeling trapped. The obstacles to living a satisfying life are often overwhelming for many families raising a child with behavior problems. Yet, being unhappy is not inevitable, even if you have a very challenging child.

Within the pages of this book I make a radical claim—how you approach the challenges posed by your child can give you a new sense of what is important and lead to a happier and more satisfying life. Yes, in fact, the very child who tests your patience on a daily basis, who makes you question your ability as a parent and who may be the source of many sleepless nights could be the secret to a better, more fulfilling life. In turn, a happier you—along with some "tricks of the trade"—can lead to improvements in your child's behavior.

I recently spoke with one mother about her son and his intractable ways. Michael always had to sit in the same chair, eat with the same fork, and drink from the same cup. His food preferences were also very limited and he refused to try anything new or different. If his mealtime routine was interrupted in any way, he would scream and yell and hit himself. As we discussed ways to handle these outbursts, Michael's mother reflected, "I know this sounds odd, but we're pretty lucky. Michael doesn't get sick like he used to, and his teacher this year is great." Here was a woman who juggles home and work; has three children, including one with autism; and who rarely has a meal without a major meltdown by her child. And she feels lucky. How could someone who faces so many challenges feel fortunate and be happy?

Researchers are learning more and more about the keys to living a fulfilling life. Behavioral and brain researchers are discovering fascinating interconnections between what people do and with whom they interact each day and how this can affect the brain—and, in turn, satisfaction with life. As you have probably discovered, having a bigger car or a more impressive house does not automatically lead to happiness. Instead, incorporating concepts such as optimism and appreciating the small things in life can have a profound influence in how people feel about themselves and others. As you will see as you read through the book, many of these ideas are not new. All of the great religions of the world, for example, incorporate these concepts in their practices, and this partly accounts for why people who describe themselves as religious also tend to be happier. The difference is that now researchers are getting a clearer picture about which specific things—for example, "counting your blessings"—really do make people happier.

GOALS

The goal of this book is to provide both help and hope to you and other families like yours. I introduce you to several exciting new techniques from the burgeoning field of positive psychology that are designed to help you not only improve your child's behavior but also to help you become happier and more hopeful.

Help is necessary for families to deal with the day-to-day challenges of raising a child with special needs. Fortunately, now there are techniques with strong scientific backing that are known to produce meaningful change in the behavior of challenging children. This book gives you a helpful guide to understanding your child's behaviors and practical and effective suggestions for how to reduce those that are problems. The majority of the research that I (and my colleagues around the world) have conducted has been with children having some of the most severe problems and with families most profoundly affected by their child's difficulties. Lest you think, "This won't work for my child or for me," you can feel comfortable knowing that there is good evidence that it will.

Unfortunately, help is not enough. Many families just can't seem to address their child's challenging behaviors by using these valuable tools. When discussing this obstacle, I like to use the comparison with people who are trying to lose weight. Obesity is one of the major factors leading to significant health problems among adults and increasingly among children. But losing weight is simple, isn't it? Just eat fewer calories and exercise (eat less and move more) and you will lose weight. All of the research over the past several decades on weight loss comes down to those two simple steps, and it works—if you can do it! However, many people can't do this. Why? The reason is that it is not enough for many people just to know what to do, whether it is about dieting or parenting. Thoughts and emotions get in the way of the rational brain. Yes, I know I shouldn't eat chocolate cake at midnight, but when I'm anxious or depressed, I feel better eating that delicious dessert—at least for a while. I'll feel guilty tomorrow, but right now I opt for the relief.

The same pattern affects your ability to be a better parent. You know you shouldn't let your child have the candy bar to stop her tantrum in the supermarket, but if you give in she'll stop crying. Your spouse knows that your son's teeth need to be brushed each night, but skipping one night won't be that bad and it will be a quieter night, won't it? To be a better parent you need to know what to do and you need the strength to be able to do it. Confidence without knowledge or knowledge without confidence—neither is enough to be a successful parent. This book is one of the first to combine the best techniques for addressing children's challenging behavior with new research that shows how to summon up the strength and confidence to do it.

TRIED AND TRUE TECHNIQUES

This book is based on the science of happiness and the science of positive child behavioral techniques. It is not about what I think will increase your happiness or improve your child's behavior. There are plenty of books, magazine articles, television shows, and web sites that can give you interesting and far more entertaining perspectives on how to handle personal adversity. What I have written about in the pages of this book are techniques that researchers have shown can work with real families facing real challenges. Think about it. Most people would be very nervous if someone recommended taking a drug or trying surgery that had not been fully tested. What if it doesn't work—or, worse, what if there are bad side effects? Yet, many of these same people try things with their child because they sound good, even though there is no research to back up their effectiveness and safety. I respect your time too much to waste it. Here I describe only those approaches that have been shown to work. Don't worry. I will not be describing the research in great (read *boring*) detail. My goal with this book is to make decades of effective practice accessible to every parent.

ORGANIZATION OF THIS BOOK

The next chapter—in the "Hope" section of the book—introduces you to the concept of Optimistic Parenting—what I am calling this exciting new approach to help parents deal with challenging children in a way that enriches their own lives. Evidence-based work from the burgeoning field of positive psychology is combined with the latest work in behavioral interventions to help families become happier and more hopeful. The next chapters introduce parents to the techniques professionals use with the Optimistic Parenting approach. These techniques help parents become more confident and happier in their parenting role—thus providing the hope for good outcomes for them and their child. These easy-to-use steps will aid parents to become more satisfied with their own lives and will serve as the foundation they need to make them better able to take on the challenges required for dealing with child behavior problems. I describe research from the rapidly increasing scientific field that studies the concept of subjective well-being, providing tested methods that parents can use when working with their child. Just as important, these approaches can also serve as life lessons that can help make their lives more fulfilling overall.

The second section of the book—"Help"—includes several chapters designed to introduce families to the fields of behavioral analysis and positive behavior support. My focus is on how to understand why children misbehave— an essential first step before one starts planning an approach to reducing these behaviors. The next chapters then cover common motivations for behavior problems, how to strategize about changing the child's world, and how you respond to difficulties. All of these steps—including both hope and help—have been successfully tested in an important long-term study. In this study, my colleagues and I found that teaching parents to be more optimistic about their child and their own abilities led to much better results with their children's behavior problems.[1]

There are, however, some situations that can be particularly challenging for families and that may require additional attention. The last section of the book— "Special Topics"—takes all of what I discuss in the previous chapters and applies them to special problems posed by some children's challenging behaviors. These special concerns include problems around transitions (e.g., trying to get your child to the dinner table or onto the school bus) and problems involving sleep. Each chapter provides step-by-step techniques for analyzing the problems and easy-to-follow approaches for improving a family's ability to deal with these circumstances. Cases from families facing these challenges help bring to life the approaches that are useful for overcoming them.

Again, throughout these chapters I incorporate the concepts learned in the previous "Hope" section. When beginning to understand behavior problems, for example, I also help you examine what you are thinking and feeling when you experience your child misbehaving. Then, as I introduce suggestions for helping your child, I provide guidance for how to modify your own thoughts and feelings in order to reduce obstacles and enhance the parenting experience. Research by my colleagues and I suggests that this addition to behavioral plans increases the likelihood that you will successfully help your child develop more productive habits and lead a more independent life. And, again, along the way it is likely that if you follow the advice in the book, you will feel better about yourself as well.

I encourage you to read through the whole book. It may be tempting to skip to the "Help" section to get ideas about new techniques to use with your child. Let me warn you that this would be like trying only part of a new diet plan. You may find, for example, that a few tips are helpful in getting your child to sleep better or to get on the school bus in the morning. However, the goal is obtaining meaningful and lasting changes in you and your child—because, inevitably, there will be setbacks. For instance, my colleagues and I often find that we have successfully helped children to sleep better, only for them to once again have their sleep disrupted by major changes in routines (e.g., vacations). The key to real success is knowing how to regroup and get the children back on a good course of sleep. Sometimes parents get so frustrated by these stumbling blocks that they abandon a potentially successful approach ("See, it didn't work") and miss opportunities to be successful again. This is true not just for sleep but for all child problems. The "Hope" section is designed in part to get you through these rough patches. It provides tools for you to be able to dust yourself off and try one more time. Again, researchers are finding that this makes parents feel better about themselves overall and leads to improved quality of life for the whole family.

If you are like me and tend to be impatient, review each of the chapters. But then promise yourself that you will take the time to go through each one carefully, because this is about you. It is about doing something for you that will benefit your child as well. This is not selfish. This is necessary.

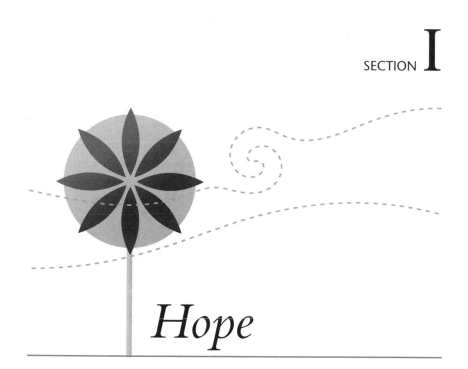

Hope

Hope is the thing with feathers
That perches in the soul.

—Emily Dickinson
"Hope Is the Thing with Feathers"

CHAPTER 1

Optimistic Parenting

Your toddler is screaming in the supermarket, and everyone is staring at you. A quick stop at the drugstore now seems like a major chore because your daughter is whining to go home. It's after midnight, and your son shows no sign of being ready for bed. Your youngest child just ran out into the street but miraculously was not hurt. Once again, your 3-year old is refusing to eat anything but potato chips.

These scenes are repeated in hundreds of thousands of homes each day. But not to worry! There certainly is no shortage of people stepping forward to give you advice. The cashier at the supermarket suggests that maybe you shouldn't give your child candy because the sugar could be making him so difficult. The doctor on the car radio claims that children who watch too much television will have delayed social development. Your mother suggests that you should exercise with your son before bedtime so that he will be tired and fall asleep. A neighbor sees your child dashing across the street and tells your husband that you really should keep a closer eye on him. Your pediatrician expresses concern about your daughter's diet of potato chips, but her only advice is to give your daughter more choices. It is unfortunate to note that these scenes are played out each day for families from all walks of life.

On the one hand, minute by minute you are faced with a difficult child. On the other hand, you receive abundant but sometimes conflicting advice. To make matters worse, you often defeat yourself. You occasionally feel that things will never change and you will never have your own life. You see so many parents who seem to handle their child's problems so much better than you do. You feel responsible for your child's difficulties, and sometimes this guilt and the rest of life's stress make you give in to your child's tantrums when you know you shouldn't. When faced with it all, it feels overwhelming and beyond the ability of even the strongest and most loving parent.

But there is good news. A growing group of behavioral scientists, including myself and my colleagues, are uncovering the reasons behind child behavior problems. More and more, we are able to get inside the minds of children with behavior problems and figure out just what they are trying to tell us. And, we are taking advantage of these new insights by developing innovative approaches to helping parents with their children who have behavior problems. These innovations emphasize the positive. Punishment is avoided; instead, the goal is to teach skills to children that help them navigate an often unforgiving world. These new discoveries are bright lights in what has been a rather dim outlook for many children. Significant improvements in the behaviors of thousands of children are realized each day because of this scientific approach to a perennial problem.

Despite these advances, however, these approaches have not been successful with all families. A great many parents are not ready to implement the suggestions for making their children behave better. For a variety of reasons, some families have a difficult time working with their children in ways that are helpful. Since the early 2000s, the struggles of these families motivated us to turn our attention to these parents. In our research on child behavior problems, we started to ask a new question: "How can we help parents who want to be more successful with their difficult children but just can't?" In addition to developing strategies that could help their children, could we assist these families with the close-to-impossible task of parenting a difficult child?

THE GOOD NEWS

Throughout the pages of this book, I describe an exciting new approach that not only will help your child but also will help you feel more confident in your child-rearing ability. What I am calling Optimistic Parenting is actually a collection of tips and techniques that are successful even with families who have extremely difficult children. In this chapter, I outline the lessons we in the field of behavioral science have learned from extensive research with the families of children who have very severe behavior problems. The following chapters will help you achieve the success we have seen with hundreds of these families.

At the same time as I am suggesting that you can achieve success with your child, I am also setting my sights much higher. In this book, I'm making a revolutionary claim: What we in the field have learned in our research cannot only help you with your child's struggles but also can get *you* on the way to a happier and more fulfilling life. I am convinced that you can use the experiences presented by your challenging child to find meaning and purpose in your *own* life. Rather than feeling trapped or constantly at wits' end due to the endless battles you face, the lessons learned from your child can help you become happier. As I explain throughout this book, behavioral scientists are discovering the keys to what they call "subjective well-being," or the feeling of a satisfying life. And, central to being happier and more content with your life are concepts such as finding a purpose, being hopeful and grateful, and enjoying the good things that happen to you. Our research shows that how you approach your challenging child can actually be turned on its head and can lead to improved life satisfaction rather than depression, anxiety, or frustration.

Because you are reading this book, I assume that part of the life circumstance affecting your happiness is your child. I have spent decades working with children, some of whom had life-threatening challenging behavior. I have been privileged to work with some amazing parents, all of whom were devoted to their children. Each of these parents had one major assumption: "If my child's behavior improves, that will make me happy." And, for many years, I believed this too. If I could help them help their child, the improvements in their child's life would result in increased happiness for the family. What better goal could there be?

Three decades of research on child behavior problems, however—including work on understanding why children misbehave and the development of treatments to improve behavior—has lead me to the opposite conclusion. Improved child behavior does not always make families happier. As you will see, the absence of stress, anxiety, or depression does not equal happiness and life satisfaction. This is worth repeating. There are people who are highly stressed yet feel good about themselves and their lives. And, there are people who manage to relieve themselves of things that make them upset only to find that they are not automatically happier. Trying to change difficult child behavior is much more complicated if families are struggling themselves. What we are learning is that confidence and optimism—having hope—are prerequisites to successful parenting. In a sense, what I am saying is that *improving child behavior may not make you happier, but being happier may help you improve your child's behavior.*

Why are there so many people who are not happy? Today, rates of anxiety and depression are at levels that could be described as epidemic. People spend billions of dollars each year on medications in an attempt to handle life's stresses. Is it life circumstances, or is it something else? The more we learn about happiness and fulfillment, the more we understand that some people are born different than others—with a level of optimism that makes them resilient to most of life's slings and arrows. Other individuals, however, have a much more difficult time handling the challenges they face. A combination of genetics and life circumstances dictates how each person confronts life's inevitable obstacles. However, even people who are prone to difficulties such as anxiety and depression can be helped. In this book, I walk you through some ways to see what will work best for you.

BEING HAPPY

What does it mean to take care of yourself? Does it mean an hour a night of alone time? Time during the day with friends? Building in exercise time during the week? This will obviously change with each person. What makes one person feel better may increase stress in another. However, what I am talking about here is more than a brief change of pace each week. Instead, I am suggesting that to be a good parent you must be happy. A happy parent? Isn't that an oxymoron? No. Not only is it important that you are happy as a parent and as a person, it is essential.

I can hear you now. "Oh great. He's suggesting that I should walk around saying I don't care that my child just started screaming in line at the grocery store. Or smile as my child's school threatens to throw him out of the program I worked so hard to get him into. This sounds like a bunch of New Age nonsense to me!" You're right. Being unrealistically positive—wearing "rose colored glasses"—is not what I mean by being happy. Instead, being truly happy means being content. Being genuinely happy is feeling good about yourself as a person and as a parent and feeling that your life has meaning. It means that after confronting a personal obstacle, you are able to find that personal reserve of emotional energy to move on. This type of happiness—called *subjective well-being*—is obtainable; in addition, it can result in improvements in health and can make you a better parent.

ONE FAMILY'S LESSONS

Before I describe this very exciting new advance in our work, the story of one family provides a good perspective on where professionals in the field of behavioral science have been successful and where we have failed families up until now. My first professional experience more than a quarter of a century ago emphasizes just how disruptive a child's behavior problems can be for families.

In the late 1970s, I was a young psychology graduate student fresh out of college and armed mainly with the best of intentions. My first day in the graduate program included an important assignment working in a clinic for children with severe developmental disabilities. Today, many of these children would be diagnosed as having autism or a related disorder. My first case assignment was a young boy named Timmy, whom I was told was a handful. Little did I know that being described as a "handful" was a euphemistic way of saying he was the most challenging child in the clinic. To this day, I can remember almost everything about my first glimpse of him.

Timmy was sitting at a plain table in a small, unadorned room that had only a door and a one-way mirror. I was watching him from behind the mirror under the guidance of my supervisor, who—I think—was talking about Timmy. To be honest, I wasn't really sure what he was saying because I could not hear a word of it. Instead, I was fixated on the scene unfolding before me. As my supervisor's words were going in one ear and out of the other, Timmy was in a chair slapping his face and biting the back of his hand. Throughout this time, he was crying and screaming, and once he tried to bite his foot through his shoe. Occasionally, the woman who was working with him would lean over and say something to him, and he would respond by attacking her. He scratched her face and slapped her and was desperately trying to get away from her. She was clearly upset and seemed embarrassed but did not let his attacks stop her. Only later did I find out that the haggard-looking woman sitting across from Timmy was his mother. I had never seen anything like this in my life.

Later that morning I was sitting in my supervisor's office. He continued talking, but I was still lost in thought. Finally, I interrupted him by blurting out, "Why would he do that?" He was caught off guard by my question. "What?" "Why would he do that?" I said. "Why would he hurt himself like that, and why would he attack his mother?" I just could not get my head around what I had witnessed back in that room. It was like having passed a car accident and trying to make sense of the carnage. My supervisor sat back in his chair and waited a bit before answering. This was clearly a question he had faced before, and he was reading my face to study my reactions. "We don't ask why," he finally said. An unusual thing for a psychologist to say, I thought. Wasn't that what psychologists did? "For many years, people have theorized about why these kids hit themselves and why they hurt other people. And, unfortunately, some of these theories have done more harm than good. None of them have led to treatments that we can use to help them stop this self-injury and aggression. Here in this clinic, we don't ask why. Instead, we ask how many times the behavior occurs. Then, we try some treatment; and if the child improves, we continue that technique. If the child stays the same or gets worse, we try something else." I nodded and took notes, but his answer was quite unsatisfying. In fact, it was just these types of questions that would fuel 3 decades of my later research on these challenging behaviors.

Months after my first observations of Timmy and his mother, Ruth, and following several of my failed attempts to improve his behavior, I paid a visit to Timmy's home. Ruth suggested I stop by to discuss the latest plans for his behavior problems. These new plans were designed to be implemented at home, and I now suspect she wanted to give me a reality check. Through the clinic's parent-training program, we had designed a home-teaching plan for Timmy that would focus on improving his language skills—he could say only two or three words—as well as attempt to reduce his very serious behavior problems. The new plan required that his mother begin working with him as soon as he arrived home from school and continue until bedtime. Autism professionals believed at the time that if we were to make any meaningful progress with children such as Timmy, teaching had to occur during almost every waking moment. Every interaction was to be a teachable moment. During the initial presentation of the plan in my office, Ruth looked quite uncomfortable but said very little. Her silence was odd because she was a veteran of these plans—a now 7-year-old Timmy had been at the clinic for several years—and she was so experienced that we often asked her to help the other parents who came with their children to the clinic. But it was a more animated and upbeat Ruth who greeted me at the front door of her home.

As I was welcomed into the rather modest living room, my initial impression was that this was a very family-oriented home. Signs of children and smells of cooking dominated, and it was clearly a very comfortable place to be. Nothing fancy here—there was worn carpeting on the floors and old blinds on the windows—just a place where one family experienced its joys and sorrows. Looking around the room, the first thing that caught my eye was a picnic table. In the middle of the almost empty room was a well-worn wooden table with benches on each side. Ruth noticed my curiosity but said nothing. I later learned that Timmy destroyed furniture at home, something we didn't see at the clinic, so the dinner table as well as the rest of the family's furnishings had to be "Timmy proof."

Timmy's mother led me into the kitchen to sit and to meet her other children. There at a small dinette table were her two little girls trying to do their homework. Timmy was there too, interrupting his sisters by constantly grabbing papers and shredding them. The girls looked at me almost apologetically, as if it was their fault he wasn't behaving. After we exchanged hellos, I looked around and noticed that the kitchen cabinets had combination locks that were crudely attached to the well-worn cupboards. The back door also was locked in this way. This time Ruth offered that Timmy would sneak food and eat until he became sick if the cabinets were unlocked. In addition, he would sometimes leave the house alone at night and roam the neighborhood, which is why the doors were locked from the inside. Family routines were carefully choreographed to avoid having Timmy get into trouble or hurt himself. In a physical sense, the whole family was trapped in the house, and I was slowly learning that they were also trapped emotionally by Timmy's seemingly unending needs.

We went back into the living room with Timmy (to keep him away from the girls) and sat at the picnic table while Ruth described a typical day in his life. As we spoke, it became clear that Ruth, now a single parent, spent almost every moment of her life dealing with Timmy and his disruptive behaviors. While he was home, he could never be left alone; and while he was in our program during the day, his mother attended meetings with other professionals about his schooling and treatment and also volunteered to help other parents who had children like Timmy. As a result of these constant demands on her time, Ruth had little of herself left over for her other two children and felt extremely guilty about that. In fact, it seemed that she felt guilty almost constantly. It was becoming clear that she felt responsible for Timmy's many problems, despite the fact that she was the one person saving him from seriously harming himself or others. She felt guilty about the break-up of her marriage and thought it was mostly her fault that now the children did not have a live-in father. In one revealing comment, she told me that she secretly longed for a different life and felt guilty about that too. My plan for Timmy's behaviors—a plan that would be almost impossible for Ruth to carry out given the realities of her life—added just one more layer of guilt.

I would like to be able to say that I fully appreciated her situation and helped her deal not only with Timmy but also with the multitude of feelings and emotions that were causing her such pain. I would like to say that, but I can't. I believe I was sympathetic at the time. I encouraged her to talk more with other parents with the hope that she could gain strength and perspective from families going through the same experiences. I was well-meaning, but I lacked any real insight into her difficulties. I didn't recognize that her feelings of guilt and inadequacy, combined with a resignation about Timmy's future, were major obstacles to her ability to help her son and lead a happier life herself. These feelings were not going to go away just by talking to other parents. Like many of my fellow clinicians at the time, I was so focused on my behavior plans and getting families to carry them out that I missed signs that should have been as obvious as Las Vegas billboards. Ruth needed fairly intensive help herself, but I had nothing to offer her.

Behavioral consultants are people too, and we sometimes don't listen closely enough to important people in a child's life, such as family members, teachers, and others. Chalk it up to arrogance ("Yeah, yeah—I figured they would say that!"), ignorance, or even our own insecurity (never show weakness!), but consultants sometimes miss essential information. One of the interesting findings from our research is that there is a common dynamic between families struggling with a difficult child and the professionals with whom they interact. These families are confronted daily with people and institutions that make demands on them. When these demands appear too difficult and seem out of reach, sometimes families push back. This push back can take the form of saying things such as "Oh, that won't work with my child" or "I've already tried that." Later chapters explore these interactions more fully, but this type of response can push away professionals who are well-meaning but may not fully understand why parents are being so "uncooperative."

A program is not effective if people will not or cannot do it. This book is all about what we learned by really listening to families in crisis. Unfortunately, it wasn't until years later that I began to appreciate Timmy's mother and her situation. At the time, I was so focused on getting her to continue our program at home that I didn't realize how unrealistic this was. The time and effort to carry out these plans would have been difficult for anyone, let alone a single mom with two other children. Her resistance and lack of "compliance" with my requests was a constant source of frustration for me. "If only she would run the program each night," I told a colleague, "I'm sure Timmy would be making much better progress." It was easy to blame our failure with Timmy in the clinic on his mother's lack of follow-up at home.

Timmy's mom taught me that parents cannot hope to be effective if they are unsure about their abilities as parents or are pessimistic about their child's ability to change. Feelings of guilt, inadequacy, anger, and so forth will get in the way of being an effective parent. Just telling parents not to feel that way does not help. Parents need to help themselves before professionals can ask them to help their children.

It is unfortunate that Timmy's story doesn't end there. Fast-forward some 15 years later to the early 1990s. I was walking down the hall of a residential facility that was home to more than 80 adults with significant disabilities. It was staffed by people who seemed to care about the folks living there, although the techniques they used to teach skills and react to behavior problems had not evolved substantially from the approaches we had used years before. As our group walked by one particular room, I had a déjà vu experience. It was triggered by a clicking sound that was as familiar to me as if I had heard it every day for more than a decade. A rush of memories swept over me, both good and bad. Without looking into the room, I turned to the person conducting the tour and said, "Wow, that's Timmy! I would recognize his 'clicking' anywhere." She smiled and said, "We call him Tim now." Tim was at this point almost 23 years old and much bigger than me. His mom had reluctantly placed him in a series of facilities once he became too big and aggressive for her to handle anymore. Tim now required two rather large men to be with him most of the day. They protected the other residents from his frequent violent outbursts and interrupted him when he tried to hit himself. It was devastating to realize that everything we did for Tim years earlier had no visible impact on him. It broke my heart to see his still beautiful (although now more mature) face, still unable to reveal what thoughts lay behind those mischievous eyes. After all of these years, his ability to communicate with us remained limited (only using the few words we had taught him at age 7), and clearly our behavior plans had not prevented him from becoming dangerous to himself and to others. What might have been the outcome for Tim and his family if we knew then what we know now?

BACKGROUND

The story of Timmy and his mother provides a backdrop for what behavioral scientists have learned about severe child behaviors since the 1970s. When I worked with Timmy and many other children like him, treatment was usually a series of trial and error experiments. Fortunately, there was some information to help guide us. We knew that children could be encouraged to learn if they were rewarded and could, at least temporarily, stop acting up if they were punished. So we pushed ahead with these two simple but important ideas, trying an almost infinite number of variations until something succeeded. In Timmy's case, I taught his teachers how to provide him with pieces of food and praise if he got close to imitating what they said—for example, "Timmy, look at me. Say, 'apple.'" Timmy learned to say several words that helped him get some basic needs met (e.g., "drink," "no"), but his progress was very slow and ultimately extremely limited.

The biggest reason for our slow progress with Timmy's education was how he behaved. His way of acting up was very destructive, both to himself and to those around him. Obviously, it is very difficult to teach someone who is hitting you, so reducing Timmy's self-destructive and aggressive behavior was our top priority. We first tried to encourage him to do things that would prevent him from hitting. We would praise him if he sat nicely at his desk. He was given treats if he worked on a task even for a very short period of time without becoming too disruptive. The reasoning here was that if we could increase the amount of time Timmy was well behaved, then we would decrease the amount of time he acted out. Unfortunately, although there were days when he would behave better, there also were still days when he would lash out quite violently. After many months of effort, it was time to take a different approach.

What we did next may shock you. Remember, this was in the 1970s when the options for children such as Timmy were quite limited. Few schools would take responsibility for a child with his severe behavior problems, and our clinic was the only one in that region of the state that would even attempt to teach him the skills he needed to succeed in life. If his family had lived even a little further away from our program, he would not be able to attend and would have been kept at home all day with only limited support from professionals. So, we met with his mother Ruth and discussed our options. Should we just give up (not really an option any of us considered)? Should we try other types of rewards for Timmy, despite having exhausted all of the options we could think of? Or, should we try some form of punishment with the understanding that other children were reported to have improved with this approach?

Using punishment was not considered lightly. No one wanted to use punishment with Timmy. In fact, the teachers and staff felt a great deal of affection for Timmy despite his aggression toward us. At times he could be most endearing, with a smile that would melt your heart. If he was comfortable, he would back into you (never looking at your face or making eye contact), cock his head to one side, smile, and make his clicking sound. In fact, if he did this to you it was considered quite an honor because he was very selective. Everyone who worked at the clinic would check on Timmy's daily progress, and they invested a great deal of emotional energy in the hopes that he would make significant gains.

I remember back to that time having very vivid dreams about Timmy. In one recurring dream, he could talk and carry on sophisticated conversations. We would sit next to each other in his classroom, and he would be looking at me as we spoke to each other. A common theme in this dream was talking with him about his behavior, and I recall asking him why he would hit himself and why he would hit me. What I can't remember is what he said in response to my questioning. Did he tell me something then that I should have used to help him? I vaguely remember him responding to these types of questions by just looking at me with an enigmatic smile. Certainly there was a part of me that yearned to know what he thought and felt and how he saw the world around him. The tragic part of the dream always came after I woke up and remembered the talking Timmy. It was heartrending to gradually wake up and remember that Timmy couldn't talk, that he couldn't have carried on that discussion with me, and yet that locked inside of that beautiful boy may have been the key to help him let us know his secrets.

So, with much hesitancy and trepidation, wondering whether we would be doing more harm than good, we all agreed to try some form of punishment to respond to Timmy's outbursts. Timmy's mother gave us her permission to design a new plan that included both rewards for good behavior as well as a punishment should Timmy hit us or himself. As we discussed the options, it was decided that it had to be a single event—something that wasn't done in anger and that could be delivered by each of his teachers in the same way. It also had to be something that didn't cause Timmy any lasting harm. A traditional spank with the palm of the hand was suggested, but in the end it was agreed that each time he hit someone or hit or bit himself, a supervisor would hit him on the behind with a ruler. His mother would try it first in the clinic and then would instruct us on how to do it—how to hold him, how hard to swing the ruler, and so forth. Why a ruler? One rationale was that children in the past were disciplined by teachers with a ruler and, therefore, our use of the ruler could be justified based on this cultural practice. Some of the staff thought that the symbolism provided by the ruler was a weak justification for using it with Timmy, but clearly the options for Timmy at that time were quite limited.

Looking back to that time more than 3 decades ago, I can see that we meant well but were just grasping at straws. We wanted something, anything, that would get Timmy to be less disruptive. Our logic was first to get him to behave better and only then to try teaching him to better communicate with others. It was only some time later that we would learn that we had it exactly backward; we needed to teach him to let us know what he wanted as a way of making him better behaved.

So, we put our plan in place. A trial period was selected, and Timmy's mother taught us how to use the ruler. This was not something she did at home, and, in fact, I don't think she ever physically punished Timmy before this plan.

However, we prevailed upon her to take the lead because we felt more comfortable having her instruct us to be sure the punishment was carried out with all of the sensitivity it deserved. When my turn came, I sat in the same room that I had observed Timmy and his mother in all of those months ago and watched as Ruth went through some of his typical tasks. Not surprisingly, he started to become upset and hit her. Ruth proceeded to stand up and say a loud "No hitting!" Then we stood him up, turned him around, and Ruth talked me through the ruler spank. We were all quite tense, and I knew others were watching this unfold through the one-way mirror in the next room. When I hit him with the ruler, it broke in half. Timmy didn't respond, perhaps because the act of breaking softened the blow, but I was horrified. What had I done? Did I hurt him? Ruth's reaction to this was characteristic. She began to apologize to me as if it was her fault. I could hear muffled voices in the next room and knew everyone saw this. It was mortifying to me to think I was capable of doing such a thing. Was this what I wanted to do with my life—hit children with rulers?

We ended that session and soon thereafter terminated the plan because of a lack of progress. The program that included the ruler spank seemed to have a minimal impact on Timmy's behavior. Unfortunately (or perhaps fortunately), it had a significant impact on me. I was ashamed to be part of this type of plan; and somewhere inside of me, I became determined to find out why children such as Timmy behave the way they do and to design plans that were both effective and humane. In many ways, Timmy and his mother taught me most of what I needed to know about behavior problems and how to treat them. Some of the lessons were obvious at the time. Others took years to sink in.

KNOWING WHY IS IMPORTANT

Timmy's behavior problems defied easy explanation. Timmy challenged my best efforts at the time, and I struggled to understand why he continued to behave in such strange ways. I realized then that if I were to help other children like him, I needed to learn why they did these things. Over the years, my research and the research of a number of my very talented colleagues has opened our eyes as to why children may become disruptive.

Soon after working at the clinic where I first met Timmy and Ruth, I worked in an institution for people with severe intellectual disabilities (previously called *mental retardation*). I soon was put in charge of a unit that cared for about 30 youth who had severe behavior problems like Timmy. Some were very aggressive to the point of being dangerous, others hurt themselves, and many of them showed a number of other unusual behaviors. For example, one young 17-year-old man had spent most of his childhood living almost as a feral child. His parents were unable to control him, so he wandered in the woods around his home most of the time and sometimes even slept outside. He came to us never having learned basic skills such as how to use a toilet or how to use utensils for eating. However, the biggest challenge was his habit of eating things off of the ground (a problem technically referred to as pica, from the Latin word for *magpie,* a bird that scavenges for food and will eat almost anything). His indiscriminate eating probably originated during his wanderings in the woods but was now so entrenched in his being that we feared for his health. He would eat discarded cigarette butts and also hoarded things in his underwear, presumably so that he could keep them secret and eat them later.

The extent of this problem entered the realm of legend one day as we were leading a tour of people through the residence. I was showing inspectors around to make sure the environment was safe and respectful of the rights and privacy of the individuals who lived there. As we walked into the room of the young man who ate everything, someone asked to see his clothes closet. Because some of the other residents would sometimes "borrow" clothes from others, we had locked wooden doors on the closets to keep their possessions safe. As I opened the door, it fell off its hinges in my hand. This surprised the visitors and me because the closets were relatively new and built to withstand a great deal of abuse. A closer inspection revealed that our resident had been picking at and eating the veneer on the closet door; over time, he had consumed enough to literally eat the door off of its hinges. A hospital visit showed that he appeared to suffer no ill effects, and this part of the institution's history became an often-told story. I am pleased to say that months of training with this young man significantly improved his behavior, and he learned many new skills that helped him live more independently.

As with Timmy, however, many of the other residents acted in ways that defied our best efforts. One 16-year-old named David did not speak but was generally well behaved. He always had a very sincere look on his face—an expression that would conjure up images of a reflective soul that for some reason just could not or would not reveal itself to us. He was usually amiable and fun to work with, except after dinner. Like clockwork, upon his arrival back at the residence after the evening meal, he would fall to the floor and start screaming and would repeatedly bite his hand and hit himself. These were very disturbing episodes that prompted endless discussions among the staff and clinical professionals about their origins. Perhaps he was allergic to some food he had at dinner? Was he constipated? Was there something about the night staff that upset him? Was he having seizures triggered by the florescent lights in the hallway? Everyone had their favorite theory.

Shortly after I arrived to work on this unit, I decided to attempt to unravel the secret behind David's outbursts. I followed him to dinner and back to the unit over the course of several nights, trying to see if there were any patterns that would reveal themselves. Each night, he ate different foods and the staff interacted with him well. I monitored his bowel movements (something the staff did regularly for all of the residents) and compared this with his food intake. After consulting with our physician, it appeared that his digestion was just fine. Of course, because we could not "get inside" of his head, we could never be sure that he was not experiencing some physical discomfort; however, all evidence seemed to argue against this. On the third night, David did something different. On the other nights, he would walk into the residence and immediately sit down on the floor and start his tantrum. He had a very unique way of sliding down on the floor and folding his legs behind him, a position that made restraining him complicated and potentially dangerous. However, this night he walked in and moved toward the staff office. As usual, the door was closed and locked, although there was a large Plexiglas panel so that staff could see out and the residents could see in. Once he got to the door, David fell to the floor and commenced screaming. This was a subtle change but one that caused me to wonder: Was there something in the office that triggered these episodes?

Driving home that night, I remembered a conversation I had with the overnight staff. They told me that sometimes David would awaken in the middle of the night. Asked how they handled this, they told me that he just did not seem tired on these nights, so they let him join them in the staff office. He would hang out with them for awhile until he seemed sleepy, and then they would lead him back to bed. The overnight staff at the residence were difficult to supervise, and we sometimes had discipline problems. In fact, the week before, I had to reprimand one staff member for bringing his portable television to work with him. In one of those "aha" moments, it hit me. Was David spending some nights with the staff watching television, and was that what he wanted when he came into the residence each evening? Was this what he was trying to tell us?

The next night we tried an experiment. As we approached the door to the residence and before we went inside, I told the staff to ask David if he wanted to watch television. To say they were skeptical of his ability to understand this would be a massive understatement, but to their credit, they did it. As soon as they said "television," his head came up. They immediately led him to the television room in the back of the residence, turned on the set, and let him sit in front of it. He was mesmerized, and miraculously there was no tantrum! We repeated this sequence over the next several nights, each time ending with the same results. David would eagerly follow the staff and plant himself in front of the television after dinner, and his nightly disruptions disappeared. Eventually, we bought him his own television, which he could operate himself. David's life of simple routines changed dramatically that night—the result of our ability to look at him and his seemingly irrational behavior in this new light. Could it really be that David's nightly tantrums were simply a way of telling us what he wanted?

Watching David walk into his residence each night and indicate that he wanted his television was the definition of happiness for me. Here, in a small way, I was able to positively affect his life and make him happier. I felt that at this brief moment in time we were able to understand him just a little bit, and this glimpse into his inner world gave us the clues we needed to help him—without having to spank him with a ruler! David and his television took on mythic proportions at work, and staff from other residences quickly learned of our success. The staff members at the residence were quite proud of what we accomplished and felt empowered to look more closely at the behavior of the other residents living there. David and his success injected a healthy dose of hope in all of us. Maybe it was possible to help all of the residents as we had helped David! We all were, for a time, happier. It felt good to come to work and to feel as if we made a difference. Although I didn't realize it then, this was to become an important part of what we could offer parents. Being aware of successes and being grateful for them are genuine keys for happiness and fulfillment. And being hopeful helps people persist, even when the future looks darkest.

David's story illustrates another important lesson when it comes to dealing with challenging behaviors. I believed that David had abilities he wasn't showing us. I believed that he could understand us if we asked about the television, or at least he could learn to understand us. I believed he was capable of changing how he behaved each night as he entered the residence. The staff, conversely, who had far more experience with David than I did and who were involved in the hundreds of daily interactions with him over the course of each day, thought he understood very little. He had no speech, although he would grunt in response to some of the things they said to him, and he did not respond in meaningful ways to their instructions to him (e.g., "Brush your teeth, David," "Time to get out of bed"). This was just David—just the way he was. His nightly tantrum was a fact of David's life that was troublesome but that was seemingly inevitable. Although the staff wanted to end these disruptions, conversations about the tantrums were primarily about how they should respond to them (e.g., "Should we put a mat in the entrance so that when he falls to the floor he doesn't get hurt?") and less about what could be done to prevent them from occurring. Lowered expectations are self-fulfilling; asking little gets little in return. Alternatively, expect more, and more will be returned. For David, these lowered expectations were transmitted from staff members to each new staff member until they became his reality. One of the keys to Optimistic Parenting is the belief that a child can change—something called child efficacy. This is fundamental. Unless you believe your child has it within him- or herself to improve his or her behavior, you will ultimately fail in your efforts.

Please be forewarned; expecting too much can sometimes lead to disappointment and can be as detrimental as expecting too little. Some of our parents who describe themselves as perfectionists expect a great deal from their children. For example, a 5-year-old soccer player wanders around the field generally enjoying herself but not being the aggressive go-getter her parents had envisioned. The parents scream from the sidelines to "go for the ball" or to "get in the right position" and are genuinely disappointed at her performance. What should be an enjoyable family day becomes a battle of wills and a frustrating experience for all. In these cases, we try to remind parents that some things in life should just be fun. Their daughter will probably never be a world–class athlete in this sport given her lack of interest and drive, and that's okay. As parents, we strive to find the right balance between ambitions and acceptance of what is "good enough" for our children. We need to maintain our optimism that things will improve and at the same time appreciate those precious little positive moments that too often get lost in our quest for *more* and *better.*

LESSONS FROM THE RESEARCH

My first inkling that concepts such as *hope* and *happiness* were essential for succeeding with child behavior problems came with a large research study I conducted some years ago. Having worked for so many years with children, youth, and adults who presented their families, schools, and communities with very severe behavior problems, my thoughts naturally turned to prevention. Could outcomes be improved and behavior problems possibly prevented altogether by working with very young children before their difficulties escalated into such disruptive episodes? If that was even possible, what could we do with these children?

Some children provide more challenges than others. I've worked with families whose child would be disruptive in some places (e.g., when asked to stop watching a favorite video and come to the dinner table) but generally well behaved in most other settings. Other children, even those with the same diagnoses and skill levels, are a handful everywhere. They may have limited attention spans and become easily frustrated, and they make navigating almost any situation a cause for concern. The thought of having to do even the simplest chores such as washing up or dressing with these children creates a sense of dread because of the inevitable battle that will likely result. But what causes this difference? What makes one child disruptive and another well behaved?

Much more research is needed to answer the question of cause. It is likely that some combination of biology (including genetics) and how one responds to behavior problems leads children down these different paths. For example, children come into this world with different personalities (known by behavioral scientists as *temperaments*). Some children are just born *easy*—they eat well, sleep well, and generally adapt to new situations without much fuss. Other children, unfortunately, are more prone to be difficult. These children might be picky eaters, have trouble around bedtime, and generally have trouble maintaining their attention or transitioning from activity to activity. Almost all of the children we work with in our research would fall on the difficult end on measures of temperament. It is important for parents to understand that this is not their doing. Again, children can be born with different personalities; however, how one responds to them can help direct them toward better behavior. There is still much to learn about the complex interaction between childhood temperament and parental styles, and I expect that creative studies will get researchers closer to some of the answers.

In our research, we posed this important question: Why do some children become more and more disruptive as they get older whereas others seem to change very little or even get better? In other words, are there things that we can do that would help children from developing new and even more disruptive behaviors? If researchers and professionals can begin to answer these questions, maybe we can provide families with advice that will help stop future problems from developing. Working with a young child who is disruptive can be much more manageable than negotiating with an adolescent whose physical development and emotional unpredictability can compound already difficult situations. Prevention is always easier than treatment.

To answer this question, I planned a study[1] to see why some children became increasingly disruptive as they grew older. This first study was difficult to do for several reasons. First, my research colleagues and I had to follow the children and their families over several years. In today's increasingly mobile society, keeping track of families over the years can be quite challenging because it is very common for people to move out of town and even out of state for a variety of reasons. Second, because we didn't know what might be important for predicting later problems, we had to take a "shotgun" approach, looking at a lot of different possible influences at the same time. For example, we looked at the child's diagnosis and cognitive skills as well as social and communication skills. I suspected that a child's communication skills would be the most important factor. I've conducted research since the early 1980s looking at how behavior problems can be seen as a form of communication—something explored in this book—and so I expected that those children who had more difficulty expressing their needs and wants would be the ones having the most trouble later on.

In addition to assessing different aspects of each child, we looked at factors affecting the family, such as stress and the family members' views of themselves and their child. We knew quite clearly that child problems can negatively affect family life, but we also wanted to see whether problems in the family could, in turn, further influence how a child behaves. Once we conducted all of these assessments, we followed these children for 3 years—from age 3 to age 6. Over the course of time, we anticipated that some of the children would show improvements in their behavior, some would continue to be challenging, and others would become even more difficult to handle. So, in our study, we attempted to determine what characteristics of the child or the family when the child was 3 years old could tell us which child would be better behaved or more disruptive by age 6.

The findings from this study were surprising. For example, many people believe that the best predictor of future behavior is past behavior. It would seem that children who were the most disruptive when they were younger would be the most challenging children as they got older. At the same time, it would seem that children who were relatively easy to handle when they were young would continue to be the easiest children to manage as they grew older. This was not always the case.

Even more surprising (at least to me!) was that my guess about how communication affected behavior was wrong. The children were very different in their ability to communicate their needs, yet whether they could let us know what they wanted wasn't the best way to tell which children would go on to become the most challenging. In fact, the best thing that predicted future problems caught me off guard, at least until I thought about it for awhile. At around the time that we were first untangling the results from this rather complex study, a personal interaction with several of the mothers who participated in our research illuminated for me what we were finding in the larger study.

A group of parents had invited me to lead a discussion for their book club at the local bookstore. It was a small group—less than 10 parents were there that night—and we were discussing a new book on child behavior problems. In general, we all agreed that the book was good, providing some new tips for parents to use with their kids. The discussion was animated, with a lot of joking and laughing as the parents shared anecdotes about some of their child's escapades, sometimes making for startling eavesdropping for nearby book shoppers. Most of the mothers in the group were obviously comfortable discussing these potentially embarrassing situations (e.g., the time one of their sons "relieved himself" behind a potted tree at the mall, presumably because his father did that when they were hiking in the woods; the story of one young girl who would imitate her teacher and say "Good sitting!" when one of her brothers sat down at the dinner table). The book club provided a safe haven for these shared experiences and cherished moments during which these mothers could just be themselves. One mother, however, who was also a participant in our study, said very little. She seemed uncomfortable in the group, and I learned later that she was only there because her good friend, who was also in our study, had dragged her along.

As the group broke up, these two mothers were the last to leave, and we lingered for awhile talking about their children. I had known them at that point for 3 years through their work in our study, and it was good to get a chance to catch up on a more personal level. The mom who was uncomfortable in the group now seemed a bit more relaxed, and we talked frankly about her difficulties with her son. When he first entered our study, he clearly was not one of the more disruptive children in our group. He would whine and cry a bit when he was asked to do something he didn't want to do, but it seemed more manipulative than anything else. Despite this, both of his parents had a great deal of difficulty with even these relatively minor outbursts. His mom would describe "walking on eggshells" around him, hoping not to trigger any problems. She always had many rationales about why he was being fussy that day, such as "I think maybe he's catching a cold," or "We're taking him to the doctor. We think he might have allergies." The family had fairly elaborate routines for many daily activities (e.g., letting the child eat dinner in the living room while watching his favorite DVD) because these adjustments in their lives seemed to avoid some of the problems. The mother was embarrassed by the child's behavior when he got upset in public, in part because she felt it reflected poorly on her. She described how they rarely went out anymore with him and even felt uncomfortable leaving him with someone for several hours out of concern for what a babysitter might think of them and their inability to control their son. As part of our study, we offered parenting advice, but both the mother and father never seemed able to carry out any of the suggestions we offered. In the 3 years since we had first met, the child's behavior had become much more difficult to handle and his teacher at school was talking about some alternative placement.

This mother's friend had a completely different story. When she first signed up for our study, her son was perhaps one of the more disruptive 3-year-olds in the group. He was very aggressive toward other children, and he threw major tantrums at home and in the community when he didn't get what he wanted. His mother was a strong advocate for him and was described by many of the staff in our study as a "pistol." As she told us, she didn't take guff (she used a different word) from anyone about her son's behavior. If her son was screaming in the supermarket and someone made the mistake of commenting (saying, e.g., "You really should control your child"), she would whip out a prepared card explaining his diagnosis and tell them in no uncertain terms that they really should educate themselves about this condition and, by the way, mind their own business. She never let her son's behavior stop her from continually challenging him. Even though he too would be difficult at dinner, she maintained that he was part of the family and he was to eat at the table with his parents. Many early battles ensued, but over time it became accepted and his behavior improved. She deliberately took him out shopping with her for the same reason, not wanting to give in to his outbursts. This was not easy, but with some help from us, his behavior outside the home improved as well.

Here, in these two families that I could now observe in stark relief, was what we found in our study. Although a number of factors seemed to contribute to the outcomes for these children, the best predictor of successful outcomes was *parental optimism*. More than a child's diagnosis, how the child behaved at age 3, or the skills the child showed us at this early stage in development, the best way to know which children would either not become more disruptive or even improve in their behavior was if the parents persisted with efforts to help their child behave better. This persistence occurred in families that seemed to have a "can-do" attitude. They believed their child could change, and, just as important, they believed they were capable of helping their child change.

In contrast, if parents gave up on many efforts to help their child behave better and if they went out of their way to avoid problems to the point of changing major aspects of their lives so as to not rock the boat, they were likely to have a child whose behavior became more challenging in time. So, on the flip side, *parental pessimism* appeared to be a good predictor of later problems. Pessimistic families seemed to be less sure their child was capable of making meaningful changes in his or her behavior. And, unlike the more optimistic families, they had nagging doubts about their own ability to carry out the often difficult tasks required for helping a challenging child. We saw these differences (optimistic versus pessimistic) in the families in our study when the child was 3 years of age and found that these factors foretold outcomes that were only partly the result of their child's behavior or abilities.

WHO IS TO BLAME?

So, how do you look at the important results we found about the influence of parental attitudes on child outcomes? Well, if you are one of the pessimistic parents, you will blame yourself for your child's problems. You might secretly think, "See, I knew it is my fault that my daughter is so disruptive," or "Nothing seems to help." Or, deep down you might say to yourself, "My child has this disorder, so there is really very little that can be done. We just need to learn to live with chaos." You might also view our finding as blaming the victims. Here is just one more professional pointing the finger at parents for the problems of their children. Are we blaming parents? No.

First of all, our study didn't answer the question of which came first, child problems or parental pessimism. So, for example, it could be just as possible that disruptive behavior seen very early in children causes some parents to become more negative about their parenting skills and about their child's capabilities. Pessimism could be the result of child problems and not the cause of them. For some families, I believe that's true. It is hard to imagine not being profoundly affected by a child who presents so many challenges.

I do believe there are parents who have self-doubt from the beginning or, at least, are prone to these insecurities. Seeing your child continue to act up no matter what you try, and hearing friends, family members, and even strangers tell you that you're doing it all wrong will drag down even the most upbeat person. Fears of repeated fiascoes with a child who acts up dramatically and persistently can be a self-fulfilling prophesy, confirming what these parents secretly believed anyway—that they were not good parents. Pretty defeating. How a person will react to becoming a parent, especially with a child who may have special needs, is not something that can be predicted. I've seen couples who weren't sure they wanted a child turn into highly confident parents; yet, I've also worked with couples who idealized their lives with children only to find the unexpected challenges almost too much to bear.

However this played out in your family—your experience with your child from an early age made you lower your expectations, you tend to be pessimistic about your child because of a diagnosis, or maybe you or your partner have secret doubts about your parenting skills—the need for extra help is still there. In fact, I suspect that most parents can benefit from examining how they view their child and themselves as parents regardless of their child's diagnosis or the extent of his or her problem behaviors.

As a researcher, I looked at these results and believed that just as we have worked with very challenging children and have been able to make meaningful progress, we might be able to help parents as well. Again, whether you became a parent of a challenging child and the experience occasionally gets the better of you or you tend to look at the world as half empty rather than half full and this further complicates an already daunting task, some additional guidance might be of great value to you. We are able to assist parents to look at their world differently—to see that in fact they are good parents and that their child is capable of much more than they might think. In addition to helping your child, I think you can use these techniques to grow as a person. In fact, there is evidence from psychological research that people who view the world pessimistically can be helped to be more optimistic. People can be taught to examine the things they say to themselves that tend to get in the way and can learn to change these thoughts to more helpful ones. So, the next big questions are as follows: Can parents of very challenging children learn to think about themselves and their child in a more positive and helpful way, and will this assist them to more successfully apply the techniques that are known to improve their child's behavior?

PUTTING IT ALL TOGETHER

When I first wrestled with this concept and informally described my thoughts to professionals in the field, often a light went off in their heads and the concept immediately made sense to them. This was especially true for those professionals who sometimes struggled mightily to help families only to see them drop out or stop coming to parent-training sessions. Good, caring people who devote their professional (and sometimes personal) lives to helping parents with challenging children struggle constantly to help all families. These professionals know that they are not able to reach every family; however, here was a different way to look at these families. Rather than making judgments that parents who do not complete their training programs are "noncompliant," "difficult," or even "bad" parents, they could instead view them through different eyes and see them as humans like all of us who need a little extra, specially designed, help that few have even thought to provide. So why not tell the world about this years ago?

As I promised in the beginning of this book, all of my recommendations are "tried and true" techniques, meaning I won't recommend something that has not been researched and shown to be effective. So? Does it work? Can we help parents become more confident in their abilities, and does this lead to improvements in their ability to work with their child? In a word, yes. In addition, it is important to note that our research is showing that this new approach is leading to even more improvements in child behavior. This rather large and extensive study is described in later sections of the book, but be assured for now that we can recommend this approach without hesitation.

Of the many lessons learned from the thousands of families we have worked with over the years, the two that follow are the most important: 1) Find out why the child is misbehaving, and 2) find out if the thoughts and feelings of mothers and fathers will get in the way of their being successful parents. Armed with this information, strategies can be developed to fit the needs of the whole family and help the child on the road to better behavior.

What follows next are the big lessons I have learned that will help you along the way. I expand on these lessons in the next few chapters. Then, the remaining chapters focus on your child and how to deal with challenging behavior while also taking care of yourself. Because you are busy, there is often not enough time to work with your child and, at a different time, work on yourself. There are ways to do both at the same time. Over a brief few weeks, you will be able to help your child to behave better and help yourself to feel better and happier.

These changes are probably something you have dreamt about for some time. What would it be like to have a quiet dinner as a family? What if getting on the school bus in the morning, getting washed up at night, or going to bed happened uneventfully? Imagine going shopping with your child without a meltdown! What is an everyday occurrence for most families seems like an impossible fantasy for others. We have shown with hundreds of families that these outcomes are within your reach. But, even though these outcomes are highly desirable, I don't think that they are enough. I think families want and deserve more—more than just the absence of problems. You want and deserve to be happy. You want and deserve to enjoy being a parent and the time spent together as a family.

For those of you who would like a "hint" about what we do with parents to help them along the way, here are our top ten tips. I explain each in more detail later and take you step by step through the process of making this work for you and your child.

Ten Tips for Optimistic Parenting

1. *Explore your thoughts and feelings before, during, and after meltdowns.* Practice noticing these feelings so that you can see later if they help or hurt your parenting skills. Most parents need help with doing this in a way that is productive, and I show you how this can be done in a relatively short amount of time.

2. *If your spouse or partner doesn't help, ask why.* Just as your thoughts and feelings interfere with good parenting, so might your spouse's self-doubts or doubts about your child. This involves the seemingly obvious but often very difficult issue that confronts most couples—communication. I provide examples about how we work through these challenges with couples.

3. *Believe you are a good parent.* When you add up all you do for your child, the positives far outweigh any occasional lapses you may experience. Focus on the positive. If you are reading this book, it means you want to be an even better parent—a sign that you already are a good one!

4. *Believe your child can change.* All of our experience tells us *any* child can improve his or her challenging behavior. It helps to believe this and expect more from your child.

5. *Take care of yourself.* You cannot help your child if you are hurting. Give yourself permission to be "selfish" occasionally.

6. *Leverage—don't multitask.* Doing two things at once means you may be doing two things poorly. If you are stretched, try to combine activities with your child that achieve multiple goals (e.g., having your child help set the table, which gets the chore done but also provides a learning experience).

7. *Parent in the moment.* Keep reminding yourself to focus on what is happening right now with your child (e.g., having a good bath) rather than other things (e.g., thinking about what to make for dinner while bathing your child). I devote a major section of a chapter to this important topic and show you how this can be one of the most valuable tools to help you be a better parent and a happier person.

8. *Recognize and appreciatie the good things in life.* We sometimes have a tendency to focus too much on negative events (e.g., a bad tantrum in the car) rather than on the positive ones (e.g., playing nicely with siblings). Each night, practice reminding yourself of the good things that happened that day.

9. *Express gratitude toward those who help you.* One of the most powerful exercises in becoming a happier person is expressing gratitude. Thanking those who help you with your child (including your spouse or partner, if appropriate) will make you feel better and will make the other person feel better as well.

10. *Sometimes bad is okay.* Feeling bad sometimes is inevitable for everyone. Accept the fact that there will be "down times," and don't fight them. As they say, "What doesn't kill you will only make you stronger."

Optimistic Parenting is an approach to handling child behavior problems that stresses the importance of being ready to take on this challenge. Only when you feel capable of tackling these problems will you truly be able to carry out the techniques that lead to success. If these techniques seem either too simplistic or too difficult for you to carry out, give them a chance. Again, our research shows that people from all walks of life have gained tremendously by following our steps. Not only have they observed important changes in their child's disruptive behavior, they also report important improvements in their own quality of life. They feel better and more confident about themselves. They are…happier.

Take the time to work your way through this book. Use it to find ideas for improving your child's behavior but also for you to build a happier life. You may find that you already practice some aspects of what we recommend. That is fairly common among families with whom I have worked. The trick is to try all of the suggestions to see what works best for you. Life is short. Use every opportunity to make the best life you can.

CHAPTER 2

Confident Parenting

You gain strength, courage and confidence by every experience in which you really stop to look fear in the face. You are able to say to yourself, "I have lived through this horror. I can take the next thing that comes along." You must do the thing you think you cannot do.

—Eleanor Roosevelt (1884–1962)

This chapter expands on the idea that being a more confident parent will improve your parenting skills—a key component of Optimistic Parenting. Researchers have long known that confidence is an important component to parenting. Successful parents are those who know what they are doing and respond to their child's needs without hesitation. Not believing in what one is doing or that one is doing the right thing with one's child is a surefire path to failure. If a parent does not feel confident in his or her approach to helping a child, the likelihood is great that he or she will give up if his or her attempts are not immediately successful. Any hint of a failure will confirm that what the parent is doing is wrong. Following an introduction to this aspect of my colleagues' and my work in this chapter, the next chapter (Chapter 3—"Insight into Your Thoughts and Feelings") walks you through the same exercises we use in our research to help you get a glimpse of your own views of yourself and your child.

Unfortunately, my colleagues and I see far too many parents who do not buy into approaches that are likely to help their child. For example, parents often tell us, "I tried it but it didn't work!" or, "That won't work with my child!" It is true that families may have tried approaches that ultimately were not successful or that parents may strongly suspect that their child will not respond to a particular strategy; however, sometimes what really happens is that the parents do not believe in the proposed strategy or have confidence in their ability to carry it out successfully. Then, when the child has a brief relapse—for example, a screaming tantrum at dinner—the parents' lack of faith in the approach or in their ability to parent is reinforced. As professionals in the field, our job is to design plans that are believable and to help parents feel good about their ability to carry the plans out.

"Children can smell fear," a mother once told me in jest. There may be some truth in this bit of humor. Behavioral scientists discovered some time ago that human emotions are contagious. This means that if a person approaches another person with a sad face and speaks in a slow and depressed tone of voice, the other person is likely to start to feel sad as well. The opposite also is true; one person can pick up another person's happy demeanor. Humans appear to be born with the ability to experience empathy—literally feeling the emotions of other people.

This emotion contagion happens with children as well. Awhile back, my colleagues and I conducted some research showing that if a teacher approaches a difficult task with a smile and a lot of positive energy, the child is more likely to attempt and complete the task; however, if the teacher shows hesitancy and is more neutral, the child is more likely to resist the work. As one can imagine, this happens every day at school. A teacher might have a history with a particular child who really fights doing math problems. When the teacher is ready to sit down and go over the math, he or she may approach the session with a great deal of dread (perhaps thinking, "Ugh, this is always such a hassle!"). The child is likely to pick up this emotion and also dread what is to come and resist the work. This cycle then becomes self-fulfilling and just reinforces the teacher's initial fear—that math with this student will always be a struggle. Believing and acting as if something will be unpleasant (e.g., "Please don't give me a hard time tonight about going to bed!") makes it more likely that a child will pick up on that emotion and increases the chance that a problem will ensue. Approaching difficult situations with a positive attitude is not a panacea for all child problems; however, it does seem to make situations just a little bit easier. Therefore, being confident in your ability as a parent may not only help you persist in the face of resistance but may also send a signal to your child that you mean business and that "resistance is futile!" Confidence alone is not enough to fix all problems, but it is an important prerequisite to successful parenting.

Keep in mind that you do not need to be perfect to be successful! Successful parents make mistakes all the time. Almost all parents have thought at one time or another that they should not have said or done something with their child who was acting up or that they should have followed through on a problem but for a variety of reasons did not trust their own instincts. The difference between successful parents and those who feel defeated, however, is how they learn from their successes and failures. This is also, by the way, what researchers find to be true among good business leaders. Successful leaders are not the ones with the most experience and are not people who never fail. Instead, the best leaders are those who learn larger lessons from their failures and find ways to take advantage of those experiences (thus the cliché "when life gives you lemons, make lemonade"). One important message of this book is to stop feeling guilty if you are not a "perfect parent." Instead, strive to get better and better at being a parent. The good news is that children are not irreparably harmed by a few mistakes. They tend to be fairly resilient and can bounce back from occasional inconsistencies. Do not forget that parenting is a voyage, and try to enjoy the trip!

This next story about my father holds a great deal of significance to me; I am sharing it with you to illustrate the true meaning of confidence and its role in helping you become a more optimistic parent.

FATHER AND SON

It was a simple but extraordinary moment. Anyone looking on would have seen just a father and son having a conversation in a car. We had just finished having lunch at a local restaurant—the first time my father and I ever had a meal together alone. What we discussed over our food escapes me now, in part because it was more than 35 years ago but mostly because our lunch conversation was overshadowed by the brief interchange we had in the car.

I was home during a break from my sophomore year at college. My father unexpectedly invited me to lunch and then to go with him while he had an interview for a new job. After a 30-year career as a civilian employee with the U.S. Army, he had retired at the age of 59. Only a few months after his retirement, he was now looking for another job. His government pension was adequate for my parents, but because his children needed help with college tuition, he delayed his retirement to earn some extra income. He never complained or resented having to put off a well-deserved rest.

As my father pulled up to the building where he was to have his job interview, I began to empathize with him. Here he was, almost 60 years old, yet he needed to prove himself to some interviewer who might be younger and less experienced than he. I could recall waiting to be interviewed for jobs and being anxious about what was to come. What would they ask? How would I come across? I asked him, "Are you nervous?" He looked over at me without vanity or arrogance and said, "No. I know I can do this job. I can do it as well as anyone." Looking at him in that moment, I saw him in a way I never did before. Although he was a good-natured and loving father and husband, it was my mother everyone looked to as being the strength in the family. She was the one who went to battle with our school when a teacher displayed anti-Semitism. She disciplined the children when it was necessary. The words "Wait until your father gets home!" were never uttered in my house. Yet, here was "good old dad," stronger and more confident than I had ever seen him.

When I look back on that day, I feel fortunate in many ways. I caught a glimpse of my father not as his child but through the eyes of an adult. Here was a model not for unbridled or unwarranted confidence but for how a true optimist might see the world and consequently feel that he could succeed. My father showed a confidence that said despite whatever weaknesses or failings he might have (which he recognized), he could do the job and do it well. He would do whatever needed to be done. He would persist. He would be successful.

That lunch was not only the first time my father and I had a meal together alone; it was also the last. A short while after returning to college that year I got a call from a relative saying that I needed to come home. My father had died. He had collapsed at his new job and died instantly. It was more than 3 decades ago, but I still can't write this without tears.

I share this example with you because it gets to the heart of what I mean by confidence and optimism. Optimism does not always carry a smile. Bad things happen to people, but optimists find a way to go on. When my father died, I briefly flirted with the idea of quitting school and going back home to be a support for my mother. His sudden and unexpected death was so overwhelming to the whole family, and school was the last thing on my mind. When I mentioned this idea to my mother, however, she very simply said that she appreciated the thought but would be okay—"Go back to school and move on." There was nothing conditional in her words or tone of voice. We would all carry on. As I drove back to the university, I couldn't imagine how I would be able to concentrate enough to resume my studies and finish the semester. It was a daily struggle, but I did it and completed the year with all *A*s.

OPTIMISM AND PESSIMISM

My father was a confident person and parent. He trusted his judgment but was able to learn from the mistakes he made; this made him an optimist in the most basic sense. He did not think that everything was terrific or that good things would just happen to him. He knew you had to work hard in life to achieve meaningful things—a loving family, security, and daily joy. He also knew that hard work made these things that much more precious. He knew that bad things could and would happen to even the best of people. Throughout my father's too-short life, he never made a lot of money, and we grew up in a working-class neighborhood. For several years as I was growing up, my mother's sister and her two sons moved into our small house, meaning that seven people had to squeeze into three bedrooms and share only one full bathroom, all on my father's modest income. Although this produced a great deal of stress and strain for the whole family, my father approached the situation as a pragmatist. We needed more privacy, so he divided a bedroom into two by himself, learning as he went how to frame a wall, install a door, and put in drywall. He certainly had his down times, but they did not seem to last and he was able to find the good side to most situations. How did he do it? He did it through optimistic thinking.

More is now known about how optimists and pessimists think. They look at the world in very different and predictable ways. A conversation I had with a parent named Trish who was in one of our programs may help to describe these differences. My colleagues and I had been working on getting Trish's young daughter to fall asleep at night on her own without a tantrum. During the second week of our program, the young girl cried for only about a minute at bedtime (as opposed to her usual hour-long tantrum), fell asleep, and slept peacefully through the night. "Wow!" I said over the telephone while checking in with Trish the next day. "That's terrific. You must feel very good about how hard you worked to get her to this point." Without skipping a beat, Trish replied, "I think it was the hotdogs." The hotdogs? I thought about this for a bit. Over the years, I believed I had heard every explanation for child behavior, but this one was new to me. "Yeah, she likes hotdogs, and she ate two for dinner. I think that's why she slept okay last night."

There are various differences between optimists and pessimists, and Trish's response illustrates the first one: *Pessimists see positive things as being caused by some outside influence and not as something they accomplished.* Trish did not take credit for working for more than a week on her daughter's bedtime tantrums; instead, she found a way to give credit to an outside influence—what her daughter had eaten for dinner. An optimist would have seen this as a personal accomplishment— "Yes, I've gone through a lot; however, I'm proud of how patient I've been, and it's starting to pay off."

At the same time, Trish blamed herself for her daughter's bedtime sleep problems. She once shared, "I think I spoiled her when she was little. I let her sleep with me and now she can't do it alone." This statement aptly illustrates the second difference between pessimists and optimists: *Pessimists see negative things as their fault.* Now, it may be true that by letting her daughter sleep with her, Trish contributed to her daughter's current sleep problems. An optimist, however, also would give credit to factors outside of his or her control (e.g., "She was always a fussy baby"). Optimists see that there are reasons for a child's misbehavior that may have nothing to do with their parenting. Trish could not take credit for her own successful efforts and blamed herself for her child's sleep problems.

After recovering from Trish's hotdog theory of sleep therapy, I tried to give Trish more encouragement. "This is really a good sign. If you look at her progress, she's crying less and less each night. I'll bet that if you keep up what you are doing with her she will soon start to fall asleep without much crying or fussiness at all." "I don't know what I'm going to do," she replied, as if I had not just spoken, "This crying every night just wears me down. It takes me hours to fall asleep after these meltdowns, and I just don't know how I can keep doing everything without sleep." Despite my pep talk, Trish displayed another classic pessimistic style of thinking: *Pessimists see negative things as likely to continue and positive things as temporary.* I tried to point out to Trish that all of her efforts were now starting to pay off and her daughter was doing better each night. Trish's pessimistic style of looking at these situations, however, led her to feel that her daughter's problems were permanent and not likely to end no matter what we did. This one good night was a fluke to her. Optimists, in contrast, would have embraced this sign of progress, because they tend to see negative things as temporary obstacles that can be overcome. To an optimist, the good nights would be seen as true signs of progress and indications of more good things to come.

As we continued to speak, the conversation turned from Trish's daughter's tantrums to the effects the late bedtimes had on her daughter in school. "Her teacher complains that she's tired at school. She doesn't pay attention and gets in trouble. How will she ever get through the next grade? I think she is going to get kicked out of this program and I just don't know what I will do when that happens." Trish obviously has many rational concerns about her daughter's future; however, in this instance, she is letting these concerns distract her from the positive direction things are taking. *Pessimists overgeneralize problems, seeing them as likely to affect many parts of their lives.* Trish's daughter's sleep problems were just the tip of the iceberg, and Trish felt overwhelmed by the many implications of the problem because she believed they could not be fixed. The term *catastrophizing* is sometimes used for this tendency. It is an irrational thought that something is far worse than it actually is. For example, after one bad episode in a doctor's office with his child, a father might describe the occurrence as "a disaster" and state that "this always happens when we go out in public," overlooking any good episodes that may have happened that day. A more optimistic view would recognize that the trip to the doctor was bad but might attribute the misbehavior to a long wait or a lack of toys in the waiting room. An optimistic view of the situation leads to strategies to improve the situation the next time (e.g., "I need to bring something with us to keep her occupied"). The pessimistic reaction (e.g., "A disaster always happens when we go out") leaves little room for improvement short of completely avoiding trips out in public.

As I described previously, pessimists look at child rearing in a way that seems to interfere with their ability to be better parents. If a parent always sees behavior problems as his or her own fault and believes that the problems will spill over to other situations and times, he or she will begin to feel hopeless. When a person feels hopeless, he or she often cannot think of any good options other than some form of escape. Many parents who have seen the world through pessimistic eyes have been able to learn a new way of perceiving life's events, helping them to wake up the next day ready to take on new and old challenges.

Again, knowing what to do and being able to carry it out day after day are two different parts of successful parenting. Part of the job of professionals in the field is to figure out who needs help in which area (e.g., who needs to learn strategies for changing their child's behavior, who needs help persisting when things inevitably go wrong). At this point, it may be helpful to take a closer look inside the minds of one set of pessimistic parents to see how they view the world and see if some of these attitudes seem familiar. The story of the next family illustrates many of the concepts that are characteristic of pessimistic parents.

A PESSIMISTIC FAMILY

During their first visit with our project, Marcie and Dave appeared to be the poster family for confidence. They were an attractive couple in their early 30s who made it clear from the start that they were comfortable financially and really didn't need to be in our study (which was free to all participants). They were very much in sync with each other, often finishing each other's sentences. They had only one child, a 5-year-old boy named Jeremy who had received a number of different diagnoses over the past few months, including attention-deficit/hyperactivity disorder (ADHD), bipolar disorder, and oppositional defiant disorder. Jeremy's school referred the family to us because of Jeremy's problems at school and because his family had been extremely difficult to work with. Jeremy was described by his parents as being a bundle of energy who resisted almost everything they tried to get him to do. Dressing was always a fight (e.g., "I don't like that shirt; it's itchy!"); mealtimes frequently became a battle of wills, which Jeremy usually won (e.g., "This is yuck!"); and going out in public was almost out of the question because of his loud protests about wanting to leave and go home. The teachers at Jeremy's school described his behavior as being out of control. As Marcie and Dave discussed these challenges with us, however, their demeanor was odd. One of the first things taught to new clinicians as they start conducting therapy is to notice how people communicate good and bad situations. One would expect people to appear upbeat and happy when recalling good times and somewhat sad or anxious when talking about bad times. As the couple spoke of their significant problems with Jeremy, however, they would look back and forth at each other and smile or wink. As we listened to them tell us their family story, it seemed that they thought these problems were all pretty humorous despite the fairly significant impact they had on Jeremy and on their family life. Jeremy's difficulties seemed like their own private, shared piece of the world—a situation that brought them together. One might imagine that given the problems their child presented they would feel unsure about themselves as parents. Our first impression while listening to them talk, however, was that they were completely in control. In fact, their discourse reminded me of an unusual form of psychosis, a shared psychotic disorder called *folie à deux* in which an individual develops delusions simply as a result of a close relationship with a delusional individual.

But Marcie and Dave were not delusional. As the sessions went on, it became clear that they were realistic about Jeremy's problems but had very little insight into their own thoughts about his behavior. In addition, they each seemed to have little to no understanding of what the other parent really thought and felt. What Dave eventually communicated to us was that he saw Jeremy as being evil. He saw his behavior problems as aimed intentionally at them in an effort to anger his parents. Screaming at dinnertime was just Jeremy's way of disrupting the meal. The fights to get him to use a seat belt in the car were attempts to ruin Dave's day. He told us about how his own older brother was a similar child growing up and that he continued to have a strained relationship with him. He saw his brother and Jeremy as both fundamentally flawed and bad people. Dave believed his son was not capable of changing and there was nothing that he, as a parent, could change. Marcie, conversely, was more conflicted. Although she was disturbed and stressed out by Jeremy's outbursts, she felt that Jeremy had little control over himself. The constant search for a diagnosis was Marcie's way of finding the cause of these episodes that appeared to take over her unfortunate son. She was sure that the right label would explain the problems that ruled most aspects of their lives and help them to determine a cure.

Despite the fact that Dave's and Marcie's views of Jeremy's behavior differed so dramatically from each other (i.e., evil versus caused by a disorder), they actually had something in common. Both of their views were pessimistic ways of looking at Jeremy's behavior. For Dave, the fact that his son was essentially born an evil child meant to him that he could not change. Dave expected his son to grow up like his brother and be troubled for the rest of his life. Again, it is important to reiterate that pessimists see bad situations as relatively permanent. In Dave's eyes, therefore, treatment for Jeremy was fruitless; anything he and Marcie were asked to try with Jeremy would ultimately fail because Jeremy could not change. Dave would halfheartedly try some of the procedures suggested by the school, but when Jeremy did not change immediately, it just confirmed Dave's feeling that Jeremy's problems were permanent and inevitable. Similarly, Marcie's view also was one that implied that Jeremy had no control over his behavior; she believed that whatever disorder Jeremy had was unchangeable. Just as Dave believed that Jeremy's was an inborn problem (i.e., he was born bad), Marcie thought that one of Jeremy's disorders was responsible for his bad behavior. What this means from a treatment perspective is that deep down Marcie did not feel that a treatment plan would work unless it involved curing Jeremy of his many diagnosed problems—ADHD, bipolar disorder, and oppositional defiant disorder. On top of all of this, she felt guilty about her inability to help her son—a feeling she had never shared with Dave.

In scientific terms, both Dave and Marcie would be said to have low child efficacy—they had little faith that their child could improve. Obviously, this lack of faith in Jeremy's ability to change would seriously interfere with any attempts to help Jeremy at home or at school. This belief was likely behind their lack of cooperation with the school program. For example, if Jeremy's teacher wanted to discuss a new plan to help Jeremy behave better in the classroom, Marcie and Dave often reverted to statements such as "Oh, we've tried that at home, but it just doesn't faze him." Marcie and Dave's lack of willingness to try new approaches with Jeremy resulted in a great deal of frustration among school staff, who were doing the best they could with Jeremy. The staff members racked their brains to develop new and creative approaches that Jeremy's parents could use at home, but all of their suggestions were met with similar skepticism. Dave and Marcie were savvy enough not to say, "He's just a bad kid" or "He has bipolar disorder, why don't you just leave him alone." Instead, they would just smile knowingly at each other and communicate nonverbally that they thought the teachers just didn't get it. Not having any insight into how Jeremy's parents felt about Jeremy's problems led to suspicions among Jeremy's teachers and professionals in the school district that Marcie and Dave were uncaring and neglectful parents. This was an understandable conclusion, but one that was far from the truth.

Dave and Marcie also had what we would call low self-efficacy—a term that indicates how much they felt they could control Jeremy's behavior. So, not only did they doubt Jeremy's ability to change but they also had doubts about their own ability to parent him effectively. Getting at their self-doubts took a great deal of our effort in working with Dave and Marcie. After a few preliminary sessions, a critical conversation with them about their beliefs as parents went something like this: "Marcie, when Jeremy demanded to open the box of cereal in the supermarket, what were you thinking and feeling?" "He was being a brat," she offered succinctly. "Okay, but what were you feeling at the time? Were you angry or anxious, or did it just not bother you?" "Well of course it bothered me!" She seemed annoyed at the question, but we persisted. "Were you angry at him?" "No." "Why not?" "Because I told you he has these other problems that make him act up like that. It's not his fault!" She looked exasperated at us. "What do you think the other people in the supermarket thought?" Here she hesitated a bit and looked at her husband. He smiled knowingly, appearing to send the message that all of the other people in the world just don't understand. "Why should I care what they think?" she fired back. We responded carefully. "You shouldn't. But what do you think they thought of his tantrum?" Here she became teary eyed. "Well, I don't know. Maybe they think I'm a bad mother. They just don't understand. But…" We waited a bit until she was ready to collect herself and complete her thought. "But maybe I am a bad mother. I've seen other parents with kids who scream when they are out in public, and they seem to know what to do. They don't get upset. They don't yell like I do. I just feel so out of control and don't know what the right thing is to do!" Dave leaned over and comforted her and looked as lost as she did.

Here it was. Here was what was behind the bravado—the brave front Marcie and Dave communicated to the world. They had each other, and together they battled daily a highly difficult child without really knowing where to turn. Dave had a difficult time showing any weakness, and Marcie went along with this strategy for dealing with other people who were just trying to help. Here, in one 15-minute conversation, my colleagues and I saw that this seemingly uncaring family did in fact care a great deal, but their lack of insight into their own doubts about Jeremy and their abilities as parents was getting in the way of any help they could receive. They were profoundly unhappy, and their only source of support and solace was each other and their shared battle with Jeremy and the rest of the outside world.

Many people engage in some form of these psychological battles throughout their lives. Psychoanalysts—mental health professionals whose work is based on the psychoanalytic theories of Sigmund Freud and his disciples— would call Dave and Marcie's responses to Jeremy's teachers a defense mechanism. From this perspective, a defense mechanism is a type of coping style that protects us from being consciously aware of an uncomfortable thought or feeling (e.g., "I'm not a good and caring parent"). Behaviorists—professionals who look at behavior in terms of reinforcing events—might see Dave and Marcie as escaping or avoiding unpleasant confrontations by making statements that end the conversation (e.g., saying "That won't work" tends to limit the discussion about a new plan). A behaviorist would call Marcie and Dave's actions "escape behavior," which gets negatively reinforced by the ending of the discussion. Most human beings have been in situations that make them uncomfortable (e.g., a conversation about politics or religion) and have tried to steer the conversation to some safer and less stressful topic. This is an example of an escape strategy (although not a defense mechanism if a person was aware of what he or she was doing).

However one labels it, many pessimistic parents use a style of behavior or speaking that makes other people back away from discussions or confrontations. This could be the active style used by Dave and Marcie (e.g., saying, "We tried that already; we know it doesn't work") or a more passive style involving just not following through with a plan that one does not believe in. And, these styles make sense. It is difficult and uncomfortable to confront thoughts and feeling that result in feeling bad. The key to resolving these dilemmas and changing strategies is to recognize what is going on and to examine how and why one is reacting that way.

Being a confident parent means looking at child rearing through the eyes of an optimist. That does not mean being unrealistically positive that everything is going to be fine or that you know everything you need to know about your child. What it means is seeing setbacks as inevitable but temporary. It means seeing that you can—with a little help—be the parent your child needs and that you want to be. It means recognizing when you've worked hard and made progress with your child and that, despite some mistakes, his or her misbehavior is not your fault. It means learning from these setbacks and getting up the next morning ready to try again. A confident parent analyzes complete disasters and sees them as isolated incidents and possible to fix.

Any one of the pessimistic views of parenting (e.g., seeing your child as out of control, doubting your abilities as a parent) will interfere with being the best parent you can be. Fortunately, there are techniques that can help you identify these thoughts and beliefs and, most important, how to change them. We use your views of your child and of yourself as a parent as the example throughout the book but recognize that this analysis of how you view the world reaches beyond just parenting. It may provide you with some understanding about why other relationships are problematic for you. The next chapters outline important steps that have helped many families such as yours become more confident and successful.

CHAPTER 3

Insight into Your Thoughts and Feelings

The unexamined life is not worth living.

—Socrates, in Plato's *The Apology*

This chapter focuses on how to take a close look at your thoughts and feelings to determine whether they are getting in the way of your being the most successful parent you can be. You will learn how to become more optimistic in your approach to the world—a skill that will help you both as a parent and as a human being. Having more confidence is a key to leading a happier life. Thanks to pioneering researchers such as Martin Seligman (author of *Learned Optimism*[1]), it is now known that people who tend to be more pessimistic in their world view can be helped to become more optimistic in the way they view their lives. Our research shows that family members can significantly increase their parental effectiveness by examining the things they say to themselves that interfere with their ability to help their child, essentially becoming more optimistic parents. Many parents find these exercises to be enlightening because they give parents new insights into their own thoughts and provide them with a different way of looking at the world. As with all of the exercises in this book, I encourage you to look at these exercises not only as a way to help your child but also as a way to help yourself. It is now known that reorienting the way you look at your parenting can increase your confidence and, therefore, make you feel better overall.

THE JOURNAL

The first step in taking a closer look at your thoughts and feelings involves a bit of homework on your part. Appendix A at the end of the book contains a Self-

Talk Journal. Use copies of these formatted journal pages to help record situations that occur with your child and what you think and feel during these times. To begin, the journal asks you to write down one example of a difficulty you faced this week with your child (e.g., screaming while getting dressed in the morning). At the same time, try to recall what you thought and how you felt during these times. Additional journal forms in Appendix A have space for more information, such as consequences, but first focus on the situation (i.e., what your child did), your thoughts (i.e., what you were thinking at the time), and your feelings (i.e., your emotions and physical feelings during that time).

Next is the first journal form completed by Joyce, the mother of 4-year-old Mike, who was very difficult when it came time to do things he didn't like to do—sitting at the dinner table, going to bed at night, or leaving a favorite activity (e.g., watching television). This example of Joyce's entry for that day illustrates how many parents begin this task and also some of the problems they face when they first start this exercise.

JOYCE'S JOURNAL: INITIAL ENTRY

SITUATION What happened (success or difficulty)?	THOUGHTS What did you think or say to yourself when this happened?	FEELINGS What emotions did you experience and how did you react physically when this happened?
When Mike sat down for dinner, he started getting upset. (difficulty)	I thought, "ugh, I hate dinnertime."	I felt tired.

Now let's examine each of Joyce's entries.

Situation: Describing the Problem Behavior

Joyce's description of Mike's difficulty (i.e., the situation) does not describe the behaviors in enough detail for us to know exactly what Mike was doing.

- -

SITUATION What happened (success or difficulty)?
When Mike sat down for dinner, he started getting upset. (difficulty)

- -

For example, does "he started getting upset" mean he cried, stamped his feet, threw dishes across the room, or merely frowned and crossed his arms? Additional detail is needed to get a good idea about just how disruptive this problem is to the family. Specifying this also will help later in the process to figure out whether Mike is improving. For example, in this case, what Mike actually did was whine (saying, "I don't want that icky dinner!") and cry loudly. As any parent knows, a child's constant whining can be like fingernails on a blackboard and can be a source of stress that wears a parent down over time. In addition, loud crying or screaming can disrupt dinner for everyone. If later, Mike continues to "get upset" when called to dinner but "getting upset" only involves frowning, it is possible to see that he is making progress.

During this process, my colleagues and I typically ask parents to describe the difficulty their child presents in enough detail so that someone unfamiliar with their child and the situation would be able to picture in his or her mind what has happened. Simply saying one's child "tantrums" is another example of a description that does not allow someone reading the description to imagine what happened. Instead, saying "she ran around the room pulling things off of the walls and screamed" is more helpful. As we asked Joyce to describe again what Mike did at dinnertime, she revised her journal.

SITUATION What happened (success or difficulty)?
When Mike sat down at the dinner table and the food was put in front of him, he started whining and crying. (difficulty)

This description is better, not just because now Joyce elaborates to say that "getting upset" means "whining and crying" but also because it is now known that Mike didn't start his disruptive behavior until the food was put down in front of him. Knowing exactly what might be triggering Mike's problem (e.g., perhaps it is the type of food being served rather than the physical act of sitting at the table) will be very helpful when it is time to design a plan to help him. The concept of *triggers*—what seems to set off a problem—is important not just for the child's problem behavior (e.g., placing food in front of a child) but also for parents' thoughts and feelings. Before continuing to investigate what might be contributing to Mike's difficulties—remember, this exercise is first about Joyce—it will be useful to look at Joyce's other entries. What is Joyce thinking and feeling during Mike's problem episodes? The next section provides a closer look at how Joyce initially described her reactions.

Thoughts: Describing What You Think or Say to Yourself

Being aware of what you think or say to yourself when your child misbehaves is fundamental to Optimistic Parenting. Because it may be necessary to change what you say to yourself in difficult situations (and in good situations), the obvious first step is to become conscious of these thoughts. Unfortunately, it is also one of the more difficult things for many parents to do. In fact, when we train professionals who will be teaching families Optimistic Parenting, it is astonishing just how many of these individuals—professionals, no less!—are not aware of their own thoughts when they face difficulties. Part of the training we conduct involves having the professionals use situations from their own lives so that they have a better feeling for what the families with whom they work are going through. The professionals also struggle to put into words what they are thinking when their own child acts up. Although it may take a bit of practice on your part, be assured that we have been successful in teaching all of our families to get a better insight into their thoughts when it comes to their child's misbehavior.

The following quotes again show how Joyce first described her thoughts when Mike started whining and crying at the dinner table.

SITUATION What happened (success or difficulty)?
When Mike sat down at the dinner table and the food was put in front of him, he started whining and crying. (difficulty)

THOUGHTS What did you think or say to yourself when this happened?
I thought, "Ugh, I hate dinnertime."

Recording that she was thinking, "Ugh, I hate dinnertime" is a start; however, as with her description of Mike's behavior, it is not enough. It is important to know what Joyce is thinking about herself, about Mike, and about other people who either are witnessing this problem or who might have an opinion about it. In psychotherapy terms, this is referred to as having insight into a situation. In Joyce's case, just thinking "I hate dinnertime" does not reveal enough about her real thoughts about this episode.

It is important to point out that in our clinical work with families, we do not try to get people to have insight into complex family relationships that may have occurred long ago. For example, we do not try to figure out if how a parent was treated as a child is influencing how they act as parents themselves. This relative lack of attention to the distant past is not because we think that having access to this kind of background information is unimportant. For example, it may be very helpful to know if Joyce had fond memories of dinnertime with her family when she was a child (e.g., everyone sitting around talking and laughing and enjoying each other's company) and if this is why disruption at dinnertime in her own home is so upsetting or if her parents required silence during meals and her lack of success at having quiet dinnertimes is making her feel inadequate as a parent. The reason why we do not go into great deal about the past is simply a matter of time. Sometimes this information is revealed along the way, but we focus our discussions on what is happening in the present. We want to help parents become more confident and successful, and we need to help them relatively quickly—over weeks rather than months or years. Fortunately, our research tells us that we can be very successful in improving how parents look at themselves as parents and how they view their child's problems and, most important, we see significant improvements in child behavior problems as a result.

This part of Optimistic Parenting is so important that we have spent many hours poring over the transcripts of the conversations between the parents and our therapists in our Optimistic Parenting project. In doing so, we have observed some important and repeating themes in what parents report about their thoughts during difficult times. I expect that this information will help you examine your own thoughts as well. To get started, think through a difficult situation with your child that occurred recently and then take the Thoughts Quiz (see Appendix A at the end of the book). The following sections explore each statement in the quiz individually and consider what your response suggests about your thoughts about yourself, your child, and others. The discussion then will return to Joyce's journal entry and how she changed it.

I Have Little or No Control over This Situation   If you tended to agree with this statement about your thoughts at the time your child misbehaved, you are not alone. More than 80% of the families with whom we work express some form of concern that occasionally or often things get out of their control. How often have you envied other parents who seem to have everything planned out and who seem to be holding up well even when things are chaotic? What we know from watching hundreds of families with their difficult children is that often those parents who seem to be cool and calm are instead thinking they wish they could be managing things better. In fact, it is a rare parent who always feels competent when faced with a difficult child.

> *I feel like I don't have any control over my husband. I don't have any control over my son. I don't have any control over my dog. And at that point I really don't have any control over myself because I'm just reacting to these things going on because I am so overwhelmed that I lose control of myself and forget all the good things I know I do and just kind of react. (A mother's description about a chaotic afternoon at home)*

The belief that one has some control over problem situations with one's child is essential for becoming a more optimistic parent and is crucial for one's mental and perhaps even one's physical health. The concept of control has been studied for some time now, and the results of these research studies provide valuable information for helping families such as yours to become more successful and happier. For example, in the mid-1960s, Martin Seligman and Steve Maier, two psychological researchers, conducted a series of experiments with dogs to see what would happen if the dogs had no control over an unpleasant situation.[2] The details of these studies may be disturbing to some, and this type of research would most likely not be conducted today; however, the principles Seligman and Maier uncovered have implications for helping people who struggle daily with minor as well as major problems with life.

Seligman and Maier began their first study by giving dogs painful electric shocks. Some of the dogs could stop receiving the shocks by pressing on a lever, and they quickly learned this task. They still received the painful shocks but had control over this unpleasant situation. Another group of dogs, however, could do nothing to stop the shocks. The researchers added a very clever twist to this experiment. They made sure that the dogs who could not control their electric shocks received the same number of shocks at the same time as the dogs that could turn them off with the lever. Therefore, the only difference between the two groups of dogs was this concept of control. In a second study, Seligman and Maier put these same dogs in a small area where they would again receive shocks but could avoid the shocks by simply jumping over a partition into a different area. The dogs that previously had the ability to turn off the shocks with the lever quickly learned to jump into the new, safer area. However, many of the dogs that could not control the shocks simply lay down and gave up. They whined and, to the researchers, looked sad and depressed. Despite the fact that safety was just a few feet away, they appeared to have learned that they were helpless to do anything about their fate.

This series of studies served as the basis for a theory of depression called learned helplessness. At the heart of this theory is that some people become depressed after repeatedly experiencing not being able to control important aspects of their lives. So, for example, the death of someone close or having someone one cares about abandon him or her would be experiences out of one's control that would make one feel helpless and, therefore, sad and depressed. The same thing is true with experiences with one's child. Repeatedly feeling that one cannot control unpleasant situations will lead to a feeling of helplessness. In Joyce's example, the fact that she could not stop her son Mike from whining and crying at dinnertime could make her feel out of control and, over time, depressed.

However, people are not dogs. What researchers discovered when they studied learned helplessness with people (don't worry—they did not shock them!) was that it was not actually being out of control that caused depression but simply the *perception* that the person had no control. In other words, simply thinking one has no control is enough to make one feel helpless. An example from one of our families can serve as an illustration.

At the time she contacted us, Ashley was a 26-year-old mother of three young children who came to us for help with her 4-year-old son Jeffrey. All three of Ashley's children were very active, but Jeffrey often got into trouble. He was impulsive—moving from activity to activity without ever finishing anything—and had difficulty focusing his attention. For example, if he was told not to touch something (e.g., a flower vase on a table), he would listen at the time but minutes later pick it up and play with it as if he forgot the warning.

In completing her journal entry about a particularly difficult situation with Jeffrey, Ashley recalled an incident during the past week when she brought her family to her brother's house for an afternoon barbeque. As she related the incident to us during a session, it was clear that almost as soon as she arrived at her brother's house with her children, things started to fall apart. As they walked into the backyard, Jeffrey immediately ran over to his uncle's dog and started playing with her. Concerned that Jeffrey's playing with the dog might get out of hand (which had happened in the past, resulting in a bite), Ashley redirected him to a play area on the other side of the yard. Jeffrey resisted at first but then saw the swing set and rushed over to claim a swing. Unfortunately, Jeffrey's brother and sister were already sitting on the two swings. Seeing this, Ashley quickly tried to get him on the slide, but Jeffrey would have none of it. He cried and pushed his sister, trying to force her off of the swing. His sister began crying and grabbed on even more tightly to the chains of the swing in defiance.

After separating the children for several minutes, Ashley brought them inside, hoping that they could get along in a calmer setting. Unfortunately, unlike her house, her brother's house was filled with breakable things in easy reach, and Jeffrey proceeded to play with most of them. After about 10 minutes of intervening to protect her brother's valuables, Ashley gathered up the three children and went home.

This situation was very upsetting to Ashley, and she described her thoughts and feelings to us in the next session. "I had no control over anything. Nothing I did worked, and the kids were just crazy." We asked her what she believed her brother thought about what was going on, and she considered our question for a moment and then answered: "I guess I was embarrassed and thought that he thinks I'm a bad mother. He can keep his kids under control, but mine ran around like wild children. Nothing I do works!" As Ashley related this to us, you could see the sadness in her eyes.

During our first meeting with Ashley several weeks earlier, she described herself as having been a "party girl" before the kids were born. At times you could see flashes of that persona in Ashley, especially when she joked with her husband; however, the increasingly difficult situation with Jeffrey was melting away that self-image. The feeling of often having no control with her children was affecting other parts of Ashley's life. She described how she now didn't want to go out except as an escape. She didn't enjoy things like she did before and was eating more and sleeping less. These changes—loss of interest in previously pleasurable activities as well as changes in eating and sleeping habits—are all signs of depression. Ashley's perception of being out of control was making her more and more depressed.

To give you an idea of how we help parents who have thoughts such as Ashley's, here is how we started. We began by asking the following question: "At the barbeque, is it true you really had no control at all?" "Yes," Ashley replied. "But you were able to take your children out of that situation. You also said that next time you would ask your brother to make his house more kid friendly and put away things that could be broken easily. That would make it better to visit. So, did you have no control at all?" "Well, I guess I had some control." In fact, Ashley did have some control. From the outside, others probably would have seen what happened and thought that her children were difficult but that she handled it well. She didn't yell or scream (too much), and she took charge by moving the children indoors and finally taking them home. Yet, her perception of the situation was very different from what it looked like to others. Her thoughts about being out of control—regardless of whether she actually was—were enough to make her upset and sad.

Psychological researchers describe what is called a pessimistic attributional style—a way of looking at situations that is common among people who are depressed but is also seen in others. I described this way of thinking in Chapter 2 when illustrating the differences in how optimists and pessimists look at the same situations. To review, people who exhibit pessimistic attribution styles interpret what happens to them in the following ways:

- Pessimists see positive things as being caused by some outside influence and not as something they accomplished.
- Pessimists see negative things as their fault.
- Pessimists see negative things as likely to continue and positive things as temporary.
- Pessimists overgeneralize problems, seeing them as likely to affect many parts of their lives.

In Ashley's case, Ashley would discount good interactions with Jeffrey as a result of the amount of sleep he had or the food he ate (outside influences) but his impulsivity and activity as her own doing. His behaviors were probably signs of ADHD—a genetic disorder that has little to do with her parenting skills—yet she saw them as her failures. When Jeffrey was well behaved, Ashley saw this as a fluke (temporary); when Jeffrey misbehaved, Ashley could not envision an end to his disruption (permanent). Finally, she would catastrophize and overgeneralize—describing these episodes as being more disruptive than they actually were.

The other questions from the quiz are examined in the sections that follow. I highlighted thoughts of being out of control in the previous section because these thoughts are so important. First, they can cause you to give up too easily on efforts that could help your child. Again, believing in yourself and your abilities as a parent is the first step toward Optimistic Parenting. Second, thoughts of being out of control in your life can directly and negatively affect you, causing you discomfort and possibly even influencing your health. Some research, for example, suggests that looking at the world as a pessimist can put you at increased risk for infectious diseases and may even shorten your life.[3] Finally, in the sections that follow, some of the themes that parents describe may be related to thoughts of being out of control.

I'm Not Sure How Best to Handle This Situation   If your thoughts in your problem situation include doubts about how you should have handled the episode, then this too can affect your ability to respond properly to your child. This thought is similar to worrying about being out of control but is more specific to your own knowledge or ability to respond to problems.

How am I going to get my son to eat new foods? This is really hard. This is harder than I thought it was going to be. My son's situation is very complicated. His food issues are very complex. (A mother's description of her reactions after taking her son to be assessed by a therapist for his picky eating)

I include the concept of self-doubt in the same category as the concern about being out of control (self-efficacy). A great deal of research has been done on the overall notion of self-efficacy—thoughts related to your ability to assist your child. One of the findings from parents who have low self-efficacy (those who feel out of control and/or doubt their parenting abilities) is that they will tend to have negative emotional reactions such as anger or sadness in response to their child's problem behavior. Later chapters address the idea that what you think (e.g., "I am a bad parent") affects how you feel (e.g., angry, resigned, frustrated, helpless). Our goal is to improve your self-efficacy, and this, in turn, will improve your emotional reactions to problem situations.

In This Situation, Others Are Judging Me Negatively as a Parent

If you agreed with this response to your child's behavior, your concern switches from what you think about yourself to what others think about you as a parent. These two different concepts can overlap (i.e., feeling both insecure and judged) but also can be separate (i.e., being sure about what to do but still thinking that others are critical of your skills or approach). If you have expressed this concern to friends or other people who are important to you, you likely have heard in response, "Oh, what do you care what others think?" Although it is true that the opinions of others should not matter, to you they do.

The hardest part is when people stare and they don't understand. I heard an airline employee say, "I'm sorry we have parents who can't control their children." They don't know my son is autistic. It's embarrassing. (A mother's reflections about her family's recent plane trip and her son's tantrums)

If you think back to Ashley and the episode at her brother's house, she told us that she was thinking that her brother was judging her as a parent because she could not keep her children from misbehaving at his house. Although she was doing all she could to handle the problems with Jeffrey and her other children, at the same time she felt that her brother was keeping an eye on all of this and was thinking that she was incompetent. When we later checked on her feelings, she told us that this made her feel inadequate and highly anxious. These thoughts and feelings clearly interfered with her ability to handle some of the situation in a way she typically would.

Some fascinating research has been done on the concept of using one's gut instinct in situations when one is faced with difficult choices (in this case, how to handle a child's problems out in public).[4] Scientists believe that the human brain is only capable of handling up to seven pieces of information at a time and that when faced with more options than that, we begin to have difficulty choosing. In fact, although people will report that they prefer more choices (e.g., 20 types of breakfast cereal, 30 different types of new cars), we are more likely to purchase something if the choices are somewhat limited. With increasing choices, our rational brain becomes less helpful because humans are not able to judge so many options. In this case, the emotional brain helps out. For example, when a person goes down the snack chip aisle in the supermarket and dozens of options jump out at him or her, he or she is likely to pick the most familiar option (e.g., the brand name chips). Marketing depends on this, which is why our society is faced with so much advertising; a familiar product is more likely than an unfamiliar product to be chosen in a store. Researchers in the field of marketing understand that the emotional choice will be one of familiarity when faced with conflicting options.

But what happens if the emotional brain is distracted? If an individual is upset or otherwise thinking and feeling something else, he or she will have difficulty using emotional thinking, otherwise referred to as a gut reaction. Let me explain with a personal example. I have spent decades driving cars with a stick shift (manual transmission). My first car was a Volkswagen; and in the following years, I mostly drove cars that required manual gear shifting. Typically, driving with a stick shift is not something I think about when I am traveling around town or on a trip. My rational brain is not being used and I am not thinking, "Put it in second gear now" or "Start downshifting as you approach the red light." I just drive—using my emotional brain, which is partly out of my awareness. However, whenever I have someone in the car with me besides members of my family, I start to think. And when I think about shifting gears, inevitably I make a mistake (grinding the gears!). This thing that usually comes naturally to me becomes stilted when I am concerned about what someone might think about my driving. Being anxious about someone's opinion of my driving actually contributes to my driving poorly.

This same phenomenon occurs with parenting. Much of what you do with your child happens without thinking—a kiss on the head, a smile, a warning not to touch someone; all of these things usually happen from instinct, from your gut. However, if you think you are being observed and judged, then you become more self-conscious about each of these gestures. You might hesitate to do things because now you are not trusting your instincts. There are ways to begin to change this pattern, which will be covered later in the book; for now, it is enough to begin to become aware of whether these types of thoughts are going through your mind when you are parenting your child in a difficult situation.

In This Situation, Others Are Judging My Child Negatively   Being concerned about the opinions of other people is not limited to how they view

you as a parent. Parents often will report that when their child acts up in front of others, they are concerned that others are judging their child. This concern extends to friends, relatives, or other children. Some families who have children with more severe problems can become extremely embarrassed for their child, reading into the looks being made by others.

> *I really worry about that, especially with other children seeing it. I don't mind so much adults seeing it or if she does it in the store and somebody says something. I could care less. I worry about the other kids seeing that because they know she is not in any way, shape, or form normal. I hate to use that word. I don't want other children saying, "Well you know, that's the freak." I hate to use that word too but I don't want them thinking that way. (A mother's concern about how other children view her daughter and her behaviors)*

In Chapter 1, I described two mothers at a book club meeting who had participated in some of our early research. Each of these parents had a child with significant problems, but they each looked at their child's abilities quite differently. One mother was riddled with self-doubt, whereas the other was confident in her abilities. Similarly, the mother with low self-efficacy also became embarrassed for her child when he had tantrums in public. She felt the eyes of other parents on both her and her child, and she feared that other children thought her child was "weird." As a result, she began limiting her outings with her child, and they were becoming more and more isolated.

In contrast, the mother who expressed more confidence in herself also expressed that she did not care what others thought of her or her child. When her child acted up in a public place such as a supermarket and someone made a negative comment, she would give that person a lecture on the nature of her child's problems and would communicate quite clearly how rude and ignorant the person was. She simply did not care what others thought. Again, this is easier said than done; later in this book (Chapter 5) I describe how to deal with this concern for your child without having to resort to the tongue lashing this mother chose as her style.

My Child Is Not Able to Control This Behavior and My Child's Disability or Condition Is Causing or Contributing to This Problem

Thinking that your child's problem behaviors are out of his or her control is another significant obstacle to effective behavior change. If your child has a psychological diagnosis (e.g., ADHD, bipolar disorder, autism spectrum disorder), you may be tempted to believe that the disorder or problem is responsible for the way your child behaves in all situations. For example, in my colleagues' and my research on the sleep problems of children with special needs,[5] we often find that parents attribute their child's problems at bedtime or their night waking to the child's disorder (e.g., "Most children with autism have sleep problems, so he probably has difficulty sleeping through the night because of his disorder").

What we have to point out to families is that although sleep problems may be more common among children with certain disorders, more often than not the difficulties themselves may not differ from the sleep problems of children without disabilities; the way we approach fixing the sleep problems is the same as well.

> *That's the autistic thing, but why does he do that? I really sometimes think something is hurting him. Because he can play with me and he is perfectly okay…and then all of a sudden he has to stand up and he has to jump. So then I think something has to be…the word* hurt *may not be correct but something sensory. (A father tries to explain his son's jumping up and down at seemingly unpredictable times as caused by his disorder)*

Even if your child has no specific diagnosis, sometimes the nature of your child's problems makes them seem as if they could not possibly be controlled. Often, for example, a tantrum can be so violent and emotion ridden that it appears as if the child is possessed by some outside force. Again, however, research shows time and time again that the reasons why children misbehave do not differ substantially among children, regardless of how the behavior problems appear from the outside. Fortunately, we are able to help all of our families improve their child's problem behaviors.

Regardless of why you think that your child's behavior may be at least partly out of his or her control, thinking that your child cannot manage to behave better (what we call having low child efficacy) will affect how you respond to him or her. Any doubt about your own ability or, in this case, your child's ability to change will introduce a level of uncertainty into parenting situations. As a result, any temporary setbacks will be attributed to your child's inability rather than to the typical changes that inevitably occur. Again, using an example from our sleep work, my colleagues and I find that once we have helped a child to sleep better, minor changes can interrupt our progress. A weekend of staying up too late or a long trip that changes a child's sleep pattern can cause some of the sleep problems to return. If the parents see these changes as temporary (i.e., "Once we get back home and get back on schedule, he'll start to sleep better again"), then they will regroup and go back to the plans that worked before. However, if this setback is seen as a sign that the child will never really be able to sleep better (i.e., "Ugh, that plan didn't really work!"), then they are more likely to give up and not persist.

Being effective as a parent requires persistence more than anything else. Having any doubts about your child's ability to change will make continuing on a difficult course just that much more difficult.

This Type of Situation Is Always a Problem for My Child   This type of thought about a situation may reflect how pervasive you think a problem is for your child. If parents in our program tend to have these types of thoughts

often, we examine them further to see how realistic they are. It very well may be that a particular situation is always (or almost always) a problem for your child. For example, getting dressed in the morning may be a trigger for a major tantrum, and this may occur every morning. In this case, thinking that it is always a problem is rational and realistic. Having parents become aware that they are thinking this as they begin to get their child dressed is important, however, because these thoughts may actually contribute to the problem.

They've been horrible all week. It's like nothing is so much different as my son is starting to really see that when he has a temper tantrum and we don't want to deal with it and we give in he sees that if I do this, this is what will happen. Now he tantrums all the time. (A mother describes her son's tantrums as if they are happening continuously)

If you recall, in Chapter 2 I discussed the interesting phenomenon of "emotion contagion." In this case, if a parent begins a particular task or activity (e.g., getting dressed, going to the store) that is usually a problem with the thought that it will be a problem again, then the child may pick up the parent's negative emotion about what is about to happen. The parent's dread may be a signal to the child that the situation is going to be a problem, and he or she will pick up on that negative emotion.

Although in some cases these thoughts are reality-based, this type of thought in some parents may not be entirely realistic. Thinking that a particular situation is always a problem may not reflect reality as much as be a result of the pervasive style of thinking that is common in people with pessimistic attributional styles of thinking. Mealtime, for example, might be a common time for a particular child to tantrum but in reality may only happen once or twice per week. The tantrums, however, may result in such a commotion that at the time it seems as if it happens at every meal. This exaggerated view of the problem can cause a parent to feel helpless—much like the dogs in the learned helplessness experiments—and lead to a sense of defeat (e.g., "Shopping with my child is always a disaster—I don't take her with me anymore").

Many of these thoughts can cause an individual to start avoiding certain problem situations. For example, one of the families in our program related the following story to us about their teenage son.

Just when he turned 13, he started closing his bedroom door. Of course, we remember what it is like being a teenager and the importance of privacy. But more and more, it is getting difficult to talk to him. If we knock on his door now, he says from inside, "Yes?" as if talking to us is a major imposition. We think that talking through doors is rude, and we tell him that. He will then crack open the door about a half an inch and repeat "Yes?" but with even more impatience. In the past, we would have talked about a variety of things, but we are beginning to avoid these interactions because they are so unpleasant. Now, we only knock on his door when we absolutely have to, usually to remind him to do his homework or to do a chore around the house. Increasingly, our only communication is negative. In fact, now we avoid getting him to do chores such as taking out the garbage because it is such a hassle. He seems to be the one in control of things and although we know it's not right, we feel trapped.

Avoiding problems is natural. Every parent learns the concept of "picking your battles" at some point and understands when and when not to push certain things. But, in the case just described and for most of the families with whom we work, this avoidance of problems starts to become a problem in and of itself. I have called this progression of avoiding more and more situations the *concession process*. Again, it is natural that as parents we all learn that children need room to grow and make their own decisions. However, many parents who are faced with an extremely challenging child begin to fashion a world around them that becomes extremely limited—essentially conceding all problem situations to the child—and start to feel trapped in their child's world.

I do that a lot. I am avoiding a lot with him. I just don't have the energy to fight with him. It's just, "Here, I'll get you dressed. Here take this snack. Here, here, here..." (A mother describes how she constantly gives in to her son's demands despite knowing she should not)

The concession process begins insidiously—without parents really knowing it's happening. It starts with little things; for example, you might give your child a candy bar in a supermarket after he or she begins to whine about it. You know you probably shouldn't give in to his or her whining, but what harm will come from doing it just this once? You might put your child's shirt on him or her yourself, even though he or she can do it on his or her own, just because it's easier and faster if you do it. Perhaps you serve your child dinner in the living room in front of the television, because then the rest of the family can eat in peace. Over time, much in the house begins to revolve around your child who has problem behavior. Maybe you don't go to restaurants or to the park to avoid negative incidents. You might not invite friends over to your house because it is likely that your child will act out and ruin the evening.

This process of concession—giving in to the needs and demands of your child at the expense of your needs and those of the rest of your family—can progress to a level that is so extreme it can lead to feeling trapped inside your home and in your life. I remember one case in which I visited a mother (Bridget) at her home just after she had met her son's bus following a particularly difficult day at school. Her son Jamie was 14 years old, weighed approximately 250 pounds, had a limited ability to speak, and had significant cognitive impairments. When I arrived, Jamie was sitting in the hallway off of the living room, leaning against the wall, and eating his afterschool snack. His snack was a rather large bowl of grits smothered in butter, and he was wearing only his underpants. Bridget related to me that as soon as Jamie would come home from school he would strip and demand grits. In fact, he would hit his mother or anyone else who got in the way if he didn't get his snack immediately.

Bridget further described her life with her son and how the family accommodated his needs. Her younger daughter never had friends over because they were afraid of Jamie. They rarely went out and only went to one fast food restaurant because it had a separate room. When the family was in that side room, no one else came in because of the odd noises Jamie would make. This was embarrassing to Bridget and her family so they never went anywhere else where other people might be around.

As Bridget continued to describe all of the things they did to keep Jamie and themselves safe, I asked her how she was doing. I guess she didn't quite understand my question because she started to defend how they dealt with Jamie. "No," I said. "I want to know how you are doing. It must be very hard on you to handle all of this mostly by yourself." She finally looked up, as if she was going "off script." It was obvious she told these stories hundreds of times before—to friends, relatives, teachers, and other professionals—and felt defensive each time she did. She had her story straight, and my question caught her off guard. She started to cry. After a moment she collected herself somewhat and managed to get out, "No one ever asks about me. Everyone comes here to tell me why I shouldn't give him so much food or why I shouldn't let him take his clothes off at home. They try to get me to fill out endless forms or to get me to try to teach him things. I'm just doing the best that I can! And I feel trapped and like I will never have my own life. And then I feel guilty thinking that because this should all be about what's best for Jamie."

Bridget and her family had lived the concession process for 14 years. Little by little, they had found ways to survive with limited injury and disruption from Jamie by creating an artificial world around him. It was all understandable given the circumstances, but the cumulative effect of all of the changes over the years and the tears was a way of interacting that left the rest of the family prisoners in their own home and community. The case of Bridget and Jamie is an extreme one, but it is certainly not unique. In fact, we see these types of interactions to some extent in all of the homes that we visit.

The concession process is not limited to families. Teachers also fall prey to this process. It is not uncommon for us to see a teacher rearranging where a child sits, how close she stands next to a child, and the activities required of a child, all to avoid problems. I sometimes can walk into a classroom and immediately tell the concession process is occurring by looking at the room arrangement and seeing what the child is doing. For example, other children might be working at their desks on a task, whereas the child I am there to see is sitting in a corner playing with a toy, all in an effort to avoid behavior problems. The teacher has probably learned that avoiding tasks makes the child behave better—a classic case of the concession process. In fact, some programs for students with special needs are designed specifically to avoid any possibility of problems. The students eat in the cafeteria at different times to avoid conflict with other students. They may sit at assigned seats throughout the day to avoid interactions with each other. They follow rigid schedules to avoid the problems that accompany unpredictable situations that can trigger problem behavior in some children.

Is this wrong? Why shouldn't teachers try to adapt the activities in their classrooms to meet the needs of their students? As I mentioned before, some level of concession is typical and is a part of dealing with diverse groups of people regardless of their behavior problems. For example, a woman may concede to the desires of her husband by watching a Sunday afternoon football game even if this is not something she enjoys herself. However, when the level of concession starts to be confining and when other aspects of one's world become a problem because excessive amounts of one's time or activities are conceded to others, then it bares reflection. Let's take the classroom example. If a student is better behaved when she is allowed to sit alone in the corner listening to her favorite music all day, is this good? The teacher might be happy because the child no longer has tantrums when asked to do regular class activities. The other students might be happy as well now that there is less disruption in the room. In fact, I have seen teachers praised by their supervisors for making just these changes (saying, e.g., "She is the best teacher he has ever had; he hasn't had a major tantrum all semester!"). Of course, the problem here is obvious. Just because a student is well behaved does not mean his or her academic and social needs are being met. Sitting listening to music in a corner does not further a student's math or reading skills or prepare him or her for being in a classroom with demands. Having students follow rigid schedules to avoid problems associated with uncertainty limits their ability to handle the inevitable times when the schedule cannot be followed. Again, there is a fine line between being flexible and creating environments around a child that are so idiosyncratic and specific as to interfere with his or her future independence and the family's happiness.

Has your family been affected by the concession process? One way to test whether this has occurred in your own family is to ask yourself if you often feel trapped. Have the changes you have made in your life and in the lives of the other members of the family caused serious disruptions in your own lives? In addition, are the changes likely to get in the way of your child's ability to succeed in other settings? For example, years ago I tried to teach a child in a residential setting where I worked to tie his shoes. After much effort and no success, he was just given shoes with no laces. This concession reduced his resistance to our teaching him shoe tying, he could now successfully put on his own shoes, and he would not have trouble later in life without this skill. At the same time, I persisted in my efforts to get him to put on his own shirt. I could have conceded to him by just dressing him myself, which would have been much easier and taken less time, but I wanted him to be able to dress himself. He could be far more independent in life if he had this skill. Ultimately, he learned to put on T-shirts but was unable to learn to button shirts; this, at least, was enough for him to dress himself minimally.

How would you assess the concessions made by Bridget for her son Jamie? Would it be okay for her to continue to allow him to strip when he comes home, sit on the floor in the hall, and eat high-calorie grits? Of course, this really was not our decision; Bridget was just doing her best to find ways to survive day to day. With Bridget's approval, however, we did begin to target these behaviors at home. Because Bridget hoped that one day Jamie would be able to live semi-independently in a group home, his habit of stripping and sitting on the floor eating a snack needed to be addressed; these behaviors certainly would have interfered with his success in such a setting. At the same time, his ballooning weight was becoming a major health concern; at 14 years of age, he already was showing signs of diabetes. Having him consume so much high-fat food during the day was shortening his life span. Before I introduced any intervention at home for Jamie, however, I needed to understand the thoughts Bridget had that led her to this point. Did she feel incapable of helping Jamie (low self-efficacy)? Did she feel Jamie was not capable of learning to eat in a more typical way (low child efficacy)? Were there other thoughts that interfered with her gut reactions about the best way to handle these problems?

The issue of the concession process is addressed again in Chapters 5, 6, and 11. Many of the interfering thoughts described here can lead to this pattern of concession and can have serious consequences for a child's ability to be more independent and for a family's happiness.

This Will Never Get Better or May Become Worse   The previous thought (e.g., "This type of situation is always a problem for my child") involves the idea that problems cut across all situations regardless of whether this is really true. This next statement (i.e., "This will never get better or may become worse") gets to what we typically think of when we talk about pessimism. Obviously, if one thinks that a problem is not likely to improve, one will have a great deal of difficulty persisting with any plan designed to work on the problem. If you find that you have this thought when a negative situation is occurring with your child, it may be a result of your own tendency to look at difficult situations in a negative light. As I mentioned before, some people are more likely to look at difficult situations as permanent, thus making efforts to improve these situations futile. However, more often than not, this thought involves a combination of how you look at the world and your experiences. So, for example, if you have tried a number of different ways (e.g., bribing, threatening, dragging despite kicking and screaming) of getting your child to get on the school bus in the morning without crying but have been unsuccessful, these negative experiences can make you believe that getting your child on the bus will always be a problem. Again, if you approach a situation such as this as if it will always be a problem, it likely will be.

> *It's kind of like people that have arthritis. They learn to live with the pain. (A mother describes her difficulties dealing with her son's behavior problems)*

It is important to examine your thoughts during these problem situations and see if this type of pessimistic thought is creeping into your mind. Later, I will describe how to start to view these situations from a more optimistic point of view (e.g., "This can get better").

I Will Never Have Time for Just Me   This is a summary of a variety of thoughts that center on how your child's problem behavior is affecting you. It often takes some of the parents in our program a little time to admit that they are thinking not only about their child and the impact of his or her challenging behaviors on the rest of the family but also about how their child's behavior affects their own lives. When I asked Bridget, Jamie's mother, how she was doing, she released a torrent of emotions and finally said, "I'm just doing the best that I can! And I feel trapped and that I will never have my own life. And then I feel guilty thinking that because this should all be about what's best for Jamie." In the following quotation, another mother describes how she would like some time for herself, away from her children:

> *Sometimes I feel like I just want to go watch a movie. Just leave the kids with some-one and go watch a good movie or just go out to eat. Just be by myself, have some time to do some stuff, maybe go to the gym, work out.*

A great deal of sacrificing occurs when one becomes a parent. Even the most well-behaved children require their parents to change their lives to meet the children's needs. However, having a challenging child multiplies the amount of time and emotional energy required of the parent. In Bridget's case, she was doing what she thought was expected of her. Because of his many behavioral as well as medical needs, Bridget took total control over his care. Her background was as a nurse, so she was used to putting the needs of other people over her own. When I asked her how she was handling it all, she revealed that I was the first professional to ever ask about her. All of the others seemed to approach her with an agenda about her son (e.g., "How can we get Jamie to lose some weight?" "How can we get the family to work with him like we do at school?"), and usually there was a subtext of somehow blaming her for not being a better parent.

For a time, Bridget went to a parent support group for families who had children with problems similar to her son's. This was recommended by the school as part of their routine recommendations for families with very challenging children. The idea was to put her in touch with other families facing similar experiences and that somehow that might help her. Bridget did recognize that there was some value in this group. She said she learned from another parent in the group about a dentist who would be sensitive to Jamie's needs and that this was a major find. However, Bridget also experienced a downside to this group; she often left the meeting feeling sad. When I pressed her for details, she revealed that she felt inadequate among some of the other mothers. There were some, she said, who not only seemed to handle their child's outbursts but also seemed to be conversant in the latest research; one parent in the group even presented information about her experiences at a local conference. Although she never shared this with the group, these accomplishments made her feel inadequate. "I can barely get out of bed some mornings, and here they are on major committees, going to conferences, and keeping on top of everything. I never feel like I'm doing enough." On top of all of this, Bridget was longing for a life of her own—some part of her that did not have to focus on her son and his many needs; however, even the thought of this made her feel guilty.

It is not selfish to want your life to include something in addition to being a parent. In fact, I would argue that it is healthy to have aspects of your life apart from caring for your challenging child. We sometimes get so enmeshed in helping others that we forget to help ourselves. In Chapter 6 I will come back to this concept and help you achieve a more balanced life.

My Child Is Doing This on Purpose   This thought is common among some parents and is the opposite of one of the other common things parents say to themselves—"My child is not able to control this behavior."

Because he's got the devil in him. He's got "666" on his forehead. I'm just coming up with some other terminology for you to write down. That could be a possibility. (A mother's humorous explanation for why her son seems to intentionally misbehave with her)

Sometimes in our program, we see families in which one parent thinks the child has no control and the other parent believes it is all intentional. If you think back to the description of Dave and Marcie in Chapter 2, you will see a perfect example of this pattern. They were the couple who appeared on the surface to be so confident; yet, when we delved into their thoughts about their son Jeremy's problems, it became clear that they were not. Marcie believed that her son had no control over his outbursts and that some disorder (e.g., ADHD) probably was to blame. Dave, conversely, felt that Jeremy was intentionally screaming and carrying on in situations to get back at his father and to control the situation. Who interpreted Jeremy's behavior correctly? When later we discuss how to determine why your child misbehaves, we will see that in a way both of them were correct. But for now, we will keep our focus on what you are thinking during these episodes (e.g., yelling and screaming at dinnertime) and then go over better ways to look at the same situations.

This Situation Is (Spouse's, Partner's, Family Member's, or Other's) Fault for Not Handling This Like I Suggested   Another common theme in the inner dialogue that goes through the minds of parents in difficult child situations is blame—finding who is responsible for the outburst that is now causing so much disruption.

My son wouldn't eat dinner, so I agreed to make him something different—chicken nuggets—but he keeps screaming. I put him in time-out in his bedroom, but he wouldn't stay. My husband took him out of time-out and gave him the chicken nuggets. If he hadn't intervened I would have gotten my son to calm down. When dad is around, my son knows he will rescue him. And the same thing happens at my parent's house—they give in to him too. (A mother describes her frustration with her husband and her parents for interfering with her efforts to discipline her child)

Blame is a funny thing. When there is a problem or things do not turn out as planned, often one's first instinct is to judge one's own behavior or the actions of others—what, in our society, we call "finding fault." In fact, much of the day's news is reported as a presentation of facts (e.g., "A young girl was hit by a car crossing Main Street today") followed by some presentation of why the incident occurred (e.g., "Neighbors blame the lack of a more visible police presence for the speeding downtown"). Politics is all about who is responsible. Rarely do we in American society see thoughtful discussions of how things might be changed for the better without fingers pointing in the direction of who is to blame for the terrible state of our town, city, state, country, world, environment, and so forth. One only needs to read the comments made by readers of news stories online to see the outpouring of blame that occurs in any troubling event, from the ridiculous (e.g., "Why was the girl crossing the street anyway?") to the personal (e.g., "I keep saying that the mayor doesn't care about the safety of our citizens").

For some parents, the same instincts play out when their child misbehaves. If your inclination is to find fault, your first reaction may be to blame yourself (self-blame, which I discuss next) or to blame other people. Although neither of these thoughts is particularly productive, blaming someone else (e.g., "If you had only put him to bed at his regular bedtime, we wouldn't be seeing this tantrum now") may make you feel less guilty (e.g., "It isn't my fault that he is overtired and crying now"). Again, it is part of human nature to judge a situation and to try to find out why it occurred. The real question—which is addressed later in this chapter in the section titled "What Are the Consequences of Your Thoughts and Feelings?"—is whether these thoughts are valuable or help you be a better parent.

It Is My Fault that This Is a Problem   Again, trying to find blame for a difficult situation is a natural reaction; however, excessive self-blame is a destructive process that can significantly interfere with one's ability to be a better parent. Equally as important, self-blame can, over time, lead to anxiety and depression.

It makes me feel horrible. Sometimes I feel like a failure. I've done so well with all these other kids and I've potty-trained all these other kids and my daughter is 3 and still in Pull-Ups. Sometimes I feel like I just completely don't know what to do with this child. (A mother describes how she feels it is her fault that her daughter has such a difficult time with toileting)

The very first case I described in Chapter 1—the case of Timmy (the boy with autism who hit himself and others) and his mother Ruth—is a classic case of self-blame. Ruth felt that it was her fault that Timmy had so many problems. In fact, she had what I call "genetic guilt"—the guilty feeling that comes along with believing that you passed along the genes that are responsible for your child's difficulties (in this case, autism). Despite the fact that Ruth spent all of her waking moments caring for Timmy, she felt that she wasn't doing enough. Compounding this feeling of guilt for Timmy's problems was the blame Ruth put on herself for her failed marriage and for therefore depriving her children of having a father figure in the house. All of this self-blame contributed to Ruth's growing sense of helplessness and responsibility for the difficult time her children were having. She was sad and probably clinically depressed most of the time that I knew her.

You probably think I am going to say that parents are not to blame for their child's misbehavior. Well, you are wrong. Parents are to blame. And, the child is to blame. And, biology is to blame. And, the surrounding environment (e.g., school, friends, other family members, professionals and their advice, diet, medications) is to blame as well. At some level, all parents influence how their children behave. The real question that is explored in this book is not who should be blamed but what things can be changed to help your child behave better. Regardless of your religious or spiritual beliefs, the "Serenity Prayer," popularized by Alcoholics Anonymous and often attributed to Reinhold Niebuhr, sums up this concept:

God, grant me the serenity
To accept the things I cannot change;
Courage to change the things I can;
And wisdom to know the difference.

It is the "wisdom to know the difference" and the "courage to change the things I can" that guide the remainder of this book.

Why Am I Always Responsible for My Child's Behavior?   Even though we refer to our program as "parent training," it is typically the mothers with whom we work. Despite enormous changes in the family—with more and more mothers working outside of the home—mothers continue to take on a majority of the household and child-rearing responsibilities. Even in families in which the husband, boyfriend, partner, or grandparents pitch in, it is still typically the mother who takes responsibility for organizing all child care jobs. Although this is not always true—some men or other family members do take on the main caregiver role in a small number of families—in the vast majority of families, the mother (or grandmother) is in charge.

A lot of times I do feel like I'm handling everything myself because my husband is not there a lot of the time. He's at work. But then also sometimes when he is home I feel that I'm a much more active parent than my husband is. (A mother describes how she feels she is always responsible for her child)

Because one parent (again, usually the mother) typically takes the lead with regard to the children, the other parental partner is likely to be on the sidelines. In some ways, this makes sense. It is easier to run a household or even a business if one person oversees the day-to-day operations and takes ultimate responsibility. Having more than one person share responsibilities can become complicated, with important things (e.g., scheduling a doctor's appointment, signing a permission slip for school) sometimes being missed because one person thought the other would follow through. Although it is easy to understand why a family would run this way, having one parent handle most of the child-related responsibilities can place an enormous burden on that person's shoulders and, in some cases, lead to resentment.

It should not be surprising, then, that a common theme in the thoughts of mothers who have children with challenging behavior is some version of "Why am I always responsible for my child's behavior?" Sometimes, this is the theme of ongoing conflict in the family, a continuous discussion of this problem that dominates how a couple communicates. In other families, this theme is submerged. The thoughts are there (e.g., "Why is it always up to me?"), but they do not get communicated in a way that helps get the problem resolved. When we have the opportunity in our sessions to work with both partners, it is sometimes the case that the man is relatively silent. Such was the case for Henry. This case will be examined in some detail because it not only illustrates this type of conflict but also shows some of the other thoughts that parents have about their child's behavior.

Henry and his wife Dani had been married for 7 years. By all accounts, it had been a happy marriage—at least until the birth of their first child about 3 years earlier. They had been trying to have a child for some time and, in fact, had just begun to discuss adopting a child. Then, Dani became pregnant. Dani was ill during most of the pregnancy, but she reports that Henry was very attentive and helpful; it actually was the most positive time of their marriage. This all changed when Chelsea was born.

Both Dani and Henry were only children and, therefore, never grew up with other children in the house. They had no experience with other children with which to compare Chelsea's progress; therefore, they were not alarmed when, during Chelsea's first year, she didn't babble and didn't seem to be interested in typical infant games. Chelsea seemed to scream almost constantly, but Dani and Henry saw other children crying at the mall or at the supermarket and told themselves that it was just part of being an infant.

Waiting in the pediatrician's office for Chelsea's 18-month checkup, Henry started to read the chart on the wall that described developmental milestones and became anxious. His daughter was fine when it came to things such as running and climbing or scribbling with a crayon but didn't measure up when it came to her language or social skills. He didn't share his concern with Dani.

Later, in the doctor's examining room, things seemed to go well. Chelsea tolerated the poking and probing better than they expected, especially when the doctor let her play with his stethoscope. However, when the pediatrician started to listen to her parent's answers to questions about social development and language, his face took on a look of concern. He tried playing "Peekaboo" with Chelsea, but she didn't seem interested. When he asked Chelsea to point to the toy dog on the table, she looked over at it but didn't point to it or look at him. The doctor started to ask more questions. Later, Henry would tell us that he couldn't remember too much else about that visit except that it was as if the lights in the exam room were getting dimmer and he was having trouble focusing. He thought he might pass out. When Henry and Dani walked back to their car, they knew without speaking that their world had just fundamentally changed.

Over the next few months, they began their crash course in new terms—autism, speech and language pathology, pervasive developmental disorder-not otherwise specified (PDD-NOS)—and new acronyms—IDEA (Individuals with Disabilities Education Act), IEP (individualized education program), ABA (applied behavior analysis), PBS (positive behavioral support), and so forth. Dani, as she usually did, took control. She went online, met and talked to other parents of children such as Chelsea, and generally immersed herself in this new world.

Henry's reaction was quite different. He seemed to resist talk of a diagnosis. In his world, everything seemed to be fine. Sure, his daughter was different, but she was not *abnormal*. If Chelsea wanted to sit on the floor and eat her lunch, what was wrong with that? She would scream if they tried to get her to wear shoes outside, so why did they have to force her? Chelsea's mom, on the other hand, pushed her to do the things that other children her age did. Dani took Chelsea shopping and on other errands around town even though it often ended in a tantrum.

This conflict in style between Henry and Dani worsened until it became all-consuming. By the time they came to our center for help with Chelsea, they had begun discussing separation.

In our sessions, Dani did most of the talking and Henry seemed to be totally withdrawn. It didn't take long before Dani expressed her frustration with Henry. "He just doesn't seem to care! Chelsea could be playing with macaroni and cheese on the living room rug, and he just sits there." Henry folded his arms over his chest and sank down in his chair. Dani looked over at him with disgust. "And why am I always the one to get her dressed? To take her to the doctor's office? To brush her teeth?" Henry looked at her, not angry or resentful at her attacks, but with a blank expression.

"Is it true?" the therapist asked. "Do you really not care about these things?" Henry just shrugged.

Before we return to this family, it is worth pointing out a few issues that this case has in common with that of other families who ask for our help. It is not unusual to have a couple disagree over how to raise a child. Like too many couples, however, Henry and Dani didn't just disagree on Chelsea's care; they didn't seem to have any way to resolve their differences in dealing with Chelsea. In addition, Henry just seems to have shut down. But, does Henry really not care about his daughter? Early on, all of the signs pointed to a caring father. What could have caused him to pull back?

Because this is a very common pattern among the families in our program, it may be useful to take a look at what might have led to this style of interacting. In the 1950s, a family involved a married man and woman with children. It was common for the man to spend most of the day away from home, at work. The woman usually was responsible for running the home and taking care of the children. With changing times, however, families also have changed. More and more women are taking on jobs outside of the home, in part as a result of financial necessity but also because of changing views of women in the workplace. In many families, however, the woman continues to be the one responsible for most of the household chores and for child rearing even if she holds a full-time job.

As I pointed out, the good news is that men are helping out more in this changing family structure; however, this usually involves their carrying out chores identified by the mother. The mother, therefore, is still responsible, even if the father helps. Let's look at how this affects the father.

To provide some insight into Henry's view of the world, picture this scenario told to me and my colleagues by Henry and Dani. One night, Dani asked, "Would you give Chelsea a bath tonight? I promised I would go over to my sister's and help her with wedding plans." Henry dreaded bath time because Chelsea often fought it, but he agreed. Henry and Dani had just made up from an argument, and he was trying to be conciliatory. To Henry's relief, Chelsea's bath went fairly well. Chelsea loved rubber ducks, and they had just bought a few new ones. Chelsea would throw them around the bathroom, but it helped distract her enough for Henry to get her clean. Dani wasn't home by bedtime, so he took this on too, lying down next to Chelsea until she fell asleep. He was upstairs in the bedroom when he heard Dani come home. He felt pretty good, having succeeded in getting Chelsea bathed and into bed. When Dani walked into the bedroom, however, she was angry. "That bathroom is a mess! There's water all over the place, towels are on the floor, and the tub's dirty. Do you think I'm your maid? I ask you to do one thing...." Henry was crushed. Here he thought he would be the hero, but instead, despite all his efforts and good intentions, they were back in the same place with Dani angry at him.

How did this affect Henry? Did it make him determined to do a better job next time or to take on more chores? This is what Dani thought would happen. She told us that she expected he would feel bad, see the world through her eyes, and be better at helping. In fact, it had the opposite effect. After considerable prodding, Henry told us, "Nothing I do is right. Even when I go out of my way to help, she gets mad at me anyway." So, did he tell his wife this? Did he express his frustration and try to get her to see things from his perspective? "No," he told us. "If I told her she was wrong and she shouldn't have gotten upset with me, she probably would let loose with the usual, 'I work too, you know. I'm tired too. But I also have to take care of you and Chelsea and my sister. Who helps me?'" So, instead, Henry learned to say nothing. And he just withdrew. Sometimes he helped out. But when he did he didn't expect, nor did he receive, anything positive back from Dani.

So whose fault is this? Is Dani wrong for not being more supportive of Henry? Is Henry wrong for expecting Dani to take the lead and also to praise him when he helped? Well, actually, it's no one's fault. Or at least, it's not helpful to try to assign blame. Finding a "winner" means that someone has to be the "loser." Instead, what we try to do is get each person to see how his or her behavior affects the other. For example, my guess is that if Dani held back on the criticism about the dirty bathroom and instead said something such as, "You really helped me out tonight. It was so great to come home and not have to bathe Chelsea or get her to bed" this would have made Henry feel good and, most important, more likely to do it again. At the same time, if Henry had told her, "I'm sorry about the bathroom. I guess I forgot to clean it up because she was being fussy. But it makes me feel bad that I did all of this and your only reaction was to get mad at me," that might have completely changed Dani's view of him.

My colleagues and I cannot help families with these situations if each parent is not fully aware of what he or she—as well as his or her partner—is thinking during these episodes. In a marriage or relationship, it is often expected that one partner will understand what the other is thinking and feeling, and experience situations in the same way as the other partner. But, often, they do not. Too many times we hear one parent say to the other, "I'm not a mind reader you know!"

This whole exercise of writing down what you are thinking during a problem episode actually has multiple purposes. First, I want you to be aware of what you are thinking during these times in case your thoughts are interfering with how you would like to react. In addition, one of the next steps in our process of helping families is to examine how these thoughts might make your parenting more difficult. Second, however, what you are thinking is sometimes a revelation to your partner and vice versa. It was shocking to Dani to hear Henry say that he thought he was being a fantastic father by giving Dani a bath and getting her to bed. Her perception of the situation was completely different—he couldn't even manage to clean up the bathroom, which she then had to handle. It helped their perceptions of each other to know how they saw these situations and led the way to improving their communication with each other. In marriage therapy, therapists sometimes will ask couples to take each other's perspective on a situation to do this very thing—help each partner know how the other partner sees the world. Often, this helps couples get closer, knowing that each partner is well intentioned but might have a very different view about what is going on.

I hope that this extended explanation of the outcomes of your Thought Quiz helps you examine the things that you might be thinking while your child is misbehaving. Again, you will rely a great deal on this information as you move through the next steps of the process of Optimistic Parenting. It can take some time to get comfortable with this exercise—especially if your child is being extremely disruptive and you are just trying to get through it—so be patient. If you need to, go back to using the Thoughts Quiz each time you are recording your thoughts. It provides a structure for thinking through most of the more common thoughts shared by other families in this situation.

Return to Journal Example   Using Joyce's journal entries as examples, remember that her first effort at writing down her thoughts about her son Mike's difficulties during dinner (i.e., whining and crying) was, "Ugh, I hate dinnertime." Now that you have taken the Thought Quiz, you can see that much more information is needed about what she might have been thinking about her son or herself. We went through the range of thoughts that may have gone through her mind at the time and she changed the entry as shown next.

JOYCE'S JOURNAL: REVISED THOUGHTS

SITUATION What happened (success or difficulty)?	THOUGHTS What did you think or say to yourself when this happened?
When Mike sat down at the dinner table and the food was put in front of him, he started whining and crying. (difficulty)	I thought, "I'm a bad mother, and I'm not able to control his behavior."

This change to "I thought 'I'm a bad mother and I'm not able to control his behavior'" is a good start. You can see two themes in her response. First, the idea that she might be a "bad mother" reflects self-blame. She is thinking that it is her fault that Mike acts up at dinnertime. Second, she feels out of control—a theme that we saw is highly common among parents in these situations. Clearly, it is going to be difficult for Joyce to implement any plan for Mike's disruption if she is blaming herself and thinks this is all uncontrollable. The following is a second entry Joyce made about Mike, which in this case was about a success.

JOYCE'S JOURNAL: SUCCESS NOTED

SITUATION What happened (success or difficulty)?	THOUGHTS What did you think or say to yourself when this happened?
Mike was watching a DVD and I told him it was time for lunch. He came to the table and started eating without getting upset. (success)	I thought "He had a good night's sleep and a nap, so he wasn't so upset at lunch."

What is the difference between the types of thoughts Joyce has when Mike has a difficult time and gets upset (e.g., "I'm a bad mother and I'm not able to control his behavior") and those she has when he handles a similar situation with more success (e.g., "He had a good night's sleep and a nap, so he wasn't so upset at lunch")? In the case of the difficulty, Joyce blamed herself; in the case of the success, Joyce attributed Mike's good behavior to an outside influence—in this case, his sleeping pattern. Remember back when I discussed the pessimistic attributional style. Joyce's responses fit this pattern. She sees her son's difficulties as somehow her fault but her son's successes not as her successes but as a result of some other factor. We also saw in Joyce's responses hints of the other characteristics of pessimistic thinking. When pressed about mealtime problems, she expressed concern that they would probably always be a problem (permanent) and that the problem would occur not only at dinnertime but during any other food-related activities as well (pervasive). And again, in the case of a success such as when Mike ate lunch with no problem, Joyce saw this as just a one-time event because he happened to be well rested and didn't think it would affect his eating at other times.

When you begin to examine your thoughts in problem situations and your successes with your child, you will likely find your own common patterns of viewing these situations. We find many different styles for parents; some have only one recurring theme (e.g., "This is out of my control"), whereas others have many of the themes running through their minds depending on the situation. Again, examining your thoughts can be the most challenging part of Optimistic Parenting, but I think you will find it helpful and probably a little enlightening as well.

One Final "Thought"   About 40%–50% of the families we encounter who have children with challenging behavior have multiple pessimistic thoughts as they try to deal with these difficulties on a day-to-day basis. As I mentioned, the patterns of thoughts differ—sometimes from situation to situation and sometimes day to day or week to week. What if, however, you are part of the other half of parents who do not frequently struggle with pessimistic ideas about your child or your situation? What if you feel you are competent to handle most problems, that your child is capable of changing, and that things will get better, but you are just not happy with your life as it is? Is Optimistic Parenting still for you? In short, the answer is yes.

Part of what my colleagues and I are trying to do through the Optimistic Parenting process is to help parents make the experience of parenting a positive one—even in the face of difficult challenges. In Chapter 5 I cover techniques all parents can use—regardless of whether they are pessimistic or optimistic thinkers—to leverage these parenting experiences (yes, even the unpleasant ones) into activities that can lead to a more satisfying and fulfilling life.

I encourage all parents to review Chapter 5 because at some point almost all of us can use the techniques described for examining our thoughts and feelings and helping us gain insight into important situations. This may include problem situations with your child, but it also can extend to those difficulties you may have with your partner, family members, friends, or even co-workers. The next section discusses the emotions and feelings that go along with these thoughts and describes their role in our approach to helping parents.

Feelings: Describing What Emotions You Experience and How You React Physically

Getting in touch with what you are feeling during difficulties and successes can be as complicated a task as being aware of what you are thinking. It is surprisingly easy to be out of touch in these situations. A good friend of mine once told me, for example, that while she was in a therapy session to help her deal with her father's impending death, she seemed to hold her breath as she discussed him. "You're not breathing," the therapist told her. "What?" my friend replied. "You're not breathing. When you talk about your father you hold your breath. Stop for a second and take a few deep breaths." The therapist looked at her and waited. My friend took a few deep breaths and then, quite to her surprise, started crying. In her mind, she was calmly discussing his illness and the details surrounding his care, and she was not aware of how her complicated feelings (i.e., sadness about her father's illness, long-standing anger at him for his treatment of her) were making her react physically. It was as if she was both physically (i.e., holding her breath) and emotionally (i.e., holding back her feelings) avoiding this painful experience.

My wife can always tell when I am tense—often before I am even aware of it myself—by looking at my hand. She describes it as my "claw." If she sees that I have the claw (with my fingers tensed up as if I am holding a baseball), she usually responds by saying, "What's wrong?" It has become so commonplace now that as soon as she looks at my hand, I become aware that I am tense, and we both smile. By giving me feedback on how my body reacts to stress, she taught me to be more aware of it in myself. The exercise we use with families is designed to do the same thing—get individuals to be more aware of what they are feeling in certain situations.

When I work with families in our program, I do not attempt to change their emotions directly. This is in contrast to how I work with families regarding their thoughts. I will very clearly discuss your thoughts as they relate to specific situations, discuss how certain thoughts may help or hurt your ability to deal with a problem situation, and then give you some techniques for improving what you say to yourself; however, I will not do the same thing for how you feel. Although I want you to become aware of what you are feeling, I will not ask you to change your feelings.

Imagine, for example, if you told me that your child's screaming out in public makes you angry and I reacted by telling you not to be angry! Or, imagine if you told me that the way your son interacts with other children embarrasses you and I told you instead to feel proud about how he acts. Telling people not to feel a certain way invalidates their feelings. Saying, for example, that you feel sad and then having someone tell you that instead you should feel happy misses the point of communicating emotions. You might feel that the person was not listening to and did not understand you. Often, people share their feelings to get support. Let's return to Joyce's journal and see how she completed the next section of the form by telling us what she thought or felt when her child whined and cried at mealtimes.

JOYCE'S JOURNAL: FEELINGS NOTED

SITUATION What happened (success or difficulty)?	THOUGHTS What did you think or say to yourself when this happened?	FEELINGS What emotions did you experience and how did you react physically when this happened?
When Mike sat down at the dinner table and the food was put in front of him, he started whining and crying. (difficulty)	I thought, "Ugh, I hate dinnertime." I also thought "I'm a bad mother, and I'm not able to control his behavior."	I felt tired.

What I ask of parents is to write down what emotions they feel and how they feel physically in both positive and negative situations. In Joyce's case, the negative situation was the problem at the dinner table, and Joyce expressed thoughts of being a bad mother and being out of control. Her report of her feelings was at first brief— "I felt tired." We wanted to know more about Joyce's feelings, but this was actually a good start. She previously was not even aware that these mealtime tantrums made her feel tired. Why is it good to know what you felt previously? First, these journal entries will serve as a record of how your thoughts and feelings have changed as you progress through the program. In Joyce's case, perhaps as she finds successful ways of dealing with Mike's behavior and starts to think of herself as a good mother who has control over these situations, she will start to feel less tired and perhaps even invigorated by her success.

Second, being required to complete these kinds of journal entries helps you become more aware of your feelings. It forces you to examine what goes on in these situations and, just like my wife looking at my "claw," can help to remind you that you are reacting in particular ways that may not be helpful. If you become aware of some physical reactions, such as feeling tense, you can respond with a technique that will help you feel better. For example, in the case I just described with my friend, once she became aware of her tendency not to breathe when she was highly stressed, she learned to stop and take a few deep breaths. This made her feel a little better at the time. It certainly did not take away the source of her stress and did not minimize the difficulties she was having, but it was a way to deal with this feeling in a productive and positive way. She used the technique and then further reflected on what specifically was making her feel tense.

This last point is an important one and is worth highlighting. *Just expressing your emotions will not solve your problems.* There is a school of thought that the problems people face in life are primarily an inability to express how they feel. For example, if someone cuts ahead of a person in line in a movie theater and the person does not react, some view this as harmful because the person is "bottling up" his or her emotions. From this point of view, emotions are like fluids or gas that can build up until they explode. This way of looking at emotions is particularly popular among professionals who work with children, especially those children who may have limited communication skills. I have seen hundreds (if not thousands) of school plans that focus primarily on having a child "express emotions." Even before teaching children to communicate their needs (e.g., "I am thirsty," "Can you spend some time with me?" "Can I take a break?"), many teachers and other professionals focus on having the child express emotions ("I am angry!").

The problem with just expressing emotions involves others' reactions. For example, if I say "I'm angry" and someone congratulates me on expressing myself, I will only feel a little bit better if my concern is expressing myself and now I feel better that at least I said something. But if I said "I'm angry" because you interrupted me, and you congratulate me on expressing my emotions and then proceed to interrupt me again, I will still be angry! Or, if you tell your partner that it makes you anxious to put your son to bed at night because you know it will be a major problem and your partner does not respond, the fact that you have expressed yourself probably will have little effect on your anxious feelings; you may, however, now feel angry at your partner!

To reiterate, if it makes you feel bad about yourself because you do not tell people how you feel about certain situations, then expressing these feelings may be helpful; however, just saying the words "You hurt my feelings" to someone will probably not be helpful if he or she does not respond in a way that you expect or hope for. For some parents, my colleagues' and my goal becomes teaching them how to express their emotions in a way that will lead to their desired outcomes (e.g., expressing the need for help with child care, which in turn leads to others helping you out more). Similarly, as described later, we might teach a child to express an emotion as a behavior change strategy, but only if it leads to an outcome the child desires.

As was just pointed out, recording your emotional reactions to certain situations will help you monitor any changes that may occur over time. For example, at the beginning of this process, you may have gotten angry when your child made a mess, but now his behavior has improved and you rarely get angry at him anymore. This success will be an important reminder to you that your feelings can change and can help you through other rough times. Second, getting used to recording your emotions can help you become more aware or in touch with how you are reacting to problems. But there is actually a third, and perhaps more sensitive, reason for you to keep a record of your emotions. In our sessions with families, we look at how these emotions do or do not get expressed. For example, if you get angry when your child makes a mess in a room you just spent hours cleaning, do you yell and scream at your child? Do you complain to important others about how you feel? Or do you just keep the anger to yourself? Are your emotions inner directed (e.g., "I'm angry with myself," "I feel inadequate and helpless") or outer directed (e.g., "Why can't you be a better husband and help me out?" "My child is doing this on purpose!")?

The reason we look at how these feelings get expressed is we want to see if there is any other reason why you keep getting upset. Obviously, a child who presents constant or even occasional challenges is certainly reason enough to create unpleasant emotions. And, as we discussed, feeling out of control can lead to some of the inner-directed emotional responses such as sadness, hopelessness, or depression. At the same time, however, some parents inadvertently learn that expressing emotions in a certain way can have its own rewards. Sometimes, this is good. For example, if you feel frustrated and alone when you are constantly dealing with your child's problems, expressing these thoughts and feelings to a partner or a friend can make you feel better. In part, this can be one of the real advantages to participating in a support group. Being among other parents who struggle with similar situations day to day can be comforting and make you feel as if you are not alone. This feeling of comradeship or solidarity can even be uplifting and motivating. There are times, however, when what and how you express your emotional feelings can be encouraged in a way that is not helpful. The reactions of other people may be such that they only serve to continue and reinforce feelings such as anger or feeling sorry for yourself. An example here might be helpful.

Cindy was a 38-year-old mother of two children, one of whom (Jesse) was a handful and required constant attention to keep him from breaking things throughout the house and from running out the front door into the busy street in their neighborhood. Most activities that required an effort on 4-year-old Jesse's part were usually met with resistance. Cindy and her husband, Mack, had been married for 20 years and, as Cindy described it, "had had their ups and downs." The birth of Jesse 4 years earlier was unexpected, as were Jesse's constant demands. Both Cindy and Mack worked outside the home—Mack as a landscaper and Cindy as a greeter at a local big chain store. They arranged their schedules so that one of them could be home at all times; however, it was Cindy who maintained responsibility for most of the household and the child care needs. When my colleagues and I had her complete the journal, one of her early entries described her difficulties getting her son Jesse to brush his teeth at night.

CINDY'S JOURNAL: EARLY ENTRY

SITUATION What happened (success or difficulty)?	THOUGHTS What did you think or say to yourself when this happened?	FEELINGS What emotions did you experience and how did you react physically when this happened?
I got Jesse into the bathroom to wash up. When I took out the toothbrush and toothpaste, he started crying and tried to leave the bathroom. (difficulty)	I thought, "Why is he doing this to me? I'm tired from working all day and I don't need this. Why didn't my husband brush his teeth earlier? I guess this is my 'job' and no one else can do it."	I felt upset at Jesse and angry with my husband. I felt the muscles in my neck tighten up.

This scenario may be familiar to many readers. It is not uncommon to have difficulties such as brushing your child's teeth if he or she tends to be challenging in general. And, the circumstances surrounding this situation—feeling resentment at others—is common as well. In Cindy's case, however, there was more. As we asked her more about the toothbrushing incident, she spent a considerable amount of time making remarks such as, "I guess I must have a special 'gift'—being the only one in the house who can ask Jesse to brush his teeth. His older brother or his father could have done this before I got home, but no, it's my job. Why is it that mothers always have to do these things? Men are so incompetent." Cindy had a very good sense of humor, and much of what she was saying was tinged with some not-so-subtle sarcasm.

As we proceeded to discuss ways of dealing with toothbrushing, we asked, "Have your husband or son ever offered to help Jesse brush his teeth and get him ready for bed?" Cindy smiled a wry smile. "Them? Oh, they've tried. But when they do it, Jesse still has food between his teeth." She rolled her eyes. "Each time they do it, I look in Jesse's mouth and show them what a crummy job they did. Then, I just have to take him back into the bathroom and do it again—this time, the right way."

Just as the scenario of difficult toothbrushing and the sense of frustration that you and only you are responsible are common, so too is the type of dynamic being described. Sometimes, as parents, we focus a great deal on getting things done "the right way." This alone is not a problem. Obviously, Cindy wants her son's teeth to be clean for hygiene and appearance reasons. That's just being a good parent. But, if her goal really was to have her husband and son help out with this chore, she would have given them feedback and asked them to do it again. But, she didn't. Instead, she reminded them almost nightly how she was the only one doing the task. One reason for not requesting her husband and older son to repeat the toothbrushing and do a better job could have been because they resisted. They could have given her a hard time about doing it a second time (e.g., "It looks fine to me!"). But, that actually was not the case here. Whenever Cindy asked for their help and they did not complete the task to her satisfaction, her response was to take back the responsibility but to complain about how difficult it was on her.

This is the other, sometimes sensitive, part of recording your emotional reactions to situations. We want to see if sometimes your emotional reactions serve a purpose for you. In Cindy's case, complaining to her family and friends about how hard caring for Jesse alone was on her elicited a great deal of sympathy. Friends would relate stories about their husbands (roll your eyes here) and how they never helped out either. Her own mother would commiserate about how her husband never "lifted a finger around the house" and that if you wanted to get anything done right, you had to do it yourself. Cindy received more emotional support from others if she pointed out how she had to do everything herself than if she just expressed her real concerns (e.g., "Why am I not able to get him to behave better?"). In behavioral terms, Cindy was getting reinforced for complaining about the lack of help she was getting at home.

Recall that we saw a similar pattern in the case of Dani and Henry, who I described earlier in this chapter. Dani, too, would complain about Henry's inability to help around the house, which caused her to take on all of the responsibilities. Her complaints would sometimes get Henry to feel guilty and do something nice for her such as buy her a gift or take her out to dinner. Let me be clear here. This isn't bad. It was good of Henry to show his appreciation for what his wife was taking on, just as it was good of Cindy's friends and mother to express their support for all she did for her son; however, if you find yourself maintaining problem scenarios without trying to seriously resolve them (e.g., getting your partner to help out even if the chores are not completed perfectly), then you need to examine why. "Am I getting something out of expressing myself this way that gets in the way of things getting better?" Going through the steps of Optimistic Parenting will help you explore these feelings and emotional expressions and provide alternative strategies for both expressing yourself in a healthy manner and getting the practical and emotional support you need.

Let's go back to Joyce's journal entry as a further illustration as to how to complete the Feelings side of the journal. We asked Joyce to elaborate a bit more on the emotional side of her feelings. The fact that she felt tired (i.e., what she felt physically) is important to know, but we asked her to think about the emotions that went along with feeling tired. Joyce's revised journal entry included her feelings.

JOYCE'S JOURNAL: FEELINGS NOTED

SITUATION What happened (success or difficulty)?	THOUGHTS What did you think or say to yourself when this happened?	FEELINGS What emotions did you experience and how did you react physically when this happened?
When Mike sat down at the dinner table and the food was put in front of him, he started whining and crying. (difficulty)	I thought, "ugh, I hate dinnertime." I also thought, "I'm a bad mother, and I'm not able to control his behavior."	I felt tired and sad. Sometimes this all makes me feel depressed.

When Joyce had time to reflect further about her feelings at the time, she revealed that her emotions included sadness and depression. If you look at her thoughts and her emotions together, you can see that thinking she is a "bad mother" and that she cannot control Mike's behavior may be contributing to these feelings of sadness and depression. If you think back to our previous discussion about helplessness, you will remember that thinking one has no control can make one feel helpless and perhaps even hopeless. Our goal for Joyce, later in the program, was to see if we could help her change how she thought about the situation with Mike and if that, in turn, would make her feel less sad and depressed. Again, note that our goal was to change Joyce's thoughts but not directly change her emotions. We find that successes in parenting and changes in the way parents view themselves can by themselves lead to improved emotions that accompany these situations.

In our program, we try to help parents become aware of their emotions by giving them examples from other parents; however, it is difficult to completely list all of the possible emotions, in part because there are many subtleties in the way people feel and because people sometimes use terms differently. The following quotations from parents talking about their positive and negative emotions can provide a starting place for you to start to explore your own feelings.

Examples of Positive Emotions   Clearly, our goal is to help you along the way to increase the amount of time you experience positive emotions and decrease the amount of time you feel negative emotions. Even in the most difficult times, parents will express positive feelings surrounding parenting such as confidence, hopefulness, happiness, joy, pride, and warmth toward their child and others. Consider the following quotations from parents in our program:

> *I was really relieved, proud of him and myself and happy that it was a nice trip for everyone. (A mother describing a pleasant trip to a local store with the whole family)*

> *When I see bits of that, you know, when you see bits of normalcy here and there you kinda get a feeling that we're gonna be okay. (A mother describing how her daughter's older brother taught her to blow kisses and how this made her feel more optimistic about their future)*

> *I always know I can find a solution. It's about finding it. I don't ever feel there's no solution. It's just a question of how long is it going to take to find a solution that works. (A mother describes her feelings of confidence in being able to find solutions for her son's problem behaviors)*

Examples of Negative Emotions   At the same time, especially when dealing with very challenging children, parents often report a great number of negative emotions such as guilt, hopelessness, helplessness, fear, anger, incompetence, frustration, resignation, embarrassment, sadness, and anxiousness. Consider the following quotations from parents:

> *I'm sick of this. We have not slept through the night in 4 years. (A mother sharing her frustration and anger over her son's chronic sleep problems)*

> *It wears me out sometimes, but I can't, I won't… All I can think of… I feel like I'm in a pool and I'm drowning and all that I'm doing is making sure that I'm holding my kids up above the water to breathe. Just as long as they survive and they can get through this. That's kind of how I feel about it. (A mother talking about her feelings of sadness and hopelessness over her own future)*

> *I gave up my job. I gave everything for my son and sometimes I think I gave up my life. I cannot tell this to anyone, but I feel this. You know the life I have is not the life I ever wanted to have. So I feel like I do whatever I can just for him. But I also feel guilty even thinking about myself and my life when he has so many problems. I'm supposed to be his mother. (A mother sharing her secret feelings about her own life and feeling guilty that she has these thoughts)*

Again, the goal of the Feelings section of the journal is to help you become more aware of the physical and emotional reactions you have when faced with both successes and difficult situations. Overall, the journal at this point is designed to get you used to being conscious of how you are reacting to situations—both through what you say to yourself (thoughts) and how you respond emotionally (feelings). The next chapter describes how we take this information and help parents view the world, themselves, and their child in a more productive and healthy way.

WHAT ARE THE CONSEQUENCES
OF YOUR THOUGHTS AND FEELINGS?

Once you have become comfortable keeping track of your thoughts and feelings in situations involving your child, the next step involves looking at the consequences of these reactions. That is to say, does it help you to think that everything is out of your control, that you are a bad parent, or that your child is not capable of change? Or, do some of these thoughts actually interfere with your ability to be a good parent? To demonstrate the impact of these thoughts and feelings, the journal entry expands to include consequences, or what happens as a result of these thoughts and feelings. The example of Joyce and Mike from earlier in this chapter is used to illustrate the consequences of reactions. Joyce's journal entry, complete with consequences, appears next.

JOYCE'S JOURNAL: CONSEQUENCES NOTED

SITUATION What happened (success or difficulty)?	THOUGHTS What did you think or say to yourself when this happened?	FEELINGS What emotions did you experience and how did you react physically when this happened?	CONSEQUENCES What happened as a result of your thoughts and feelings?
When Mike sat down at the dinner table and the food was put in front of him, he started whining and crying. (difficulty)	I thought, "ugh, I hate dinnertime." I also thought, "I'm a bad mother, and I'm not able to control his behavior."	I felt tired and sad. Sometimes this all makes me feel depressed.	I gave him cookies so he would stop crying.

    As shown previously, this situation, during which Mike whined and cried at the dinner table, led to thoughts by Joyce that she was a bad mother and that Mike's behavior was out of her control. These thoughts made Joyce feel tired and sad. Partly because of these thoughts and feelings, Joyce gave Mike cookies for dinner to stop him from being disruptive. As she told us in the session when we discussed the consequences, she knew that she should not give him cookies at this time. She knew that her action might make dinnertime that much more difficult for them in the future; however, because this was all so overwhelming to her, she gave in and gave him the cookies. In this scenario, the consequence of Joyce having these pessimistic thoughts was to act against her own good instincts (i.e., "I shouldn't give in to his demands when he is misbehaving"). This is what we mean by *consequences* in the journal—what happened as a result of your thoughts and feelings?

    Sometimes, parents can have these difficult reactions (e.g., feeling anxious or depressed) and still follow through with what they think is best for their child; however, in the Consequences step, we are looking to see if and how your thoughts and feelings make you respond to your child. The question is, "Are you changing how you respond to behavior problems because of the way you think and feel?"

The example of Joyce and Mike also points out a pattern that will be revisited—how your child's behavior affects what you do. This act of "giving in" and improving your child's behavior in the present can cause your child to continue to misbehave in the future and may encourage you to give in again to restore peace for a short time. In Joyce's case, Mike's whining and crying upset her so much that she gave in and gave him cookies. Let's take this scenario one step further. When Mike got his cookies to eat, he stopped whining and crying. Peace was felt throughout the house! What effect do you think this had on Joyce the next time Mike whined and cried and she was stressed out? She was more likely to give in to him because it "worked" so well before. Giving Mike cookies stopped him from disrupting dinner for everyone. Joyce and the rest of the family were reinforced for giving in and, therefore, were more likely to do it again in the future. So, even though Joyce knew that giving Mike cookies was not the correct way to handle his disruptive behavior, it certainly felt good when he stopped crying. The consequence for Joyce's thinking she was out of control and feeling depressed was that she was more likely to give in to Mike's demands.

There was one more consequence to this sequence. Giving in to Mike's demands temporarily stopped the problem, but it also reinforced Joyce's earlier feelings of inadequacy. When we asked her to elaborate, she edited her journal entry one more time to reveal her thoughts about the situation.

JOYCE'S JOURNAL: CONSEQUENCES IN DETAIL

SITUATION What happened (success or difficulty)?	THOUGHTS What did you think or say to yourself when this happened?	FEELINGS What emotions did you experience and how did you react physically when this happened?	CONSEQUENCES What happened as a result of your thoughts and feelings?
When Mike sat down at the dinner table and the food was put in front of him, he started whining and crying. (difficulty)	I thought, "ugh, I hate dinnertime." I also thought, "I'm a bad mother, and I'm not able to control his behavior."	I felt tired and sad. Sometimes this all makes me feel depressed.	I gave him cookies so he would stop crying. I felt like I had lost this battle and that I am really a failure as a parent.

The comment, "I felt like I lost this battle and that I am really a failure as a parent," illustrates how reacting to one's thoughts and feelings by giving in to one's child can become a self-perpetuating cycle.

If you brought together a group of professionals and described Joyce's scenario—Mike whined and cried and Joyce gave him cookies to quiet him down—the recommendation from the vast majority of them would likely be the same. Most would suggest that Joyce needs parent training to teach her how not to encourage Mike's crying. In other words, the professionals would assume that

Joyce did not understand that it was not a good thing to reinforce Mike's behavior by giving him the cookies and, therefore, what she needs is a simple education about what to do and what not to do. As I state throughout this book, however, in our work over the years we have found that many parents have good instincts when it comes to parenting their children. In cases such as Joyce's, maybe parents need information about how to react. Perhaps more important, though, they need help with being able to follow through with these approaches. Joyce, for example, needs help understanding that she is a good mother and that she is capable of helping Mike behave better. All of the parenting instruction in the world will not get her to follow through unless her unproductive thoughts are addressed. In this case, education is not enough.

Again, Joyce's example showed how her thoughts led to her "giving in" to Mike's demands. Let's look at another example from a different parent (Annie) to further examine this concept of consequences.

ANNIE'S JOURNAL: INITIAL ENTRY

SITUATION What happened (success or difficulty)?	THOUGHTS What did you think or say to yourself when this happened?	FEELINGS What emotions did you experience and how did you react physically when this happened?	CONSEQUENCES What happened as a result of your thoughts and feelings?
My older daughter was playing with a toy and Kathy took it away from her because she wanted it. When my other daughter grabbed it back, Kathy started to cry and hit herself. She started having one of her "spells." (difficulty)	I thought, "Poor Kathy. She is not able to control herself because of her autism. She seems so unhappy."	I felt sad for her and began to worry about her future.	I comforted her until she calmed down, and then I gave her the toy to play with.

In this case, Kathy was a 4-year-old girl with a diagnosis of autism. Her mother Annie was a single parent of three young children and relied on government assistance to help feed, clothe, and shelter her family. As you can see by her journal entry of her thoughts about Kathy's behavior problems (including some serious tantrums that involved hitting her own face), Annie looked at Kathy's behaviors as being part of her disorder. To Annie, this meant that Kathy had no control over what she did. Her tantrums were pitiful for Annie to watch, and this resulted in her holding and comforting her whenever Kathy had one of these "spells." Annie told us that in the past, professionals told her to ignore these tantrums and that would make them go away; however, she was never able to ignore her daughter when she cried.

The professionals who referred Annie and her family to our program told us that Annie was a "noncompliant" mother who did not follow through on any of their recommendations. In fact, because Kathy's behaviors were increasing in frequency and intensity, they were concerned that Annie's unwillingness to cooperate with them was making Kathy's behavior worse and, therefore, bordered on abuse. There had been some talk about taking Kathy away from Annie to protect her from Annie's influence.

What is striking here is that the professionals looked at Annie simply as being a bad mother who did not listen to their advice and was therefore uncooperative and noncompliant. At no time did they ask Annie what she was thinking and feeling when it came to her daughter's difficulties. As was the case with Joyce, the professionals who worked with Annie and Kathy believed that Annie's lack of adherence and follow-through to instruction she had received during several parenting education classes was a result of her being willful and a bad mother. In fact, however, Annie was a very loving mother. She cared very much for daughter as well as her other children. Annie's belief, however, that Kathy had no control over her behavior made Annie respond to Kathy's tantrums in the exact opposite way that the professionals thought was appropriate. Hugging Kathy to calm her down makes perfect sense if one believes that Kathy's autism is causing her tantrums. Our job was first to get Annie to examine her thoughts and feelings and then to look at how those thoughts and feelings influenced the way that Annie responded to Kathy's behavior problems. Once we were able to help Annie gain this insight, we implemented some of the techniques I describe later to give her a different perspective on Kathy's behavior (i.e., Kathy did indeed have control over how she behaved). Armed with these techniques and her new perspective, Annie was able to respond to Kathy's tantrums in a more productive way.

Before moving on to the next step in the process of changing how you might view these situations, I present one more example of a different family and a different scenario.

GRACE'S JOURNAL: INITIAL ENTRY

SITUATION What happened (success or difficulty)?	THOUGHTS What did you think or say to yourself when this happened?	FEELINGS What emotions did you experience and how did you react physically when this happened?	CONSEQUENCES What happened as a result of your thoughts and feelings?
We were in the grocery store, and Jason started to run around grabbing things off the shelves. (difficulty)	I thought, "Everyone is looking at me and thinking I'm a terrible parent."	I was embarrassed and started to have an anxiety attack.	We left the store immediately, and I didn't get to do the shopping.

This journal entry belongs to Grace, a 39-year-old first-time parent. Grace waited to have a child because she wanted to follow up on her career goals (she was a highly placed advertising executive) and because she had some concerns about her ability to be a mother. Now in her late 30s, she felt a little out of place among the mothers of her son Jason's friends, most of whom were 5–10 years younger than she. Jason, now age 6, was willful and often did not listen to Grace when she asked him to behave. As shown in the example journal entry, he acted up in the grocery store and started touching and grabbing things. At first, Grace tried to reason with him (by saying, e.g., "Now, Jason, what did I say about taking things off of the shelves?"); when he did not stop, she began yelling at him. She told us she "lost it" in the store because she was so frustrated with him. Rather than feeling good about expressing this emotion, however, she felt bad and believed that the other parents in the store were judging her negatively.

Grace's thoughts about what others were thinking triggered an anxiety attack. She reported that she felt a tightness in her chest, that she started to sweat, and that her heart was racing. This had happened to her in the past, usually in highly stressful situations at work (e.g., when she had to make a major presentation to important clients in front of her boss); however, they were occurring increasingly in problem situations with her son. When the anxiety attacks first began, Grace thought she was having a heart attack and that she was going to die. Fortunately, after an extensive medical evaluation it was clear that her heart was fine and she was diagnosed with an anxiety disorder. Her doctor suggested she reduce the stress in her life—obviously difficult for a woman with a full-time job outside of the home and another full-time job as a mother.

It is apparent from looking at Grace's journal that the trigger for her anxiety attack in the grocery store was having thoughts that she was being judged (i.e., "Everyone is looking at me and thinking I'm a terrible parent"). As a result of her negative thoughts and feelings, she did something that is quite common—she escaped (i.e., "We left the store immediately and I didn't get to do the shopping"). This only makes sense. When someone finds him- or herself in an uncomfortable position, the first reaction often is to find a way to escape or avoid what is making the person anxious. So, for Grace, the consequence of her thoughts and feelings was to leave the store.

There are two problems with this type of reaction. The first problem is that Grace's decision to escape and leave the store initiated the concession process, introduced earlier in this chapter. Because Grace was concerned about being judged and the resulting anxiety it caused for her, she started to avoid going to grocery stores with Jason. Then, she started to avoid other stores as well. A trip to a shopping mall with Jason could be extremely chaotic, so Grace arranged for her husband to take care of Jason if she needed to shop. Then, the family stopped going to restaurants or even playgrounds because of Jason's behavior. This was obviously becoming a major problem for the whole family; over time, Grace felt like a prisoner in her own home.

The second problem, in addition to the concession process, is that Grace's strategy of escaping these anxiety-provoking situations also was affecting her anxiety attacks. She was starting to have more of these attacks in situations in which she had never had them before. Why would this happen? In Chapter 4, I describe groundbreaking research on OCD, one of the most debilitating of the anxiety disorders. The most effective treatment for OCD is exposure and response prevention; namely, exposing people to the things that cause fear and anxiety and not letting them escape. This is more commonly referred to as "facing your fears." In the case of people with OCD, this means that they may be asked to open the door to a public building (something anxiety-provoking for some because of germs) and not be allowed to wash their hands immediately afterward. Over time, these individuals begin to see that there are no immediate negative consequences (e.g., they do not become ill) and their anxiety lessens.

Some of Grace's anxiety involves being in situations in which she could be judged by others (e.g., performing in front of her boss, trying to handle her disruptive child in public). By escaping these situations, she is avoiding exposure to situations that make her anxious. Without this exposure, however, her anxiety will not be reduced. For Grace, therefore, the consequence of her thoughts and feelings (i.e., "We left the store immediately and I didn't get to do the shopping") will affect her parenting success (i.e., by conceding to each of these problem situations, which will likely make them worse) as well as her own emotional well-being (i.e., helping her avoid exposure to anxiety-provoking situations).

In Chapter 4, I provide many more examples of consequences and how we use this information to assist parents to change the way they think. For you, these changes in self-talk will help improve how you feel about yourself and others and help you parent in a more positive way. Before moving to the section on changing the way you think, be sure to have at least 2 weeks worth of journal entries completed documenting your successes and challenges with your child; make sure to include your thoughts and feelings as well as the consequences of your thoughts and feelings. Once you are fairly comfortable with the journal, then move on to the next chapter.

CHAPTER 4

Changing the Way You Think

If my mind can conceive it, and my heart can believe it, I know I can achieve it.

—attributed to Jesse Jackson, American Civil
Rights Leader, Baptist Minister, and Politician, b. 1941

One of the most remarkable successes in the field of psychology over the past few decades is an approach called cognitive-behavioral therapy (CBT). Cognitive behavioral therapy actually is an umbrella term under which exist a number of different approaches. These methods have been used and found effective for helping people with numerous problems of daily living as well as with severe psychological problems such as clinical levels of anxiety, depression, eating disorders, addiction, and many other serious conditions. Despite some differences in the approaches, they all have something in common—they assume that how you think can affect the way you feel and the way you behave. Optimistic Parenting uses techniques from CBT. We look at how parents think about situations with their child as affecting how they are likely to respond, especially when they are under stress. When these thoughts interfere with responding the way they would like to (e.g., giving their child a candy bar when he is screaming in the supermarket despite knowing that this is not a good reaction), then we help parents change these thoughts.

Some of the more startling discoveries about how CBT can help people have come with the advent of brain imaging techniques. These techniques—once only used in highly sophisticated research laboratories—are now becoming a commonly used approach for diagnosing medical problems. In addition to their use in finding and diagnosing illnesses, they are increasingly being employed to look at how the brain might be involved in psychological problems. For instance, brain imaging research is underway to help explore a highly debilitating anxiety disorder known as obsessive-compulsive disorder (OCD). This should not be confused with the tendency of some people to be highly ordered and to like things being done "just so." People with OCD constantly endure intrusive and frightening thoughts. For example, a person might believe that everything around him is contaminated with deadly bacteria and that touching anything that has not been sterilized will lead to infections and death. These obsessive thoughts are so anxiety producing that the only way to make them more bearable is to act in ways to help reduce the anxiety. As a result of this belief that everything around him is contaminated (i.e., the "obsessive" part of OCD), this person might wash his hands and use disinfectants to sanitize door knobs, table tops, and so forth (i.e., the "compulsive" part of OCD) to relieve anxiety. People who are constantly "checking"—such as looking to be sure the stove is turned off numerous times a day—are behaving in this ritualistic way to make sure that they did not forget something important (e.g., turning off the stove) and that no catastrophic consequences (e.g., burning down their home) will occur as a result. The level of dysfunction among people with OCD can be among the most serious of any of the psychological disorders.

The good news for people who are so debilitated by these types of intrusive and frightening thoughts is that a particular form of CBT, mentioned briefly in Chapter 3—*exposure and response prevention*—is highly effective in helping these individuals lead more typical lives. Therapy includes examining the individual's thoughts (e.g., "I will become deathly ill if I come in contact with these germs") and then exposing him or her to the things or situations that he or she fears (e.g., touching a door knob on a public building). This type of CBT changes how individuals with OCD think about fearful things and also reduces their anxiety.

One research group led by Lewis R. Baxter studied a group of people who suffered from OCD and had them participate in brain imaging studies. Certain areas of their brains thought to be involved with feeling anxiety were not working in the same way as those same areas of the brain in people without this disorder. The meaning of this is clear—how your brain works can affect what you feel. After this brain scan assessment, some of the participants received medication to help reduce their symptoms and other participants went through sessions of CBT. After treatment, the researchers again had them go through brain imaging to see if and how the two treatments affected their brain functioning. In one of the most remarkable findings in our field, Baxter and his colleagues found that both the medication and the CBT changed the way that the individuals' brains were working—with the new patterns now looking more like people who did not have OCD.[1] In other words, CBT not only improved their symptoms of OCD but actually changed the way their brains functioned!

Human beings tend to think of the brain as influencing the way one thinks, feels, and behaves; however, more and more researchers are discovering that this works in the other direction as well. What one thinks, feels, and does also can affect brain functioning. I mention this important work here because it reinforces an important point. The changes that can occur for you if you follow through with our efforts to help you view the world in a more optimistic way can be profound. These are not just a few tricks or tips to somehow distract you from the difficulties you are facing. These are scientifically tested techniques that can change your life—not a claim I make lightly. It is possible to make changes in the very way your brain works—in this case, in a positive and constructive direction.

In our work with parents, we use several components of CBT. Once parents are comfortable and proficient at examining their thoughts and feelings in situations with their child, we then practice several different techniques for helping them look at these situations in a more productive way. These techniques include *disputation* (in which we challenge parents to defend their thoughts to see if they are rational or helpful), *distraction* (in which we work on having parents become aware of a problem thought and then refocus their attention on something else) and *substitution* (in which the goal is to replace a problem thought with one that is more useful). Again, although I will be illustrating these techniques with examples from our work with the parents of challenging children, you may find them useful in other situations as well. For example, if you find that at your child's school you have problem situations with a teacher or an administrator, this approach may help you determine your thought patterns and whether they are getting in the way of more successful interactions. One of our parents told us how she applied the techniques we taught her for dealing with her daughter to her daughter's teacher. Geralyn was a single parent of a 16-year-old girl named Tina who had significant cognitive impairments and also displayed aggressive behavior at home and at school. As we worked through the journal with her, Geralyn reported frequent thoughts about being an incompetent parent. "I go to all of the trainings the school provides. I attend weekly parent support meetings and read everything I can about my daughter's condition. Yet, when Tina acts up in public I still feel that I should know how to deal with this better." Our sessions with Geralyn were very sensitive because her emotions were always at the surface. At first she expressed a great deal of anger at us when we would discuss her situation and difficulties. She seemed very defensive whenever we went over some of the things that went on at home. As Geralyn became better at examining her thoughts and emotions, however, it became clear to her and to us that much of her anger was her reaction to feeling as if she was being criticized. "My friends tell me I'm too touchy. That I need to lighten up a bit. They say I'm a perfectionist and that my trying to make things perfect is going to make me crazy!" For example, Geralyn was trying to work on getting Tina to feed herself at meals, but her progress was limited. When Tina became frustrated with all of her mother's prompting (e.g., "No, hold your spoon this way"), she would often hit her mother until her mother gave up. In her journal, Geralyn reported that Tina's lack of progress made her feel that she was not good at parenting, which would eventually lead her to give up. "I'm such a loser at this. I watch others and even videos of other children like Tina who can learn to do this. Why can't I teach her?"

As we worked through Geralyn's thoughts about her interactions with Tina, Geralyn also reported her frustrations with Tina's teacher. "She sends home these notes everyday and they just drive me crazy. They say things like, 'Tina hit another child on the playground today, but there was no injury.' Or, 'Tina still refuses to use a spoon at lunch.' I don't write back like I'm supposed to because it makes me so upset. What good is it to tell me these things?" We asked Geralyn to write down her thoughts and feelings about these notes and her interactions with Tina's teacher because there was a growing rift between school and home and this was hurting Tina's progress. What Geralyn discovered as she included these interactions in her journal was that just as Tina's lack of progress made her feel inadequate as a parent, so did the notes home from school. Each time Tina's teacher reported some problem incident (e.g., "Tina threw her silverware on the floor in the cafeteria"), Geralyn reported that this too made her feel like a failure as a mother. "When I read these notes, I feel like the teacher is accusing me of being a bad parent." In addition to reading these notes as accusations, we also discovered that Geralyn would discount the good notes. Just as you would expect from someone with a pessimistic attributional style, Geralyn read the notes of problem incidents as somehow her fault (interestingly, not the teacher's fault) while ignoring or downplaying the good notes (e.g., "Tina put her work away all by herself!"). Geralyn told us that just having this perspective on the communications with school was helpful and made it easier for her not to blame the teacher for something (e.g., saying she is a bad mother) that was clearly not the teacher's intent.

Other parents report using the journal for analyzing their thoughts about difficulties and successes with their partners, relatives, and friends. I encourage you to do this as well. It is always helpful to have a better view of your interactions with others; if you do observe some patterns, certain sections in this chapter will help you to resolve these as well. First, I briefly discuss how to assess if you are ready for these next steps.

ARE YOU READY TO CHANGE?

"How many therapists does it take to change a light bulb?
Only one. But the light bulb has to want to change."

—Unknown author

One of the clichés of therapy is that you cannot help people who do not want to change. But it is more than a cliché. Psychologists, psychiatrists, and other types of therapists have no magic that assists them with helping another person who does not want their services. Sometimes, parents come to us for help with their child but are really looking to us to somehow "fix" their child. They are looking for a trick or a magic pill that will somehow make all of the problems go away. Unfortunately, that is not possible; in fact, I would venture to guess that there will always be a need for helping parents with their challenging children.

In this chapter, I discuss your journal entries and provide ways of improving the way you view the situations you have identified as troublesome. But how do you know if you are ready for this next step? To help you figure this out, I devised a "readiness quiz" to assess if you are at the point where you are able to take this next step. Here it is:

Are you reading this book?

If you answered "yes" to this question, then you are ready. If you are looking for help with your child's problems and for ways to make your life more satisfying, then you are ready. To illustrate what it means to be ready, here is a brief description of the difficulties I faced with one family over the sleep problems presented by their son. This case was an early one in our work that focused on sleep problems and taught me some very valuable lessons.

James was a 3-year-old boy with multiple diagnoses. The major difficulty facing his family at the time they contacted me was his sleep. He would cry and scream at bedtime, rarely did he nap, and he woke up multiple times crying at night. As you can imagine, his family, especially his mother, was at wits' end. Because his sleep was so disrupted, so was the sleep of everyone else in the family. Nerves were frayed by the lack of good, solid sleep, and it made dealing with James during the day that much harder. His mother described losing her temper with him during the day, and she believed that her disrupted sleep was partly to blame.

To help the family, we began by designing a sleep intervention. What we recommended is not important at this point (I discuss interventions for sleep problems in Chapter 11). What was important was that each time we made a recommendation, his mother would agree to follow through with the plan. And, each time, she failed to carry it out. Obviously, her difficulties with James were significant, so we tried to be sensitive to her needs. Finally, I made a very simple suggestion: "When James gets out of bed after his bedtime, just walk him back to his room, put him back to bed, and say nothing. Let's see if that works." Now, this was not an ideal plan, but it was something that I thought his mother could carry out with little effort. The next day, I called to check on her and see how it all went. "So, how did it go last night? Did he come out of his room last night after bedtime?" "Yes, at about 10:30." "Were you able to follow our suggestion? Did you walk him back to his room?" "No," his mom replied. "I just let him sit with me watching television. I was too tired and just didn't have it in me to fight with him. He finally fell asleep in the living room and I put him into his bed."

She must have sensed my frustration because she relayed what happened with a tone of guilt in her voice.

In discussing this case with our clinical team at the time, we all came to the same conclusion: James's mom was not ready. Although James's sleep difficulties were clearly significant, she was not ready to deal with them. We believed that once she was motivated to really work on his sleep problems, she would come back to us for help. Our assumption was that the lack of success was her fault. We thought we did everything correctly and made multiple suggestions that would have helped James sleep better. It was our conclusion that she really did not want to do what was needed. This scene is repeated thousands of times each day in clinical work with children and their families. If the family does not follow the parenting plan of the clinician, it is obviously the fault of the family.

What is ironic about this conclusion is that long ago we stopped blaming the child when our plans were not successful. In fact, one of the first things I was taught when working with children who displayed significant challenges was that if your plan is not working, then you (the clinician) did something wrong. It was not the child who was to blame for the lack of success; after all, it was your plan. For example, if you were teaching a child to put on her shirt and she was not learning the steps, then you did not blame the disorder the child may have—you changed your plan to meet her needs. Maybe you broke the task down into more or different steps or you found a way to motivate her; regardless, the onus was on you. If I am trying to get a child to behave better and it is not working, then it is my fault, and I change the plan.

Yet, if a parent is not successful with a plan we designed, we as clinicians have a tendency to blame the parent and not the plan. As I have discussed Optimistic Parenting across the country, I make sure to highlight this point to professionals. I tell them, "If the parents of the child with whom you are working are not following through with the plans you designed—then it is your fault. You designed the plan incorrectly. The difficulties families are having may require your looking more closely at what obstacles parents are facing. Then it is your job to help them with these obstacles." For my colleagues and I, this means looking closely at the thoughts parents have that may be interfering with success and incorporating this aspect into the plan.

Going back to James's sleep problems and his mother's difficulties carrying out our suggestions, we had to examine what James's mother was thinking. When we did, we found that she had real doubts about whether James would ever sleep well. She thought that his medical problems were causing his nighttime disruptions, so when he screamed and she was stressed, she acquiesced to his needs. She gave up or conceded not because she was a bad mother or because she was a noncompliant parent but because when things became difficult, she doubted they would ever get better. These doubts, in turn, interfered with her being able to carry out the plan we designed together.

We needed to help her with these thoughts before she was ever going to be successful with her son's sleeping difficulties.

So, are you ready? Yes. What is next is a way for you to "change the plans" to fit your own needs as well as the needs of your child. I learned a long time ago that any plan for the child has to fit the needs of the rest of the family as well. In our field, this is now referred to as contextual fit, or looking closely at the family environment and altering plans to fit everyone's needs. One of the ways we will fit our plans to meet your needs is to take a close look at your thoughts during the troublesome situations you examined in your journal.

DISPUTATION: CHALLENGING BELIEFS

The first strategy we use in changing thought patterns is to dispute them. *Disputation* is the name given to the technique of challenging some of the beliefs and thoughts you have about both good and bad situations. Essentially, what I ask you to do is to argue with yourself. To do this is really quite easy. Just ask yourself these two general questions about each of the thoughts you have:

1. Is what I am thinking *really* true?
2. Is what I am thinking useful?

It is easy to get so used to thinking a certain way that you fail to give your thoughts a reality check. For example, as you have completed the journal entries, did you find that some of your thoughts seemed simplistic or maybe even silly once you wrote them down on paper? This can happen, for example, if one catastrophizes or thinks that a situation is much worse than it really is. A typical example is when a parent has a hard time getting her child to do certain things at home and thinks, "I have absolutely no control over this child!" A quick check of the two questions can be helpful. In our program, we would ask the parent the following:

1. "Is this true that you have *absolutely no control* over this child?" "Yes," is a typical reply. "You say you have no control, yet you are able to get him to school each day, and he is clean and dressed. You seem to have some control." "Well, yes," the parent will answer. "I guess I do have some control."
2. "Is it helpful to think 'I have absolutely no control over this child'? Does it make the situation better for you to handle to think this?" "No. It makes me feel helpless and bad as a parent. It makes me want to give up."

This is a typical disputation discussion with parents who go through our program and is the process you can do yourself. The following illustrates the disputation process we conducted with Joyce, whose example was introduced in Chapter 3.

JOYCE'S JOURNAL: DISPUTATION EXAMPLE

SITUATION What happened (success or difficulty)?	THOUGHTS What did you think or say to yourself when this happened?	FEELINGS What emotions did you experience and how did you react physically when this happened?	CONSEQUENCES What happened as a result of your thoughts and feelings?	DISPUTATION Were your thoughts accurate and useful?
When Mike sat down at the dinner table and the food was put in front of him, he started whining and crying. (difficulty)	I thought, "ugh, I hate dinnertime." I also thought, "I'm a bad mother, and I'm not able to control his behavior."	I felt tired and sad. Sometimes this all makes me feel depressed.	I gave him cookies so he would stop crying. I felt like I had lost this battle and that I am really a failure as a parent.	Well, I spend most of my time trying to help my son. I guess I'm not a bad mother. And I can sometimes get him to eat dinner without much of a problem. These thoughts are a little exaggerated. I can see that when I think like this, I lose my ability to follow through; so I guess these thoughts are not helpful.

In this example, Joyce was beginning to learn how to accurately monitor her thoughts in these situations and was seeing that some of her thoughts were not completely accurate and may have been contributing to her difficulty in dealing with problem situations with Mike. After a little disputation discussion with her, she could see that she obviously is a very good and caring mother and it was only her frustration that caused her to doubt this. She was also much better at working with her son Mike than she gave herself credit for, which was essential to point out. As we have seen with many parents, Joyce's pessimistic style was leading her to blame herself for the negative behaviors Mike was showing and not take credit for the positive ones. Thinking these more pessimistic thoughts was not at all helpful and contributed to Joyce giving in to Mike's demands when she really did not want to.

Remember to keep track of your successes as well. The following is an entry of a success entered by Joyce.

JOYCE'S JOURNAL: DESCRIBING A SUCCESS

SITUATION What happened (success or difficulty)?	THOUGHTS What did you think or say to yourself when this happened?	FEELINGS What emotions did you experience and how did you react physically when this happened?	CONSEQUENCES What happened as a result of your thoughts and feelings?	DISPUTATION Were your thoughts accurate and useful?
I asked Mike to put away his building blocks in the toy chest. When I came back into his room, they were all picked up off the floor. (success)	I thought, "It's a miracle he finally did something I asked. Why is it always so difficult for him to help me out? All day long he has been a pain and the only thing he did right was this one little thing. He should be doing this all the time."	I felt angry at him for giving me such a hard time all day.	I didn't praise him for putting away his toys like I had asked.	I guess I was so upset from earlier in the day that I was too focused on what he hadn't done before and not focused on what he did do right. I guess it wasn't useful to be thinking about the bad parts of the day rather than the good thing he did. It made me resent having to reward him for something he did right.

You can see the pessimistic attributional style repeated here as well. This, too, is an all–too-common occurrence among parents of challenging children. They get so focused on the things that go wrong that they sometimes devalue the good interactions. In following up with Joyce about her thoughts and feelings, she confessed that the part of our plan that involved reinforcing Mike for being compliant with simple commands almost seemed like bribes. "Shouldn't he do these things anyway?" she asked. She took exception to having to praise him when he was being good. We followed through with the disputation process on this thought. "Is it accurate to think that he should be doing things such as putting his toys away or eating his dinner without a major problem?" "Yes," she responded. "I agree," the therapist replied, much to her surprise. "He should be doing these things; but, right now, he doesn't do them all the time. You are working on this and seeing improvement. The next question is, is it helpful to think these thoughts?" "I guess not," she admitted. "It just makes me upset and I don't appreciate his progress."

Whether thoughts you are having are actually helpful is an important point. I am not suggesting that *all* of your thoughts—both negative and positive—are somehow irrational or misguided. In fact, they may be right on target. In Joyce's case, she was right: Mike should have been able to put his toys away without an elaborate reinforcement system. He should have been able do it when he was asked with only a "thank you" or some brief praise as reinforcement. Joyce should *not* have had to put on a multimedia extravaganza for each small step. However, Mike did not put his toys away, and he often had a tantrum when asked. We were working on getting him to the point where he would comply with this simple request without much fanfare. But, at the time, the plan we had helped Joyce put in place was the first step. So, her thought about what he should have been doing was correct. But, my point is that it did not help Joyce to think this when she was trying to get him to that end goal. Eventually, we taught her other ways of viewing the situation and his progress that helped her persist through the process.

The following example may be helpful to further explore this disputation process. Recall that in the previous chapter I described Mack and Cindy—two parents that worked outside the home—and their extremely active son Jesse, who

CINDY'S JOURNAL: DISPUTATION EXAMPLE

SITUATION What happened (success or difficulty)?	THOUGHTS What did you think or say to yourself when this happened?	FEELINGS What emotions did you experience and how did you react physically when this happened?	CONSEQUENCES What happened as a result of your thoughts and feelings?	DISPUTATION Were your thoughts accurate and useful?
I got Jesse into the bathroom to wash up. When I took out the toothbrush and toothpaste, he started crying and tried to leave the bathroom. (difficulty)	I thought, "Why is he doing this to me? I'm tired from working all day, and I don't need this. Why didn't my husband brush his teeth earlier? I guess this is my 'job' and no one else can do it."	I felt upset at Jesse and angry with my husband. I felt the muscles in my neck tighten up.	Even though he calmed down and did cooperate with toothbrushing, I didn't praise him because I was upset. I made Mack turn off his football game and put on my show because I was upset with him, but I didn't tell him why I had him change the channel.	I guess Jesse doesn't like to brush his teeth—I guess most kids don't—and he really wasn't doing this to upset me. And it didn't help to think this because he did finally cooperate and I didn't praise him. I think it was okay for me to think that my husband should help, but I should have told him that and worked out a plan so we shared this job.

required constant monitoring. This sample shows the situation Cindy described to us along with the rest of her journal entry after we introduced disputation.

In Cindy's case, Jesse's reluctance to brush his teeth was not all that different from the reluctance seen in other young children. Again, Cindy was right to think that Jesse should be more cooperative, but her thought about his crying on purpose with the intention of upsetting her may not have been completely correct. In any case, it certainly was not helpful in getting the toothbrushing accomplished. At the same time, Cindy was thinking how her husband should be helping out more and was becoming upset with him as well. Should Mack have brushed Jesse's teeth earlier so Cindy did not have to? Yes. And no. The answer would be yes if Cindy and Mack had worked out an agreement about who should carry out this task with Jesse, but they had not. The answer would be yes if Mack was an observant and sensitive husband who saw what needed to be done around the house and did those things without prompting. Mack actually was a very good husband and father who helped out at home *when asked*. But because Cindy typically took control of most of these situations and because she did not communicate to Mack her frustration, he was not aware of the looming problem.

Cindy's thoughts about having Mack help out more were accurate but would have been more helpful if she had let him know her need for his help. Is that fair? As we saw in a previous case, it probably is not fair; however, it is a reality for many families. The goal, then, was to reduce the blaming and to work toward changes in getting Jesse's toothbrushing done but also to help Cindy and Mack let each other see the world through each other's eyes and work toward a more equitable parenting arrangement.

I hope that with the help of these examples you can see the real value in disputation. The objective is not to find fault or to determine who is right. The objective in disputation is to reality-test your thoughts—to see if they are completely accurate and, more important, to see if they are useful to you. As these examples have illustrated, sometimes a person's thoughts in emotionally charged situations are not accurate. They may be exaggerated or expose a bias (such as a pessimistic style). Other times, although someone's thoughts may be a true reflection of reality, they may do little to help that person get through rough times.

Just as you took some time to get used to writing down your thoughts and feelings in the journal, allow yourself time to reflect on and question these thoughts and feelings. If you find it helpful, you may enlist the help of another person (e.g., your partner, a sibling, a close friend) to serve as a sounding board for this process. Give this person permission to be the devil's advocate—to challenge you on the accuracy and usefulness of your thoughts and feelings. Try not to be defensive (e.g., "But he never helps me!") but instead listen to the view of a different person in an open way. Remember, the goal is not to look back (i.e., blame). The goal is to look forward to find ways of resolving current problems. We are now in "problem-solving mode"—a more optimistic approach to dealing with difficulties than lingering on past transgressions.

For some parents, just being aware of these disconnects between what they think and feel and what is accurate and helpful is enough to suggest to them different ways of handling situations. However, most parents find that additional and more specific strategies are needed, such as the next CBT strategy: distraction.

DISTRACTION: INTERRUPTING UNPRODUCTIVE AND DISTRESSING THOUGHTS

I have wandered all my life, and I have also traveled; the difference between the two being this, that we wander for distraction, but we travel for fulfillment.

—Hilaire Belloc (as cited in Braude, 1962, p. 829)

The lives of most individuals in today's society are filled with distractions. For example, if you work with a computer on a daily basis, you might find that searching the Internet for news, weather, or humor can eat into time that you should be spending at work. One survey suggests that employees waste 2 hours per day at work on Internet distractions, costing companies more than $750 billion each year.[2] Distraction while driving has become a major concern with the proliferation of cell phones and smart phones that let drivers talk or text while they should be focused on the road and other drivers. There is no lack of things to interfere with our ability to carry out daily tasks.

Despite the potential negative impact of too many distractions, there are times when distraction is helpful. Life can sometimes be so filled with stress that people need a way to escape for a time with activities that provide comfort or, at a minimum, take them away from the problems at hand. Some people find that reading can be a great way to remove themselves from the daily grind. Watching movies or television shows also are popular diversions, as are physical activities and hobbies. Distraction is good if it is done for the right reasons and if the distractions provide physical or emotional refreshment and restoration.

In my colleagues' and my work, we sometimes take advantage of distraction to help parents deal with unwanted or unproductive thoughts about themselves, their child, or others. Distraction is one of several formal techniques used in optimism training that can be very helpful with dealing with troubling thoughts. It is used to interrupt unproductive thoughts that might interfere with carrying out plans the way one wants. Let's return to the case of Joyce and her son Mike and take a look at Joyce's journal entries to see how we used distraction with her. In the previous entry, Joyce gave Mike cookies to stop crying at the dinner table. This was partly the result of her thinking that she was not a good mother and that she had no control over him at mealtimes. We used disputation with her to see if her thoughts about herself were accurate and useful, and she determined that they were not. In this similar scenario, we suggested that Joyce select something to say to herself or do that might get her through Mike's small tantrum—a mental distraction that would last long enough for Mike to stop crying and that would make Joyce feel better about herself and their progress. The results of Joyce's attempts to use distraction are documented next.

JOYCE'S JOURNAL: USE OF DISTRACTION

SITUATION What happened (success or difficulty)?	THOUGHTS What did you think or say to yourself when this happened?	FEELINGS What emotions did you experience and how did you react physically when this happened?	DISPUTATION Were your thoughts accurate and useful?	DISTRACTION What did you do to shift your attention?
When Mike started to come to the table and saw there was no food, he started to cry and say, "I want mac and cheese." (difficulty)	I started to think, "Here we go again; this is going to be a disaster."	I felt tense.	Well, I spend most of my time trying to help my son. I guess I'm not a bad mother. And I can sometimes get him to eat dinner without much of a problem. These thoughts are a little exaggerated. I can see that when I think like this, I lose my ability to follow through, so I guess they are not helpful either.	I took out the piece of paper I wrote during our session and read it to myself. It said, "This will only last for 2 more minutes. I gave birth after being in labor for 20 hours. If I can survive labor for 20 hours I can survive a 2-minute tantrum!"

Through our observations of Mike's tantrums, we discovered that they did not last very long—maybe 2–3 minutes. To help Joyce put this into perspective while the tantrums were occurring, we asked her to write this information about the duration of his tantrums down on a piece of paper that she could pull out during these disruptions. This would act as a reminder to her about how short Mike's tantrums could be. She commented that when she looked at it this way, it really wasn't that bad; after all, she had survived a long and painful labor, so surely she could survive this—assuming the tantrums would improve with the plans we put in place. The thoughts about her labor made Joyce smile, so we suggested she add this to the note to herself. The next time there was a problem with a meal, she used the note as a distraction to help her through this difficult episode and found it made her smile and feel less tense. This, in turn, helped her make it through the tantrum without giving in to Mike's crying and without giving him cookies like she would have before.

I view these types of distractions as valuable but temporary. In the short term, they can help a parent avoid reacting impulsively and give him or her time to think through what he or she would really like to do. Often, people talk about "counting to 10" before reacting. This is just another form of distraction that helps a person to calm him- or herself, collect his or her thoughts, and react in a more rational and acceptable way. Joyce's bit of humor (i.e., "If I can survive labor for 20 hours, then I can survive a 2-minute tantrum!") did just that. She said that she felt less tense once she looked at the situation from this perspective and, therefore, could wait out the tantrum, which was one part of our plan for Mike's mealtime problems. But it is important to repeat that this is only a temporary strategy. Distracting yourself is only helpful in the long term if you have a plan for ultimately resolving your child's problem. In Joyce's case, reminding herself about labor will wear thin over time and will be less effective if she is not seeing progress in Mike's behavior. After a time, if Mike is still being disruptive, it is likely that Joyce's previous thoughts about being a bad mother and not having control will creep back in, which will make her vulnerable to resorting to giving in again by quieting Mike with cookies.

Going back to the case of Cindy and Mack and their son Jesse, recall that Jesse's tantrums often left Cindy with thoughts of being unappreciated and taken advantage of by her husband. She also had thoughts that her son Jesse was misbehaving on purpose. After we worked through the disputation process with her, we agreed that perhaps there was some reason to feel resentment toward her husband, and that they needed to communicate more about how each of them viewed these situations. However, Cindy also saw that Jesse's problems with toothbrushing were probably not intended to upset her and that thinking this was not particularly helpful for dealing with this daily task. As we then moved on to the use of distraction and discussed ways for Cindy to distract herself from these thoughts, she recalled a part of a movie the family watched that made toothbrushing funny. So, we suggested that this be her strategy for distraction. The edited journal entry shown on the next page describes how Cindy used this new distraction while assisting Jesse with toothbrushing.

When Cindy mentioned in our session that the family had watched *Pee-wee's Big Adventure* on DVD and that Jesse and Mack were laughing hysterically over Pee-wee Herman's use of a giant toothbrush to brush his teeth, we decided to try to recreate this scene during toothbrushing with Jesse. Although Cindy and Mack could not find a giant toothbrush, Cindy started to sing the little song Pee-wee sang when he used the toothbrush—"Brush, brush, brush…"—which distracted Cindy for a time from her negative thoughts. This distraction also served to change the mood of both Cindy and Jesse. It made them smile and helped Jesse start to enjoy rather than avoid toothbrushing.

CINDY'S JOURNAL: USE OF DISTRACTION

SITUATION What happened (success or difficulty)?	THOUGHTS What did you think or say to yourself when this happened?	FEELINGS What emotions did you experience and how did you react physically when this happened?	DISPUTATION Were your thoughts accurate and useful?	DISTRACTION What did you do to shift your attention?
I got Jesse into the bathroom to wash up. When I took out the toothbrush and toothpaste, he started crying and tried to leave the bathroom. (difficulty)	I thought, "Why is he doing this to me? I'm tired from working all day, and I don't need this. Why didn't my husband brush his teeth earlier? I guess this is my 'job' and no one else can do it."	I felt upset at Jesse and angry with my husband. I felt the muscles in my neck tighten up.	I guess Jesse doesn't like to brush his teeth—I guess most kids don't—and he really wasn't doing this to upset me. And it didn't help to think this because he did finally cooperate and I didn't praise him. I think it was okay for me to think that my husband should help, but I should have told him that and worked out a plan so we shared this job.	I started to sing a song with Jesse about brushing his teeth. We saw this in a movie (Pee-wee's Big Adventure). This made us both smile and refocused me on a fun thing.

As I pointed out in the case of Joyce and Mike, it is important to reiterate that just using distraction without resolving the problems that contributed to negative thoughts is not the goal of this technique. In this case, Cindy had a reasonable concern with Mack's lack of participation in this and other tasks, and this concern needed to be mediated. Also, although the song made toothbrushing easier on both mother and son, numerous other situations in which Jesse misbehaved needed to be addressed. Distracting Cindy from her thoughts about Jesse's deliberately acting up and her concerns with her husband's inclusion in parenting was only a temporary fix to getting through these stressful events. We still needed to help her work better with Jesse to reduce his tantrums and to mediate the parenting duties to help them both be better partners in Jesse's progress. Having said this, the distraction technique was particularly successful for Cindy in helping Jesse with toothbrushing, which had been a source of considerable frustration in the past.

As I suggested with the use of disputation, you may find it helpful to talk the technique of distraction through with another person with whom you have a good relationship and who can help you dream up creative strategies that work for you. The goal again is to refocus your attention away from the thoughts that seem to interfere with your parenting skills (e.g., "I am a bad parent," "I have no control over this situation," "Other people are judging me," "My child will never get better") to more pleasant thoughts or different aspects of the situation.

In Chapter 3, I described the case of Ashley and her son Jeffrey. She was the mom in her mid-20s who described herself as having been a "party girl" before becoming a parent but who was quickly becoming isolated and depressed over her difficulty handling Jeffrey and her other children. A major theme of Ashley's thoughts was that she had absolutely no control over what went on with her children, and these thoughts were causing her to avoid any situation that potentially might cause problems—again, what we call the concession process. The disputation process helped Ashley see that her thought about having no control was not rational and that she did have a fair amount of control over what happened with her children. However, despite pointing this out to Ashley and getting her to articulate that the thought might indeed be irrational, she was not able to stop from thinking this and berating herself during difficult situations for her perceived inadequacies as a parent.

As a first step toward helping Ashley with these thoughts, we asked her to think of some techniques to help distract her during rough times. We gave her a few examples—writing down her belief that she had no control and throwing away the piece of paper, scheduling time to think through this belief when she had a quiet moment, or taking out a note that said "Stop!" every time she thought she was out of control. She left our session with this homework but was obviously still struggling to find something that felt real and not silly to her.

When Ashley and her husband returned the following week, she looked much more upbeat. She told us that she and her husband had friends over to play cards while the children were at a neighbor's house. They had had a great time and laughed all night. "In the middle of our partying," she said, "I thought, 'I've got it! Yippee-kay-ay!'" Her therapist looked puzzled. "You know. Yippee-kay-ay! From the movie? When I mentioned this to my friends they were hysterical and thought it was a terrific idea!" They both grinned from ear to ear each time she repeated "Yippee-kay-ay." Ashley helped her therapist out. "This is what I've been using as a distraction. Each time the kids are getting to me, I think 'Yippee-kay-ay.' If my husband is around I look at him and smile and he knows I'm thinking it and we both smile." The therapist was pleased. "Great, this is obviously a word that means something to the two of you and improves your mood. I think you should continue using it during the rough patches."

A search of famous movie lines uncovered that "Yippee-kay-ay" comes from the *Die Hard* movies and is the beginning of a line the main character says just before he shoots a bad guy. For Ashley and her husband, it was obviously a lighthearted way of putting their children's behavior in perspective, and they assured us that they had no plans of gunning down their little darlings!

The use of humor in tough situations can be a very effective way of changing your mood and distracting you from unproductive thoughts. It is difficult to be angry and laugh at the same time. Another strategy to distract yourself from thinking in ways that interfere with your parenting is a technique that I discuss in Chapter 5 on how to be a happier parent. This approach—called *mindfulness*—involves being hyperaware of what is happening to you at the moment. Rather than removing yourself from what is happening around you (e.g., your child is screaming at a supermarket, and you are attempting to distract yourself by recalling a scene from a movie), you become hyperaware and focused on what is happening with your body (e.g., your breathing) and around you (e.g., sounds of shopping carts and the beeps of cashiers ringing up customers). Used properly, mindfulness can be calming and allow you time to think through what to do next (e.g., I will slowly but surely keep moving the cart past the candy aisle while breathing deeply) without the judgmental thoughts that typically may invade your mind during these times. Again, I describe this technique in more detail in the next chapter as an overall strategy for dealing with anxiety and for providing you with more peace of mind.

SUBSTITUTION: REPLACING UNPRODUCTIVE AND DISTRESSING THOUGHTS

Another important tool used in CBT is substitution, or replacing negative thoughts with more positive and useful ways of looking at a difficult situation. In many ways, this is similar to the "half-empty" and "half-full" perspectives on the world that characterize views by pessimists and optimists. One afternoon, not long ago, my wife had a small accident in a parking lot with her 2-week-old new car. It was a larger car than she was used to driving, and she accidently backed into a cement pillar. Although the damage looked inconsequential, the bill from the body shop to fix it was shocking to put it mildly. She called to tell me what had happened and felt terrible that we now had to spend more money right after buying the car. "You're not hurt?" I asked. "No, just embarrassed." "Great! And we have insurance?" "Yes, but we will have to pay for part of it." She was still upset and felt guilty about what had happened. "Not a big deal," I said. "You know, there are so many people unemployed right now, and we can afford to fix your car; it's not so terrible, is it?" You could hear the smile in her voice when she said, "You always have a way of looking at the bright side of things!"

Actually, I do not look at the bright side of things all the time. It is not always good to be *too* optimistic. For example, if one constantly expects the very best, he or she will frequently be disappointed if he or she achieves less than was hoped for. In our parenting research, my colleagues and I work to keep the expectations of parents for their children realistic. We never find, for instance, that we can help a child go from almost constant disruption to being perfectly well behaved in a matter of weeks. Actually, very few children are perfectly well behaved, even those who appear to be flawless on the surface. This is important for families to understand. Setting achievable goals for yourself and your child helps you appreciate the achievements and avoid major disappointments and frustration.

There are times, too, when it is helpful to be a little pessimistic. If you can anticipate problems (e.g., my daughter is likely to be upset with me when I tell her that I can't take her to the park today), then you can plan for how you want to react should they occur. And, on the bright side (I did it again!), think of how you will feel if things work out better than you expect (e.g., your daughter only whines a little bit and then is fine when told she cannot play in the park). I have encouraged realistic and practical optimism throughout this book as a means of helping you and your child. This does not mean never having any expectations but rather to expect changes in small increments rather than miracle fixes.

From time to time, I do fall back on looking at the bigger picture to remind myself that I am a very lucky person, even when things are not going well. In the example I described about my wife's car, I used a strategy referred to by social psychologists as downward social comparison.[3] This is a tendency by some people to compare themselves with people or groups whose troubles are more serious than theirs. For example, this is a common phenomenon observed among women with breast cancer. Although these women need and seek the support of other women who are coping well with the disease, they find some comfort in seeing that they are luckier or more fortunate than women who have more serious forms of cancer or who have more invasive treatment (e.g., double mastectomy versus their lumpectomy). In my case, I felt better knowing that the situation with my wife's car could have been much worse, knowing others who have been seriously hurt in car accidents or who have been devastated financially by such events.

Downward social comparison is just one technique you can use to employ substitution to help you with thoughts that interfere with parenting. Look for a thought that is a more optimistic way of viewing a situation to replace the pessimistic thought that may be causing you difficulty. To provide an illustration about how this works in Optimistic Parenting, let's return to the case of Joyce and describe how my colleagues and I taught her to substitute some of her more pessimistic thoughts with more positive ways of viewing her situation. The following is her journal entry about another incident that occurred during mealtime, but this time we asked her to come up with a substitute way of thinking about what was going on that might make her feel better.

JOYCE'S JOURNAL: SUBSTITUTE THINKING

SITUATION What happened (success or difficulty)?	THOUGHTS What did you think or say to yourself when this happened?	FEELINGS What emotions did you experience and how did you react physically when this happened?	SUBSTITUTION What is a more positive way to think about this?
Mike sat down at the dinner table. Before I could get the food to the table, he climbed out of his chair and sat on the floor screaming. (difficulty)	He is so out of control. I really am at my limit, and I don't know what to do. I should be better at handling this, but I'm not.	I was starting to feel anger at him, but then I felt so defeated and guilty that if I were better at dealing with him, he would behave better. I felt tired.	I am a good mother and I am trying to help him. I am getting this training with your program, and we will get this under control.

Again, Mike's behavior at mealtime caused Joyce to think that she had no control over his behavior and that she was a bad mother. These thoughts led to a variety of feelings such as anger, sadness, and guilt. To replace these thoughts, Joyce made some good suggestions. She looked more realistically at what kind of mother she was and rightly came to the conclusion that she was caring and was working hard at helping her son be better behaved. Joyce also suggested that thinking "We will get this under control" was a better way of looking at his tantrum than "He is so out of control."

It may be helpful to review how far we have come with Joyce up to this point. Remember that we had to work with her to be more specific with us about just what Mike was doing when he had his tantrums (i.e., Situation). We also needed to work even harder to get her to be aware of and communicate what she was thinking (i.e., Thoughts) and how she was reacting emotionally (i.e., Feelings) to these disruptions. Although Joyce found it difficult, she eventually became comfortable being aware of what she was thinking and feeling while Mike was misbehaving. As we talked with Joyce about these thoughts and feelings and discussed the concepts of a pessimistic style of thinking, she was able to see that she usually looked only at the negative aspects of Mike's behavior and her life in general and needed to look at things more positively, both for her own well-being as well as for that of the rest of her family.

Suggestions for Thought Substitutions

Joyce was able to pick realistic thoughts (e.g., "I am a good mother," "We will get this under control") rather than those that might lead to disappointment later on (e.g., "He will be better by next week"). Sometimes, however, parents are not as successful as Joyce in seeing how their thoughts need to be reworked. If you find yourself in this situation or if you just need a review of these concepts, the next section revisits the themes identified in the Chapter 3 Thoughts Quiz discussion and provides some possible substitutes for pessimistic thinking.

1. How You See Yourself as a Parent (Self-Efficacy)

Current Thought (Pessimistic): *I cannot control my child.* Remember that this way of thinking in some form or another is quite common among families with challenging children. Even if you are not thinking these exact words, some aspect of this theme of low self-efficacy (believing that you are unable to manage your child) is found in many families' journal entries. It is important to point out that the extreme version of this thought—having absolutely no control—is never actually the case even if all you can do is leave a situation (e.g., leaving a friend's house during a tantrum) or prevent some problem from occurring (e.g., childproofing your house to avoid accidents).

Substitute Thought (Optimistic): *I am usually able to handle problem situations* or *I will gain more control soon.* Again, you do not have to use these exact words, but some version of these more optimistic views of difficult situations can help you see the "half-full" side of what can seem to be a chaotic or frenzied situation. One of my favorite substitutions for the thought of being out of control is "I am doing the best that I can." This thought can be a helpful, more confident, and, therefore, more optimistic way of viewing a difficult situation. This should not be viewed as "I am limited as a parent" but more along the lines of "This is difficult, I am doing my best, and there is little more to do now." These segments of the poem "If—" by Rudyard Kipling give the general feeling of this substitution:[4]

If you can keep your head when all about you
Are losing theirs and blaming it on you;
If you can trust yourself when all men doubt you,
But make allowance for their doubting too;
If you can wait and not be tired by waiting...
Yours is the Earth and everything that's in it...

This thought substitution is successful if it gets you to see that simply not panicking in a difficult situation is a triumph.

Sometimes, it is useful to look back at your journal entries for successes to see that, in fact, you did have interactions that worked well. At the same time, in each of the cases of success, make sure that you reexamine your thoughts in these successful situations to make them more in line with an optimistic view of the world. Remember, people with pessimistic styles not only have characteristic ways of viewing difficult situations but also often have unproductive ways of looking at their child's successes. This unproductive style includes looking at their child's progress as temporary (e.g., it was a fluke good day) and not taking credit for the progress. If you look back at Joyce's journal entry about a successful situation with Mike, you can see that her thoughts about the situation were not helpful.

JOYCE'S JOURNAL: UNHELPFUL
THOUGHTS ABOUT A SUCCESSFUL SITUATION

SITUATION What happened (success or difficulty)?	THOUGHTS What did you think or say to yourself when this happened?	FEELINGS What emotions did you experience and how did you react physically when this happened?	CONSEQUENCES What happened as a result of your thoughts and feelings?	SUBSTITUTION What is a more positive way to think about this?
I asked Mike to put his building blocks in the toy chest. When I came back into his room, they were all picked up off the floor. (success)	I thought, "It's a miracle he finally did something I asked. Why is it always so difficult for him to help me out? All day long he has been a pain, and the only thing he did right was this one little thing. He should be doing this all the time."	I felt angry at him for giving me such a hard time all day.	I didn't praise him for putting away his toys like I asked.	He is making progress. All of the work I have done to get him to be more responsible is beginning to pay off, and he is starting to listen to me. This is a big step forward, and there will be more.

In this situation, Joyce minimized what should have been a very positive moment—Mike actually followed her instructions and put away his toys. We taught Joyce how to substitute the more negative view of what Mike did by emphasizing his progress and her role in his success. And, later we used this as an example of how he was making progress—a thought she could keep in mind when he had temporary setbacks and did not follow her requests.

Current Thought (Pessimistic): *I have doubts about my ability to help my child improve his or her behavior.* This thought is similar to the "out-of-control" theme but is more specific about your ability as a parent. It is expected that all parents make mistakes from time to time, but this thought implies that you feel inadequate or at least not up to the challenge.

Substitute Thought (Optimistic): *I am capable of helping my child improve.* You need to believe in yourself to be a successful parent. Even if, up to this point, your efforts to change your child's behavior have been less than successful, that does not necessarily reflect on you or your abilities as a parent. Except in cases when my colleagues and I have a parent with severe cognitive impairments or psychological disorders (and not even in all of those cases), we have yet to find a parent who could not help their child improve how he or she behaves. Some of our parents simplify this thought into "I can do it" or "I will do it," almost as an affirmation that they repeat to themselves when approaching a problem situation. Notice that this is about improving your child's behavior and not "curing" it, which makes the thought realistic and achievable. For example, we had one mother who, when faced with her challenging son, would think, "I'm not capable of teaching him anything. All I do is give in to him." Yet, when we asked her through the disputation process, "Does he get dressed?" "Yes," she replied. "Does he know how to brush his teeth?" "Yes." "So," we continued, "is it true that you are not capable of teaching him anything?" "Well, no," she finally admitted. We taught her the substitute thought, "I am quite good at teaching him new things, and this is just another new thing."

One mother came up with a new way of thinking about her supposed inability to help her child. She described to us a situation at a friend's house during which her son had a screaming fit and she was thinking that she had no control. When she later reflected on the situation, she realized that she had likely stayed at her friend's house too long and that her son did not have anything with him to keep him occupied. She told us that he probably would behave better the next time if she brought some toys or a video and that just thinking this through made her feel better—like she could figure this all out. Instead of having (in her words) a "pity party" and feeling out of control, she was now substituting these types of thoughts—that she was able to figure out what was going on and come up with solutions. Part of her confidence came, in part, from our teaching her some of the parenting skills discussed in the second section of this book, titled *Help*; however, she also was learning not to panic and to trust in herself that she would "find a way."

We usually remind parents that children can have regressions that are a result of circumstances that have nothing to do with the parents (e.g., not getting a good night's sleep, being ill). It is important to keep this in mind should your child experience some temporary setbacks. There will be setbacks, but you need to keep the thought firmly in your mind that you can still make a positive difference.

2. How You Think Others See You as a Parent (Concern About Others—Self)

Current Thought (Pessimistic): *When my child misbehaves, people see me as a bad parent.* This can be a very distressing way of thinking, especially if you are in public during an episode that your child is acting up. For some parents, this can be an irrational thought; there are instances when parents are so sensitive that they are picking up judgmental signals that are just not there. However, it is also true that people have a tendency to judge the parent when a child misbehaves. As I mentioned previously, this kind of thought can be so distressing that parents get flustered and stop using their good judgment and common sense and just react.

Substitute Thoughts (Optimistic): *I know I am a good parent, Other people just don't understand, I don't care what they think,* or *Most parents have times when their child misbehaves.* As with all of the thought substitutions, which one you pick depends on what works best for you and your situation. If you remember back to Chapter 1, I described one mother who was quite capable of confronting people who questioned her ability as a parent. If someone carelessly threw out a comment about her child or her ability to parent, she would educate them on the spot about her son's disability, how it contributed to his behaving differently, and how they should keep their nose out of other people's business! In her case, no substitution was necessary because she already had an optimistic thought— "I don't care what you think."

However, this is much more difficult for other parents. They do care what other people think, and it does bother them to feel that they are being perceived as being less than successful parents. Saying, "Why let this bother you?" ignores the reality that, for some people, it does upset them and it will not change by telling them it shouldn't. If you are one of the parents bothered by this thought, one of the "tricks" we suggest is to act in ways that make it clear that you have a plan and to have your substitute thought include that plan (e.g., "I know I am a good parent, and this is how I am going to handle this situation"). It can help if you not so subtly remind your child out loud (so others can hear) what your plan is (e.g., "What did I say about screaming? One more time and you do not get to watch your video tonight."). By doing so, you remind yourself what you will be doing, which is important; reinforce that you have a strategy; remind your child of any consequences; and communicate to others that you are not panicking or just a super indulgent parent who does not care if your child is so disruptive.

I have focused on dealing with the fact that there are people who judge you. At the same time, it is important to remember that, in any crowd of parents, there are also those parents who are thinking, 1) "Thank goodness it's not me!" 2) "Boy, I remember those days with my child," or 3) "Those poor parents!" Whenever I sit near a parent of a crying child in an airplane, I make a point of commiserating how I went through the same thing. Often, the parent is somewhat relieved. Although the child is still crying, at least the parent knows I am not judging the situation negatively. Remember that the next time you see a parent facing your same challenges and "pay it forward!"

3. How You Think Others View Your Child (Concern About Others— Child)

Current Thought (Pessimistic): *I think that other people judge my child when he or she is misbehaving.* All parents worry about their children. Parents hope that their children will be happy and healthy. They want their children to be successful, to have friends, and to lead a fulfilling life. However, children who display behavior challenges provide parents with an extra layer of worry. Will they be ostracized, bullied, or made fun of by other children? Will adults judge them negatively? These can be legitimate concerns. Some people, especially those with limited experience with children having special needs, can be judgmental about children as well. Being overwhelmed by this thought, however, to the point that it begins to interfere with your parenting efforts is a problem. As we do with all of these thoughts, my colleagues and I typically ask you to consider two disputation questions—"Is what I am thinking *really* true?" and "Is what I am thinking useful?"—and then try to realistically deal with them. Sometimes this thought is not as accurate as you might think, and certainly it is not helpful.

Substitute Thought (Optimistic): *Most parents have times when their child misbehaves.* As we go through the disputation process that I described earlier, parents in our program who are concerned about how others perceive their child are challenged to defend this way of thinking. For example, my colleagues and I might ask them, "Do you think it is possible that other adults may have problems with their own children and are more concerned with you and how you are handling it?" As suggested here, sometimes the substitution of a thought such as "Most parents have times when their child misbehaves" can be very helpful for parents to remember that their child is not the only child in the world having a difficult time. In my clinical experience, I have observed thousands of children and often find that parents will say something like this—"Oh yeah, for some reason he is good out in public. People think he is so well behaved. But it is a whole different story once we get home." It is helpful to remember this when you are noticing otherwise well-behaved children in stores, at school, in playgrounds, or in other public settings. Sometimes these "good kids" are not so good all of the time.

Although not directly part of the substitution process, there are times when a parent can intervene in more active ways in these situations. In addition to examining the accuracy and usefulness of such thoughts, education of others can be helpful to both them and you. Telling someone else such as a friend or relative about your child's difficulties and how you are working on them can change their thought patterns from "That child needs some discipline" to "Wow, I didn't know she had this problem. I don't know if I could handle this as a parent." In this case, you are using the substitution process with other people—changing how they view your child.

You also can help change the thoughts of other children. For example, good school programs for children with special needs often include activities that educate other children about a child who is exhibiting problems and encourage acceptance and social interaction. There are a number of excellent examples of these programs that could be helpful if concern remains about your child's interactions with other children.[5] These programs help put your child's behavior in a new light for other children and are designed to encourage a more optimistic approach to interacting with and viewing children with behavior challenges.

4. How You See Your Child's Ability to Control His or Her Behavior (Child Efficacy)

Current Thought (Pessimistic): *My child is not capable of behaving better.* This is one of the more difficult thoughts to get parents to realize they possess in a situation. Often this belief is so entrenched in the parents' way of looking at their child that they do not even realize they hold this assumption. It is usually not articulated this way (i.e., "My child cannot behave better") but rather comes out in how the parents deal with their child on a day-to-day basis. Parents may have had so many negative experiences in their efforts to change their child's behavior (e.g., getting them to wait a period of time before getting something they want) that they stop trying; their belief becomes that their child cannot change. This concept of low child efficacy (or the belief that one's child has a limited ability to learn something new or behave in a better way) is an important part of why some families give up in more and more situations (i.e., the concession process). It is obvious that holding this assumption will seriously interfere with the parents' ability to make meaningful changes in their child's behavior.

Substitute Thought (Optimistic): *My child is capable of behaving better.* Part of our educational process with parents when we start designing behavior plans is the assumption that their child is, in fact, quite capable of change. Just as we have worked with families from all walks of life with all manner of problems and obstacles, so too have we worked with children, youth, and adults with a range of challenges. We have seen improvements in communication skills and behavior problems in children with dual sensory impairments (i.e., are both deaf and blind) and in children who have significant cognitive impairments. I also have worked with individuals in psychiatric settings, group homes, schools, vocational settings, and the community; in all cases (with the proper cooperation), I have seen important improvements in behavior.

I am not saying everyone can be helped to do anything (e.g., I still can't speak Spanish properly because I am not able to trill my tongue—a source of great disappointment to my high school Spanish teacher). Some children will need additional supports throughout their lives. Others will struggle with problems such as attentional difficulties, impulsivity, anxiety, or depression or will have other challenges to overcome. However, any child who is displaying significant challenging behavior can be helped to behave better. The belief that "My child is capable of behaving better" needs to be implanted in your head at all times.

Current Thought (Pessimistic): *My child's behavior is related to his or her disability.* This thought is similar to the previous low child efficacy belief (i.e.,

"My child is not capable of behaving better") but is more specific to a particular disability or disorder. I have spent a great deal of my career working with families who have children with autism spectrum disorders, and often the parents hold a shared belief that the behavior difficulties displayed by their children are directly related to their diagnosis. And, sometimes this is true. A child with autism who constantly twirls around in circles probably behaves this way because of perceptual or sensory issues related to his or her disorder. At the same time, there are many behaviors that parents believe are directly related to a particular diagnosis that are common among children without this diagnosis. Many children who do not have specific diagnoses hit others, scream, or refuse to do things they do not want to do. This is important to remember as you work with your child.

Substitute Thought (Optimistic): *My child is capable of behaving better.* The same type of substitution can be used for this type of child efficacy thought as for the previous version. As I have pointed out, even those difficult behaviors that are directly attributable to a disorder (e.g., the distraction exhibited by a child with ADHD) usually can be improved. At the same time, research since the 1970s clearly shows that most, if not all, challenging behaviors can be improved, regardless of the child's abilities or disabilities.

5. How You View the Problem Situation (Pervasive)

Current Thought (Pessimistic): *All of these situations are always a major problem.* Recall that I described the concept of catastrophizing, viewing situations as much worse than they actually are. This, again, is a pessimistic way of viewing problems—that they are pervasive and occur more often or much worse than what actually happens in reality. This is a natural reaction to what may seem, at the time, as a major problem that has happened before. One mother, for example, described a problem situation she had with her daughter, who had acted up at the supermarket. Her mother had to leave a half-full cart of groceries in the store to take her home. "Shopping with my child is a disaster," she told us. "I'm never going shopping with her again." The problem with a thought like this is that—as happened in this case—the parent feels completely defeated and runs the risk of avoiding all such situations again. This is the beginning of the concession process that we saw can, if left unchecked, lead to more serious difficulties down the road.

Substitute Thought (Optimistic): *This particular incident was a problem.* It is much more helpful to isolate problems and try to see whether there are specific situations that trigger a child's behavior problems. Chapter 7 describes how to do this, but for now it is important for us to point out how to determine whether you are catastrophizing and, if you are, how to change that. In the example I just described, we reviewed with this mother different shopping trips she had taken with her daughter in the past to see if, in fact, they always were a disaster. What the mother told us was that short trips—running into the store for one or two items—usually were not a problem. Her daughter would be gener-ally well behaved under these circumstances. Even longer trips could go well, but they were hit and miss. As we talked through these different excursions, the mother started to see certain patterns. For example, if the shopping trip went on for more than about a half hour, her daughter was more likely to become rest-less and act up. Also, the mother thought her daughter handled trips better if she had eaten something right before they left the house. Being hungry at the super-market seemed to make her much more difficult. Therefore, what we did was examine whether the belief that "Shopping with my child is a disaster" was an accurate depiction of all shopping trips. Clearly, at least in this case, this was not true. We would not want to try to create a substitute thought (e.g., "Only long shopping trips are difficult") that was not accurate.

In this mother's case, the extreme thought (i.e., "Shopping with my child is a disaster") was not completely true, and she could see this once we went through a number of different scenarios. We could then help her through these situations by giving her a substitute thought that provided a better and more helpful perspective. She decided on "Long shopping trips with my daughter can be difficult" as a better way to view situations. The new, optimistic thought reminded this mother that not all of the trips were problems and also that she should try to limit how long the trips were. Being more efficient in the store and feeding her daughter first—in other words, having a plan for dealing with potential problems—made this mother feel less tense as they went out and refocused her attention on what was important—what is triggering her daughter to act up and how could she plan for and ultimately change her behavior.

As you start to examine your own thoughts, it is important to always try to put them in this perspective. In a sense, what I am asking you to do is to attempt to reduce the amount of time you react emotionally and instead try to use these difficult situations as times to observe and understand your child's behavior. So, rather than thinking "This is awful," instead use the time to deal with your child but also to think through what might be contributing to this tantrum, at this time, in this situation. Redirecting your thoughts in this way can help you see that there are good times as well as bad times and can give you ways of dealing with the tough times in the future.

6. How You View the Future (Stable)

Current Thought (Pessimistic): *Things will never get better or will get worse.* This is the ultimate pessimistic thought. Thinking that there is no hope, that nothing one does will make things better, leads to giving up. Just as Seligman and Maier's dogs did not try to jump over the barrier to avoid getting shocked, so too can parents become so defeated that they stop trying to make things better.

Substitute Thought (Optimistic): *Things can and will get better.* This is the ultimate optimistic thought. It is hopeful. It is positive. It is essential for suc-ceeding as a parent. Having said this, we do not expect parents to enthusiastically walk around with a constant grin on their face looking at all situations as wonderful. It certainly would be strange to see a parent in a group of other parents smiling and looking hopeful as her child was beating up another child ("Well, at least he didn't use a rock this time!"). I have already pointed out that being too optimistic can have its problems (e.g., reduces the likelihood that you will plan for difficult situations). You will have your moments of pessimism. That is natural and, in a limited way, helpful. However, these pessimistic thoughts need to be balanced with a view that no matter how bad things become, there is a way out and that things can and will get better. This attitude helps you try again, even when faced with pitfalls and obstacles. Thinking that things will never change causes you to abandon potentially useful approaches to helping your child because you will view minor defeats as signs of hopelessness. When you are in these difficult situations and you find yourself feeling defeated, remembering that there is hope will be important for you to be successful in the future.

Current Thought (Pessimistic): *I will never have my own life.* You can be pessimistic about your child's future prospects, and this will cause you to limit how you handle problems. Another future-oriented pessimistic thought is about you and your own life. This is a very common thought among parents in our program but one that is, for some, quite difficult to articulate to someone else. It seems selfish to some parents to think about themselves. This is especially prevalent among the parents of children who have severe and multiple problems. The expectation by friends, family, and society is that parents of a child in great need will sacrifice their lives for their child. In fact, it is common in our culture to idolize parents who do just that—sacrifice their own lives for the benefit of their child. These images ultimately make some parents feel very guilty if they start to have thoughts about their own happiness and well-being. As one parent put it, "These thoughts start to expand and become my 'pity party' and then I feel guilty for thinking about my own life."

Substitute Thought (Optimistic): *I am working toward more time for myself.* This substitute thought requires that you are, in fact, working toward finding time to help yourself heal and become your own person. Chapter 5 is dedicated to this effort to becoming happier and more fulfilled and, as I have discussed throughout the pages of this book, is essential for you to become a great parent. As you work toward this goal, it is important to remind yourself that this is an important part of parenting and that it is crucial for your mental and physical health.

7.   Who Is Responsible for a Problem Situation (Blame—Child)

Current Thought (Pessimistic): *My child is doing this on purpose.* This thought can be a difficult one for us to dispute with some parents. "But he is doing it on purpose!" Looking at it one way, all children act out on purpose. Chapter 6 examines the "purposes" of child behavior problems. Although it is not entirely wrong to view children with behavior problems in this light, other ways of looking at your child's behavior are more helpful when dealing with difficult situations.

Substitute Thought (Optimistic): *My child is not being disruptive intentionally.* This difference between what is being done on purpose (i.e., what is intentional) and what is not is a tricky but important distinction. For example, suppose a 2-month-old child is hungry. What would you expect this child to do? Obviously, we know that children at this age will cry when they are hungry, and a parent's job is to recognize this need and help satisfy it. Is this infant crying on purpose? Well, in one sense, yes. Without having any other way to communicate the need for food, the infant will cry. For some new parents or for those who have limited patience, this crying can be annoying. For some, this behavior may be so irritating that they resort to abusive behavior to stop the crying. There are many cases each year of young children being seriously abused for crying "on purpose."

We view most problem behavior among children in this light. Children will misbehave if they do not have better ways of getting what they want or need. Our job as parents and professionals is to try to understand what the messages behind their behaviors might be (e.g., "Will you spend more time with me?" "I don't want to do this") and then give them better ways of getting what they need. This process is less about blame than it is about gaining an understanding of what might be causing the problems. Rarely, for example, do we find that children will act up to make Mommy angry. Instead, what may be happening is that a child wants more of his or her mother's time (in a good way) but does not have the skills to gain this positive attention; therefore, he or she settles for negative attention. I spend a great deal of time in the later chapters of this book on this concept. But for the process of substitution, it is important to recognize that children rarely act up intentionally to hurt or annoy their parents but instead are trying to obtain some other goal. Similarly, children rarely misbehave to harm a sibling or friend but may do it to get some reaction from other people. The first step is to recognize this and to remind yourself that these challenges are not intentional.

8. Who Is Responsible for a Problem Situation (Blame—Others)

Current Thought (Pessimistic): *If only others would follow my suggestions correctly, my child would be better behaved.* It can be exasperating to believe that other people (e.g., your partner, grandparents) are sabotaging your efforts to help your child. It is difficult enough to follow through with your own strategies without feeling that the actions of others are undermining all of your hard work. I discussed the issue of blame briefly in Chapter 3 and noted how unproductive these thoughts can be, regardless of how legitimate the concern. The question now is how can you learn to deal with this thought in a way that is helpful to you and to your child?

Substitute Thought (Optimistic): *Everyone is doing his or her best under the circumstances.* One way to look at the concern that others are interfering with your parenting is to recognize that 1) there may be other ways to deal with your child's behavior that are equally legitimate and 2) others may have their own thoughts and feelings that get in the way of doing what is best for your child. The first alternative view can be the most difficult to adopt. Most individuals have opinions on the "right" way to handle a situation, and it can be upsetting if others follow a different course. One parent I worked with, Janet, was consumed with this thought when it came to parenting her child. Her ex-husband, Pete, would have their daughter over to his house every other weekend and, in Janet's words, would spoil her the whole time to win her favor. "He just gives her anything she wants. If she wants ice cream for dinner, she gets it. Then she comes home and wants ice cream for dinner. It drives me nuts! I don't want her eating ice cream at all, and I certainly don't want her eating it instead of a healthy dinner." It was clear from our discussions that we needed to get Pete involved in the program for their daughter's good. Both parents agreed to this, and the next session Pete and Janet arrived together.

As we discussed their daughter and their differences of opinion, Janet repeated her concern. "I'm the one who has to make sure she has healthy meals, and you just feed her junk like ice cream for dinner. I always look like the 'bad guy' in these situations. I'm the one who has to be strict and lay down the rules." Pete looked a little surprised. "I don't give her ice cream for dinner. The rule is that if she finishes what I made her, she can have ice cream." It seems that their daughter was misleading her mom into believing it was okay to have ice cream for dinner because that's what daddy did at his house. There is an important rule in parenting that can be summed up by Ronald Reagan's favorite saying when dealing with the old Soviet Union: "Trust, but verify."

In this case, Janet should trust both her daughter as well as her ex-husband. It is good to have a healthy bit of skepticism when it comes to what others say, and in this case, their daughter was partially correct. She did have ice cream at dinner, but it was for dessert and not the main course. As we discussed this further, Janet agreed to Pete using ice cream as an enticement for their daughter to finish dinner at his house and felt better that she was wrong in her assumption about what might be going on. This was a good compromise and also made Janet feel that perhaps her ex-husband was not intentionally sabotaging her own efforts with their daughter.

One of the problems with believing that others are not dealing with one's child in the correct way is that occasionally parents respond to these conflicts by going in and rescuing the situation. They micromanage the situation so that it is "perfect." Have you ever taken over a child care job such as bath time, toothbrushing, or dressing because your partner didn't do it correctly? And then, did you feel resentful that you have to do everything yourself? In this case, the substitute thought perhaps should be "I don't need to be perfect. Others can help me, even if it is not done exactly the way I would do it."

It also can be helpful to remember that others may have their own thoughts and feelings that get in their way of doing what they know are the right things to do. Your mother, for example, might be giving in to all of your son's demands when you are not around (e.g., letting him fall asleep on the living room floor while watching television, letting him eat with his hands) because she feels he cannot do any better because of his "problems" or because she does not feel that *she* has any control. Your mother may not express these thoughts and concerns—saying instead things such as "What's wrong if he sleeps in the living room?"—not because she believes you are wrong, but because of her own pessimistic thoughts. Until or unless you can help her change this way of looking at the world (have her borrow this book or, better yet, buy her a copy of her own), it may be helpful to recognize the situation for what it is (her limitation and not yours) and use a substitute thought such as "She is doing her best under the circumstances." Again, rather than blaming everyone else, try other ways of viewing these obstacles that will help you with your own efforts with your child.

9. Who Is Responsible for a Problem Situation (Blame—Self)

Current Thought (Pessimistic): *It is my fault that things are going wrong.* Self-blame is one of the most unproductive and destructive thoughts experienced by parents. Looking back (e.g., "I should have handled that differently") is only of value if it provides a lesson and the motivation to do something different. Otherwise, it is a waste of time and can lead to lingering sadness and regret.

Substitute Thought (Optimistic): *I am doing the best that I can under the circumstances.* This is a more optimistic version of the self-blame attitude. Although we could all do better as parents, it is important to remember that there are things out of our control that can interfere with our best efforts. This does not mean that you should not try harder or have higher expectations for yourself; however, sometimes the best you can do under extreme circumstances is just to hold it together and not do something you will regret later. Repeating this thought as a substitute for "It's all my fault" can help you move forward and feel better about yourself.

Remember, too, that it is important to recall successes in these situations. Take credit for the good days, or even the good minutes, and summon up these situations in your mind when you are having doubts.

10. Who Should Be Responsible for the Problem Situation (Self-Concern)

Current Thought (Pessimistic): *Why am I always the one who has to be responsible for these situations?* This thought can be similar to blaming others for interfering with your child-rearing plans; however, it is slightly different in that it is a way of lamenting that you are the one who has to make the important decisions and remember at all times what your child needs and that you are the one who feels guilty if things do not go well.

When examining this way of thinking, it is essential that you go through the full disputation process discussed previously. The two questions my colleagues and I ask in disputation (i.e., "Is what I am thinking *really* true?" "Is what I am thinking useful?") are important to bring up here again, and it is important that you take a close and honest look at these. Is it really true that you are always the one who has to be responsible, or does it just feel that way at times? This distinction will be helpful in deciding what type of substitution you might want to use. It may be true that you are always the one responsible. The issue then is how it makes you feel (resentful?) and how you can remedy this. At the same time, it might not be completely true; others (e.g., your spouse or partner, a family member) may be helping out and taking some responsibility and at times it just feels overwhelming to you. In this case, it would be helpful to examine how rational the thought is and how you might replace it.

The second question—Is what I am thinking useful?—is the one that will require the real soul searching on your part. If you are in a constant state of anger and resentment because you feel as if all of the responsibilities of parenting your challenging child fall unfairly on your shoulders, then you need to answer the question about whether it is helpful to think this way. Why does this require introspection and soul searching? Because sometimes expressing this to others gets you something. It may not get you any extra help or relieve you of any important responsibilities, but it may give you attention. It may help to shine a light on you that you are not able to do any other way. Communicating to others how difficult things are can be a way of getting people to respond in supportive ways (e.g., "Wow, I don't know how you do it!" "You're a saint"). Is that bad? Let's look at one of our cases to illustrate this pattern and to see whether it was a useful strategy to constantly resent the responsibilities of parenting.

Helen and Peter were a couple in their 40s who were "late" to parenthood. Both were highly successful in their respective careers, although at different times. Peter was a sales manager for a number of different start-up companies and was a natural at selling highly innovative products. He would travel the world going to important meetings with staff of large corporations and was as comfortable in the board room as he was with his next-door neighbor. With some downturns in the economy, however, there came a time when he lost his job and there were fewer and fewer opportunities for him. Just as this was happening, Helen's career as an attorney was taking off. She was a bankruptcy attorney, and the poor economy meant that she had more and more employment options. She was very good at what she did and landed an important position at a major firm.

In the middle of these events, Helen and Peter had Hanna. Hanna was born while Helen was working part-time and Peter was in the upswing of his career. That meant that Helen took on the major responsibilities for raising Hanna, which was quite a challenge. Hanna was a fussy infant and was ultimately diagnosed with Asperger syndrome, an autism spectrum disorder with a number of distinctive characteristics. Children with this disorder do not have the problems with speech as do children with autism. Although they can communicate, they lack some of the subtle social skills that are important for successful communication. When Hanna was older, for example, she was very literal in her understanding of another's communication. If she were told to "pick up her room," she would interpret this as a request to somehow lift her room up. Helen described how she left the store with Hanna once to discover that Hanna had taken a small toy from the store and hidden it in her shirt. Helen was upset. "I told you that you couldn't have things from the store without asking!" "I did ask," Hanna replied quite calmly. Helen thought back and recalled that Hanna asked for the toy but was told she could not have it. Hanna interpreted her request as following the letter of the law—she asked for it so she could take it.

Hanna, like other children with Asperger syndrome, followed a series of rituals (e.g., lining up her silverware at mealtime) and would scream loudly and hit others if the rituals were not followed. She also loved horses and could recite almost everything there is to know about them.

At about the time that Hanna was to enter preschool, Peter and Helen experienced their career shifts. This meant that now Peter spent most of his time at home while Helen was off at work, and Peter now became responsible for Hanna's care and for the multiple arrangements needed for making Hanna's school placement a success. At first, Peter took some pride in this because the situation was a bit similar to sales positions he had held. He would visit with schools and teachers and explain Hanna's special needs. He would charm the school personnel and could be quite persuasive in getting them to accommodate Hanna and her behaviors. However, the weight of the responsibilities at home and at school quickly wore on him. Peter and Helen came to us for help because of Hanna's behavior and because they were beginning to have difficulties as a couple.

When we went through the journal (shown on the next page), Peter reported on one particular incident with Hanna that week that precipitated a fight between him and Helen.

Peter's description of the problem at breakfast helped to make clear for us a number of different issues. It was easy to see that Peter's impatience with Hanna actually made getting ready worse, but there was another issue that we needed to explore. Peter was feeling that he should not have to have all of this responsibility, and he resented it. Helen was quick to point out that for Hanna's first few years she was the one responsible and handled it without major complaints. Now, it was Peter's turn, and he seemed to forget that Helen was still helping as much as she could. The biggest problem for Helen, though, was Peter's constant sarcastic comments to her when they were alone and, even

PETER'S JOURNAL: DESCRIPTION OF
A PROBLEM AT BREAKFAST

SITUATION What happened (success or difficulty)?	THOUGHTS What did you think or say to yourself when this happened?	FEELINGS What emotions did you experience and how did you react physically when this happened?	CONSEQUENCES What happened as a result of your thoughts and feelings?	DISPUTATION Were your thoughts accurate and useful?
We were rushing to get to the preschool on time, and I didn't let Hanna line up her silverware for breakfast. She started to scream and yell, but we were late so I had to drive her to the program screaming all the way. (difficulty)	I thought, "This will never end. She will always have these problems." I also questioned why this was now all up to me. Why am I the one to get her ready? Why am I the one who is responsible for all of this?	I was anxious not to be late. I felt angry at her for giving me such a hard time and felt sorry for myself.	My impatience led to my not taking the 60 seconds necessary to let her line up her silverware, which resulted in her tantrum.	She is getting better at these things—not taking quite so long to get ready. I guess my thoughts weren't useful because dealing with her tantrum took more time than if I had allowed her to line up the silverware. I am responsible—so that's accurate—but I guess it doesn't help to think this way.

worse, when they were with family and friends. According to Helen, Peter would always find a way to make a quip about a problem with Hanna that had occurred during the day and, in Helen's words, communicate "Oh poor me!" "I know it's tough," she said. "I did it for years. But I never whined about it like he does. Every conversation we have with friends revolves around Hanna and how much of a handful she is and what a courageous father Peter is. Although I appreciate that he takes care of her during the day, it has become annoying that he takes on this martyr role all of the time."

The case of Peter and Helen illustrates how thinking "Why am I the one who always has to be responsible for these situations?" and also communicating this to others can sometimes serve a purpose for the person in this situation. Although he was not fully aware of it, Peter was getting a great deal of attention and sympathy from others by constantly bringing up his challenges. Let me be clear: I am not saying that Peter should not have communicated to others what he was thinking and feeling. What I am trying to clarify with this case is that sometimes these thoughts and how one deals with them take on a life of their own. Again, what Peter was experiencing was a great deal of anxiety and frustration, and he was learning that pointing this out to friends and family members got them to respond to him in ways that were satisfying. Was he aware of this? In other words, did he deliberately plan to make these comments so that others would feel sorry for him? I don't think so. I think he was encouraged by the support and, without realizing it, was doing it more and more. And, his complaints made Helen feel guilty that she was not home more and could not help out as much as she would like.

Our work with Helen and Peter—especially with his thoughts of being overwhelmed by child care responsibilities—first centered on clarifying the dynamic interchange from Hanna's behavior to Peter's reactions and how they affected his parenting and Helen's feelings. The journal was helpful to both Helen and Peter because it allowed them to see how each was thinking and feeling and gave them a forum to discuss this without assigning blame or making judgments (e.g., who was a good or a bad parent).

There are times when thinking you have too much responsibility is both accurate and useful. If you can become aware of these thoughts and appropriately communicate them to others, then you may be able to help resolve your concerns. In the case just described, Peter and Helen were able to work out alternate arrangements (including getting a babysitter at times) that helped Peter with the responsibilities of taking care of Hanna and also acknowledged that his concerns were legitimate. Peter then learned not to use this style of interacting with other people and, instead, to take a more positive spin on situations.

Substitute Thought (Optimistic): *Everyone is doing the best that he or she can under the circumstances.* In Peter's case, he was able to substitute a more optimistic view of his situation in place of his feeling overwhelmed by responsibility. He decided that a more useful thought for him was "If I need help, Helen is always there for me." Rather than thoughts of resentment (e.g., "I'm doing more than she is"), he reminded himself that he did not have to take this on alone and that he could reach out for help in a more positive way. These discussions were beneficial for him and also turned into a very loving interchange between Peter and Helen. It reaffirmed that they were in their situation together and that they were both willing to do whatever it took to help Hanna but also to help and support each other. They left that session holding hands.

Peter later discovered that he would get as much attention from others by pointing out areas of Hanna's progress. So, rather than saying, "You won't believe what Hanna did at the gas station today!" and reliving a bad situation, he was learning to point out the more positive events and how she was making progress (e.g., "Hanna calmed down quickly when we drove by a stable and I told her we could not stop today to pet the horses; I think she is becoming more tolerant").

Chapter 7 describes how everybody—including children with special needs—requires a certain level of attention. And that is not bad. What is a struggle for most people is how to solicit this attention from others in positive and constructive ways. Just thinking and communicating "Why is this always my job?" does not help you in the long run unless it leads to getting additional support.

GAINING PERSPECTIVE

As a young student of psychology, I once watched a researcher look at the behavior of rats in a small cage. It was pretty simple. Two rats lived in the cage together, and there was a little slot out of which food came when they pressed a lever. They looked content in their little world and seemed to get along despite the cramped quarters. Then, the experimenter changed their situation. He started to restrict the amount of food they could get when they pressed the lever. Quickly, the rats seemed to pick up on the change and spent a great deal of time huddled around the lever, pressing it constantly. However, something else happened. Their peaceful existence came to an end, and they began to fight with each other. Whereas before they were happy to take turns getting food, now they bit at each other to compete for the food. The researcher explained how the restricted resources (in this case, food) led to an increase in aggression and that there were parallels in the larger world around us.

What interested me in this experiment was how narrow the rats' world view was. Here they were fighting with each other when the real reason they had less food was the experimenter! Of course, you would not really expect rats to be able to figure out that the large man who came by the cage each day was responsible for their current dilemma; however, this story plays back in my mind often, especially when I suspect someone is taking a narrow view of the world. Sometimes we as human beings are just like those two rats—unable to look beyond our current problems and see what might be behind our difficulties. Have you ever seen an airline passenger get angry at a ticket agent because his flight is late or canceled? Did the ticket agent make the flight late? Could the agent do anything about it? Of course not! Yet, like the rats, the passenger got upset and lashed out at the closest target.

One of the ways of becoming more optimistic is to take a step back from your current difficulties and see if there are better ways of dealing with them. Rather than responding emotionally, it is useful to take a problem-solving approach to an obstacle. This is really what we are trying to accomplish with the thought-changing exercises in this chapter. This can help you calm down and react to problems more systematically and thoughtfully. A funny incident with some friends may serve to illustrate this concept.

My wife and I went out one night with some good friends to a local restaurant for dinner. Several of us ordered tacos, one of the specialties, and asked for a side order of guacamole (which was an extra charge). The woman who was serving us that night was very helpful and pleasant, and we were all having a good time; however, shortly after we ordered, the server returned to our table to tell us—very apologetically—that they were out of guacamole. After a few good-natured jokes ("I'm sorry, but I can't possibly eat tacos without guacamole!"), we went back to our conversation. Later, when one of the other servers delivered our meals, our friend joked, "What, no guacamole?" The server then told us that they were making a fresh batch in the kitchen. This made everyone happy (it doesn't take much). Our original server returned minutes later to check on us and we asked about the guacamole. "Oh, I think they are preparing some in the kitchen, but they told me it will not be ready for at least 30 minutes." Well, this started a conversation about how long it takes to make guacamole, should we wait, isn't there anything she could do to speed it up, and so forth. The conversation was getting a bit uncomfortable, but our server was being as accommodating as she could. Finally, I said, "Could we get some slices of avocado instead? That would be great for me." Everyone turned to me and smiled at my brilliant solution to this monumental problem.

If I could have had each person at the table as well as our server fill out the journal, it would have been interesting to see how they would have responded. "How could you have a taco special without making enough guacamole?" "Something *always* goes wrong when we eat here!" "Is our server just too lazy to go in the kitchen and move them along?" "I can never get a meal just the way I like it." "She should have told us they were out of guacamole when we ordered the tacos." "Why are these people giving me such a hard time about guacamole?" Regardless of their thoughts, what none of them were doing was problem solving. You have a problem situation—no guacamole. Rather than getting upset or trying to educate the restaurant or the server about how to run their business, what could be done realistically to make things better? Avocado slices were the savior—and she did not charge us for them!

This frivolous example (which I exaggerated a bit) shows the tendency of human beings to react to difficulties with our emotional brain rather than our rationale one. In the case of your child's problem behavior, there also is that natural response of reacting rather than problem solving. Clearly, a child screaming uncontrollably at night is a much different situation than not getting a side dish you want with your meal, but the principle is the same. They both require the ability to step back, look at what's going on, and try to find a useful solution. Throughout this chapter, I have tried to help you by providing you with a structured way of looking at your thoughts, checking on how real and useful they are, and then, when necessary, finding alternative ways of looking at the same situation.

In our research, we are finding that helping people look at the problems they experience with their children in a more optimistic way also helps them persist and follow through with the strategies that will help their children behave better. But there is more than that. We have some evidence that these changes in the way you feel may lead to less anxiety and less stress. Decreasing stress is extremely important; too much stress over too long a time can result in serious mental as well as physical consequences. However, as I have pointed out before, simply being less stressed or anxious does not make you happy. What does? Read on.

CHAPTER 5

How to Become a Happier Parent

In the unlikely event of a sudden loss of cabin pressure, oxygen masks will drop from the compartment above. Place the mask over your nose and mouth and breathe normally. Please put on your own mask before attempting to assist others.

—In-flight safety instructions, original author unknown

The instructions flight attendants provide to air travelers sum up the theme of this book—you need to take care of yourself before you can assist your child or anyone else. You really cannot be an effective parent if you are too tired or stressed or lack confidence in yourself. These ideas seems so obvious, yet most parents "run on empty" much of the time, and most professionals seem to miss this important part of helping families.

So what's stopping you? Why are you, like so many other parents, probably reluctant to take the time and effort to work on such a vital part of succeeding as a parent? One of the more surprising things my colleagues and I learned in working with families over the years is that many parents feel guilty when it comes to taking care of their own needs. A common reaction is "This is supposed to be about my child!" You spend so much time and effort to make a better life for your child and family that any thought of the things you would like to do (e.g., a quiet night out with your spouse or friends) triggers the thought that you are being selfish. I have worked with parents who devote countless hours to child care as well as enormous amounts of time attending endless meetings about their child, often with a great deal of frustration. They are people who have put their own lives and ambitions on hold to make a better life for their family; yet, the thought of taking even a day off from this challenge sets off waves of guilt. They are so used to focusing on their child—and getting others to focus on their child—that any break seems like a betrayal. If this sounds like you, I encourage you to read on.

The other reason that parents often think of themselves last is time. There never seems to be enough time to get everything accomplished that needs to be done in a day, so you prioritize—or "triage"—to get to the emergencies first. You put out fires, running from one urgent task to another; unfortunately, this approach often does not leave any time for you.

This is one of the more important lessons I have learned from the many families who participate in our research. People who are racked with guilt or who feel insecure about their abilities as parents cannot help their children in the most efficient way. Parents who sacrifice too much become less effective. They must feel better themselves to be successful. My wife pointed this out about me and my work years ago. When I was in graduate school working on my Ph.D., I often would work late nights to try to catch up on my classwork and research. I thought if I could put in a few more hours, I would be that much ahead of the game; yet, what was really happening was that I was becoming *less* efficient. I found that my mind would wander and that I had trouble focusing on what was necessary to keep up. It then became necessary to work the extra hours just to do as much as I had done before. It was my wife who had to point this out to me and insisted that regardless of how far behind I felt, I needed to take a little bit of time off—away from work—each week. At first, this was extremely difficult to do. I was so used to working that I felt guilty that I was not doing more. Yet, over time (it took months), I gradually learned that time away from work both physically and mentally did help me become more effective when it was time to accomplish something.

What I hope to achieve in this chapter is to help you lead a better, more fulfilling life. Satisfying your own needs will make you a better parent. I take you step by step through the process that has helped so many parents lead more balanced lives—providing their child with needed attention while also taking care of their own needs. But first, it may be helpful to glimpse into your future to see what may happen if you do not take time to care for yourself.

THE EFFECTS OF STRESS

Warning! What I am about to tell you may, at least temporarily, cause you even more stress. I'm sorry to do this, but it is important to point out that very high levels of stress can affect both your mental and physical well-being. I already discussed (in the description of research on the brain functioning of people with OCD in Chapter 4) how changing the way you think can affect how your brain works. The good news is that learning how to think more optimistically actually can improve how your brain functions on a day-to-day basis. The bad news is that being exposed to too much stress for too long can negatively affect your brain and, in turn, other organs in your body.

Stress is actually a fairly subjective experience. An event or a situation that is stressful for one person may actually be experienced as neutral or positive for another. For example, at first glance, it likely is not surprising to learn that the death of a spouse or child tops the list of stressful events for most people. Also included on this list are life changes such as divorce and marital separation. Yet, in some circumstances, these events may not be as stressful as one might expect. The death of a loved one after a long and painful illness may provide relief that comes with the knowledge that the loved one is no longer suffering. A divorce or marital separation also may have positive aspects for some couples. It may be surprising, however, to learn that some seemingly positive events are also ranked high on lists of stressful life events. Marriage, marital reconciliation, and pregnancy are all considered stressful. Obviously, these events are typically anticipated with a great deal of joy; however, they also often come with so many details and changes in a person's life that they may take a toll on one's physical and emotional health.

One of the things being learned through research is that living with a child who exhibits high levels of problem behavior can cause extreme levels of stress for parents. In fact, the stress that a child with problem behavior produces in a family can exceed the stress caused by having a child with another type of disability. Research on families who have a child with autism, for example, finds that the parents have higher levels of stress than parents who have a child with a disorder such as Down syndrome. If the child with autism poses frequent behavior challenges, the biological stress profiles of these families (measured by a hormone called *cortisol*) begin to resemble those of other groups experiencing chronic stress, including parents of children with cancer, combat soldiers, Holocaust survivors, and individuals suffering from posttraumatic stress disorder (PTSD).[1] Dealing with challenging children can lead to long-term stress across all types of families, from those with children who have mild developmental problems to those with children who have multiple and severe disabilities.

What is the effect of experiencing high levels of stress over extended periods of time? Researchers who study the effects of stress on the brain have found that chronic stress (i.e., being under almost constant stress for weeks or months) damages a part of the brain called the *hypothalamus* in a way that can make it less efficient in turning off the stress response.[2] In other words, too much stress for too long can cause your body to have a difficult time turning off its response to stress even after the stress has ended. This process can increase the likelihood of serious health consequences (e.g., cardiovascular disease) as well as mental health consequences (e.g., anxiety, depression). Clearly, then, it is important to reduce stress levels to benefit both the way one feels on a day-to-day basis and one's overall health.

As I mentioned previously, stress is subjective. Whether an individual experiences stress under certain circumstances depends on how he or she perceives those circumstances. Things such as marriage or divorce can be viewed and experienced as stressful or not very stressful events, depending on the circumstances. What is the key to experiencing less stress? Control. If one feels as if he or she has control over a situation, he or she is less likely to respond to the event as stressful. For example, if a woman is getting married and feels as if most of the details are controllable and that the changes that she may experience in her lifestyle are anticipated and manageable, then she can experience the event positively. If, however, she feels as if she has less control than she desires, then she will become upset when things do not go the way she expects (e.g., in the extreme case, "bridezillas").

The same is true for interactions involving your child. If you feel out of control—which is one of the most common experiences of raising a challenging child—then you will experience high levels of stress. At the same time, if you feel that you have some control over a situation with your child, you are less likely to feel stress. So, for example, picture a child screaming while his mother waits in line at the dry cleaners. If what is going through her mind is, "This is so embarrassing. What am I going to do and how do I get out of here?" then this mother will experience a high level of stress. Picture the same situation with a different mother who has and implements a plan: "I told the manager about his problem, and he is looking at me with understanding. I will remind my son that we have to wait 3 minutes and then, if he is better, we get to do something he likes." She also reminds herself that her son is actually waiting better than he has in the past and that soon it will be much less of a problem. In this second scenario—despite going through the same situation—the mother will experience much less stress. Although on the surface, these two mothers appear to be in the same situation, the way that they perceive the child's tantrum makes all the difference on their level of stress. All of the techniques covered in the previous chapter not only contribute to helping you interact better with your child but also are designed to help you feel more in control and, therefore, less stressed.

Pain is inevitable. Suffering is optional.

—Buddhist proverb

I was at mile 21 and felt like I was going to die. I am a long-distance runner (a stress reducer) and have run three marathons. The cliché about marathons is that they are actually two races. The first race goes from the start to about mile 20, and the second race is the last 6.2 miles. Somewhere around mile 20, most people "hit the wall"—the point at which one's brain screams "That's enough running!" At mile 21 in this race, my legs felt like tree trunks attached to my body, and I was just dragging them along step by step. My back hurt and my mind was ready to quit. Then, something even worse happened. Out of the corner of my eye I could see that there was another marathoner slowly shuffling along with me but going just fast enough to start to pass me. Soon, I could see that not only was he going to pass by me, but he was about 90 years old. Yikes! Wasn't it bad enough that I was having trouble picturing myself running another 5 or so miles without having to be beaten by someone old enough to be my grandfather? Whatever motivation I had left was slowly draining out of my body.

As he passed me, I could vaguely make out some writing on the back of his shirt. These messages can sometimes be entertaining (e.g., "At least I'm in front of you," "I run to eat," "I'm the slow twin") when one has spent hours on the road, so I tried to focus on what he had written there. One's brain works a little more slowly when one is at the edge of exhaustion, so it took some time for the words to sink in. "Pain is inevitable. Suffering is optional." "What does that mean?" I thought. After a while, it started to make some sense. If one runs a marathon, it will be painful. Something (or everything) will hurt. But how one chooses to deal with the pain is what really matters. One can focus on it and worry (e.g., "Is my foot broken?" "Will my back ever get better?"), or one can accept the pain and focus on the positive (e.g., "There are several hundred people still behind me!" "My wife is at the finish line"). This thought helped me over the finish line into my wife's waiting arms.

Despite what you might be thinking, this type of experience is one of the wonderful parts of running marathons. You learn a great deal about yourself throughout the months of training. But even on the day of a marathon, there are incredible experiences. Marathons typically begin early in the morning, usually to avoid the heat of the day. Picture if you can, being among thousands of very different but like-minded people at 6:00 a.m. in the middle of a closed-off road, most awaiting the race of their lives. As you look around, you see groups of young people in their teens and 20s, middle-age folks like me, and older adults— all of whom are either smiling and joking or are expressing some anxiety. There are men and women; people of all sizes and shapes; and people of all political persuasions, races, and creeds. If you step back a bit and take in this crowd, you know that if you asked any one of these people for assistance, he or she would go out of his or her way to help you. In this mass of humanity is a united feeling of hope. Every one of these runners will experience pain in the next few hours; yet, they are prepared physically and, more importantly, mentally for this. Experienced runners no longer fear it. They know that how much you suffer is up to you.

Pain is inevitable if you are the parent of any child. Trying to steer through life a child who poses significant challenges will at times seem unbearable, and I am not suggesting that anything in this book will somehow make that journey always pleasant. However, how much you suffer through these challenges is up to you. Stress is up to you. How you experience bad circumstances can be changed in ways that make them more bearable.

Just as the early morning throngs of marathoners look forward to their running adventure, I hope to convince you that as a parent of a challenging child you are in a similar group. There is a tough road ahead, and there will inevitably be pain. But if you look around, there are thousands of people like you who will be sharing your journey and who are willing to help. You share common goals and, hopefully, will share common attitudes about how to handle the tough times.

We have already gone through an important step in this process, which involved examining your thoughts in both difficult and successful situations and trying to change thoughts that get in your way of being a better parent. Again, this change in your point of view can help you realize that you have more control over events than you might think and that there is hope for the future—all thoughts that will reduce your level of stress when it is needed. And, reducing your stress is one step toward being a happier person.

ON HAPPINESS

What is pleasant is the activity of the present, the hope of the future, and the memory of the past.

—Aristotle (350 B.C.E.)

Recently, I saw a cartoon of a man in an electronics store looking over the latest high-tech gadget. Next to him was a salesperson, and it looked as if they were discussing the features of this new electronic "toy." The caption on the cartoon read, "And, will it make me happy?" Many individuals long to be happier. Books on the nature of happiness and how to become happier are routinely bestsellers. The pharmaceutical industry makes billions of dollars in profits each year, with much of it selling the promise of happiness. But what does it mean to be happy?

The ancient philosopher Aristotle wrote a great deal about happiness. In some of his writings, he made an important distinction.[3] He saw that there are two types of experiences that are positive for people. The first—which he called hedonism—is the pursuit of pleasure and the focus on positive feelings. Most people have their hedonistic pleasures. It could be an expensive bottle of wine, watching reruns of *Sex in the City,* a piece (or two) of chocolate cake, a trashy novel, a manicure and pedicure, or an exotic vacation. Occasional hedonism is fine; however, these indulgences tend to be temporary pleasures without much lasting benefit. Aristotle also described a second type of positive experience—what he called eudaimonia—sometimes translated as *human flourishment* or the fulfillment that comes from engaging in meaningful activity and the actualization of one's potential. One of the important differences between hedonism and eudaimonia is that engaging in hedonistic activities begins to lose its luster over time. I might long for chocolate cake, for example, but too much chocolate cake makes it much less interesting. A fun weekend with my wife, however, just doing regular things together, never gets old. An example might serve as a good illustration.

I teach a course about the science of happiness and usually lead off the first class with a description of a yacht. Our campus is on the water and is one of the more beautiful urban universities you will find. Just a block away from our campus is a port where once in a while very large boats dock for repairs. On several occasions, a private yacht has been docked there and is a sight to behold. The yacht is a little more than 300 feet long and has five decks. On board, there is a helicopter, a power boat, and a sailboat. Inside is a swimming pool, a movie theater, and even a room with a limestone fireplace. It is larger than any home I have ever been in!

I pose this question to my class: "If you owned this yacht, would you be happy?" I add that it would come with a staff that would take care of you and the yacht and take you to exotic lands whenever the spirit moved you, and you would not have to worry about how to pay for any of it. The class is usually split. Typically, most of the younger students (19- to 21-year-olds) smile broadly and report that absolutely they would be happy! Older students are less sure. Then I ask, is the owner happy? As a billionaire, the owner probably has every *thing* he ever wanted. Again, the age split usually pops up, with the younger students convinced that he must be very happy and the older students having mixed feelings. Then I point out that the owner has another *larger* (416-foot) yacht. Why would someone need an even larger yacht? Is that the sign of someone who is happy?

I use this example to describe the difference between hedonism and eudaimonia. Having a large yacht with many toys is usually an effort to pack in as much pleasure as one can. The idea behind this view of happiness is that if a 100-foot yacht is fun, a 300-foot yacht with more toys should be that much more fun. As I mentioned, the yacht owner actually had purchased an even larger yacht. That is hedonism. However, if he volunteered the yacht to help out sick children (along the lines of the Make-A-Wish Foundation) or used it as a floating hospital during a disaster, he might feel good about himself because he was doing something meaningful. That is eudaimonia.*

Why is it that hedonism is so short-lived? One concept scientists have used is called the hedonic treadmill—an analogy that explains why there may be limits as to how money and material things can influence one's happiness. The hedonic treadmill concept suggests that people tend to remain relatively stable in their level of happiness regardless of major changes in their wealth. In the case of the yacht, it may be that having one 300-foot yacht did not make the owner that much happier, so he purchased an even bigger one in an effort to

---

*There are actually a number of different translations of the term *eudaimonia,* but for the purposes of this book I take it to mean *the fulfillment that comes from engaging in meaningful activity and the actualization of one's potential.*

achieve some desired degree of satisfaction. (I do not know the owner, and he may be very happy. This story about the yachts is just used as an example.) Like being on a treadmill and getting nowhere, what scientists usually find is that having more money does not continue to increase a person's happiness. If a person has $1 million, having $2 million will not make him or her twice as happy and, in fact, may have no impact on his or her happiness at all. In today's society, people tend to think that if something makes us happy or feel good, then more of that thing should be even better. Fortunately, or unfortunately, that is not the case. By watching the rich and famous on television and in the movies, one would think that they are the happiest people on the planet. If one thinks about it, however, they also seem to get divorced more frequently and, in general, their private lives seem to be filled with a great detail of turmoil. There are exceptions, of course; however, these celebrities seem to be able to get their satisfaction from something other than faster cars, more parties, and bigger homes.

Why do *things* seem to have only a temporary effect on our happiness? One clue has to do with the way the brain works. Inside the brain is a system of cells called the pleasure pathway. These cells release a brain chemical (a neurotransmitter called dopamine) when we engage in something pleasurable. If you munch on your favorite treat, for a brief time this chemical is released in your brain and you feel good. If you drink alcohol or use any of the other mood-altering drugs (e.g., cocaine, nicotine, marijuana), then the same thing happens. Pleasurable sexual relations affect the brain in the same way. Your brain's pleasure pathway is flooded with the chemical dopamine for a time and you feel the pleasant effects. This is obviously a very positive experience and will, for a time, make people happier.

But then the brain adapts. If it is artificially filled with dopamine because of some outside influence (e.g., cocaine), then, over time, your brain will get used to having this chemical and will adjust. Your brain cells actually can change how they work to compensate for this extra chemical being added from the outside. This is why people who regularly take mood-altering drugs find that, over time, they need more of the drug to have the same effect. Whereas at one time two glasses of wine may have made a person feel good, it may start to take three glasses to have the same effect. The brain actually begins to change physically in reaction to these changes in the chemical balance. This also explains why people have withdrawal symptoms when they try to stop taking a drug. For example, if you have ever tried to stop smoking (which involves ingesting nicotine, one of the most addictive of drugs) or stop drinking coffee (with its caffeine), you likely have found that abstaining from these drugs actually makes you feel physically unwell. That is because your brain has adapted to them and craves them once they are no longer present. This process is a great deal more complicated than I've made it sound here, but those are the basics of what occurs.

So, why would someone need a 400-foot yacht when he already has a 300-foot yacht? The reason is the same as why a person might need two cups of coffee to wake him or her in the morning when years ago one cup was enough. These hedonic pleasures (e.g., having a yacht or a bigger house) by themselves cause increases in the activity of the brain's pleasure pathway, but over time one adapts to them as well. The positive feelings once experienced with these things start to lessen with more access (e.g., having chocolate cake every night) and, over time, lose their effects. Hedonism requires constant change to maintain the pleasurable experience.

Conversely, one's brain does not seem to adapt to activities that lead to eudaimonia—again, fulfillment from meaningful activities and achieving one's potential—as quickly or in the same way as to hedonistic activities. It may be that different chemical processes take place when one engages in these more meaningful experiences. For example, researchers are examining the brain chemical oxytocin, which has been dubbed "the hormone of love and bonding" or "the cuddle hormone." Oxytocin is released in the brain during labor prior to the birth of a child, during breastfeeding, and during sexual orgasms. There is some thought that this neurochemical is important in parenting and maintaining close relationships. In one research study, participants were given extra oxytocin and were found to be more generous to others compared with those participants not receiving oxytocin.[4] This may explain why people who watch telethons that portray sympathetic stories are more likely to donate money. Seeing these stories can increase oxytocin levels, making viewers feel more generous.

The distinction that Aristotle drew thousands of years ago between hedonism and eudaimonia may have its roots in the brain chemicals that cause pleasure. Scientists are now closely examining these distinctions in an effort to better understand happiness and to help people lead more fulfilling lives. Researchers tend to use the term *subjective well-being* rather than the more awkward *eudaimonia* as a term for how people think and feel about their lives. In this chapter, I focus on your subjective well-being rather than your pursuit of hedonistic pleasure when I talk about becoming a happier parent. Achieving subjective well-being is possible and is a more lasting and satisfying goal for most people.

So, how satisfied with your life are you right now? To give you some basis of comparison as to how satisfied you are compared with people in other groups, the Satisfaction with Life Scale,[5] a very short list of questions that is used frequently by scientists to gauge one aspect of subjective well-being, is included in Appendix A. Take a minute to complete this short quiz, and then we will look at your responses compared with those of others.

Does the score you received match your impression of how satisfied you are with your life? The Satisfaction with Life Scale tends to be pretty accurate when it comes to comparing how people feel about themselves. It may be interesting to see how your scores compare to others. For example, the list below illustrates how certain groups tend to see their lives through this scale. American college students, for example, tend to be slightly satisfied with their lives, whereas Chinese students are slightly dissatisfied. This may reflect the different pressures placed on these two groups, with Chinese students often under a great deal of pressure from their families to achieve. Note that women who are abused report as a group being neutral about their lives, whereas male prison inmates (not surprisingly) tend to report being dissatisfied. The following are the norms for certain groups:[6]

- American college students (23.0–25.2)
- Chinese students (16.1)
- Male prison inmates (12.3)
- Women who are abused (20.7)
- Clinical clients (14.4)

Keep a record of your score to see whether it changes in the coming weeks as you work through the suggestions I provide for you and your child.

THE PURSUIT OF HAPPINESS

We hold these truths to be self-evident, that all men are created equal, that they are endowed by their Creator with certain unalienable Rights, that among these are Life, Liberty and the pursuit of Happiness.

—The Declaration of Independence

I now turn to actually pursuing subjective well-being—the type of meaningful and long-lasting life satisfaction that can change your life. The first few suggestions on my list of 10 tips to Optimistic Parenting involve the thought assessment and change processes I described in the previous chapters. Looking at the world in general and your parenting specifically in a more confident and optimistic way can lead to improved subjective well-being. The remaining recommendations (i.e., leverage—don't multitask, parent in the moment, sometimes bad is okay, list three good things that happen each day, and express gratitude) involve specific things you can do to help yourself become less stressed and more satisfied with your life. This chapter details these remaining strategies. It first discusses one of the more important obstacles to being a happier person and parent—time. How can you "make more time" for the things that will make you more satisfied with your life?

Leverage—Don't Multitask

As one mother told me, "I don't have the time to work on me. Once my child is better behaved, then I'll work on myself. I'm not very good at multitasking."

Multitasking has taken on a negative meaning over the last few years, and for good reason. For example, a recent close call brought home how many people are trying to do two things at once. As I was driving very slowly through a parking lot, a big SUV was coming toward me from the other direction. The driver was smack in the middle of the lane and driving right at my car! I could see the driver looking down at his cell phone, likely sending someone a message or looking at his e-mail, but clearly not watching where he was going. I quickly stopped and used my car's horn in time for him to look up and stop. He smiled weakly as he drove past my car, but it took awhile for me to calm down. He was multitasking. He was driving (such as it was) and communicating with someone at the same time; he was not driving well, and my guess is he was not communicating well either. Our brains are not very good at doing two separate things at once.

Optimistic Parenting is not about multitasking. In fact, you will see that trying to do more than one thing at the same time is the cause of unhappiness among many people. Instead, the way you will help yourself and your child at the same time is by learning how to *leverage* what you do during each day. Let me give you a personal example: I remember as a child bitterly complaining to my mother about washing up for dinner. "Why do I have to wash my face and hands to eat? I'm not dirty!" My mother was rarely prone to arguing. She wasn't about to get into a lengthy discussion about hygiene or about what it meant to be a civilized human being! No—she negotiated. "Okay," she said. You don't have to wash your hands. Just wash your face before you come to the dinner table." Now, I thought I was a pretty smart child, but it took a few days for me to realize what she had done. I was taught that to wash your face you lathered up the soap in your hands and applied it to your face. Then you took clean water in your hands and rinsed your face. In other words, you washed your hands while you were washing your face! This is leveraging.

Leveraging is the strategy I use in the next few sections and in later chapters about helping your child be better behaved. If you plan it, you can do two things at once and do them both well. For example, you can practice good behavior with your child while spending "quality time" with him or her and get enjoyment out of the interaction. We don't have time to do one thing at a time, but if we do it right, we don't have to! For example, one of the mothers in our program was having a difficult time with her son around dinnertime. While she was rushing around preparing the meal, putting dishes in the dishwasher, and setting the table, her son would constantly get into trouble. During one session, she relayed the following story: "The other night, he was just a terror. He pulled some books off of the shelf while I was in the kitchen. Then he came to where I was and started to demand pots and pans so he could play with them. I tried to explain I was using them to make his favorite dinner, which was macaroni and cheese, but that didn't stop him. And then it got quiet. I learned a long time ago that that quiet doesn't mean anything good. I suddenly heard flushing sounds coming from the bathroom. He was flushing bars of soap and face towels down the toilet, which was starting to back up!"

It is obvious that this mother cannot multitask in this situation—no matter how competent she is as a parent. She cannot prepare dinner and watch her son adequately at the same time. So, we suggested that she try to combine these two goals: prepare for dinner and engage her child in some activity to keep him out of trouble. She came up with the idea of teaching her son how to fold the silverware in the paper dinner napkins like they do at some restaurants. Then, he was to place them next to the plates on the table in preparation for dinner. It took him quite a while to get the correct number of knives and forks, and his folding skills were rather crude; but, he and his mother interacted throughout this task—which is what he really wanted—and dinner was made and put on the table. It took a little longer to have him help set the table, but all in all it took less extra time than it took to deal with his constant disruptions.

Finding ways to leverage activities can take a little creativity and patience, but it is one way to really do two things at once. Ask yourself if there is a way to get what you want (e.g., dinner prepared) and what your child wants (e.g., your attention) by doing the same activity. Can you create a "win–win" situation?

Sometimes, you will not be able to combine everything you want to do into one activity. What should you do then? One way to deal with these situations is to "make more time." We can do this by appreciating the time we have—a process known as mindfulness.

Parent in the Moment

We want to make good time, but for us now this is measured with emphasis on "good" rather than "time" and when you make that shift in emphasis the whole approach changes.

—Robert M. Pirsig (1974)

There is nothing quite so luxurious as time. As any parent knows, there never seems to be enough. This is especially true for parents who are raising challenging children. Often, these children require an endless number of appointments with a variety of professionals and school personnel. Then there are the child care responsibilities themselves, which for some children almost never end. This can be especially difficult for families who have a child who also experiences sleep problems. The challenges during the day cannot be put aside for a few hours at night because that is the time when the problems escalate. I have heard numerous parents lament that they miss the period in their life when they had time to do things for themselves.

In response to this universal problem, almost every self-help book for parents recommends "making time for yourself" as an essential part of successful parenting. "Take 30 minutes each day just for you," is a common parenting tip.

Even taken just once per week, this time can be very helpful for recharging your emotional batteries. Going to the gym or for a walk, reading a book, or just wandering through a store ("retail therapy") are just a few of the suggestions made for parents to relax and give themselves a renewed sense of energy. However, in our experience with parents who have truly difficult children, this can seem to be wishful thinking. For some, the problem is that they do not have the personal or financial resources to be able to take a break from their responsibilities. There may not be another person who can take over the care of their child, and hiring someone may either be unaffordable or require someone with a great deal of training and maturity. The child may be such a handful that leaving him or her with anyone else is just not an easy option.

In the previous section, I described how to leverage activities to gain more time; however, another strategy that has proven to be very effective for parents who struggle with this problem is to learn how to appreciate the time they already have. Let me explain. Some of you reading this book are having wandering thoughts. Instead of fully focusing on what you are reading, you have these mental intrusions. "I should probably change the cat litter." "Did I remember to make my daughter's lunch for tomorrow?" "I'd better not forget to make that dentist appointment." In fact, I may have just triggered one of these thoughts, causing you to put the book down to go and change the cat litter! These thoughts can make you anxious, fearing that you will forget something or not get everything completed. This is an all-too-common problem that seems to get worse every day. I have seen countless examples of parents who are trapped by the negative or bothersome details of life and rarely ever appreciate what is happening in the present. A stream of anxiety runs at a constant pace through many parents because of the countless things that must get done each day. Although this is certainly understandable, you should recognize that these anxious thoughts can get in the way of life's little surprises. While you were planning tonight's schedule, your son may have just spent a good 10 minutes playing quietly—an amazing accomplishment for him. While you were thinking about what your daughter did not eat tonight, you may have missed the fact that she did not, for once, run away from the table.

What I call "parenting in the moment" is a skill that you can learn that lets you take care of life's details but also appreciate the wonderful little things in life. Again, you are learning to leverage in the best possible way. Instead of doing just one thing at a time such as focusing just on your child or just on you, you can focus on your child in a way that also makes you a happier person. I will help you determine how well you live in the moment and how to do this better while being a better parent to your child. But first, let's look at an example to illustrate how not being mindful can interfere with good parenting.

Angie, a mother of a 5-year-old boy with autism, arrived for a session with her therapist looking rather tired. It had been a rough week, she related, and she was looking forward to her session in part just for the break. As the therapist went over her week, they discussed bath time, usually a pretty difficult task for her son. Angie reminded the therapist about how her son typically would fight getting into the tub and then later would fight getting out. "It always puzzles me. Why does he love swimming in the pool yet seem to hate the bath?"

The therapist asked her to go over the particulars of the last bath to try to get at how disruptive he was and how she handled it. "Let's see," Angie thought aloud. "Well, last night he was actually pretty good." She said this with a look of surprise, as if this was the first time she had a chance to think about it. "He got into the bath without any crying or screaming, and, in fact," she paused to think it over, "he got out of the bath without a tantrum too." The therapist congratulated her because bath time had been a long-standing problem and Angie was working hard on his progress. "So, did you praise him for getting into the bath so well?" Looking sheepish, Angie confessed that she did not. "That's okay; did you praise him for getting out without any crying?" Again, Angie seemed to feel guilty and admitted that she didn't do that either.

The therapist didn't press the issue but instead asked what Angie was thinking during this time. "I was angry that no one had given him a bath—and here it was 8:00 at night—and after a long day of work, I had to do it myself. Why am I the only person who is responsible? I guess I was also thinking that he is usually so disruptive in the bath and will this ever improve?" The therapist pointed out that she was so preoccupied by these other thoughts that she actually missed a great bath! Because she did not focus on what was going right, she also missed an opportunity to praise her son and give him extra attention for his good behavior. What could have been a very pleasant and satisfying interaction was just a routine bath filled with thoughts of resentment and self-concern.

Why would Angie focus on the negative in this situation rather than appreciate the successful bath? One reason we have discussed already may have been her pessimistic style of thinking. Remember that she—like other parents with a pessimistic view of the world—tends to blame herself and others when things go wrong but does not take credit for when things go right. She also was spending a fair amount of time blaming others for not helping her. But, in addition to this way of thinking, Angie was not "there." In her head, she was not really giving her son a bath; she was thinking about other things.

One of the consequences of living in the modern world is to be faced constantly with complex and multiple challenges. Unfortunately, this complexity comes at a cost. People often are reacting to one situation (e.g., putting on a child's shoes) while thinking about something else (e.g., "I wonder if I have time to make dinner tonight?"). Many people never truly experience and, therefore, enjoy what they are doing in the present because their minds are constantly planning ahead.

This is a particular problem when dealing with a challenging child. In crisis situations (e.g., screaming and hitting during bath time), the parent is able to focus on the task at hand (e.g., how do I get him to calm down and not get hurt in the tub until he is clean?). The reason for this is obvious: The parent needs to focus to successfully navigate the crisis. However, what does the parent do when the child is well behaved? Under these circumstances, the parent has the luxury of planning for or doing those things he or she could not do when he or she was dealing with the emergency.

One day, I was watching a mother and her daughter in the park. The mother was on her cell phone, talking to a friend while her daughter was walking beside her. Her daughter looked down and saw a little bug on the sidewalk and tried to get her mother's attention. "Wait a minute, Claire. Mommy will be done in a minute." "It's green, Mommy! Look! Look! Look!" Her mother kept nodding but continued her conversation. Claire then reached up and hit her mother in the leg. "Claire!" She told her friend she had to go and then bent down to scold her daughter for hitting her. In this short interaction, one easily can see the dilemma. Claire's mother was trying to spend some time with her daughter but simultaneously trying to spend some time talking with her friend. Claire wanted to be with her mother and show her the colorful bug on the sidewalk. This entomological discovery by Claire (a cool green bug!) went from potentially being a positive experience to a negative one during which Claire learned how to get her mother off of the telephone to refocus her attention on Claire—hit her mother in the leg!

One of the things every professional tries to teach parents of challenging children is to catch them being good. The key to encouraging good behavior is to pay attention to it and praise the child for being well behaved. This is likely to increase the chance of the child being good again. However, too often when a child is behaving, the parent is freed to do one of the dozens of other things that need to get done, and his or her mind wanders. Only when there is a problem that needs attention does the parent refocus on what is happening in the present. The key to "making more time" is to be mindful— to be aware of what is taking place around you and your child and give yourself a chance to live in the moment and appreciate the good things that are happening.

The concept of mindfulness has a long history and is based on traditional Eastern disciplines including Buddhism. Being mindful suggests that practicing being more aware of what we as human beings are experiencing without judging it can increase our satisfaction with day-to-day activities. Researchers are just now demonstrating the physical and mental health benefits that can be derived from being mindful. For example, practicing mindfulness appears to help reduce anxiety and depression and may even improve immune system functioning.[7] Important new discoveries about how we experience our lives— including the concept of *mindfulness*—are unlocking secrets to making day-to-day events enjoyable.

Are You Mindful?   How mindful are you? Do you feel as if you are aware of and appreciate what is going on around you, or are you so concerned about the many things in your life requiring your attention that you find yourself too preoccupied to be aware of the things you are doing in the present? Mindfulness is of particular importance for people who experience anxiety. Anxiety and worry are future-oriented experiences. Although it may not seem obvious, some individuals are anxious in certain situations because they are concerned with what *might* happen in the future. For example, if you approach your child to ask her to come to dinner and that action makes you feel anxious, it is not really the act of walking toward your child but the concern about what is about to happen (e.g., perhaps a tantrum) that causes your anxiety. Or, if you wake up in the middle of the night feeling tense, it is probably the result of thinking about things that may occur in the future (e.g., tomorrow's school meeting that you are dreading). Being mindful can help you refocus on the present and has been shown to help people who have clinically diagnosed anxiety problems.

One assessment frequently used to determine a person's level of mindfulness is the Mindful Attention Awareness Scale.[8] A reference copy is included in Appendix A to help you get an idea of just how mindful you are. The scale indicates that a score is obtained by adding up the points for each question and finding the average by dividing the total by 15.

So, how would you do on this scale? For a comparison, the typical person scores an average of 3.85 on this scale. Interestingly, Zen practitioners—who cultivate mindfulness in their lives—have been found to report an average score of 4.29. It is important to point out that your level of mindfulness can change depending on the situation. You may be more or less mindful depending on the circumstances. Continue reading to learn about some exercises you can use to help improve your ability to stay aware of your surroundings and be in the moment. If you decide to go ahead and take advantage of the mindfulness exercises I describe next, think of what your score would be as a *before* indication and see if your score would improve with practice.

Mindful Parenting Exercise   Parenting in the moment—being aware of even the minor interactions with your child during the day—can require some practice. Formal mindfulness training techniques are available for you to use to help you live a more mindful life overall.[9] These techniques are a form of meditation but differ in important ways from the type of meditation with which you might be familiar.

People tend to think of meditation as focusing on a word (e.g., "Ohm") or object, relaxing your body and mind, and trying to eliminate all other thoughts. Mindfulness meditation, in contrast, involves being aware of other thoughts, sounds, and feelings. Some teachers of mindfulness meditation use an eating exercise to help clients learn this technique. They have their clients pick one grape or raisin, for example, and first focus on what it looks like and feels like in the hand. Then, they have them eat the food slowly and deliberately, noticing not only the taste and smell but also how the food feels in their mouths as well as any other sensations. They focus on how their jaws are working to chew the food and, finally, on how it feels to swallow it. This type of slow and deliberate—mindful—eating has been used to help people eat less because it can stop them from *mindlessly* eating more than they want.

I have designed a mindful parenting exercise to do something similar with how you interact with your child. You will begin with a positive activity—hopefully one that is fun—and practice how to appreciate and not judge this activity. Later, I show you how to apply these skills to situations in which your child may be misbehaving. It may take a bit of practice for you to become skilled in using these techniques, especially if you tend to let your mind wander or to be anxious in situations with your child. Be patient, because great benefits will derive from incorporating these skills into your parenting. The following are the steps of the exercise I created.

1. Begin by selecting a task or activity with your child that is unlikely to lead to problem behavior. For young children, this could be as simple as reading or coloring together or watching your child's favorite video or DVD. For older children, this activity could involve playing a video game (or at least watching your child play), doing some household chore together (e.g., setting the table), walking through a store, or even going for a walk or drive.

2. As you participate in the task, constantly remind yourself that you should be nonjudgmental. At least for this activity, there is no right way or wrong way to do things (unless they could be dangerous or harmful), and there are no correct ways for you to react. The goal is to notice how you and your child behave and feel in this activity. If, for example, your child uses a truck to serve as a building block, do not attempt to prompt your child or demonstrate the "correct" use of the truck but instead notice what you are thinking (e.g., "No, that's not how you play with that toy!") and try to bring your thoughts back to the activity.

3. During your interactions with your child, practice being aware of all of your thoughts as well as your emotional and physical feelings. If your thoughts begin to wander from what is going on around you, gently pull your attention back to the task. For example, if you find yourself thinking about work or some other chore you need to accomplish, do not judge this (e.g., "I shouldn't be thinking about work now!") but, rather, refocus you attention. Your job is simply to be here now. Similarly, if you feel tense or anxious, just be aware of this and do not form an opinion (e.g., "I should be enjoying this but I'm not"). Again, just feel what is going on with you during these interactions.

4. In addition to being aware of your own reactions, use all of your senses to experience what is going on around you. What do you hear (e.g., the sound of a crayon on the paper, your child's breathing)? What do you smell (e.g.,

the smell of new clothes in the store, the smell of your child's hair)? What do you see (e.g., your child's fingernails, how he or she sits and his or her facial expressions)? What do you feel (e.g., the movement of your table as your child colors a picture)? Again, remember not to judge any of these observations. So, for example, if you see that your child's nails are dirty or need cutting, just be aware of this thought and then bring your thinking back to what is going on around you.

5. As you go through this exercise, be particularly attentive to your breathing. Make sure that you breathe deeply and slowly and that as you breathe, you remain in tune with your surroundings.

6. When you participate in the activity, try to be as deliberate and aware of your reactions as possible. For example, if you are coloring with your child, be aware of how the crayon feels in your hand. Slowly move it back and forth to make your drawing, not trying to do it quickly but instead trying to do it slowly and deliberately. If you are reading aloud, try to look at each new word in a new light. Be aware of how you pronounce each word.

7. At the end of the activity, be sure to praise your child appropriately (i.e., not too much, not too little) just for participating (e.g., "That was fun; I really enjoyed reading with you) and not for specific accomplishments (e.g., "I like your bird picture the best"). The goal is to enjoy the experience and not make it a specific learning goal.

Practice this exercise as many times as you can but at least once per week. As you become more proficient and comfortable with this technique, try using the skills, at least briefly, in other situations. For example, if you are sitting and eating together, try to be mindful of how you are eating and how your child is eating. Does your mind tend to wander? If so, do not judge it but try to bring your thoughts back to mealtime. Try to notice what your child notices (like in the case of Claire and her little green bug). You might be surprised at what you observe. One mother relayed the following story about how she tried this exercise and what it taught her about herself and her son.

Kathleen's 4-year-old son, Jake, had cognitive impairments and also tended to have a limited attention span. Jake often would try to wander away from his mother, and that made her very tense; therefore, when they went anywhere out in public, Kathleen would hold Jake's hand as they walked. He liked walking with his mother and holding her hand, but it was often difficult for Kathleen to do things like shopping with only one free hand. In attempting to parent in the moment, she decided to use a shopping trip at the supermarket with Jake as the activity, which was fun. She also decided to buy only one or two things so she could experience the trip with Jake and not feel as if she were dragging him around the store.

"As we walked into the store," she told us, "I could feel myself getting anxious. I tried not to judge it but just to feel it. I guess I am so conditioned to having a difficult time with Jake that I wasn't even aware of it before. I started to walk with him toward the produce section, and he walked straight over to the refrigerated section. I took a chance and let go of his hand and walked after him. I tried to be aware of what I was feeling and thinking. I was somewhat less anxious because I was not afraid he would break anything. Jake held on to the side of the case, so I decided to do it too. It was very cool, and I realized he was enjoying the feeling because it was so hot out that day. I bent down and kissed the top of his head—which felt warm and smelled so innocent.

I was about to take his hand and lead him over to the section where the bread was—which is what I would usually do—but instead told him, "Let's go find the bread." This time he took my hand and led me across to the bakery— his favorite place. I watched his face as he walked me over there and the woman behind the counter recognized us. "Hi Jake! Having a good day today?" I was about to prompt him to respond, which I usually do, but instead I waited. He smiled and said "Yeah." I couldn't believe it. That small little interaction made my eyes well up. I was crying because I must have missed these little things before, and I was also crying because I felt so much love for Jake it was overwhelming."

Kathleen had other, similar little discoveries about Jake and herself that day. She was learning to be aware of herself and Jake and to take a few chances. She told us that she still had to frequently remind herself to just "be here, now" and not spend so much time worrying about what might happen. For example, she told us of a good report from a preschool teacher that prompted a series of concerns about what school might be like as Jake got older. Again, she caught herself and realized that she was not enjoying the good report but was instead letting herself quickly turn it into a cause for concern. It is good to be aware of what could go wrong in the future because this helps us plan; however, it should not become such a pattern that you deny yourself the little pleasures when they occur.

If Kathleen's reactions sound familiar to you and you find it difficult to avoid engaging in what is called "yes, but…" (e.g., "Yes, he brushed his teeth today, but it is usually a battle," "Yes, she seemed to get along with that other little girl, but I'm afraid she will never have real friends"), you may want to enlist the aid of others to help you appreciate good events and avoid letting them lead to "but what if…" fears and concerns. A partner, friend, relative, or another close person can participate in these exercises with you, and you can process your thoughts to see if you are allowing yourself to celebrate the successes, no matter how small.

Again, mindfulness is one technique to leverage your activities. You are, in a way, making more time by experiencing the time you have. So, when you cannot take a week, a day, or even an hour off from your hectic schedule, practicing mindfulness can assist you with focusing on you and your surroundings and can be a good way to escape the worries you have, however briefly.

Learning how to be more mindful also can be a way to let the experience of parenting—even parenting a challenging child—lead you to a more satisfied life overall. If you can practice being aware of all of the small successes and triumphs in your life, the quality of your experiences will improve. We will discuss this concept in more detail in a later section of this chapter.

Sometimes Bad Is Okay

Do not seek to have events happen as you want them to, but instead want them to happen as they do happen, and your life will go well.

—Epictetus (Greek philosopher, AD 55–c.135)

One of the more interesting and exciting new findings in the field of clinical psychology is that we, as professionals in the field, may have looked at some of the problems people face in the wrong way. When people experience emotional stressors such as anxiety, we have tried to help them fight the negative feelings and thoughts. A radically different view is emerging that points to the value of accepting bad thoughts and feelings that are out of our control rather than fighting them. Not to be confused with giving up (resignation), *acceptance* involves helping people experience difficult situations and the accompanying thoughts and feelings and recognizing when they can and cannot control them. Much similarity exists between this view of people's difficulties and the "Serenity Prayer" mentioned in Chapter 3 ("God, grant me the serenity to accept the things I cannot change; courage to change the things I can; and wisdom to know the difference").

This therapeutic approach comes out of the tradition of the CBT I discussed in Chapter 4 as well as the general concept of mindfulness and is called Acceptance and Commitment Therapy (ACT, pronounced "act").[10] Acceptance and Commitment Therapy has as its goals acceptance of unwanted, uncontrollable thoughts and feelings and commitment and action toward living a life one values.[11] In a way, this approach to treatment is an application of mindfulness to problem situations. Although proponents and practitioners of ACT highlight a number of other important components for their approach to treating problems, we will be using this one aspect—acceptance of unpleasant thoughts and feelings.

For example, picture your child screaming in an aisle at the supermarket. Normally, this would make any parent angry or anxious. As previously examined, parents' thoughts under these circumstances may differ but the themes are similar. You might be thinking, for example, that others are judging you as a parent, which may be making you feel anxious. As a result, you may leave your cart in the store and go home because the situation is so upsetting. If you were asked, "Why did you leave the store?" you might report, "I left the store because I was anxious about my child's behavior." The approach taken by ACT would have you rephrase that answer from "I left the store *because* I was anxious about my child's behavior" to "I left the store *and* I was anxious about my child's behavior." What is the difference? These two statements differ as to what role anxiety plays for you. As I pointed out, it might be true that people are judging you and that this thought makes you anxious. You can let your anxiety control you (by forcing you to leave the store) or you can accept that you feel anxious and not let it direct how you respond.

One of the advantages of "looking fear in the face" is that you get exposed to things that cause you to feel uncomfortable. I have mentioned this idea in several previous discussions. The only way to really feel less anxious about something or some situation is to be exposed to it. I described people with OCD and how helping them face their fears (e.g., having them touch a table at a local fast food restaurant but not letting them wash their hands) can actually decrease their anxiety once they see that no real harm results. Standing in the store with your child screaming, understanding what people might be thinking, and *not* leaving the store because of your anxiety will eventually lead you to be less anxious. Leaving the store to avoid the anxiety actually can amplify your negative feelings the next time you are in a similar situation. This is one of the goals of therapists who use the ACT approach to anxiety and one we will use next.

It is not always desirable to make yourself withstand discomfort and anxiety just to face your fears; however, there will be times when you must face them. For example, you might have spent 45 minutes shopping in the supermarket and be in the midst of checking out when your child acts up. It will be very difficult for you to leave everything and walk out. Parents face a number of different problem situations with their children that are just unavoidable. For example, getting your child to school, washing up, getting dressed, and sitting through mealtime are not situations that you can readily and easily avoid if your child is prone to misbehaving during these situations.

In our work on people's thoughts during difficult (or successful) situations discussed previously, I introduced the concepts of *disputation, distraction,* and *substitution* as ways of dealing with these problem times (see Chapter 4). Another way to approach these problem situations is to practice mindfulness when they occur. In a sense, this is a way to distract yourself when things become difficult. However, instead of using a technique such as looking at your child's disruption more humorously (remember the mother who used the term "Yippee-kay-ay!"), what would happen if you looked at the situation as an observer? What if you accepted that you will be angry or tense and just experienced it?

The next step in being a more mindful parent is to practice these skills during situations in which your child is misbehaving. I encourage you to practice first in positive situations so that you can gain the skills under less stressful conditions. Being mindful, however, may be even more valuable to you when everything feels like it is out of control. Once you feel comfortable slowing down and experiencing the good times, try the skills in the next exercise.

Acceptance Parenting Exercise

1. Begin by selecting a task or activity with your child that is highly likely to lead to a difficulty. I am not suggesting that you set up a failure situation; just prepare yourself for a problem that is likely to occur anyway. For example, if calling your child to the dinner table or telling him or her it is time for bed typically sets off a problem, select that particular time for this exercise.

2. In this exercise, you will try to be in two roles at the same time: participant and observer. As a participant, you will follow a plan for dealing with the behavior challenge. The next section of this book—*Help*—goes over specifics for handling problems, but for this task just think through how you would like to handle it. Keep conversation and explanations to a minimum (e.g., telling your child three or four times to come to the table). As the participant, try to slow down your efforts with your child so that you can fully experience what happens.

3. As the time approaches for the event, use the skills you learned in the previous chapters to analyze what you are thinking or feeling—this is your second role as an observer. In this exercise, however, do not judge these thoughts or feelings (e.g., "things are out of control") but instead just be aware of them. Remind yourself throughout the situation that you should be nonjudgmental (e.g., "I should not be thinking things are out of control"). As with the first exercise, there are no right or wrong ways to do things (unless they could be dangerous or harmful), and there are no correct ways for you to react. The goal is to notice how you and your child do behave and feel in this activity.

4. During your interactions with your child, practice being aware of all of your thoughts and emotional and physical feelings. Try to step back from what is going on and look at it as if the situation were a slow-motion movie. If your thoughts begin to wander from what is going on around you, gently pull your attention back to the task. Therefore, if you find yourself thinking negative thoughts (e.g., "I'm not a good parent," "This is just awful"), do not judge the thoughts but refocus your attention. As odd as it sounds, your task in this exercise is to experience the whole negative interaction in as neutral a way as possible.

5. In addition to being aware of your own reactions, use all of your senses to experience what is going on around you. What do you hear (e.g., your child screaming, the sound of a toy being thrown)? What do you smell (e.g., dinner on the table)? What do you see (e.g., sweat on your child's forehead)? What do you feel (e.g., the vibration of pounding on the table)? Again, remember not to judge any of your observations.

6. As you go through this exercise, be particularly attentive to your breathing. Make sure that you breathe deeply and slowly and that, as you breathe, you remain in tune with your surroundings. You likely will feel somewhat upset, so make a conscious effort to take deep cleansing breaths when you find yourself tense.

7. When you participate in this activity, try to be as deliberate and aware of your reactions as possible. For example, if you are holding your child's hand and walking him into the kitchen kicking and screaming, be aware of how his hand feels in your hand. Slowly but deliberately follow through on your plan, trying not to let your child's behavior distract or thwart your efforts. For example, if the situation involves getting dressed, there may be times when you have your daughter's foot in your hand to put on a shoe and she is struggling. Do not fight the struggling but instead be aware of it, stop briefly (but do not let go), then continue on. Your voice and your body language should communicate calmness but sureness.

8. If your child calmed down and complied sometime before the end of the activity, be sure to praise him or her appropriately (not too much, not too little) just for finishing (e.g., "Thanks for helping me put on your shoe"), and do not criticize your child for the previous resistance (e.g., "Why do you always give me such a hard time?"). The goal for you is to be fully mindful during this event and not to let any thoughts or feelings interrupt you.

This is an advanced exercise and one that should be attempted only when you have the time and emotional reserve to follow it through to completion. If the situation you choose is getting dressed, for example, you may want to avoid the exercise in the morning before school but try it instead on a weekend morning when you have more time. Similarly, if it involves mealtime, you might want to attempt this exercise when you are not rushed to be finished. This exercise will take a little bit of planning on your part so that you do not have the additional stress of trying to move things along.

The goal of this exercise is to let you see that, even at their worst, some of the problems your child presents can be handled with less stress on you. Slow things down and take each step methodically: "First I will walk into the living room and say he has 5 minutes before dinner. After 5 minutes are up, I will walk back into the living room and ask him to come to the table. If he resists, I will turn off the television and walk him to the table." To illustrate, let's go back to

Kathleen, the mother of 4-year-old Jake, who practiced the mindfulness experience and also attempted the acceptance exercise.

Kathleen reported that she actually enjoyed the mindfulness exercise with Jake and found herself being more "Zen" with him. "I like the experience of slowing things down and feeling that I am truly appreciating Jake and how he sees the world. In fact, I try to do this with some of my home chores. For example, each time I take a shower, I have to squeegee the glass shower door. I used to hate doing this—even though it didn't take much time—because it was just one more thing to do and I was in a rush to get going. Now I squeegee the door using mindfulness. I know it takes about 12 swipes to be completed, and I count them in my head. I break it down into steps—first one direction and then the other—and I just allow myself the minute or so it takes to complete the task. In fact, my husband sometimes offers to take the last shower so I don't always have to do it, but I actually like the structure of the routine—knowing for a few seconds this is my time. It sounds odd to say it, but it helps me remember to experience other things that happen during the day."

Kathleen was learning to "make more time" by experiencing the little things that make up the larger tasks such as getting ready in the morning. As we discussed the acceptance exercise, however, she was hesitant. "Why would I want to slow down and experience his tantrums? I try as much as I can to avoid them because they are so unpleasant." This was an opportunity to discuss with Kathleen the concession process (i.e., the practice of avoiding more and more problem situations) I described in Chapter 3. We pointed out that avoiding situations where Jake's behavior might be a problem may lead to more difficulties later on. For example, Jake did not like to eat at the kitchen table, so Kathleen let him eat on the floor in the family room while he watched television. Although this was not a problem for Kathleen, we pointed out that as Jake got older, this could eventually lead to an even more serious problem. When it came time for Jake to eat lunch at school, he would probably get very upset eating in a cafeteria. In essence, by avoiding this difficulty, Kathleen was simply delaying the inevitable and perhaps even making it worse.

Following this discussion, Kathleen agreed to give the exercise a try and decided that mealtime would be a good first test. She would pick Saturday night dinner because this was usually a time when the family had a more informal, relaxed meal, and if the meal dragged on it would be less of a problem. Kathleen also decided she would bring in Jake's favorite foods (a cheeseburger and French fries from a fast food restaurant) so that Jake would really want to eat. We discussed Kathleen's plan for prompting Jake to the table and how she would react if he resisted, and she agreed that the next Saturday she would put the plan into place. Unfortunately, she did not follow through that week. She reported that it was a difficult day and that she did not have the patience for one more tantrum at dinner. She did, however, agree to try the next week and relayed the outcome to us at the next session. She said,

I really didn't know what to expect. I was anxious all day knowing that I was going to try it, and my husband wasn't too thrilled to try it either. But we both talked through the plan and agreed to try it at least one night. I got his cheeseburger and fries and put them out on the dinner table. I used my mindfulness training to experience setting the table and to experience my anxiety. Then, I told Jake it was time for dinner and that we would be eating in the kitchen. At first he ignored me, and I just observed him and myself. I was anxious and a little annoyed that he was ignoring me. He kept looking toward the kitchen but didn't move. As we planned, I told him one more time that it was time for dinner and that we would be eating in the kitchen and then took his hand and led him to the table. I could feel and smell his sweatiness as he got upset and listened to his tone of voice as he yelled "No! No! No!" I kept reminding myself to take deep breaths and felt how the muscles in my neck were getting tight and that my stomach hurt. I finally got him to sit down, but he would not eat. Again, we followed our plan and ate our dinner and said nothing about his eating. He picked up one French fry and ate it and that was it. He wasn't crying but kept his head on the table. When my husband and I finished eating, we removed our plates and his. Then it started again—"No! No! No!" He kept looking at his plate and looked anxious himself. At this point, I finally experienced the slow down. I started to feel a little in control not only of the situation but of myself. It wasn't so terrible and that made me feel calmer. I could see that this was not such a tragedy and that any thoughts I had (e.g., feeling bad when I took away his food) were things I could just experience and not judge (e.g., thinking I'm a bad mother for taking away his food). I told Jake he could have his dinner only if he ate it at the table. He didn't say anything, but I brought back his plate and he ate in what seemed like seconds. I tried again just to experience what was coming in to my senses, and a feeling of calmness and confidence was part of it. It wasn't a pleasant dinner, but it wasn't a catastrophe either.

After Kathleen described her first attempt at the exercise, we went over lessons from previous sessions such as thoughts of feeling out of control, of being a bad mother, and so forth. She was now good at seeing how she judged herself, and that practice helped her in the acceptance exercise not to judge her thoughts and feelings. We also discussed how facing the dreaded dinner and realizing that it was not as bad as she had anticipated made her feel like she could commit to trying to get Jake to eat at the table once a week to start.

Kathleen also decided to use this acceptance exercise in another problem situation for her. Kathleen and her mother had always had a rocky relationship, and she reported that her mother somehow always knew how to "push her buttons." She told us that conversations with her mother always made her feel judged and that this not only included conversations about her as Jake's mother but also about how she dressed, her decisions about working outside of the home, and so forth. Kathleen dreaded her weekly telephone call with her mother, and it usually ended with Kathleen getting upset at some point during the conversation and fuming with anger for hours afterward. The next call, she said she would try to use the acceptance techniques she used with Jake's tantrums. The next week, Kathleen relayed to us her experience with her mother.

I had a knot in the pit of my stomach on Sunday morning that got worse as the time for our usual telephone call approached. I felt suffocated by this approaching call and by the ongoing hassles with my mother. I called at our usual time, and she answered as if she were surprised to hear from me. Even her tone of voice, which I was now experiencing for the first time, made me angry. I was thinking, "We talk every week at this time, and she sounds as if she is surprised that I remembered!" I tried just to be aware of this and not react. I guess in the past this would make me upset, but I would not know why, which would make me feel defensive before we even started talking. Just like with Jake, I started to feel like I was slowing the conversation down and was being more aware of her voice as well as what she said and how this made me feel. I tried not to judge any of this, which was very hard to do. We started talking about my job, and again her tone of voice seemed to suggest that she disapproved, although she didn't communicate it directly. I guess that in the past I would read into this and start to defend myself, but this time, because I was trying not to judge it, I just let it pass. This kind of interaction happened a few times, and each time I felt as if I could hear our conversation as if I were listening in on us on another line. It actually made me feel calmer and more in control. I guess I'll never be able to change my mother's opinions of my lifestyle choices, but I can see that if I do not take the bait, we can have a rather normal conversation. I am feeling more confidence in myself and in my ability to handle problems like this.

Again, these mindfulness exercises can serve as another type of distraction (i.e., thinking and feeling everything that is going on around you rather than focusing on just your negative experiences) and as a way to enjoy the good times and expose yourself to the bad ones. Being happy or having subjective well-being involves both experiencing the good as well as reducing the bad. Make sure that you plan for both.

Recognize and Appreciate the Good Things in Life

"Your father is surveying his estate." I was getting hungry (a constant state for a 14-year-old boy) and asked my mother about dinner. I knew that we would eat when my father got home from work, but it was after 6:00 and he was nowhere to be found. "He came home a little while ago, and now he's in the backyard, surveying his estate." My mother loved to repeat this line—our family joke. My father enjoyed looking at the bushes and trees in our little backyard in the suburbs of New York City. He purchased the house after World War II—a small Cape Cod house with a little bit of grass around it. It was his—his "estate." Each evening when he could, he would just walk around noticing how things had grown over the years and drink in the fact that this was his house and his land.

Both he and my mother grew up poor during the Depression years, so this was a major step up in their standard of living. My father never let a day go by without appreciating that fact.

An essential ingredient to becoming a happier person is recognizing and appreciating the good things in life. Focusing on the negative can drain away one's physical and emotional energy. This is especially critical for parents of challenging children. You are frequently forced to focus on the negative during the day because it is your job to make things right. Obviously, a parent must take charge of a temper tantrum at the store or a child's attempt to dart across the street. In addition, you may tend to relive these events with those you love—"You won't believe what happened today!"— to get needed support. Although it is good to communicate about your struggles with people who care about you, an exclusive focus on the problems in your life can worsen an already difficult situation.

Researchers are finding that one of the more reliable and powerful keys to living a happier life is to recognize the good things in life as they come to you and to experience and express gratitude. Gratitude can be described as an emotional response to a gift. In my father's case, the gifts he appreciated were the home that he owned and his loving family. They were gifts that came in part from his hard work but also, for him, came from God. Themes of gratitude can be found throughout most religions. Some people pray and express thanks for the gifts bestowed on them. For reasons not yet fully understood, this practice brings about a great deal of subjective well-being. Strong evidence exists for the ability of gratitude to improve our experience of well-being in a lasting and meaningful way.[12] The next two sections describe easy-to-complete exercises that you can do to improve your view of yourself and your life and assist you with your efforts to help your child.

Three Good Things   Most people are told from time to time to "count their blessings." In one form or another, this is a universal strategy recommended to people in an effort to make them happier. The idea, obviously, is to remind people of those good things that happen during life and to focus more on the positive aspects of life than the negative ones. Despite the common sense involved in this recommendation, does it really work?

Several studies have shown that something as simple as counting one's blessings does in fact lead to increased satisfaction with one's life.[13] The almost effortless act of thinking of the positive things that happened during the day seems to have a lasting impact on a person's report of life satisfaction. I highly recommend that you try to incorporate this task into your nightly routine. The timing is important. Some research suggests that doing this in the evening before going to bed has the most positive effect on people. Do it for at least one week, and you may find that it becomes a nightly ritual.

The task is simple. Each night, write down three things that went well that day with your challenging child and, if you know them, their causes. Do this for

1 week (7 consecutive nights). Write down even the smallest of successes, the causes, and if you observe any patterns. Also, try to briefly describe your reactions to this task and how this made you feel. Figure 5.1 provides an example of one mother's daily log—showing just a few days of her experiences and her reflections on the task itself. This mother had a 7-year-old son with ADHD as well as an infant daughter and another baby on the way. She frequently reported feeling overwhelmed and was quite hesitant about completing this task. However, as you will see, it posed less of a difficulty than she anticipated, and she reported having a very positive experience.

This mother's experience is typical of the experiences of those parents who attempt this simple task. As she so eloquently told us, it is very easy to become too focused on the negative things that happen to us during the day. The "three good things" task is a very simple way to remind oneself on a daily basis of those

---

Thursday

1. I received good results from my son's doctor about his blood tests. I had been worried about the results, so this was very good news.
2. My son came home from school and had a green sticker on his behavior report. This felt wonderful because he had received a yellow sticker the day before when he was having trouble following directions.
3. My infant daughter started holding her own bottle during feeding time, which allowed me to get some much-needed laundry folded. My son sat with me and helped me fold some of his socks.

Friday

1. Today, when I took my son to soccer practice, he did not complain once about it being so hot out. It made me happy to see him having fun with his teammates.
2. I went to the supermarket today and was able to go grocery shopping and buy everything on my list in one day! My son only wandered away a few times but came back when I called him. This was awesome because I didn't have to plan on going back when my husband got paid again.
3. My husband, kids, and I decided to go to pizza night at a local restaurant, and my son won a penguin, which he lovingly gave to his sister. What a sweet boy!

Saturday

1. Today, I went to my son's soccer game, and not only did he make his first goal of the season, but his team also won! I know I'm not supposed to keep score because the kids are only 7 years old, but everybody does.
2. My husband got off from work early, and we actually were able to get a babysitter! We went out together for the first time in months and saw a scary movie. This was good because I also got to cuddle up next to him during the scary parts. When we came home, the babysitter reported that everything went pretty well and that my son was asleep!
3. I was able to have my mother-in-law come down and babysit my daughter for free instead of having to pay the neighbor. Not only did she exhaust my daughter but she did all the dishes, watched my son, and did the rest of the laundry. God, I love her.

Figure 5.1.　Example of one mother's daily log.

Figure 5.1.   *(continued)*

My Reflections

At first I thought that this was going to be very difficult for me to do. I mean, how often does anyone actually sit down on a daily basis and recount the good things that happened throughout the day? I think that it is pretty safe to say that most of us reflect more on what went wrong (especially with a child) and how we are going to fix any issues the following day. This project enabled me to take the little things in life, often the ones that are overlooked, and appreciate them and feel good about things throughout the day. In my busy schedule as a mother, wife, and student, it is very easy for me to feel overwhelmed at times. Sometimes I wonder what exactly I am working so hard for when an obstacle presents itself. Being able to go back and think about things and how they made my day a little brighter was very helpful. I found that after Day 3, I didn't just focus on the day's events that caught me off guard or had me feeling bad. I could still see that no matter how many things happened that made me feel bad there were many other things about the day that made me feel good. I know that some people reading my three good things would think to themselves, "Why did that make you so happy?" But the truth is, it really doesn't take that much to make a person happy. These days we are conditioned to believe that we need fancy cars, endless bank accounts, days of shopping and spending without a thought, and so forth to make us happy. The truth is that none of that guarantees true happiness. As I look back throughout my week and see things that made me feel good, like my daughter holding her own bottle or my son not complaining about the heat at his soccer game, I can remember these things helping me feel positive about the rest of my day and week to come. I think that this was a wonderful project, and I have actually continued to write down my "three good things" every day. I will try to keep it up as long as I can because it is always nice whenever I start to feel discouraged to be able to remember that I have a lot to feel lucky, happy, and appreciative for.

good things that seem to fade into the background as one faces his or her daily challenges. What this mother also observed was that the good things often were quite simple things—a kind gesture by her child or the help of her mother-in-law. Despite the apparent simplicity of this exercise, research suggests that it can increase happiness and decrease depressive symptoms for up to 6 months.[14]

As with mindfulness, you can use the "three good things" exercise and expand it to include other good things not related to your child. Parents often are surprised at how such small things as finding a good parking place, spending even just a few minutes with a friend, or having a nice family meal can be so pleasant. In the practice of mindfulness, we experience these positive things at the time that they occur; in this exercise, we practice reflecting back on those good times. Both of these techniques are quite powerful ways of enjoying parenting specifically but also your life in general. This appreciation of the good things is extremely important and serves as the focus of the next exercise you can complete to help you with your life satisfaction.

The Gratitude Letter   The "three good things" exercise can help you identify and focus on the positive experiences that are daily occurrences; but, as I have discussed, another important component to subjective well-being is to feel and express gratitude for these good things. Again, research points out that gratitude can significantly increase your personal satisfaction. People who are grateful for what they have—whatever they have—tend to be happier people. All of the major religions have mechanisms for expressing gratitude to their deities (e.g., through prayer); however, expressing gratitude to other people for their contributions to our lives is also important. Unfortunately, unlike some other cultures, Western cultures have limited institutionalized rituals for expressing gratitude to other people. Thank you notes, for example, tend to be simple and lack meaningful content and therefore tend not to express the depth of gratitude toward others that leads to subjective well-being.

In one study, researchers asked people to write and then deliver a letter of gratitude in person to someone who had been especially kind to them but had never been properly thanked.[15] They found that this gratitude letter improved their feelings of happiness on average for up to a month. When we have used this technique, we provide parents with the following instructions. Write and deliver a letter of gratitude *in person* to someone who has been especially kind to you but has never been thanked properly. Try to select someone who has helped you with your challenging child. In the letter, be specific about what the person did for you and how it affected you then and now. Then, write down a brief description of the visit, including your feelings before, during, and afterward.

One parent decided to write to her son's first preschool teacher, who you will see helped her more than she realized at the time her son was in her class. Figure 5.2 shows the letter written by this parent.

Dear Tina,

I am sorry it has taken years to write to you to express my appreciation for everything you did for me and Greg while he was in your class. I frequently think about all of the lessons you taught me, and I have always wanted to thank you.

When Greg was first placed in your classroom, I could immediately feel your warmth and affection toward him and the other children. There was never a look of surprise when Greg did some of his "behaviors," and you were one of the first people I felt comfortable leaving him with. I also remember all of the advice you gave me about dealing with his behaviors at home but also how you kept telling me to treat him like any other kid. I don't think I really understood what you meant until sometime later when I found myself coddling him too much. You had me pegged from the first week!

I know there were times when we disagreed, and I still feel bad about that. I now realize that the reports you sent home about Greg's problems at school were meant to help me and him, but at the time I felt that these notes reflected on me as a parent. I also know that I sometimes resisted your suggestions, but I now realize just how smart you really were and are! Life with Greg has sometimes been very difficult, but I thank God often for having had you as his first teacher.

Please know that you have made a major impact on Greg's life and on mine. I truly appreciate all you have done.

Julie

Figure 5.2. Letter of gratitude from Julie to her son's preschool teacher, Tina.

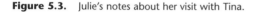

I invited Tina out for a drink after work and told her I just wanted to catch up. She seemed very pleased to hear from me and was looking forward to our talk. As we settled into the restaurant, I passed her the letter and said that this was my way of thanking her for everything she had done for me. I didn't think it would be so difficult having her read the letter in front of me! I felt like I was back in school and my teacher was reading a report I had written for class.

When Tina finished the letter, she jumped up and we both hugged and cried. She told me that my letter meant so much to her and how rarely she gets positive feedback from parents. It was so sad, in a way, to hear how hard it is for her to be a good teacher. She said that often it means telling parents things they don't want to hear or know, but that the progress in her students keeps her going.

I tried to tell her that there were probably many more parents like me who had their own issues and therefore may not be receptive to her good advice at the time; yet, like me, they were also probably grateful later on.

We talked for a few hours and ended up having dinner together. It was one of the best nights I've had in a long time. For weeks later I felt so good that I got up the courage to do that—especially having seen her reaction and how rarely this happens to her.

Figure 5.3. Julie's notes about her visit with Tina.

The second part of the exercise is to deliver the letter in person, have the person read it in front of you, and talk about it. This is perhaps the most difficult part. People often feel quite anxious about doing this because it can be a bit embarrassing. But as you will see, it can also be one of the more rewarding experiences of your life. Figure 5.3 provides Julie's account of her visit with Tina, her son's preschool teacher.

As you can see from Julie's account of her visit with Tina, her letter to her son's former teacher made her feel great and made Greg's teacher feel terrific as well. Sometimes, parents get so caught up in their own lives that they forget to thank the people who contribute to making their lives just a little bit easier. Consider using this exercise with your child's teacher, a babysitter, a relative who has pitched in to help, or even your partner. You will be surprised at how powerful this expression of gratitude can be. And, as with the other exercises, consider using it beyond your experience with your child into other aspects of your life. Figure 5.4 provides an example of how one very thoughtful father used the gratitude letter to express his appreciation to his grandmother, a very important person in his life.

Figure 5.5 contains the father's description of delivering the letter to his grandmother and their reactions. This father's experience is far from unique. I have seen parents write letters to their siblings, their parents, doctors who have helped them, and teachers who have gone above and beyond for their child. One father wrote a letter to his father who had abandoned the family when he was a young boy. Although his father was not particularly receptive, he stated that he wanted to at least thank him for the time he was a father and to give him an

Dear Gram,

I am writing you this letter to let you know how kind you have been to me. You have always treated me with love and respect, and I wanted to thank you for the kindness you have extended to me. You are truly a great person. I sincerely appreciate all of the time you took telling me stories of your life. I also appreciate you helping me with money to get through college. I couldn't have graduated without your help.

I am probably most thankful for having you here long enough to see my boys being born. It means a great deal to me that you see me as a father and not as a troubled child. I know I was difficult growing up, but I always felt that you were there when I needed you. You always stood by me, and I think about that often.

I can't imagine how difficult it must be to outlive your husband and some of your children, yet you always are a great source of strength to the family. I am sorry I haven't told you all of these things until now, but I wanted you to know.

Your loving grandson

Figure 5.4.   Letter of gratitude from a grandson to his grandmother.

opportunity to make amends. He wasn't using this to forgive him for leaving but just to give his father the opportunity to apologize. Unfortunately, his father did not apologize. "I probably won't contact him again," he told me. "But at least I can feel that I tried and that I was the bigger man. Now I know that this was not my fault and that I did everything I could to fix things. There is satisfaction in knowing this."

I was very nervous about making the trip to my grandmother's house. I called her and said I had something for her. She seemed genuinely delighted that I was coming over for a visit, but my anxiety grew as I got closer to her house. Her health has been quite poor, and in addition to being embarrassed, I didn't know what effect my visit and the letter would have on her.

She was watching television when I arrived, and I handed her the letter. "What's this?" she asked, and I told her it was just a thank-you note for her. She seemed confused and started to read the letter. My heart was pounding in my chest. I was so nervous, and then I saw her begin to cry. Once I saw her cry, tears came to my eyes too. When she finished the letter, she leaned over and held my hand. She thought she didn't deserve such a letter, which led to a long conversation about her life and my family, and it was a wonderful time.

I can honestly say that without this exercise I would never have done this, and I think I would have regretted it for the rest of my life. I felt so good having thanked her and letting her know how I felt.

As a follow-up, some weeks later she was diagnosed with a fatal illness and knew she didn't have much more time to live. She gathered the family around to discuss her impending death, and my uncle asked if she had any wishes for a ceremony once she passed. She thought for a moment and said, no, but if we did anything, she wanted me to read aloud that letter I had given her.

I was never so proud and so grateful. I think everyone needs to do this at least once in his or her life.

Figure 5.5.   A grandson's notes about his visit with his grandmother.

The gratitude exercise may be one of the more difficult things you ever do. It requires that you make yourself vulnerable and communicate feelings that may be embarrassing. In addition, as shown in the previous description, the outcome may not always be pleasant. In each case that a parent has decided to complete this exercise, however, he or she has been happy with the results and it has provided a sense of satisfaction and fulfillment that few other activities can.

FINAL THOUGHTS

The Purposeful Life

If you do it right, your child will raise you.

—Author's quote

One of the common themes running through all theories of happiness is the need to have a purpose in your life. A therapist recently described to me how she is now seeing a large number of businessmen and women in her practice who feel that their lives are empty. Even though most of these individuals continue to be financially successful, the people coming to her are confessing that what they do to make money has no meaning to them. Often, they went into their careers because family members or others told them it was a good way to make a great deal of money, and at the time, that was enticing. Yet, now they are finding that working so hard just to make money and not doing something meaningful is a bit of a trap. Remember my yacht description and how the younger students in my class often believed that having a great deal of money would make them happier. The older students, however, knew better. They knew what scientists are now making clear—that people need a certain amount of money to meet their basic living needs (e.g., enough for food, housing); if they earn more than that amount, however, the hedonic treadmill starts and, as described previously, does not bring with it life satisfaction. The problem is obvious. If making a great deal of money is your only purpose in life, you are likely to be disappointed with the direction of your life at some point in the future. As the saying goes, "No one on their deathbed ever says they wish they had spent more time at the office."

One of the secrets to a happier life is to choose to do what you love. In work, the advice is to find the things that you love and try to match your loves with a way to make a living. Making a modest living in a profession you enjoy will lead to greater satisfaction as you get older. Related to this idea of happiness and a purposeful life, scientists are studying a phenomenon referred to as optimal experience or flow.[16] *Flow* is a term used for the satisfaction you gain just by engaging in a challenging activity. In sports, players often describe this as "being in the zone." It is those brief periods of time when you are playing a sport and overcoming challenges without really thinking about it. Artists, too, describe a similar experience of being so engrossed in the challenges of painting, sculpting, molding clay, singing, or acting that they are no longer thinking—just doing. This is often described as being in a highly pleasurable state of mind. You might recognize flow in the context of parenting as one step beyond mindfulness. Flow occurs when you are so involved in what you are doing that not only do outside thoughts (e.g., doing laundry, shopping, meetings) drift away but you are no longer *thinking* parenting—you're just *doing* it. This in itself can be pleasurable.

Your life needs to have meaning and a purpose; and for better or worse, yours does. Perhaps you did not choose to have a challenging child, yet you have been given a great responsibility: the care of a life. This life will, in some way, influence the world. Some parents who have children with severe and multiple challenges find some solace in the idea that God never gives people more than they can handle. If you find that this way of looking at your current circumstances provides you with additional courage and confidence, then I encourage you to hold onto this belief. Unfortunately, there are many times when parents simply cannot handle the challenges they face. Marriages often are threatened, and some end up succumbing to the stresses that come along with parenting a challenging child. In addition, parents often report periods of anxiety and depression that are triggered by incidents or concerns with their child, and these emotions threaten the parents' own well-being.

I have provided a number of different techniques that can help you get through these difficult times; however, it is helpful to remember that the child that challenges you each day can also be the source of meaning in your life. I had a discussion with one couple whose challenging child is now an adult, and the parents reflected back on all of the emergencies and obstacles in their lives that had as their source their child. As we spoke, they each expressed some regret that they somehow had made mistakes throughout the years that caused their child to be so difficult. "If only I had not done…" was a theme that ran through our discussion. As I listened to their concerns, however, it became very clear that they were good parents doing the best they could under the circumstances. It was clear that their child had been difficult from birth and that they did everything they could to give their child a good life and to keep him on track to be a good and responsible adult.

"Is your son a drug dealer?" I asked. They looked puzzled. "No." "Has he ever been in jail?" "No." As I quizzed them about their son's current status, it was obvious that he was fine. Was he still difficult? Yes. But, somehow, they managed to help him negotiate a very complex world with few lasting negative consequences. Then I asked, "What do you think he would be like now if he had parents that didn't care what he did and didn't battle with him to help him?" They saw where I was going with this and conceded, "Yes, I know. I guess we didn't mess up too much. Yet, we still feel that there were many things we could have done better."

Every parent feels that he or she could be or could have been a better parent. The point is that if you care and you try, you'll do well. If all you do in your life is raise a child the best that you can, you have accomplished something truly special. You will have lived a life worth living. Remember that idea as we now turn our attention to helping you with your child. You never know how your child will influence the world. You may not be raising the next president or the doctor who cures cancer or the entrepreneur who ends hunger, but you may have in your hands someone who makes someone else happy or who inspires a teacher to help just one more child or who in turn helps another child. You as a parent are doing something truly heroic and meaningful.

Social Support

One last thought: It is difficult to survive challenges alone. It is known from extensive research in many different areas that the emotional support of others can reduce your stress, improve your health, and help you live longer. It can help you persist through many difficult times. This is why many professionals encourage parents who have challenging children to join a support group. These groups are sometimes organized around a disorder (e.g., ADHD, autism spectrum disorders) and can be very useful for getting help with things such as dealing with legal issues (e.g., how to work with the special education system, planning for your child's financial future) or medical issues (e.g., finding a good and understanding pediatrician or dentist). Support groups also can be a good general source of information and a wonderful forum for sharing experiences (e.g., how one parent dealt with her child being bullied at school). In general, parent support groups can be extremely valuable for getting both information and support.

For some parents who have pessimistic styles of thinking, these support groups also may be intimidating and can just reinforce thoughts of inadequacy. For instance, one mother told me about her experience with a local support group she was directed to by her son's school. She said,

> I was nervous going in to the meeting. These other parents had been getting together for awhile, and I was the newbie; but, they were very nice to me and welcomed me into the group. We all met at night in a classroom at my son's school, and it was funny to sit at those small desks. As we sat around talking, though, I became more and more uncomfortable. One mother, for example, asked the group whether they had read the latest online journal article about the disorder, and many of the parents had. They went back and forth about what it might mean for our children. Then, another parent described how he had just come back from the annual national conference during which he was part of a panel talking about parenting issues. This kind of thing went on for a while. Everyone there seemed strong and confident

and highly active in some aspect. A couple of parents field telephone calls from other parents to help them. Almost all of the parents were raising money through bake sales and car washes. I was feeling more and more alone. How could I possibly measure up to these people? They talked about being frustrated, but I didn't get the feeling that they felt like I do—defeated. Did they ever have trouble even getting out of bed in the morning like me? I was too afraid to even bring this up to this group. I didn't go back.

It is often helpful to have good models for parenting. You might look at how others handle problems and learn some tips or at least feel better about how you are handling an issue. We also frequently think back on how we were raised and use our parents as models (or perhaps as models for how you do not want to raise your child!). If the other parents to whom you are looking for support are too unlike you, however, then you are less likely to be helped. In this mother's case, the other parents in the group were support group veterans who were, at least on the surface, very confident in how they were handling things. I tried to point out to this mother there may have been many parents there feeling the same things she did. They too may have had their doubts and insecurities but felt that they could not show weakness. So, what can you do?

One solution is to create your own social support network. This can be in the form of a formal group of parents in similar situations or can just be a group of friends, relatives, and/or others who might be willing to examine their parenting experiences. One mother I know started her own Optimistic Parenting group (which she called her OP group—pronounced "ō pē"). The function of the group was primarily to go over the thoughts the group members were having about being parents. Popular topics during the first few meetings included how the media portrays parenting as a wonderful and always joyous experience; an article on the "toxic" child; how to handle unwanted parental advice from family and strangers; and the role of fathers in parenting (that was an interesting one). The group members also made sure to include as part of each meeting the positive exercises outlined in this chapter, including parenting in the moment and expressing gratitude. Some parents also provided information about other things they found helpful such as yoga and exercising, getting a pet, or just having a date night with their spouse. The founding mother set the ground rules, which were that anything was acceptable to say (e.g., "Sometimes I don't feel like I love my child") and would not be judged but that the meeting could not become a gripe session; it had to be solution focused. This included how to reorient your thinking and how to help yourself as a parent. As one of the members told the founding mother, "This is like my book club. Sometimes we talk about the book, but it's also nice to be around like-minded people and eat! But I like this better because I always leave feeling hopeful that things will get better and that I can do things just for me without feeling selfish."

Again, this support group allowed parents to say things that they felt others would judge negatively, and parents who shared these thoughts often found other parents with similar thoughts and experiences. Yet, the group also focused on how to change these ways of looking at parenting for the better and how to take care of themselves without experiencing guilt. I would encourage you to find ways of getting this type of social support, even if it requires taking the initiative yourself.

Next I describe the things you can do to help improve your child's behavior. As I go through these steps, I will remind you to keep track of your thoughts and feelings and help you to remember how to maintain a more optimistic view of these situations.

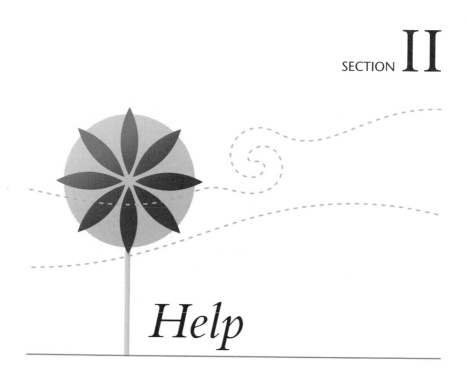

Help

He who is afraid of asking is
ashamed of learning.

—Danish Proverb

CHAPTER 6

A Close Look at Your Child's Behavior

All truths are easy to understand once they are discovered; the point is to discover them.

—Galileo Galilei (1564–1642, astronomer and physicist)

This chapter begins the section of the book designed to help you gain the knowledge and skills necessary to deal directly with your child's challenging behavior. I will continue to remind you to use the techniques outlined in the previous chapters as we go through the important steps of understanding why your child misbehaves and then designing strategies to deal with the problems. This chapter covers how to pick the behaviors to work on, how to keep track of any changes in those behaviors, and how to understand why your child is misbehaving. All of these are necessary first steps to beginning the process of improving how your child behaves.

SETTING GOALS

Your first task is to figure out which of your child's behaviors you would like to attempt to understand and try to change. Two steps are necessary for deciding which behaviors you want to work on. The first step is to think through your larger life goals for your child. The second step is then to figure out which of your child's problem behaviors are most likely to get in the way of achieving those goals. When I first mention these steps to some parents, they sometimes laugh. "I really don't need to go through these steps. I know what I want him to do. I want him to listen to me!" You may be experiencing similar thoughts. Your child may scream when it's time for bed or cry when she doesn't get her favorite food, or you just may want all tantrums to stop. This is certainly reasonable; however, it is helpful to go through the exercise anyway—it does not take long—because it often is helpful to begin with one problem (e.g., dinnertime problems) and then work through others. This process may help you prioritize which of the difficulties to tackle first.

It also is useful to spend a little time assessing what you want for your child and thinking through what might be achievable quickly (e.g., getting dressed without disruption) and what might take a little more time (e.g., getting dressed without any help). This process of assessment may lead to improved satisfaction for your whole family. A child of one of the families in our program, for example, displayed a whole range of behavior problems. When we first went over the behavior challenges, both the mother and father reported that improved efficiency in getting their daughter ready in the morning was the most important goal for them. As we went through the process of looking at broader goals, however, it became obvious that one of the largest obstacles to their child's future and to their family's satisfaction was their daughter's difficulties with traveling. She would kick and scream each time she needed to get into the car and fought being buckled into the car seat. As a result of these outbursts, the family rarely went out together; one parent usually would stay home with the daughter while the other parent ran errands or took the other children to sporting events, shopping, and so forth. As we went through the process of assessing goals, both the mother and father identified being able to go out into the community as a major goal. As a result of this examination, they decided to first focus on getting their daughter to travel with them; not only would this help their daughter be more integrated into family life but it would also allow the rest of the family more freedom to experience life outside of the home.

With these issues in mind, take a moment to work through the broader life goals that are important to you and for your challenging child. For example, these goals might include the following:

- Improving your child's physical health or emotional life
- Working on independence so that your child can go more places and experience more things
- Letting your child have more control so that he or she can make more choices in life
- Improving relationships with others to encourage friendships and other types of meaningful social relationships
- Making overall positive changes in family life

Working through these goals should be a process that is as inclusive as possible. For example, you should include your spouse, partner, or significant other in this process as well as any other family members (including your child with challenging behavior, if appropriate) who have a stake in the outcome.

In the example I gave previously, the family as a group decided that getting out more as a family was a highly desirable goal, which led to choosing the transition in and out of the car as an important short-term goal. It also may be helpful to try to coordinate this planning with your child's school to see whether you share important goals and can work on similar behavior problems at the same time.

You may end up with multiple important goals (e.g., improving your child's relationships with other children *and* eating together as a family without problem behaviors). This is common and likely means you are looking beyond just the problem of the day. In this case, examine your child's strengths and limitations when deciding on which behavior to change. For example, your child may be able to improve his or her ability to eat without problems because he or she already has all of the necessary skills. Working on friendships may take a bit longer, however, because you may need to help your child with his or her social skills in addition to working through behavior problems. However you decide to proceed, do not forget our discussion of leveraging. For example, perhaps while you work on mealtime behavior at home, the school can help by also working on mealtime behavior with peers at school. This way, at least at school your child can be working on both being well-behaved during meals as well as social relationships. Do not overlook any opportunities to combine goals into one activity.

DEFINING BEHAVIORS

Early in my career, I worked in a psychology clinic that was associated with my university. I was a therapist in training as part of my clinical psychology doctoral program, and I had the opportunity to work with a broad range of people in the local community. My training period was quite intimidating because I never knew who was going to walk through the door. In addition, all sessions were taped so that my supervisor and the other students in my group could observe the discussions and critique them. One couple I will never forget was a husband and wife in their 60s who were there to get help with their sexual incompatibilities. Here I was an unmarried 20-something-year-old, and I had to project an image of authority and wisdom. Good thing I took drama classes in high school!

One day a single mother named Claudia made an appointment and wanted to discuss her young son's behavior problems. Here was an area where I had a great deal of experience, so I felt pretty comfortable as we entered the therapy room together. I began by asking her a few basic questions and then opened the discussion with the usual line—"So what brings you here today?" This mother, who was about my age, was clearly unsure of herself and had a great deal of difficulty expressing her thoughts. Claudia said something about the problems she was having with her 4-year-old son, Marcos, but it was difficult getting specifics. "So, what is it exactly he is doing that is causing you the most problems at home?" She did not answer immediately, and I knew enough just to wait. Finally, she replied, "He just doesn't listen to me." My experience taught me that this could mean anything, so I tried again. "That must be really frustrating to you. Can you give me an example—maybe something that happened this week that was causing you a problem?" Claudia looked down at her feet and folded and unfolded her hands. "Well, he doesn't listen to anything I say." This conversation continued for a bit, and I made no further progress; therefore, I asked if I could visit her in her home to meet her son and perhaps get an idea about what it was Marcos was doing that had her concerned enough to come in for counseling. She reluctantly agreed, and we decided I would stop by after his preschool was out the next day.

Claudia's condominium was small but nicely kept, and I could see the eat-in kitchen as Claudia welcomed me in the front door. Her son was sitting at the table having a snack, and she introduced me. After saying hello, I said, "Hey, I'm Marcos too. Great name!" He barely looked up and said, "Hi." Claudia motioned for me to sit and offered me something to drink. As she brought over my glass and we started to sit down at the table with Marcos, he got up to leave the room. "Marcos, honey, you need to clean up." "No," he said simply. "Marcos, you know you need to put your cup in the sink." He stomped back into the kitchen, picked up his cup, and threw it in the sink, causing it to shatter and the glass to go flying around the room. Then, he smiled to himself and went into his room. "See," she said, as she began to pick up the pieces of glass. "He doesn't listen to me."

That scene was worth a thousand words. Within the first 5 minutes of my visit to Claudia's home, it became clear that "He doesn't listen to me" was a much bigger problem than I ever could have guessed from her description. This scenario makes it obvious that the description of the nature of the problem needs to be abundantly clear.

One reason for a good description is for everyone involved to be in complete agreement about what the problem is. For example, if you and your spouse feel that your child's tantrums are problematic and need to be eliminated but have differing ideas about what your child's tantrum actually looks like, you will run into trouble when trying to help your child. If you consider it a tantrum every time your son stamps his feet and whines but your partner only considers it a tantrum if your son also screams, then you will end up working at odds with each other.

Having a good description of your child's problem now also will help you later on. In one example from our practice, a little boy named Evan was brought to us. Evan would scream at breakfast for 10–15 minutes each morning, and his parents were at wits' end. They decided that his screaming was important to change, so my colleagues and I focused on that as our goal. Within a few weeks,

Evan was only yelling out for a second or two and then would settle down and eat his breakfast. When I asked Evan's parents about his progress, though, they were discouraged. "He is still a problem at breakfast," his father told me with some exasperation. "This really isn't working." His wife was nodding her head as well, and I was concerned that they were not able to see the progress Evan had made. You should by now be able to recognize their pessimistic style of thinking when it came to their child's progress. They were seeing his screaming as somehow intractable—something that would never improve. Because of this viewpoint, they lost perspective on the changes he had made over the last several weeks.

To help Evan's parents see the improvements in Evan's behavior at breakfast, I pulled out the records of our previous discussions. "When we first got together just last month, you wrote down that Evan would scream continuously for up to 15 minutes. If you look at your reports now, though, this is much less of a problem." "Yes, but breakfast is still so horrible," his mother responded. "I don't think we will ever have a normal breakfast at our house." If you think Evan's parents' reactions are unusual, you would be wrong. Anyone who works regularly with parents will tell you that this happens much more often than one would expect. Although it does not happen with all families, professionals see this pattern often and it creates a great deal of frustration. Despite obvious progress in a difficult child, some families just do not see it. Or, if they see it, they downplay the improvements and shift their focus to other difficulties (e.g., "Oh yes, he doesn't scream as much at breakfast, but I still can't get him to do his homework at night").

Having a good definition at the start can give you perspective over time. For example, Evan's 15-minute screaming matches were gone and had been replaced with only a few very brief outbursts, but his parents had difficulty seeing this. For this reason, you need to have objective information but also examine your thoughts in these situations to see whether they get in the way of appreciating even minor progress. Remember, the pessimistic attributional style can lead you to minimize your role in progress and overemphasize your responsibility for your child's difficulties. It also can make you see problems as larger than they are and feel as if nothing will ever change. The positive improvements must be savored (perhaps as one of the "three good things" that happened that day), and any additional challenges should be looked at as just part of the next step toward helping your child be better behaved.

One more reason to be very clear about a child's behavior is for assessment efforts. If you want to find out why your child misbehaves, you need to be very specific. For example, a number of years ago, I worked with a family for whom this caused a problem—an illustration of what can go wrong without a good definition of a child's difficulties. Arleen was a 12-year-old girl with multiple disabilities and a variety of medical and behavior challenges. One of the problem situations identified by Arleen's parents involved downtime. If Arleen was left alone in the house, for example, in front of the television, she would often begin to act up. Her parents described these tantrums as including crying, screaming, and running around. Sometimes, Arleen also would hit one of her parents. Arleen's parents had been responding to these tantrums by putting Arleen in her room. They told me that this caused her to behave a bit better but that she continued to get upset often.

As Arleen's parents and I began to go through the assessment process (which I describe next), we discovered that Arleen's tantrums seemed to serve different purposes for her. As we looked more closely, we found that she would cry to get someone to come over to her—attention-getting behavior. Conversely, we also found that Arleen would scream loudly or run around if she did not want to do something her parents were trying to get her to do (e.g., use a fork or spoon while eating). This kind of escape behavior was almost the opposite of the crying behavior; rather than wanting her parents to interact with her while she was eating, she wanted to be left alone. If her mother or father tried to instruct her on how to use utensils, she got upset. The problem was that her parents dealt with each of these types of behaviors in the same way—they sent Arleen to her room. Can you spot the problem?

Being sent to one's room without getting attention might be a successful approach to dealing with behavior problems that are an attempt to get attention from others. In Arleen's case, she seemed to use part of her tantrums—crying—to get attention. One would expect that by being sent to her room, Arleen would begin to cry less; instead of getting her parents' attention, it got her even less time with them. The problem was that Arleen's parents also used the same approach when Arleen got upset because she wanted to be left alone. When her parents started to prompt her to use a spoon to eat, Arleen would scream and run away from the table. By using the same approach that they used to deal with Arleen's crying—sending her to her room—Arleen received exactly what she wanted: to be left alone. Being sent to her room made sense for the attention-getting behavior (crying) but actually made the escape behaviors (screaming and running around) worse.

You can see the importance of being very specific about your child's behaviors as you attempt to determine why they might be occurring and then as you begin to design a plan. Some things to consider when describing your child's problem behaviors include the following:

- What does the behavior look like?
- What does the behavior sound like?
- What are several examples of this behavior?
- How can you describe the behavior with words that would be clear to other people who do not know your child?

We saw in Arleen's case that using the term *tantrum* was not helpful because it included a number of different behaviors (i.e., crying, screaming, running around) that for her were quite different in terms of their purposes (i.e., to get attention or to escape her parents' demands on her). Other terms such as *having a fit* or *having a meltdown* are also not helpful because, just as with the word *tantrum,* they have no meaning outside of your family. However, describing problems with words such as *slapping other people, screaming loudly, crying, falling to the floor,* or *stomping feet* does give you a good picture of what the problem looks like from the outside looking in.

KEEPING TRACK OF BEHAVIORS

I briefly mentioned previously why it is important to keep some records of your child's behaviors. Over time, your memory may begin to fade, and it is helpful to see if and how your child's behaviors have changed over time, especially as you begin to try out new approaches. Keeping track of your child's progress does not need to involve elaborate record keeping; in fact, I would discourage you from doing so. Unless you enjoy these types of compulsive tasks (i.e., playing with Excel spreadsheets is your favorite form of entertainment), I would suggest that you try to keep this task as simple as possible. Attempting to keep detailed descriptions at first and then later finding that you have missed days will feed right into at least one pessimistic attribution—"See, I'm not a good parent because I couldn't even keep track of my child's behavior once a day!" You already have so many demands on your time; I want you to save your emotional energy for interacting with your child.

I caution professionals about this all of the time. When dealing with a parent who has a child with challenging behavior, this is typically the professional's first request: "Take these forms and complete them. Also, keep a record of your child's behavior each hour and bring all of this to me next week." Unfortunately, there is rarely a discussion about how detailed record keeping might in itself prove to be an obstacle for a family. As one mother put it, "I interact with professionals every week, and they make constant demands on me. It depresses me to even think about it, because I know I don't live up to their expectations. Sometimes, I'm so busy I miss a day or two. Once, I filled out a week's worth of data sheets in the parking lot before I went into my son's school." Detailed record keeping will be counterproductive if it causes you additional stress and concern in your already too-full day.

To be consistent with the theme of leveraging, I suggest several ways of keeping track of your child's behavior that also can serve a second purpose—to help you understand why your child may be misbehaving. I cover this important concept next, but it may be helpful to show you how my colleagues and I have helped some families take on both of these tasks simultaneously.

Sarah was a mother in her late 20s whose son Brian was very disruptive at home. Sarah told us that 5-year-old Brian would have frequent "meltdowns" that caused a great deal of chaos. We worked through the definition process to get a good picture of Brian's problems and discovered that most of his behavior problems consisted of whining, crying, and flailing his legs and arms around. As we discussed Sarah's difficulties with Brian at home, she told us that getting him to follow through with her requests—for example, putting away his toys or getting dressed—was the major obstacle she was facing. As we went through the goal-setting exercise, it became clear that Brian's behavior was causing him to be isolated from his older brothers (who would not play with him) and from other children his age. We decided to work on this problem because it was not only a management problem at home but was also interfering with his social development (i.e., learning how to play with other children).

To get an idea about how much of a problem this was and to keep track of any changes, we asked Sarah to write down when the behaviors occurred and also what was happening before (antecedents) and after (consequences) each incident. This type of chart is usually referred to as an *ABC chart,* because you record the antecedents (A), the behaviors (B), and the consequences (C). This additional information proved critical later when we tried to figure out just why Brian was getting upset. The following is an example of Sarah's record for just part of one day.

SARAH'S ABC CHART FOR BRIAN

Day and time	ANTECEDENTS What was happening just before your child's behavior problem?	BEHAVIOR Write down the behavior(s) as well as the number of times and/or how long they occurred.		CONSEQUENCES How did you or others react to the episode?
Saturday, 10:40 a.m.	I asked Brian a second time to put his toys away.	Whining and crying	6 minutes	I put his toys away.
Saturday, noon	I asked Brian several times to change his shirt because it had gotten wet outside.	Crying, falling on the floor, kicking and screaming	2 minutes	I gave up and let him wear his shirt.

You can see from this partial record that Brian's "meltdowns" occurred several times a day and could last for several minutes. This type of tantrum going on for several minutes can be quite stressful, and it was obviously a major problem for Brian's family. It was helpful to us to see not only how often they happened and for how long but also when they were happening (e.g., when asked to put away his toys or when he was asked to change his shirt). But before examining whether there are any patterns to his behavior, let's take a look at another way to keep track of your child's behavior problems that also can serve to help in understanding why the problems might be occurring.

Jerry was a 15-year-old boy who had received a diagnosis of PDD-NOS. His language skills were fairly limited, and other people had a difficult time understanding what he was saying. Jerry attended his local school but often was placed in classes that included only students with developmental delays. At school and at home, he had been generally well behaved; however, his behavior was changing, and he was becoming increasingly noncompliant with his teachers and his mother and getting into trouble in other ways. At home, Jerry would resist doing his homework and yell at his mother when she would try to get him to help around the house. I worked with Jerry's mother, Alice, to identify important goals (e.g., more independence for Jerry) and to define his problem behaviors (e.g., not following requests from his mother, yelling, throwing things).

To try to determine how often Jerry's behaviors were a problem at home, I asked Alice to keep a record of these incidents. Alice showed some hesitancy about this, so we discussed it further. She told me that with her other children at home and her other demands, she was not sure she could keep good records. As we went over the options I suggested that she try using what is called a scatter plot.[1] A scatter plot is a fairly simple way to record when problems occur and also can provide a little information about why behaviors might be happening. This recording method is not as detailed as the ABC chart described previously, but it still can be a helpful tool. Because the scatter plot requires just simply noting when a problem occurs, Alice didn't have to stop what she was doing to write down a narrative. She seemed pleased with this, so we decided to give it a try. So that Alice didn't have to take the time to write down which of Jerry's behaviors she was documenting, we decided that she would use two scatter plots

ALICE'S SCATTER PLOT: JERRY'S NONCOMPLIANCE

Time of day	Day of the week													
	Monday	Tuesday	Wednesday	Thursday	Friday	Saturday	Sunday	Monday	Tuesday	Wednesday	Thursday	Friday	Saturday	Sunday
7:00 a.m.	X	X	X	X	X			X	X	X	X	X		
7:30	X	X	X	X	X			X	X	X	X	X		
8:00														
8:30														
9:00														

(From Touchette, P., MacDonald, R., & Langer, S. [1985]. A scatter plot for identifying stimulus control of problem behavior. *Journal of Applied Behavior Analysis, 18*[4], 344; adapted by permission.)

(which were kept on the refrigerator): one to record Jerry's noncompliance and the other to record his yelling and throwing things. To use the plots, Alice simply put an X in the box indicating the time and day a behavior occurred. The examples shown here provide a look at some of the information Alice recorded over a 2-week period. Although the examples only include her records for the morning period, Alice actually collected this information all day and into the evening.

ALICE'S SCATTER PLOT: JERRY'S YELLING AND/OR THROWING

Time of day	Day of the week													
	Monday	Tuesday	Wednesday	Thursday	Friday	Saturday	Sunday	Monday	Tuesday	Wednesday	Thursday	Friday	Saturday	Sunday
7:00 a.m.	X													
7:30			X											
8:00														
8:30														
9:00						X	X						X	X

(From Touchette, P., MacDonald, R., & Langer, S. [1985]. A scatter plot for identifying stimulus control of problem behavior. *Journal of Applied Behavior Analysis, 18*[4], 344; adapted by permission.)

It is important to note that Alice told us that keeping track of Jerry's behaviors using a scatter plot was fairly easy to do. By keeping the charts on her refrigerator, she was constantly reminded to check them off if something happened that day. And, because there really was no writing involved other than marking boxes, she found that she could do it even if she was otherwise busy. The second point to note is that Jerry engaged in some form of noncompliance every weekday morning, but his yelling and throwing were more inconsistent. Again, these patterns will be helpful for us later when we try to decipher just why Jerry might be acting this way. I will return to both Jerry's case and Brian's case (for which we used the ABC chart) in the next section.

Appendix A shows blank ABC Chart and a Scatter Plot forms. However, there are probably an unlimited number of formats you could use to keep track of your child's behaviors, and I encourage you to be creative. For example, if you have trouble keeping records all day long, you can probably take just a sample. If, like Alice, you know that weekday mornings are almost always a problem, you may want to pick just 2–3 days per week to keep records or just collect information during times when you know your child's behavior will be a problem (e.g., at mealtimes, when asked to go to bed, when coming home from school). This type of sampling can be easier, and you can still compare it to a later time (e.g., your child's behavior at bedtime before and after you try a new approach).

I described just these two types of recording forms—the ABC chart and scatter plot—because they typically provide enough information to help us understand why your child might be misbehaving. Feel free to develop your own method, however, as long as you follow the steps of assessing goals for your child and defining just what the problem behaviors look like. The fourth, and perhaps most important, step (once you have set goals for your child, defined the problem behaviors, and started to keep track of them) is to try to figure out why the behaviors are occurring. This question is addressed in the following section.

UNDERSTANDING WHY

An essential part of the process of helping your child behave better is to discover *why* your child may be engaging in problem behaviors. Understanding why is the key to unlocking a treasure trove of techniques that have been found to be very effective with even the most intractable problems. I have been fortunate in my professional career to have participated in some of the research that has uncovered these causes, and I describe some of this work in this chapter. It may be helpful, however, to revisit the case of Timmy that I described in some detail in the beginning of Chapter 1 to see why he might have been so disruptive and what we might have done with him all of those years ago had we known then what we know now.

Remember that Timmy was the young boy diagnosed with autism who would frequently bite himself and bite or hit others. My first introduction to Timmy was more than 3 decades ago, and back then we knew very little about why children and adults would behave in the manner that Timmy did. Our approach was a simple one—try to reward him when he was being good and either ignore him when he acted up (a very difficult thing to do when someone is hitting you) or use some form of punishment when he misbehaved. If you remember, we used a brief trial of punishment with Timmy—using a ruler to spank him—that proved ineffective and also was traumatizing to a number of us (and perhaps also to him) at the time.

The reason why none of these approaches was very effective was that we were guessing at which of our reactions would be reinforcing for Timmy and which would be punishing. We were looking at his world through our eyes instead of through his. We thought, for example, that if we praised him when he was working that he would like that. Don't we all like praise? Similarly, we thought that ignoring him when he hit us would be unpleasant to him. Who likes to be ignored? We were probably wrong. With hindsight, it is clear to see that Timmy probably did not like our praise and preferred to be ignored. Our educational plans and treatments were based on what we liked and disliked, and we were not able to get inside his head to see what it was like for him.

These kinds of apparent contradictions—in Timmy's case, perhaps liking to be ignored and disliking praise—have led some people to believe that certain people like to be punished. Don't some people report liking pain? Aren't there people who act in self-destructive ways—smoking and drinking too much or engaging in risky sexual behavior? If that is the case, then perhaps people like Timmy are hitting themselves because they like the pain or are trying to punish themselves. If you follow this idea, should we encourage Timmy to work by biting him? Obviously not.

This notion of liking pain or punishment is wrong. I can say unequivocally that people do not go out of their way to receive pain or to punish themselves. First of all, from a purely technical perspective, people do not encourage punishment because the definition of punishment is a thing or event (called a consequence) that will reduce the likelihood that one will engage in a behavior again. So, for example, if you accidently put your hand on a hot burner on the stove, the pain associated with that will make it much less likely that you will put your hand on the stove again. In that case, the heat and pain from touching the stove acts as a punishment. That is the technical definition. In addition, if there is any truism in psychology, it is this: People do not behave to get punished; they behave the way they do to get reinforced. Then why would someone act in ways that seem to be painful? Why would Timmy bite his hand? Wouldn't that be painful and, therefore, a punishment? Why would someone who is a masochist have someone hit them? Isn't that painful and therefore a punishment? Why would your child misbehave if he or she knows you will yell?

Again—people act the way they do to get things they want or need (reinforcement). So, then, what is the reinforcement in masochism? If you have not guessed already, the reinforcement in masochistic sexual behavior is sexual arousal. For a variety of reasons, people who are masochists have been conditioned to become aroused under certain circumstances when they are hit or restrained. What they like is the arousal, which is pleasurable, and also the anticipation of future sexual behavior. One would not, for example, find masochists who sit at home putting their hand on the hot burner on the stove. Again, it is not the pain but what is associated with the situation around the painful experience.

So, what does this tell us about people like Timmy? What it suggests is that Timmy did not bite himself because he liked the pain. It means that biting got him something he wanted. What could he have wanted that would cause him to go to such extremes? In retrospect, it is impossible to say for sure, but I have my suspicions. For example, Timmy would not bite himself if he was left alone. If he was allowed to sit by himself playing with something he liked, he would not bite his hand. He would, however, reliably bite himself if he was pushed to do something he did not want to do. For example, I can remember back to my first encounter with him and his mother. They were sitting across from each other, and his mother was trying to get Timmy to imitate her by saying "apple." She placed a picture of an apple in front of him and would begin the session by saying, "Timmy, what's this?" She would wait a few seconds, and if he did not answer, she would say, "This is an apple. Say 'apple.'" Spoken language for Timmy was very difficult, and he was obviously struggling. After just a few of these prompts, he would get visibly upset; if she continued, he would bite his hand, cry, and sometimes try to hit her as well. As strange as it seemed to me at the time, it makes perfect sense now. When he bit his hand, she would stop prompting him to answer and turn away from him. In our minds, Timmy's mother was trying not to give him any attention for biting himself; we all believed that attention was something Timmy liked and, therefore, turning attention away from him would serve as punishment. We were afraid that if Timmy's mother talked to him by saying things such as "Stop biting your hand Timmy," her attention would encourage him to continue biting. Our concern was that he would learn, "If you want your mother to talk to you, bite your hand."

In Timmy's world, however, things were likely just the opposite. My guess is that he was learning, "If you want your mother to stop hassling you, bite your hand." It worked! Once he bit his hand, she would stop asking him to say "apple" and would turn away from him for a period of time. He got a short break while we were thinking that he was being punished. At the same time, we found that praising Timmy really did not get him to behave better. For example, if Timmy was sitting nicely and working without being disruptive, his mother or his teacher would make a point of coming over to him and praising him enthusiastically: "You're doing a terrific job, Timmy! Nice sitting and working!" Unfortunately, this would occasionally trigger another bout of challenging behavior. Again, up was down, and down was up. Through Timmy's eyes, though, this probably all made sense.

Remember, Timmy was diagnosed with autism, a disorder that has at its core problems with socialization. What if instead of enthusiastic praise being something positive to him (e.g., I feel good that people are pleased with my work), it was negative (e.g., I am sitting here happily alone, and now someone is coming over and invading my space)? In this case, praise would be a punisher! In fact, in some of my research I did find this to be the case for students such as Timmy. I conducted a study some years ago with children like Timmy and found that they, in fact, did prefer to be left alone. So, when my colleagues and I used praise with them, they actually worked less! Yet, when we used a technique when the students were working hard such as the one Timmy's mother used—turning away—they actually worked more.[2] Praise, for them, was actually a punisher, and ignoring them served as a reinforcer. I will describe how to tell if your child is like one of the children in this study, but our study did confirm that Timmy's strange behavior made perfect sense. He bit himself to get something he liked—being left alone—and not for the pain.

This distinction is an important one for the next step in examining why your child may be misbehaving. You will be looking for what your child is getting out of acting up. Researchers in the field believe that challenging behaviors serve a purpose. If you can discover the reason or purpose of the behavior, then you can more easily decide how you should respond to it and perhaps what can be done to prevent it. To do this, it is necessary to look at the world through your child's eyes. A number of different techniques can be used to unveil the purpose of problem behavior, and I describe several of these that will be easy for you to use with your child. As I begin to explain the techniques that can be used to discover why your child misbehaves, I also present current views of problem behavior—what some of the most common purposes are for these behavior challenges.

REASONS FOR CHALLENGING BEHAVIOR

In order to find anything—you must be looking for something.

—J. S. Varela (1977, p. 921)

Early in my career, I can recall meeting with a psychologist who was supervising my clinical work. He was a senior member of the staff who was thoughtful and kind and highly regarded by everyone, including me. As we discussed a particular young man and his disruptive behaviors, my supervisor leaned over his desk and grabbed a worn wooden box. As he lifted open the top of the box, I could see hundreds of slightly yellowed 3-inch by 5-inch cards, each of which had notes scribbled in pencil. His small writing was neat, and the notes included references to research studies along with his own brief comments. He had placed dividers in the box to create sections for different types of studies. As we spoke, he flipped through the dividers, mumbling to himself, "Face hitting, face scratching, face slapping...hand biting! Here it is!" He looked pleased and passed the card to me. Over the years, he had read hundreds, if not thousands, of papers on different kinds of problem behaviors. Here was a true scholar who loved learning and cared deeply about the children and youth with whom we worked. He felt it was his obligation to keep up with all of the latest thinking in our field, and with his incredible memory, he could recall most of these writings by heart.

As I looked over the card, he regaled me with the details of the study. "In this case study, they used a time-out for hand biting in an adolescent male—just like the boy you're working with. Each time he bit his hand, they stood him up and led him over to the time-out room, where he had to stay for 10 minutes. If he was calm after 10 minutes, they let him out. If he was disruptive in any way, they extended the time in the room by 2 minutes. After a few weeks his hand biting was reduced by 70%. Why don't we give it a try?" He seemed satisfied that he found the right approach to helping my client stop biting his hand, and we soon ended our supervision session.

This small interaction epitomizes the state of the art in treatment planning for challenging behavior in the 1970s and the early 1980s. At that time, researchers studied different types of problem behaviors based on what the behavior looked like. For example, there were researchers who were experts on aggression (e.g., hitting or biting other people) and others who only studied self-injurious behaviors (e.g., hitting or biting oneself). Some researchers specialized in repetitive behaviors (e.g., flapping one's hand in front of one's face), and others looked only at problems around speech (e.g., echolalia—or repeating the speech of other people). My supervisor thought that if a 10-minute time-out worked for the hand-biting behaviors of the boy in the study described on his index card, then it would also work for the hand biting being displayed by the boy with whom I was working.

It is likely that you have figured out through some of the cases presented thus far that behavior specialists today now spend much less time on what a behavior problem looks like and much more time attempting to understand why the behavior is occurring. One child may bite his hand for a completely different reason than another child, even if they are the same age and have the same abilities and diagnoses. At the same time, one girl may scream for the same reason that a boy hits his mother. Knowing *why* a particular child is misbehaving is more helpful in developing a treatment plan than knowing *what* behavior the child is displaying. When a parent asks me, "What do I do if he grabs my hair?," the implication is that there must be one right way to respond to hair grabbing just as there must be another right way to respond to stomping feet, a different way to respond to throwing toys on the floor, and so forth. Unfortunately, the correct answer to "What do I do if he grabs my hair?" is the same answer I have tortured my own son with for many years—"It depends." In other words, how one should respond to any behavior depends more on the *why* driving the behavior than the *what*.

If you remember back to the discussion about the origins of your thoughts, I mentioned that people tend to focus on the here and now. For instance, if you are upset that your child is disrupting dinner, you likely do not have time to go to great lengths to try to connect your feelings with events that occurred in the distant past (e.g., how your family had meals together when you were young). I described that although this insight or awareness about your past and the way you look at the world now are important, this type of analysis would take a great deal of time. And, because you need to make relatively rapid changes in the way you think to help your child, we instead examine how events that are happening *now* affect you.

In the same way, it is important to examine what influences your child's misbehavior by looking mostly at what is happening now or in the not-so-distant past (e.g., last week or last month). Do early experiences affect how your child behaves now? Yes. However, can you change the past? No. You can, however, change the future. From a practical (and I would argue optimistic) perspective, you can look to see what is currently affecting your child's behavior and then try to modify the things you can change (i.e., "...accept the things

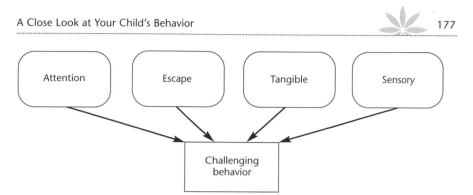

Figure 6.1.   A simple model of challenging behavior.

I cannot change; courage to change the things I can; and wisdom to know the difference").

A great deal of research since the early 1980s points to a very simple but powerful model for changing challenging behavior—a way of looking at behavior problems that can lead to important treatment approaches. The basis of this model is a simple question to ask about each behavior: "What is the child trying to tell us with this behavior?" Behavior problems serve a purpose for the child, and the parents' and professionals' job becomes one of trying to understand those purposes. Figure 6.1 illustrates one part of the model used to figure this out. I describe each part of this model in this section.

One way to look at behavior problems such as tantrums, aggression, or noncompliance is as a way for children to communicate their wants and needs. For example, crying is often the only way infants can let their parents know what they want. They cry when they are hungry, when they are cold or wet, and even if they just want someone near them. In fact, some parents are experts at reading the messages in their child's cries. At the same time, older children may use screaming in a store or hitting another child to communicate things that they cannot get any other way. A large and growing body of research in the field of behavior problems suggests that many of these difficulties can be looked at as a form of communication and that behavior problems in children can be reduced by teaching them better ways to communicate.[3]

Our research and that of others who work with people who have special needs points to several common messages that children seem to communicate through their behavior problems. Understanding what a child is communicating with his or her behavior is at the heart of any treatment plan designed to help a child with this difficulty. The top boxes in the figure represent some of the more common messages.

Attention

Attention from others is a common desire of many children and is one of the important messages. For most children, talking to a parent or friend, getting hugs, or even just being near others is something they work hard to achieve. Although some children quickly learn the ability to get attention from others in positive ways (e.g., smiling, asking "Can I play with you?"), others take a different route and use negative behaviors. Through screaming or other behaviors, some children are very successful in focusing attention on themselves. For example, I was once asked to consult on a child's behavior problems and went to his school to observe him in his classroom. As I walked into the lobby of the school, I was asked to check in and tell the woman at the desk which room I wanted to visit. I was embarrassed to say that I had forgotten and couldn't remember the teacher's name, either. As I fumbled through my briefcase for my notes, I heard a teacher yelling at a child in a nearby classroom. "I told you to sit down!" I looked at the administrative assistant in front of me and said, "That's the class. That's the class I'm supposed to be observing."

That one little clue not only helped me to quickly pick out which classroom I needed to go into but also helped me to know that the behavior problem of the child in question was probably attention getting. The teacher's yelling directed me to where the classroom was, and the fact that the teacher was yelling made me believe that the child was being very successful in getting that teacher's attention. This is an important example because it should remind us that some children would prefer even something that seems unpleasant—such as yelling—over being ignored.

As odd as it may sound that some children would prefer being yelled at over being ignored, it is actually very common. One parent relayed the story of her son's whining and constant demands and how these behaviors could escalate into a full-blown tantrum. "He is always whining about something," she told us. She seemed completely frustrated and defeated by his behavior. "Sometime I lose it and scream at him. I know this isn't good, but he almost seems to be baiting me to yell at him." "Why don't you keep a record of this?" we asked. "This way, we can get a good idea about what might be causing him to be so whiny." We asked her to keep a record of his whining using an ABC chart to see whether some patterns might exist. So that it would not be too difficult for her, we had her complete the chart just for one afternoon and bring it back to us at our next meeting. When we next got together, we took a look at the chart together and discussed it. "Did you see any patterns?" we asked. "No, not really." She shook her head and put her hand over her forehead. Her ABC chart follows. Do you see any patterns in the chart?

What you should notice first is what you do *not* see—you do not see the child whining when his mother was attending to him directly. The mother does not record any whining while she is playing with him, watching the video with him, or coloring with him. The second thing you should notice is that although whining occurred in different situations, they all had one thing in common: His mother wasn't interacting with him (e.g., when she was talking on the telephone). In addition, he would stop whining if she put down what she was doing

ABC CHART FOR A CHILD'S WHINING AND DEMANDS

Day and time	ANTECEDENTS What was happening just before your child's behavior problem?	BEHAVIOR Write down the behavior(s) as well as the number of times and/or how long they occurred.		CONSEQUENCES How did you or others react to the episode?
Sunday, 1:20 p.m.	He was watching his video, and I went to put the laundry in the machine.	He was whining that he couldn't hear the TV.	A minute or so	I came back and turned up the volume.
Sunday, 2:15 p.m.	He was playing with his sister and I was paying some bills.	He was crying about a toy she had.	2 minutes	I came over and talked to both of them about how to share.
Sunday, 2:20 p.m.	I went back to paying the bills, and they got in another fight about a toy.	He was crying.	About a minute	I came over and told them that if they didn't share nicely, then I was going to take the toy away.
Sunday 3:00 pm	I was on the telephone with my sister.	He started whining that he was hungry.	10 minutes	I had just given him a snack and told him we would eat later. He kept whining and I yelled at him. Then I felt guilty and colored with him for awhile.

and played or otherwise interacted with him. Now you might be thinking, "Well, she can't be with her child all of the time!" That's true. The first job is to find out why a child is misbehaving without judging whether it's the child's or anyone else's fault.

Another interesting thing about this chart is that the child never says, "Mom, can you come here?" He says things such as "I can't hear the TV!" or "I'm hungry." Sometimes the messages are not always what they seem on the surface. For example, I remember an incident when my son was almost 2 and he was being quite fussy. I asked him what he wanted, and he told me "milk." After getting him a glass of milk, he did not look satisfied and said, "No want milk; want water!" A glass of water still didn't satisfy him, and he said, "Want milk!" Milk, water, which was it? I was frustrated, and so was he. After going through this several times, it dawned on me that he probably did not want something to drink at all but instead just wanted to spend some time with me. He didn't know how to initiate and carry on a sophisticated conversation (e.g., "Dad, would you please come over here and spend some time with me?"), so he used his demanding requests to engage me. I was able to reduce both of our frustration during future episodes by remembering what was really motivating him and using that as a cue to spend some time with him.

When I speak with groups of parents about this message, I often point out that there is a signal in every home that alerts children to request attention. Any guesses? It is the telephone. Did you ever wonder why it is that your children can seem to play for hours with no problem but start making requests or getting into some form of trouble as soon as the telephone rings? A ringing telephone is a reliable signal that you will not be paying any attention to them for a time; without even thinking about it, it can cause them to realize that your attention is something they want.

Remember, your first task will be to figure out which of the messages seem to be important for your child's behavior problems. In no way is this a judgment of you or your child. It is simply a way to figure out whether any patterns exist to help determine why your child might be misbehaving. Also remember that your child could be whining (or doing any other disruptive thing) for a completely different reason than the one in the example I just described.

Escape

A second message that is seen quite frequently among children is escape from things that they find unpleasant. In other words, some children misbehave to get out of doing things that they do not like. For example, one child who was diagnosed with autism kept hitting his teacher, and she asked for some advice on how to make him stop. During one class, I watched them as they worked together to try to determine what message he was sending with his hitting. His teacher was working with him on sight vocabulary (i.e., learning to identify written words) and held up two cards, one of which had the word *car* written on it and the other which had the word *truck*. She was a very good teacher and showed both a great deal of enthusiasm as well as patience. "Point to the word *car*, Alex." She smiled at him and waited for him to point to the correct card. Instead, he leaned over and slapped her in the face. Her response was to very calmly ask him to stand up and sit alone in the corner. In her mind, she thought she was punishing him for hitting her; in fact, she told me that she felt guilty about using this "time-out program."

After his 10 minutes in the corner were up, Alex's teacher very calmly led him back to his chair and sat across from him again. With no hint of resentment or anger at being hit, she smiled and said, "Point to the word *car*, Alex." Once again, he hit her, and once again, she put him in the corner. As he waited there, she admitted that this program did not seem to be working; in fact, sometimes he would hit her again on the way back to the task. I asked her if I could step in for her, and she agreed. After the 10-minute time-out, I took Alex by the hand myself and led him over to the same chair. After we had settled down, I picked up the two cards and said, "Point to the word *car*, Alex." He hesitated a moment, looking back and forth at me and his teacher who was standing over to one side. Then, as if he had made his decision, he leaned over and slapped me on the side of my face. He stood up, as if he was ready to go over to the corner! "No," I said. "Sit down. Point to the word *car*, Alex." Quickly, I took his finger and prompted him to point to the right picture. When he did, I led him over to the corner so he could sit for 10 minutes. His teacher looked astounded and a bit confused. "That's not how the plan goes. You are doing it all wrong." Was I?

What I could see happening between Alex and his teacher was a classic case of escaping, and later avoiding, something unpleasant. Although I could not tell what about the task he did not like, it was clear that he did not want to be there. In his teacher's mind, she was being very positive and trying to make the task pleasant. If he happened to hit her, she would remove her positive attention and "make" him sit alone. From Alex's point of view, however, the scene played out very differently. Again, something about the task was unpleasant, but Alex was learning that if he hit the teacher, she would stop the task and let him have a 10-minute break by himself. Being allowed to stop working and instead sit away from his desk was exactly what he wanted! He learned that the way to get out of doing any schoolwork was to hit his teacher. In fact, the additional clue was that he started hitting the teacher as she was bringing him back to work. For him, this was perfect: "I don't even have to go all the way back to my seat. If I hit her, I just get another 10 minutes off!"

School principals and guidance personnel find this view of certain behaviors fascinating. It is common practice in schools to send a student to the principal's office if he or she is misbehaving in class. For some students, this can be embarrassing and cause a great deal of fear that parents will be called. However, for others, this is the perfect "punishment." A student who is bored in class or otherwise hates what is going on (e.g., a test) just needs to act up and gets to leave. When I speak with school administrators about this, they typically start to take furious notes at this time; the very thing they think they are using as a punishment may actually be making the problem worse!

Sometimes, children act up to get out of doing things that are too difficult for them. Other times, the requests they are trying to escape with their misbehavior may be for things that are too monotonous and mundane; in short, the child may be bored. Whatever the reason for wanting to escape, it is important to look for escape from demands as a message and use that to help the child with this problem. One family described to us how their daughter would misbehave at the dinner table. "When we try to get her to eat dinner at the table, she cries. But even when she stops crying, she will do things like drop her food on the floor. Once, she spilled a glass of milk, but I could swear she did it on purpose." Again, for these parents, we asked them to record several weeks' worth of these incidents and try to get her to eat at the table. We also asked them to write down what happened if she was allowed to eat somewhere else (usually in front of the television in the family room). When the family finished their recording, they were able to see a clear pattern. "I didn't realize it until now, but it seems that she will also act up in the family room. The only time she doesn't act up is if she is eating alone! I never realized it. It isn't the dinner table that is the problem. It's us!"

In other words, a child may act out to escape from attention rather than (or in addition to) escaping from demands. The message may not be "I don't want to do that" but instead it may be "I want to be alone." Often, children with autism hit themselves or others to be left alone. Although researchers do not fully understand what makes it unpleasant for these children to be around other people, it is critical to know that their behavior problems are occurring for this reason. Some children without autism also may misbehave to avoid being around people they do not like or to escape from unpleasant conversation (e.g., "Sit up in your chair," "Wipe your mouth," "How was school today?"). Knowing whether a child is acting up to get attention or to avoid attention is important to discern to help these children be better behaved.

One mother described her interactions with her teenage son this way.

I feel like he doesn't like us. He holes up in his room, which makes it difficult to carry on any type of conversation. We have gotten to the point that we do not talk unless we absolutely have to. I know this isn't good for our relationship, but it is just too difficult. The other day, for example, I knocked on his door, and from inside I heard, "Yes?" It was in that tone of voice that makes you feel as if you are asking him to do you a big favor by talking. I told him to open the door because I will not talk to him through the door. After a minute, his door creaked open—just a crack—and he repeated the impatient "Yes?" "I need you to take out the garbage," I told him. He rolled his eyes and closed the door. Eventually, he emerged and took it out, but I felt as if this was a major chore for him. You start to wonder, "What is he doing in there?" Occasionally, I check when he's at school just to make sure there are no bomb-making materials or needles!

This mother is describing how her son avoids interactions. As we discussed her situation, it became clear that part of the problem was that they only talked about unpleasant things. Because of his reluctance to engage in any long or meaningful conversations, his parents typically just communicated requests (e.g., "Take out the garbage") or mentioned topics tinged with anxiety (e.g., "Have you done your homework?" "Did you call back your friend?"). All of these questions and requests seemed to set off unpleasant interactions. The son was avoiding and escaping from conversations because the vast majority of them were unpleasant.

It is helpful to point out that when researchers look at newly married couples, they can predict with some accuracy which couples will and will not get divorced later. Research by John Gottman suggests that the "magic ratio is 5 to 1—five positive comments for every negative one."[4] In other words, if spouses are critical of each other and make more than one negative comment for every five positive ones, they are likely to split. There are no comparable studies for parents and their children, although this may be a good benchmark. If you find that most of your interactions are negative, that may explain why your child is trying to escape. Escape messages are common in children with challenging behavior, and I cover how to respond to these problems and how to prevent them from occurring in the future.

Tangible

Sometimes, the goal of a child's misbehavior is to get some thing or activity he or she likes. Behavior problems that occur to get things, or tangibles, are quite common and can be seen on almost a daily basis in any supermarket or toy store. I usually dislike food shopping (my wife says it's because I still think bread should cost about 50 cents), but occasionally I do go by myself. To make it a bit more interesting, I will wait outside of the store until a parent and a young child enter ahead of me. I like to watch their interactions—you can always learn something new. (It occurs to me at times that because many states now have stalking laws, I need to be careful!) As we enter the supermarket, the first section of the store typically contains produce. In this part of the store, most children are little angels. You can watch parents trying to educate their children about all sorts of things. "What's this honey?" "That's lettuce, Mommy." "That's right! Very good! And what color is the lettuce?" "Green?" "Very good!" Other adults are looking on with affection and admiration at these types of heartwarming interactions, but I'm more interested in what is to come. As I do my shopping, I also keep an eye on the mother and child. Soon, we are both going down the cereal aisle (I try not to be too obvious), and I can hear the little girl ask her mother for a box of cereal. "I want the Cocoa Puffs." "No honey, no Cocoa Puffs today." "I want the Cocoa Puffs!" You start to hear the anxiety in the mother's voice, nicely masked by her attempt to be polite to her daughter. "No, honey—we have three boxes at home and you don't like Cocoa Puffs." "I want *that* Cocoa Puffs!" Logic is obviously failing, so the mother pushes the cart just a little bit faster to get to the next aisle. I follow along, trying not to be spotted.

The next section of the store is where the trip really starts to be educational—the dreaded candy aisle. I usually hang back in adjacent aisles so I can hear. "I want a Snickers." "No honey, chocolate is not good for you." "I want Snickers!" The daughter is now screaming. "Honey, you know that sugar makes you hyperactive!" Now the mother's voice is starting to rise in pitch, and the daughter is becoming more insistent. I can hear that the mother is pushing the cart even faster in hopes of making it to a safe zone (maybe housewares?). Soon, I can tell that the daughter is on the floor kicking and screaming. As I turn the corner, however, I can see the daughter has stopped crying and is munching on something—the Snickers bar.

These types of interactions have been described from the parent's perspective (e.g., feelings of anxiety and panic, thoughts about being judged by others and of being an inadequate parent). What, however, is going on here from the child's perspective? Obviously, this little girl wanted Cocoa Puffs and, later, a Snickers bar. She could even say it—something not all children can do. But when her mother would not give her what she asked for, the daughter used another form of communication—her screaming and her tantrum (kicking and flailing around on the floor). It is almost as if the little girl is saying to her mother, "Perhaps you didn't understand me the first time. I really do want the Snickers bar!" For the mother, this screaming began to trigger all of those pessimistic thoughts and, despite knowing she should not be giving her daughter the candy bar when she was misbehaving, in her mind she had little choice: Deal with all of the negatives associated with a tantrum or give in and have peace.

I once witnessed a similar scene between a mother and perhaps the most perceptive and insightful little boy I have ever seen. It began in the same way as the shopping trip with the little girl and her mother. This cute, adorable little boy—no more than 3 years old—was nicely holding his mother's hand walking around the store; however, as soon as they got to an aisle with toys, he began demanding one. "I want the truck!!!" His mother was doing her best to completely ignore him and started walking away. "I want the truck! I want the truck! I want the truck!" Again, the mother kept moving away trying to look as if this was not bothering her. Then, in a flash of brilliance, the boy sat down on the floor and started yelling at the top of his lungs, "Don't hit me, Mommy! Don't hit me!" You could almost hear people in the store looking up the telephone number for child protective services. The mother quickly scooped him up (along with the truck) and tried to disappear into the masses.

These scenes demonstrate cases of behaviors that are tangibly motivated—acting up to get things you want. In addition to toys or foods, the thing a child may want could be an activity. For example, being told he cannot go outside because it is raining may cause a child to become aggressive because he is being denied this favorite activity. Why do children continue to act this way? Because, similar to the other just-mentioned messages, sometimes the negative behaviors work! Cry enough in a supermarket and your parent is likely to give in and give you what you want. Unfortunately, this giving in will increase the chance that the child will cry again the next time he or she really wants something. But giving in is also understandable considering the pressures parents are under. Fortunately, there are good ways of dealing with these types of problems. I explore ways to avoid these situations with your child later in this chapter.

Sensory

The final message is somewhat different from those just covered and, in a sense, is not a form of communication at all. Here, the goal is sensory feedback—the child acts in a particular way because it looks, feels, tastes, or sounds good to do it. In other words, the behavior itself is pleasant in some way to the child, and he or she keeps doing it because the sensory input is enjoyable. A child who rocks back and forth for hours at a time may be doing this just because it feels good and not because he or she wants attention, escape, or tangibles. Sometimes, children with severe disabilities will hit themselves lightly but constantly, which may be because of the sensory feedback it provides them. Knowing that a behavior is occurring for sensory reasons is important, because it indicates that simply ignoring the behavior will not work. In fact, being ignored and not having anything else with which to occupy themselves can be at the heart of why children act in ways to keep themselves stimulated. Other behavior plans such as time-out (e.g., removing the child to a corner of the classroom) also will be ineffective if the child is not misbehaving to get attention but rather just because of the way it feels.

Are these the only reasons why children misbehave? No. There are many things that influence whether your child will have a bad day or act up in a particular situation. What is important to point out is that these messages are at the heart of most problem behaviors and are also aspects of the behavior problems that can be changed quite readily. Consider the example that follows.

A father once told me that, in general, his son was very well behaved. Getting his son ready for school was the father's job, and it usually went pretty well. His son didn't like to wear certain clothes and sometimes would resist a bit (perhaps escape behavior), but eventually he would get dressed. Occasionally, if the boy's father became distracted with a telephone call, his son would pick that time to want to talk to him (maybe attention getting), but all that his father had to say was "Give me just a minute" and his son would wait patiently. If there was dessert from the previous night's dinner in the house, his son sometimes whined a bit to have that for breakfast (tangible), but a simple "No, you know that's not for breakfast" would suffice to move on to a healthy meal. On some mornings, however, the scenario was quite different. Occasionally, when getting dressed in the morning, his son would get very upset if he had to wear something he did not like and would voice his objections loudly (e.g., "I hate that shirt! It's too itchy."). A telephone call on these mornings would be a signal for a great deal of clinginess on the part of his son. Being told he couldn't have chocolate cake would trigger big tears and screaming. "Why," this father asked, "does my son have such a difficult time with these things on some days and not others? The reason for this type of inconsistency is related to the concept of "setting events"—which is discussed next.

Setting Events

Clearly, factors other than those already listed influence whether a child misbehaves. Behavioral scientists sometimes refer to these other factors as *setting events* (or the even more technical term *motivating operations*). Simply put, setting events are factors or conditions that change how things such as attention, escape, tangibles, or sensory influences affect a person. In the case just described, perhaps the son might have been getting sick or did not have a good night's sleep the night before. Both of these conditions (i.e., illness and fatigue) are examples of setting events. In other words, if the son was tired and irritable in the morning because he did not sleep well, having to wear a shirt that was uncomfortable may have felt more difficult than usual for him, making him try harder to escape. Not having his father's undivided attention may have been even more unbearable on this day, causing his son to act clingy. Wanting something (e.g., the chocolate cake) he could not have may have been that much more stressful because the child was not feeling well.

Before I point out some of the more important and prevalent setting events that my colleagues and I look for in children, it is essential that I make something clear. Simply being tired or sick, under normal circumstances, does not make a child cry and scream. Note that in the case I mentioned, the son acted up to escape (i.e., not wear a certain shirt), get attention (i.e., when his father was ignoring him), and get tangibles (i.e., dessert for breakfast). Being tired or sick just made these situations a bit more unbearable; therefore, the child acted up. This is what is meant by a setting event. As I show in Figure 6.2, the setting events lead to the messages, which in turn lead to the behavior problems.

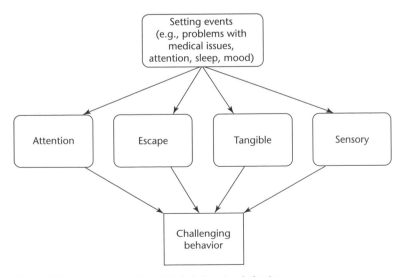

Figure 6.2. An expanded model of challenging behavior.

It is good that setting events in and of themselves do not cause behavior problems, because sometimes it is not possible to change the setting event. If a child is ill, for example, does that mean that the parent cannot do anything about the behavior problem until the child feels better? No. What my colleagues and I have found over and over again is that we can help children to be better behaved *despite* some of the setting events. We can help them with their messages to let us know what they may need or want even though they might be tired or irritable. This is important for many families to hear and learn. I often experience situations in which a family is waiting to deal with problem behavior until some other issue gets resolved. "He has been having ear infections, so we are waiting to see if he needs any surgery before we work on his crying." "Her school situation is so chaotic that we are going to delay the behavior plans until things settle down." There is no reason to delay. You can go ahead with the plans I outline without waiting until "things settle down." Things will never "settle down" (sorry!). We certainly will want to wait until *you* are ready—when you have confidence in your abilities—but your child is ready now.

Whenever we work with a child who has behavior challenges, especially behaviors that are new or that have recently become much worse, we look to see if there might be a medical issue contributing to the child's problems. We always try to rule out physical causes for behavior problems. Although it is relatively rare for a medical problem to be the cause of your child's misbehavior, overlooking this possibility can lead to a frustrating situation that could have been avoided. It is important to point out again, however, that although medical problems can make behavior problems worse, they usually are not the sole cause of a child's difficulties. This means that even if you find a medical problem and can cure the illness, it may not lead to the complete elimination of the behavior that is so disruptive.

With regard to a potential medical problem, what should you look for? Any illness that causes pain, for example, may be at the bottom of an increase in problems. An ear infection, headache, or stomachache will make your child more irritable, which in turn will make him or her more likely to have problems. Children with special needs often are more prone to physical problems; therefore, it is important to be more vigilant with the children in looking for a possible medical condition contributing to misbehavior. For example, a child who uses a wheelchair and cannot shift his or her position can get extremely uncomfortable after only a few minutes of sitting, and this can cause fussiness and anger outbursts. Simply shifting the child in his or her seat periodically may help reduce behavior problems. In general, children who are not verbal or who do not express themselves well often cannot tell you when they are in pain; therefore, a complete physical examination may be in order, especially if a child has a sudden increase in behavior problems.

As an example of how a medical condition can contribute to behavior problems, I once worked with a young woman who was having sporadic bouts of aggression. Her parents and teachers were doing a good job keeping track of her outbursts, but the behavior was difficult to predict. Getting up in the morning, for example, was usually fine; yet, during some weeks, it would be a major battle. Similar problems were occurring at school. She could go for weeks being very well behaved but then have a stretch of time during which if you placed demands on her she would hit you. We worked out that these behaviors were likely to be escape messages (e.g., "Leave me alone!"), but we could not determine why they would occur during certain time periods and not others. I then asked her parents if she had allergies. They said she did but seemed puzzled about why I had asked. Finally, we figured out that she likely was not sleeping well during certain seasons when she was reacting to pollen and mold and that this may have been contributing to her outbursts. We used her problem behavior as an "early warning system" about when she was having problems with allergies and—with the help of her physician—were able to adjust her medications accordingly. In turn, this along with our behavior plan for her escape messages greatly reduced her aggression.

Although not technically a medical problem, some children are very impulsive by nature, which can lead to a number of difficulties. Children with ADHD, for example, sometimes blurt out the first thing that comes to mind, stop playing in the middle of a game to move on to something else, or do not finish cleaning their room because they are distracted by some other interesting activity. These types of behaviors can frustrate teachers, friends, and family members and can have some rather negative long-term consequences. Teachers may only give these children negative feedback (e.g., "Would you sit down!"), which can eventually make the child feel quite bad about himself or herself. Friends may reject such a child, which can stunt the development of good social skills. Family members also can begin to see the child as only a bother and may feel too drained at the end of the day to give the child much "quality time." It is important to remember that these types of behaviors by the child are not intentional acts aimed at annoying people but rather are the result of the child's difficulty reining in his or her impulses. I discuss how you can help such a child gain more control over these impulses in Chapter 8.

One area that parents often have trouble understanding is the limit of their child's attention span. What some parents consider noncompliance sometimes simply can be a difficulty on the part of the child remembering what he or she was supposed to do. For example, asking a young child in the middle of a television program to clean his room during the next commercial is an invitation to disaster. By the time the commercial rolls around, the parent's request likely is out of mind; the fact that the child did not clean his room probably is just a difficulty in remembering rather than deliberate noncompliance. If the parent waited for the commercial to start to make the request (e.g., "While the commercial is on, I want you to go into your room and put your dirty clothes in the hamper"), the child would be more likely to cooperate. In addition to young children, some older children with special needs also may have difficulty with this skill. Look to see whether this might be the cause of your child's behavior problem and, if so, try to make requests 1) that are clear (e.g., "Put your shoes in your closet" versus "Clean up this mess") and, 2) that can be completed immediately (e.g., "Put your dishes in the sink" versus "Put your books away when you come home from school").

Another common contributing factor to behavior problems is fatigue. A lack of sleep can influence your child's behavior throughout the day. You probably know from your own experience that having a bad night's sleep can cause you to be irritable. The things that happen to you during the day may, in turn, start to be seen in a different light. For example, the person in front of you in the checkout line at the store who is taking forever to find a misplaced coupon may be tolerable when you are well rested but may start to make you crazy when you are not. Dirty clothes on the bedroom floor may be an inconvenience on a good day but may be the source of marital strife after a bad night's sleep. In the same way, your child may be affected by poor sleep as well. Both parents and teachers often say that this pattern can be puzzling: "I don't get it. He was fine doing his homework all week, but now, all of a sudden, he is giving me a hard time!" Tasks at home or at school may be seen as more demanding if a child is tired. Again, note that what the child is responding to is the homework, and he is using his misbehavior to try to escape. Remember, the child can be helped with the escape part even if it takes some time to resolve the sleep problems.

Sleep problems are very common among children with special needs; because they can play an important role in challenging behavior, I devote a full chapter, Chapter 11, to this special problem. In Chapter 11, I walk you through how to tell whether your child's sleep is disrupted, why this might be going on, and special plans for dealing with problems associated with sleep.

I once asked a teacher about a particular child in her class who was causing significant problems during the day and who was a handful at home as well. As we spoke, it was clear that the child had both good and bad days at school. "Can you tell when it will be a bad day?" I asked. "Oh yes," she smiled. She continued,

> I can tell the minute he gets off the bus what kind of day it will be. In fact, there are days when I see that look on his face and think to myself that I should have called in sick. We have a code for these days. They're called "red carpet" days. A red carpet day is a bad day. The red carpet is the place where a child sits in time-out, and I can tell by his face if it is going to be one of those days.

What this teacher could tell at a glance was the student's mood. If he bounded off the bus with a smile, he was in as good mood and it would be a good day. However, if he had the frown and came off the bus reluctantly, it was going to be a red carpet day.

As with being tired, a person's *mood* also can serve as a setting event (and, in fact, can sometimes be caused by a lack of sleep or being ill). Again, you likely know from your own experience that you can have red carpet days yourself. For a variety of reasons (known or unknown), you too have bad days, and on these days, others should probably watch out. Sometimes these moods can be short-lived, lasting only a few minutes, whereas sometimes they can last all day.

We have conducted research with children with developmental disabilities and looked at how their moods affect their behavior problems. In one study, we used mood-inducing music to influence the participants' moods.[5] We used music because its effects are universal (people from around the world respond to music in the same ways), and these students were nonverbal so they could not simply tell us the mood they were in at the time of the study. One aspect of music that influences people is the tempo. For example, playing music with a fast beat (we used the theme from the movie *Rocky*) is likely to pick up a person's mood. However, listening to music with a slow tempo is likely to make a person feel sad. If you have ever attended a funeral, you will recall that the music played is usually slow-beat music (sometimes referred to as funeral dirges). It is an odd thing, if you think about it. Here you are already sad, and the music that is played is likely to make you even sadder. I have a promise from my wife that if any music is played for me after I die, it will be fast-beat music (and some beer will be involved as well!).

In our study, we first determined why each child was misbehaving; in other words, we figured out their messages. Then, on top of that, we played either fast-beat or slow-beat music. What we found was that when the children heard the slow-beat music, we were more apt to see behavior problems in the situations that usually set them off. So, if a child was likely to get upset if we gave him a difficult task, we often saw behavior problems when we asked him to work on a task while playing the slow, sad music. However, if we asked him to work on the same task as we played the fast-beat, happier music, we saw fewer behavior problems. What seemed to be happening was that the fast-beat music put the children in a good mood, and this, in turn, seemed to help them deal with difficult situations more easily. This study showed that a person's mood can influence his or her behavior in much the same way that being tired because of a lack of sleep or being irritable does. In other words, it was a setting event for behavior problems.

Lest you run out and start recommending that everyone play only fast or upbeat music continuously for your child, we also observed that these effects were temporary. In one situation, for example, we and the student with whom we had been working were leaving the classroom after one of these sessions, and the student was in a very good mood. However, in the hall, another child made a negative comment about the way she was dressed, and that good mood vanished. I will show later how to take advantage of moods to improve behavior problems; however, it is not a cure, just as helping a child sleep better or helping with allergies will not completely eliminate problems. Setting events can influence behavior problems, but we still need to get at the child's messages to make lasting changes.

HOW TO FIND OUT WHY

If you are already familiar with the federal law about how schools should deal with children who have significant behavior challenges, you should recognize the term *functional behavior assessment*. A functional behavior assessment is simply a way to get clues as to why a particular child might be engaging in certain challenging behaviors. I have just covered some of the important things to look for (e.g., the messages the child may be attempting to send, setting events that might be affecting the messages), and now I describe a few example tools used for helping us to figure this out. At the heart of these assessments is looking for patterns. Can we find reliable patterns in why your child misbehaves, and then can we use this information to help your child behave better?

Motivation Assessment Scale

Early in my career, a colleague and I developed a rating scale called the Motivation Assessment Scale (MAS)[6] that was designed to provide an easy way to obtain information about the messages that children might be trying to send with their behavior problems. The MAS is a 16-item questionnaire that is designed to see which messages (i.e., attention, escape, tangible, sensory) seem to be involved with a child's behavior problems. Let's take a look at a few of the questions from the scale to help illustrate its design.

1. **Would the behavior occur continuously, over and over, if this person was left alone for long periods of time? (For example, several hours.)** This question is designed to see whether a child's behavior problem is occurring just for the sensory feedback it provides. So, for example, if a child likes to make noises and would do this even if she were alone in her room with no one around, this might be a sensory behavior. An important issue here is that the behavior does not seem to be a way to force people away (i.e., escape), get them to interact (i.e., attention), or get them to give the person something (i.e., tangible). Instead, it seems to occur simply because the child likes doing it. I have observed some children line up blocks for hours at a time. Others will pick up lint, hold it up to the light, and watch as it falls. Still others will do things like play with their saliva. All of these types of behaviors often occur simply because the child enjoys the activity. This first question is one of four sensory questions on the MAS.

2. **Does the behavior occur following a request to perform a difficult task?** Can you guess which of the four messages (i.e., attention, escape, tangible, sensory) this question is designed to assess? This question is designed to see whether escape (in this case, escape from demands) is at the heart of the child's problem behavior. The word *difficult* is obviously subjective (i.e., what is difficult for one child might be easy for another), but in this case it is relative to your child. If you ask your child to do something he or she does not want to do and he or she then performs the problem behavior, then you would indicate that under this question. There are a total of four escape questions on the MAS.

3. **Does the behavior seem to occur in response to your talking to other persons in the room?** This question examines whether removing your attention from your child for a time seems to trigger a behavior problem. This is similar to my telephone example, in which I explained that your child is likely to misbehave if he or she does not have your full and undivided attention. If your lack of attention to your child seems to precede his or her misbehavior, then you would indicate it under this question. Again, there are four similar questions about attention on the MAS.

4. **Does the behavior ever occur to get a toy, food or activity that this person has been told that he or she can't have?** Finally, this fourth question is designed to see whether your child is misbehaving to get something he or she wants. Sometimes, this could be a favorite object (e.g., a toy or something your child just likes to hold) that when taken away or simply unavailable seems to cause problem behaviors. Also under this category would be times when your child wants to do something—perhaps play outside—but cannot (e.g., it is raining). This question is designed to see if tangible is the message for the behavior problem; as with the other message types, four questions related to tangible are on the MAS.

Although the MAS is relatively easy to complete, several procedures should be followed before filling it out. The first thing to consider is which behavior you want to assess. Earlier in this chapter (under the section titled Defining Behaviors), I described the importance of being very specific when it comes to describing your child's behavior problems. This is very important when you begin to try to figure out why certain behaviors are happening. For example, I pointed out that the terms *tantrum, fit,* or *meltdown* are not good descriptions, in part because they could mean so many different things. When completing the MAS, it is important to tease out the separate behaviors (e.g., screaming, hitting others, stamping feet) and then complete the MAS for *each separate behavior.* Sometimes, all of the behaviors are happening for the same reason (e.g., to get your attention), but sometimes they can happen for different reasons (e.g.,

Motivation Assessment Scale

By V. Mark Durand and Daniel B. Crimmins

Name __JONATHAN__   Rater __DAN__   Date __9 / 3 / 2010__

Behavior Description __HAND BITING - ANY TIME HIS TEETH TOUCH HIS HAND__

Setting Description __DURING ONE-ON-ONE TRAINING SESSIONS__

ITEM

For each item circle one response.

RESPONSE

	Never	Almost Never	Seldom	Half the Time	Usually	Almost Always	Always
	0	1	2	3	4	5	6

1. Would the behavior occur continuously, over and over, if this person was left alone for long periods of time? (For example, several hours.) — *Seldom (2) circled*

2. Does the behavior occur following a request to perform a difficult task? — *Almost Always (5) circled*

3. Does the behavior seem to occur in response to your talking to other persons in the room? — *Half the Time (3) circled*

4. Does the behavior ever occur to get a toy, food or activity that this person has been told that he or she can't have? — *Almost Always (5) circled*

5. Would the behavior occur repeatedly, in the same way, for very long periods of time, if no one was around? (For example, rocking back and forth for over an hour.) — *Almost Never (1) circled*

6. Does the behavior occur when any request is made of this person? — *Always (6) circled*

7. Does the behavior occur whenever you stop attending to this person? — *Almost Never (1) circled*

8. Does the behavior occur when you take away a favorite toy, food, or activity? — *Almost Never (1) circled*

9. Does it appear to you that this person enjoys performing the behavior? (It feels, tastes, looks, smells, and/or sounds pleasing.) — *Never (0) circled*

10. Does this person seem to do the behavior to upset or annoy you when you are trying to get him or her to do what you ask? — *Usually (4) circled*

11. Does this person seem to do the behavior to upset or annoy you when you are not paying attention to him or her? (For example, if you are sitting in a separate room, interacting with another person.) — *Usually (4) circled*

12. Does the behavior stop occurring shortly after you give this person the toy, food or activity he or she has requested? — *Almost Always (5) circled*

13. When the behavior is occurring, does this person seem calm and unaware of anything else going on around him or her? — *Almost Never (1) circled*

14. Does the behavior stop occurring shortly after (one to five minutes) you stop working or making demands of this person? — *Almost Always (5) circled*

15. Does this person seem to do the behavior to get you to spend some time with him or her? — *Seldom (2) circled*

16. Does this behavior seem to occur when this person has been told that he or she can't do something he or she had wanted to do? — *Usually (4) circled*

SCORING

	Sensory		Escape		Attention		Tangible
1.	2	2.	5	3.	3	4.	5
5.	1	6.	6	7.	1	8.	1
9.	0	10.	4	11.	4	12.	5
13.	1	14.	5	15.	2	16.	4
Total score =	4		20		10		15
Mean score =	1.00		5.0		2.50		3.75
Relative ranking =	4		1		3		2

Figure 6.3. Sample completed Motivation Assessment Scale (MAS). (From Durand, V.M., & Crimmins, D.B. [1992]. *The Motivation Assessment Scale [MAS] administration guide.* Topeka, KS: Monaco and Associates. Reprinted by permission.)

screaming to get attention, hitting you to get you to stop making a demand). Because filling out the MAS does not take too long, I would encourage you to answer the questions separately for each behavior.

A parent asked to complete the MAS might be given the following guidance. As you start to complete the MAS, you will notice a space for setting description (see Figure 6.3). You need to decide *where* the behavior is a problem. You can refer back to the Setting Goals section of this chapter and decide where you may first want to work on a behavior problem. For example, your child may scream in many different situations, but your priorities may be at mealtimes and during toothbrushing. You would then fill out one MAS for screaming at meals and then a separate form for screaming while brushing teeth. The reason for this extra effort is the same reason for separating out the behaviors. Your child might scream at mealtime to get a favorite food (i.e., tangible) but during toothbrushing to avoid this task (i.e., escape). In this example, because screaming happens for different reasons in different places, we would actually recommend different approaches to dealing with these two different settings.

If this is all starting to make your head spin (e.g., "Do I have to fill out 50 forms?"), don't worry. Most of the time behavior problems occur for the same or similar reasons for a child. And especially because we begin with one or two problems based on your goals, this should all be very manageable. Fear not—you can do this!

Once you have decided on the behavior (e.g., screaming) and the situation that is a problem (e.g., brushing teeth), you then answer the 16 questions. Notice that the answers are not *yes* or *no* but instead require you to record about how often the behavior occurs under these conditions. See Figure 6.4 for an example of Question 2. Therefore, if the question is "Does the behavior occur following a request to perform a difficult task?" you would circle *Never, Almost Never, Seldom, Half the Time, Usually, Almost Always, or Always. Never* and *Always* are easy. But what is *Usually* or *Seldom?* The idea when completing this scale is to indicate how often the behavior occurs relative to your child. So, if your child screams every time he or she is asked to brush his or her teeth, then you would probably circle *Always.* You can look at asking your child to brush his or her teeth as a *difficult task* if that is how your child responds. However, if the misbehavior happens only about every fifth or sixth time you ask him or her to brush his or her teeth, then you might circle *Seldom.* If screaming has happened only once or twice over the course of many requests, then you would indicate *Almost Never.*

2. Does the behavior occur following a request to perform a difficult task?	Never	Almost Never	Seldom	Half the Time	Usually	Almost Always	Always
	0	1	2	3	4	5	6

Figure 6.4. Question 2 from the Motivation Assessment Scale (MAS). (From Durand, V.M., & Crimmins, D.B. [1992]. *The Motivation Assessment Scale [MAS] administration guide.* Topeka, KS: Monaco and Associates. Reprinted by permission.)

SCORING	Sensory	Escape	Attention	Tangible
	1. _0_	2. _5_	3. _1_	4. _3_
	5. _1_	6. _5_	7. _2_	8. _4_
	9. _0_	10. _4_	11. _1_	12. _6_
	13. _0_	14. _6_	15. _0_	16. _4_
Total score =	1	20	4	17
Mean score =	0.25	5.0	1.0	4.25
Relative ranking =	4	1	3	2

Figure 6.5. Motivation Assessment Scale (MAS) scores for Brian's screaming behavior. (From Durand, V.M., & Crimmins, D.B. [1992]. *The Motivation Assessment Scale [MAS] administration guide.* Topeka, KS: Monaco and Associates. Adapted by permission.)

Once you have answered all of the questions on the MAS, transfer the score from each question to the table in the scoring section at the end of the assessment. Figure 6.5 shows how Sarah, the mother of Brian (whose reports on the ABC charts appeared in the beginning of this chapter), scored the MAS for Brian. Brian's behavior problems included whining, crying, falling on the floor, and kicking and screaming. Sarah told us that the biggest problem situations were asking him to do things such as getting dressed or putting away his toys. Because her answers were similar for each of these behaviors in these settings, I am showing you just her scores for Brian's screaming.

Before discussing the interpretation of the scores, note that Sarah put the scores for each question next to the corresponding number in the table. So, you can see she answered *0* (or *Never*) to Question 1, *5* (or *Almost Always*) to Question 2, *1* (or *Almost Never*) to Question 3, and so forth. What you can see from the scoring table is that Questions 1, 5, 9, and 13 are *Sensory* questions; Questions 2, 6, 10, and 14 are *Escape* questions; Questions 3, 7, 11, 15 are *Attention* questions; and Questions 4, 8, 12, and 16 are *Tangible* questions. Sarah then added up the total score for each set of questions, calculated a mean (or average, by dividing by 4) and then indicated the rank of each. So, for Brian's screaming, you can see that *Escape* had the highest score, followed by *Tangible. Attention* and *Sensory* had relatively low scores. We usually look to see what number is the highest and whether there is a second score within about a point or so.

How would you interpret these scores? When we discussed with Sarah her answers on the MAS, she indicated that the results made a great deal of sense to her. First, it confirmed that her son Brian seemed to scream (and act up in other ways) to escape things he didn't want to do. On Question 14, for example (Does the behavior stop occurring shortly after [one to five minutes] you stop working or making demands of this person?), Sarah answered *Always* (see Figure 6.6), indicating that Brian calmed down almost immediately if his mother stopped

12. Does the behavior stop occurring shortly after you give this person the toy, food or activity he or she has requested?	Never 0	Almost Never 1	Seldom 2	Half the Time 3	Usually 4	Almost Always 5	Always ⑥
14. Does the behavior stop occurring shortly after (one to five minutes) you stop working or making demands on the person?	Never 0	Almost Never 1	Seldom 2	Half the Time 3	Usually 4	Almost Always 5	Always ⑥

Figure 6.6. Sarah's answers to Questions 12 and 14 on the Motivation Assessment Scale (MAS). (From Durand, V.M., & Crimmins, D.B. [1992]. *The Motivation Assessment Scale [MAS] administration guide*. Topeka, KS: Monaco and Associates. Adapted by permission.)

asking him to do something. But similarly, she tended to answer the tangible questions with high scores as well. For example, Sarah also answered *Always* to Question 12 (i.e., Does the behavior stop occurring shortly after you give this person the toy, food or activity he or she has requested?), suggesting that Brian also used screaming to get something he wanted (i.e., tangible). At the same time, Brian rarely if ever misbehaved this way to get attention or because screaming and yelling made him feel good (sensory).

When you complete the MAS for your child, be careful not to answer the questions with some idea in your head about what you want to see as the outcome. For example, I had one teacher complete the MAS on a child's behavior problem (i.e., hitting the teacher) in class. When the teacher handed me the completed form, I noticed that his answers were very unusual. He had answered all of the attention questions with *Always* and all of the rest of the questions with *Never*. I asked him about this because the usual pattern is never that clear. "Well," he admitted, "I think he hits me to get attention. So I answered all of those questions with the highest scores and gave zeros to the others questions." I explained to him that it is best not to complete the MAS in this manner. As you saw previously, for example, Sarah's responses to the MAS supported her guess that Brian's screaming was being used to escape situations but also pointed out something she had not though of—that Brian also screamed to get things he wanted. So, be careful as you answer these questions. Just answer them as best and as honestly as you can.

Let's look at one more example that may be helpful when using the MAS. Earlier, I described Jerry, a 15-year-old boy with PDD-NOS. His mother, Alice, told us that he had two types of problems—noncompliance (refusing to follow

SCORING	Sensory	Escape	Attention	Tangible
	1. 0	2. 6	3. 0	4. 2
	5. 2	6. 4	7. 3	8. 0
	9. 0	10. 6	11. 0	12. 2
	13. 0	14. 5	15. 1	16. 0
Total score =	2	21	4	4
Mean score =	0.5	5.25	1.0	1.0
Relative ranking =	4	1	2	2

Figure 6.7. Motivation Assessment Scale (MAS) scores for Jerry's noncompliant behaviors. (From Durand, V.M., & Crimmins, D.B. [1992]. *The Motivation Assessment Scale [MAS] administration guide.* Topeka, KS: Monaco and Associates. Adapted by permission.)

her requests) and yelling and throwing things. I asked her to complete the MAS separately for both of these behaviors: one MAS for noncompliance to her requests and another for yelling and throwing things. Alice picked the setting for Jerry's noncompliance fairly easily—these behaviors occurred whenever Alice asked Jerry to do a chore. However, picking the setting for yelling and throwing things was more difficult for her because she could not pinpoint a situation during which these behaviors typically occurred. Based on this difficulty, we decided to have Alice fill out the MAS for Jerry's yelling and throwing behaviors without specifying the setting. The scores for Jerry's noncompliance are shown in Figure 6.7. Alice's scores on the MAS were pretty clear for Jerry's noncompliance and made sense to her. Jerry would refuse to follow requests to perform chores, and his noncompliance was his way of escaping this unpleasant task. However, her scores on the MAS for Jerry's yelling and throwing were quite different. Alice's scores for these behaviors appear in Figure 6.8.

You can see that the pattern for Jerry's other problem behaviors was very different from that for noncompliance. Rather than getting high scores for *Escape*, his scores for his yelling and throwing were highest under the category for *Attention*. Alice was surprised to discover that Jerry might be yelling and

SCORING	Sensory	Escape	Attention	Tangible
	1. 4	2. 2	3. 5	4. 1
	5. 4	6. 0	7. 4	8. 0
	9. 0	10. 1	11. 5	12. 0
	13. 0	14. 1	15. 6	16. 1
Total score =	8	4	20	2
Mean score =	2.0	1.0	4.0	0.5
Relative ranking =	2	3	1	4

Figure 6.8. Motivation Assessment Scale (MAS) scores for Jerry's yelling and throwing behaviors. (From Durand, V.M., & Crimmins, D.B. [1992]. *The Motivation Assessment Scale [MAS] administration guide.* Topeka, KS: Monaco and Associates. Adapted by permission.)

throwing things to get her attention. "You, know, it has always been confusing," she told me. "Just out of the blue he would get upset. At first I thought he might be sick or in pain. Or that things at school were getting to him and that this was what was causing the problems. But once I thought about the 'triggers,' it was always when I was busy and couldn't spend time with him. He never did this when I was with him—only when he was alone. Of course, when he would do this I would sit down with him and try to talk through what was wrong. I can see this may have been his way of asking me to spend time with him."

Your answers and the scores on the MAS can give you a quick look at what your child might be telling you with his or her behavior problems. But consider this information carefully. It is important never to rely solely on these scores in starting to design a plan for dealing with behavior challenges. It is always helpful to use other methods to see whether they, too, give you the same information (e.g., the behavior problem attracts attention). In a way, this is like getting a second opinion, only it is not coming from a second doctor but rather from another way of looking for the message behind your child's behavior. Fortunately, there are other easy ways of determining what that message might be. I already briefly introduced you to two of these methods—ABC charts and scatter plots—when I discussed keeping track of your child's behavior.

ABC Chart

The ABC chart is another method you can use to determine what messages your child is trying to communicate with his or her problem behavior. I described this charting previously as a way to keep track of behavior problems, but it also can be used to find out *why* your child is misbehaving. Remember that this type of chart is referred to as an *ABC* chart because you record what was happening just before or as your child started misbehaving (the *antecedents,* or *A*), the *behavior* itself (*B*), and what happened right after the behavior occurred (the *consequences,* or *C*). Refer back to the example of Sarah's ABC chart for Brian (in the "Keeping Track of Behaviors" section of this chapter).

As with the MAS, it is important to take care with how you describe your child's behavior. In this example, Sarah included each type of behavior (i.e., whining and crying; crying, falling on the floor, kicking and screaming) when it occurred to see whether there was any distinguishable pattern. For Sarah's ABC chart, we were looking for the pattern of antecedents and consequences to see whether that pattern might provide us with information about Brian's messages. In the first instance, Brian started to whine and cry just as his mother was repeating her request to have him put his toys away. This told us that the demand (i.e., "Put your toys away") might be something unpleasant to Brian that he wants to escape. Next, we looked at the consequence—what happened as a result of Brian's whining and crying. Once Brian gave Sarah a hard time, Sarah ended up cleaning up his toys. To her, this was just easier than fighting with him. But what might have happened as a result of handling Brian's behavior this way? I hope you can see that Sarah's response to Brian's behavior likely has encouraged Brian to react to her requests by getting upset; he has learned that when he misbehaves he will not have to follow through.

Before going any further with this case, let me give you a little relationship advice. Escape messages are not just for children with challenging behavior. Adults without challenging behaviors can behave similarly. For example, if you find yourself always cleaning the dishes because no one else does but then wonder why no one helps, just look at Brian's behavior. He learned that if he did not put his toys away, eventually his mother would. We often hear from parents who report "bailing out" their spouse (e.g., doing the laundry late at night because someone forgot to put it in the washing machine as promised). This could be a learned behavior just like Brian's whining and resistance. Just something to consider!

What we are looking for with your child's behavior is similar to what we looked for with your own thoughts. We want to see whether there are any triggers to the problem behavior (i.e., antecedents) and if there are outcomes (i.e., consequences) that might be leading your child to continue to behave this way. Often, the trigger for your child's behavior (e.g., asking your child to put away toys) can become your trigger for pessimistic thinking (e.g., "This is going to be a problem"). Recognizing this connection may help you better understand your child and your own thoughts.

ALICE'S ABC CHART FOR JERRY

Day and time	ANTECEDENTS What was happening just before your child's behavior problem?	BEHAVIOR Write down the behavior(s) as well as the number of times and/or how long they occurred.		CONSEQUENCES How did you or others react to the episode?
Monday, 7:00 a.m.	I asked Jerry to put his clothes in the hamper three times.	Noncom- pliance	3 times	I put his clothes in the hamper.
Monday, 7:10 a.m.	I asked Jerry to put his towel on the hook in the bathroom.	Noncom- pliance	1 time	I put his towel away.
Monday, 7:30 a.m.	I was making breakfast in the kitchen.	Threw his shoe against the wall.	1 time	I went to see what was wrong.
Monday, 7:45 a.m.	I was on the telephone with my sister.	He started yelling.	30 seconds	I hung up quickly and asked him how he felt.

Let's go back to Jerry and his mother, Alice. Alice filled out an ABC chart for Jerry's noncompliant behavior and for his yelling and throwing things. Alice's chart appears on the previous page.

The pattern of results for Jerry's behavior problems mirrored what we saw in the results from his MAS. His noncompliance occurred as a response to being asked to do things he did not want to do. In the case here, you can see that his mother would make requests of him (sometimes several times), and he would essentially just ignore them. This was especially a problem in the morning when Jerry and his mother were getting ready for school and work. Alice was busy and would ask him to do things such as clean up his room; but, either because he did not want to do the tasks or because he had a relatively short attention span, he would ignore or forget his mother's requests and end up not completing the tasks. And, as you can see on the ABC chart, Alice ended up doing the tasks herself.

The ABC chart also confirmed what the MAS uncovered about Jerry's yelling and screaming: These behaviors typically occurred when Alice was preoccupied. As we discussed these results, Alice seemed confused. "He could just ask me to come over to him. Why doesn't he just ask? He has the words." As I will discuss later, sometimes children have the capability of communicating the things they want (e.g., Jerry's need for attention) but need help learning *how* to communicate it. In a way, children often need help getting insight into their own behavior (e.g., "I want my mother's attention") and then learning how to communicate this message in a good way rather than through their behavior problems. Just as you may have needed help to understand your own thoughts (e.g., "I don't think my child is capable of doing this") so, too, do children. The next few chapters discuss how to accomplish this.

It is important to point out that in both of these kinds of situations with Jerry, Alice would blame herself for being a "bad" parent. When Jerry wouldn't follow through on a request, Alice said she felt like a failure. At the same time, she also felt inadequate when Jerry would throw things or yell and she couldn't determine the cause. "It seems like so many parents know exactly what their child wants or needs. I remember as an infant Jerry would cry, and I couldn't tell the difference between hungry cries or discomfort. Other parents told me they could tell these things in their children. What's wrong with me?" Once again, a pessimistic way of thinking led to problems for Alice. It never occurred to Alice that maybe, through no fault of her own, Jerry's cries were simply difficult to distinguish. In other words, it was not her fault. Regardless of the origins of this problem, I needed to make clear to Alice that she was now getting a close look at Jerry's needs and wants. By looking for and finding these patterns, she was now better able to figure out what it was that Jerry needed to help himself.

Just as people sometimes complete the MAS in the wrong way (e.g., by second-guessing the answers to fit the pattern you think is occurring),

EXAMPLE OF HOW *NOT* TO COMPLETE AN ABC CHART

Day and time	ANTECEDENTS What was happening just before your child's behavior problem?	BEHAVIOR Write down the behavior(s) as well as the number of times and/or how long they occurred.		CONSEQUENCES How did you or others react to the episode?
Saturday, 9:45 a.m.	Nothing	She screamed.	3 minutes	I ignored it.
Saturday, 10:11 a.m.	Nothing	She screamed.	2 minutes	I ignored it.
Saturday, 10:22 a.m.	Nothing	She hit me.	4 times	I ignored it.
Saturday, 11:00 a.m.	Nothing	She hit me.	Once	I ignored it.

sometimes people have a difficult time completing ABC charts properly. The hypothetical ABC chart here can serve as a counterexample of how to complete the chart.

First, the good news: This chart does a good job of describing the child's different negative behaviors (i.e., screaming versus hitting). The bad news, however, is that neither the description of the antecedents (*As*) nor the consequences (*Cs*) is adequate. As far as the antecedents are concerned, it is not possible that *nothing* was happening just before the girl screamed or hit. Was she alone or with someone? Was she in the living room or the bedroom? Did someone just ask her something? Was it noisy or quiet? Did she ask for something and it was denied? Clearly, there are many things going on just before a behavior occurs, and what is going on is critical to understanding the behavior.

Similarly, let's look at the consequences. What does *I ignored it* mean? Does it mean that the parent was with the girl and walked away when the girl screamed? Or, does it mean that the girl was by herself and started to scream and the parent did not respond? These are very different types of *ignoring* and could provide clues to very different types of messages.

The key to properly completing the ABC chart is to keep in mind the messages that your child might be trying to send with his or her problem behaviors. Table 6.1 provides some guidance for what kinds of things to look for when recording antecedents and consequences. As you can see, certain antecedents and consequences are fairly common when it comes to the behavior problems of children. It is important to note, however, that this list is in no way exhaustive and there may be other things that trigger your child's behaviors. As always, be as specific as possible in your descriptions to get the best information.

Table 6.1.   Potential antecedents and consequences

Possible message	Antecedents (i.e., triggers)	Consequences
Sensory	Is your child alone or not engaged in another activity? Does your child seem disengaged with everything around him or her except for the behavior?	Is your child allowed to continue the behavior uninterrupted? Does the behavior continue for long periods of time?
Escape	Was there a request for the child to perform a task or engage in an unpleasant activity (e.g., a chore)? Did something unpleasant occur (e.g., loud noise)? Be specific about the task or unpleasant activity or occurrence.	Does your child escape or avoid the request or activity?
Attention	Was your child alone? Are you or others engaged in something else other than attending to your child?	Do you attend to the child in some way (e.g., yelling, comforting, providing explanations)? Be specific.
Tangible	Was your child told that he or she could not have some favorite thing or activity? Did you take away a favorite thing or activity? Be specific about the thing or activity that was denied or taken away.	Did your child end up getting the thing or activity?

Scatter Plot

As I described previously, the scatter plot is an easy way to keep track of your child's behavior problems; however, the chart also can be used to get clues about what might be triggering your child's behavior problems. For example, earlier in the chapter I included portions of Jerry's scatter plots for his noncompliance and yelling and throwing. Keep in mind that so far we have learned that Jerry might be noncompliant to escape from things he does not want to do (although his behaviors also may be partly a result of his short attention span). In addition, Jerry's mother, Alice, was coming to the conclusion that his yelling and throwing might be happening to get her to pay more attention to him. Let's see if there are any clues on the scatter plot.

In analyzing scatter plots, there are two important things to look for—when the behavior problem occurs and, perhaps equally as important, when it does not occur. For Jerry's noncompliance, the related scatter plot in this chapter's "Keeping Track of Behaviors" section (see p. 170) shows that this behavior problem occurred regularly in the morning during the week but not on weekends. When I questioned Alice about this, she told me that weekday mornings were when they were getting ready for school and also when she asked Jerry to help with chores. She did not typically ask for Jerry's help on weekends because it was easier for her to just do the chores herself. This pattern should be recognizable by now as the concession process. Alice was changing how she dealt with Jerry to avoid problems. The scatter plot seems to show this pattern, confirming the other pieces of information we collected through the MAS and ABC charts.

At first glance, Jerry's scatter plot for yelling and throwing (shown on p. 171 in the related scatter plot found in the "Keeping Track of Behaviors" section) seems to hold few clues to why he was acting this way; however, this is where the information from the MAS and the ABC charts was helpful. Notice that, unlike with his noncompliant behaviors, Jerry rarely yelled or threw things in the morning while getting ready for school. Looking back, his mother realized that this was probably because she was with him most of the morning trying to get him ready and out of the house. It was only at those times when she was otherwise occupied (e.g., on the telephone, doing household chores) that he would act up this way.

Again, the scatter plot can be an easy way to track behavior and at times also can provide clues about triggers for problem behaviors. My colleagues and I do not usually ask parents to complete all of these types of assessments (i.e., MAS, ABC charts, scatter plots); instead, we consult with the family to see what makes the most sense given their present circumstances. Use your best judgment and see whether you can find clues to your child's behavior with several of these tools.

Look at Your Own Behavior

Sometimes, you can look at your own behavior to see what your child might be trying to tell you through his or her behavior problems. I often find parents and teachers doing what I call *zone defense*. Zone defense is a term used in sports (e.g., basketball) in which players focus on an area of the playing field rather than just focusing on a player from the other team. At home or at school, this involves a parent or teacher strategically placing him- or herself around a child who has behavior challenges. Often, the parent or teacher will do this without being aware of it; he or she has inadvertently discovered that if he or she is always nearby, then the child does not act up as much. If the individual goes outside of the zone, however—perhaps to another room at home or to work with another child on the other side of the classroom—then the child typically starts displaying behavior problems. This kind of behavior often is a sign that the child has attention-getting behavior problems and parents and teachers have learned not to venture too far away in order to avoid outbursts.

If you find yourself avoiding certain requests or situations, this too could provide you with clues about possible triggers for your child's behavior problems. This is a common observation in classrooms. Many times, I see a child sitting alone working on a different task than the other students. Sometimes, the explanation for this can be as simple as the child needing more individual attention on a particular task; however, it also can be a sign that the child typically gets upset with a particular task (e.g., math, writing) so the teacher has learned to provide the child with a different task. Or, it may be the case that the child tends to act up in the presence of another child and the teacher has found that keeping them separate helps them be better behaved. In both of these cases, the need to *escape* is the message being sent by the child. In the first instance, the child has taught the teacher, "Don't make me do this task, otherwise I'll get upset!" Again, this is not stated explicitly but, rather, is communicated through the child's behaviors (e.g., screaming, ripping up math papers). Or, the problem is that the child prefers to be alone and has taught the teacher, "Let me sit by myself; otherwise, I'll be disruptive." The bottom line here is that often the teacher is not aware that he or she has changed the classroom routine to accommodate the child. This kind of change can evolve slowly over time until the teacher has changed so much that the child has a very different routine from the other children. We can look at what has been changed to give us clues about why the child might be misbehaving.

The same kind of situation can happen at home as well. Little by little, a parent can learn how to approach his or her child in a way that avoids problems. As I described before in the discussion of the concession process, all parents learn to do this to some extent. You might find yourself, for example, folding laundry in the playroom because, this way, you can keep an eye on things and fewer problems occur. You might wait to make telephone calls until your children are asleep because it is just calmer that way. You may find yourself making two or more versions of dinner because your child will not eat what everyone else eats. To obtain clues about why your child may be getting upset, it can be helpful to see if any patterns have developed in how you have changed things with your child. Are you finding that you, too, play "zone defense" to be near your child at all times? This might be a sign that your child is engaging in behavior problems to get attention. Do you find yourself avoiding certain requests or activities? Again, you should be able to see by now that changes in your behavior could indicate a reaction to an attempt by your child to escape or avoid problems.

I need to repeat here that most parents concede to their child's needs to some extent; however, when these concessions get to the point that they interfere with your life or your family's life or are holding back your child's progress, then it may be time to look at the strategies I describe in the chapters that follow.

Hypothetical Situations

One last easy way we can get information about your child's behavior is to ask several very simple questions: "Can you picture a situation in which your child would be well behaved?" "Can you picture a situation in which your child would get upset?" Sometimes, this line of questioning seems so obvious that parents say things such as, "Well, of course; if I just let him sit by himself in the corner he would be fine!" or, "If I let him watch his favorite DVD over and over again, he would sit quietly for hours." Conversely, they will say things such as,

"If I make him eat anything without ketchup, he wouldn't be too happy" Or, "If I tried to take away his blanket, he would scream at the top of his lungs!" By posing these questions we are not suggesting that you actually do these things, but it certainly gives us clues about what might be going on. If you find that your child is well behaved in certain situations (e.g., sitting by himself), then ask yourself why. Is it because there are no demands (escape)? Is it because she gets upset if favorite things are taken away (tangible)? Again, we wouldn't rely solely on these simple questions to determine the cause of your child's misbehavior, but often they can be a very simple and quick way to get a handle on just what might be causing your child's problems.

FINAL THOUGHTS

Do not be intimidated by this process of determining why your child may be misbehaving. Oftentimes, the reasons for challenging behavior are simple and obvious. If the reasons are not clear, you will find that we can still proceed to help your child be better behaved. It also can be helpful to use this process as a way to be more mindful (see Chapter 5). As you go about your day with your child, in addition to reacting to problems, try to become aware of the world through your child's eyes. What was going on just as your child started screaming in the supermarket? Why does your child ask for endless glasses of water or just one more story before bedtime? Is it thirst, or is it an attempt to delay? Look at all of these interactions through the lens of the messages I described (i.e., attention, escape, tangible, sensory), and you may gain important insight into your child's challenging behavior that will be invaluable in proceeding on the road to improvement.

CHAPTER 7

Emergency Strategies

He who every morning plans the transaction of the day and follows out that plan, carries a thread that will guide him through the maze of the most busy life. But where no plan is laid, where the disposal of time is surrendered merely to the chance of incidence, chaos will soon reign.

—Victor Hugo (1802–1885, writer)

Once you understand what might be triggering your child's behavior problems, you can respond to your child in a number of different ways or set up situations that will temporarily reduce the problems you face. I titled this chapter "Emergency Strategies," however, to make it clear that these strategies are not substitutes for real plans that will help your child behave better in the future. My goal is to be able to help your child behave reasonably in a world that is some-times challenging itself, that is not predictable, and that often knows very little about children with special needs. This should not be confused with expecting children (or anyone else) to be subjected to poor treatment and just "suck it up." Everyone deserves to be treated with dignity and to have the opportunity to pursue happiness; however, life itself has its challenges, and it is not the job of parents and professionals to eliminate all of those challenges but rather to try to help children obtain the skills they will need should they encounter difficulties.

I recently had an experience that taught me that I should have been listening to my own advice. After running one of the world's most beautiful races—the San Francisco Half Marathon (13.1 miles) that takes you over the Golden Gate Bridge—I ended up with a stress fracture. It wasn't anything terribly serious, but it did stop me from running for months and forced me to wear an orthopedic walking boot to keep me from further injuring my foot. For the most part, the stress fracture was just an inconvenience, and my wife drove me around town when I needed help. However, I did need to go to a conference out of town to give a talk, and I was dreading the airport experience. My expectations for an unpleasant experience were fully realized. The wait in the check-in line was long, and the security line was longer still. All told, it took more than an hour to finally get to the security screening machines, and here I had been hoping that someone would take pity on this old man in a boot who by now was in some pain. However, the guards either did not see my distress or did not care. In addition to the distress I had already experienced, I was one of only a few special passengers "lucky" enough to be specially selected to go through a "sniffer" machine. Here I was, hopping around on one foot trying to make it over to the special screening area. Then, the magic words: "Okay, now hold your hands up over your head." Huh? Couldn't they see that I was having difficulty standing and that letting go of the arm rail was likely to make me fall over? Once my ordeal was over, I was in pain, sweating, and pretty angry that I had been put through all of this. My experience was repeated on the way home (except this time I didn't have to be "sniffed"), and I couldn't wait to regale my wife with these indignities. She listened politely at first and then said very bluntly, "Why didn't you ask them to give you a wheelchair? They probably would have put you right through the lines." What I had wanted was for the world to guess my needs and help me out. What my wife was saying is what I have been telling parents for decades: I should have just asked for help.

Advocates for children with special needs are making great strides in getting schools and other settings to be sensitive to the needs of these children. In just one example, when I first entered the disabilities field and told people that I worked with "autistic children," it was common for people to respond as if I had said "artistic children." Today, if I say that I work with children with autism, people ask knowledgeable questions about the rising prevalence rates or about any link between the measles, mumps, and rubella (MMR) vaccine and autism. Despite these advances, however, the world will never be able to adapt to everyone's needs. We need to help children be ready for this world.

This is a long-winded way of telling you to be careful about how you use the emergency strategies outlined in this chapter. Too often, these strategies become the solution to the problem and never get changed. For example, a teacher may learn to avoid asking a student to go through the cafeteria line because the request causes problems. As a result, the student may never learn how to get his lunch on his own. Or, a parent may find that always taking the same route to school or to stores prevents tantrums in the car. Unfortunately, her daughter never experiences how to deal with changes in routines. As a final example, a father may find that giving his son candy for dinner prevents mealtime problems; however, as a result, the child has difficulty learning good eating habits.

Sometimes, however, emergencies happen. For example, your child might be causing such a commotion in the middle of the night that the family is not sleeping and the neighbors are complaining. Or, your son may be having a tantrum in the car, and you are afraid he will get hurt. Behavior problems may be getting in the way of getting to school or eating the right foods. There are any number of situations that require immediate intervention to avoid serious problems. In these cases, short-term solutions can help you with these difficulties. These solutions, as you will see, often rely on information about why your child is misbehaving.

AVOIDING DIFFICULT SITUATIONS

Patient, raising his arm above his head: "Doctor, doctor, it hurts when I do this!" Doctor: "Well, then don't do that!"

As obvious as this old joke seems, so too is the advice to avoid difficult situations. As much as I have recommended against this as a long-term approach to dealing with problem behaviors, there are times when avoiding situations known to cause behavior problems is necessary and may be helpful. For example, if you are working on teaching your child to be better behaved out in public, it may be helpful to start off small. Instead of taking your child on long shopping trips, for example, you may want to start by avoiding lengthy adventures and practice on short in-and-out store visits. Or, if you have found that he or she seems to get upset more often when there are a lot of people around, then shopping during quieter times (if possible) can be a solution.

You also may have found that your child does better in a predictable environment. Certain routines, for example, may prove to be calming (e.g., how you prepare for bed, getting ready to leave the house). There are many school programs that rely on predictable routines. The value in this predictability is that it makes it easier for children to learn what to do next; as a side benefit, routines often prevent problem behavior among children who have a difficult time with change. Some programs provide picture schedules, showing the child what to work on in each situation. Although providing your child with a predictable environment can be very successful, it should be used with caution. Some children fixate on routines and then the routines become difficult to change without behavior problems. If changes in routines trigger problem behavior in your child, then that should be considered. Using routines with an eye toward changing them up a bit over time can be a way to get started on a plan with less disruption. Again, my point is that the world is not always predictable (e.g., buses are late, teachers and staff change), and trying to rely only on avoiding unpredictability as a strategy for reducing problem behavior only delays the inevitable difficulties that are likely to occur.

One type of situation that almost begs you to go out of your way to avoid difficult situations is when you suspect your child is sick, overly tired, or perhaps hungry. As discussed in Chapter 6, these setting events may lead to more problems. We often tell teachers that it is alright if you back off on difficult situations on a day when you know a child is not feeling well. This should not become a habit, but it is a reasonable accommodation for any child. In our home, for example, if my wife is not feeling well, I will pick up most if not all of her tasks at home. She does the same for me. In fact, I have often suggested to my wife that twice a year we should each have our own "sick week"; for 7 days, we could get treated as if we were really ill. If your child is not feeling well or is perhaps tired from having a poor night's sleep, it is recommended that you reduce your demands; however, make sure that this "strategy" is used only occasionally. If you find yourself constantly explaining away problem behaviors for these types of reasons ("Maybe he is just not feeling well"), you may be reading too much into a difficulty. Behavior challenges do not by themselves mean that your child is sick or tired.

What if you have discovered that your child seems to be disruptive to get your attention? In this case, the strategy for avoiding difficult situations would be to provide your child with a great deal of attention. Again, this should be a strategy limited to emergency situations. If you are on a family vacation, for example, and there are places or times when you cannot afford a major tantrum (e.g., standing in line at an attraction at Disney World or sleeping together in a hotel room), you should try to plan ahead and not expect your child to be perfectly well behaved without some extra attention.

In another example, you may have discovered that your child is likely to get upset if you ask him or her to stop a favorite activity. In circumstances during which this may become a problem (e.g., watching a favorite video at a relative's house), planning ahead for extended time might prove to be useful. Again, none of these suggestions should be confused with a good plan for long-term improvement in your child's behavior.

IMPROVING DIFFICULT SITUATIONS

Although I promised my wife and son not to include them in this book, one story illustrates the concept of improving difficult situations quite clearly; therefore, I will have to ask their forgiveness. When my son was very young, he would often have a difficult time waking up in the morning to get ready for school. Because I am the same way, the task of awakening him always caused me a little concern. He would frequently not respond to my requests to get out of bed, and it took many prompts to get him up and going. However, on one morning, when it was my wife's turn to awaken him, I listened to how she did it. I could hear her lie down next to him in his bed and say very weakly, "I'm the sleepiest person in this house." Then there was a pause, and this time she said it a little stronger. "Oh, yes—it's true. I'm the sleepiest person in the whole house." Then I could hear my son, and it was clear that he was smiling: "No, I'm the sleepiest person in this house." After a few minutes of this, he was out of bed and getting ready for the day. What my wife had discovered was that making getting up fun made it a much easier task. My own grumpiness probably just contributed to my son's difficulty and made the task that much more unpleasant for him.

In much the same way, you can make many difficult situations more bearable for your child, which, in turn, can reduce the likelihood that he or she will act up. For example, if cleaning up toys is the goal, perhaps asking your child to do only a small part (e.g., pick up the red blocks and put them in the toy chest) can make it easier for him or her to finish the task and ultimately more pleasant. It also can serve as a start to a process of asking for more over time (e.g., pick up the red and the blue blocks).

Turning a difficult task into a game (e.g., "Who can do it faster?") also can add a positive spin on something that would otherwise be unpleasant. This type of strategy has sometimes been referred to as embedding positives into difficult situations. In my case, I know if I play some favorite music while working in the house, it makes whatever task I am doing that much more pleasant. In school, we often recommend that teachers embed difficult questions within a string of easy ones. This can make the whole task just a little less challenging, making the child less likely to act up to avoid it.

If your child seems to have difficulties with attention—that is, he or she becomes disrupted if left alone for periods of time—you may want to plan a favorite activity for a time when you will be occupied. For example, one of the mothers in our program had a difficult time with her child while she was trying to make dinner. The little girl, Katee, would be very demanding during this time, wanting to play with the pots and pans, getting into the refrigerator, and otherwise making it very difficult for her mother to cook. In discussing the afternoon schedule, the mother told us that Katee's favorite thing to do was to watch a particular DVD, and she usually did this right after returning home from preschool. We agreed to try to change this schedule and have Katee's mom spend time interacting with Katee when she got home; then, when it was time for dinner, Katee's mom would put on the DVD. After a few days, Katee seemed to accept this new schedule, which allowed her mother the time she needed to get everything ready for dinner without disruption. A little planning, along with understanding what Katee was trying to tell us through her challenging behavior (i.e., "I want to spend time with you."), helped tremendously with this previously difficult situation.

Chapter 10, "Transitions," explains that using positive routines as a "warm-up" before moving on to something your child may not like also can help avoid a problem situation. One mother told us about how her daughter did not like to take baths at night. The mother discovered on her own that following a certain routine made getting her daughter into the bath less troublesome. Because her daughter loved different clothes, the mother would start the bath routine by first asking her daughter to pick out the pajamas she wanted to wear that night. She also bought her daughter several fake feather boas that she was allowed to wear to bed if she had taken a bath. (The mother would tell her, "You have to be very clean to wear a boa!") This routine combined a fun activity (picking out clothes) with a consequence (only being allowed to wear the boa if she had taken a bath), which led to great improvements in bath time. You can see that trying to look at these sometimes difficult situations in a more positive light (i.e., "How can we have fun with this?") rather than dreading them can lead to some really successful outcomes.

Chapter 4 described one of these strategies in the case of Jesse and how his mother Cindy looked at his problem behaviors. As you can see in the thought journal (please refer back to p. 99), Cindy's difficulties getting Jesse to brush his teeth caused her to feel tense and think that he was trying on purpose to upset her. Once we disputed this thought, her distraction technique was to sing a song about toothbrushing. This not only helped her mood but also made the task more positive and Jesse less resistant to brushing his teeth.

Do you have some hesitancy about taking this type of approach? Sometimes, parents express the opinion that children should just take baths, come to dinner, or play by themselves without elaborate games. "Why do I have to jump through hoops," one father told me, "just to get him to do things he should be doing on his own?" There is a logic to this. We all have to do things we do not like from time to time; however, as adults, we also have a bit more freedom to make unpleasant tasks more pleasant. As I mentioned before, I often listen to music while I do chores around the house. At work, I also can listen to music through my ear buds and can take a break whenever I want and walk around when I get tired or bored. Unfortunately, our children either do not have these freedoms or do not have the skills to do these things without causing problems. Because this is designed as a temporary emergency strategy, I am not suggesting that this become a lifelong way of dealing with your child under difficult situations. It is a way to address the problem quickly but at the same time work on other approaches that will have more lasting effects.

PROVIDING CHOICES

At some level, everyone likes to have some control over important aspects of their lives. This especially can be true for children with special needs because they often are in the position of having most of what happens to them be decided by someone else. In fact, one way to view challenging behaviors is as a way for these children to gain some control over these important parts of their daily activities. Kicking and screaming to get someone to stop making a request might be the only way the child can control a situation. The situation can, however, be turned on its ear, and the child can be allowed some control but in a better way.

Presenting acceptable choices to a child can be used to make difficult situations more bearable. For example, Dina, the mother of Reggie, was having a very difficult time getting Reggie dressed in the morning. Dina would struggle with her son to get his shirt on, and he would yell "No, no, no…" throughout the ordeal. This was repeated with Reggie's pants and his socks. Dina was extremely frustrated with Reggie because it made every morning very anxiety producing for her and delayed Reggie's getting ready for school. As Dina and I discussed this situation, I recommended trying to give Reggie some choices about the clothes he would wear that day. So, instead of starting out the process of getting dressed by saying "Put your shirt on," the request instead would be, "Which shirt do you want to put on today?" In this way, Reggie could have some control but ultimately still end up dressed. This was repeated with his pants (i.e., "Which pants do you want to wear?") and his socks (i.e., "Pick out a pair of socks"). Giving Reggie choices worked out extremely well. Rather than fighting, Reggie seemed happy about getting dressed. Unfortunately, there was an unforeseen side effect. Reggie ended up wearing a rather unusual combination of clothes that day. The next day, Dina figured out that it might be better to pick out several different outfits (matching pairs of shirts, pants, and socks that would go together), thus allowing Reggie to make choices but be a little more stylish.

Choice making can be incorporated into most situations—even those times, as we saw with Dina and Reggie, when there does not seem to be an option (i.e., Reggie had to get dressed, but he still could choose what he wore). But, is it possible to give too many choices? I once visited a school program that a child I had worked with in the past who had very serious behavior problems attended. The child had been reported to have been behaving much better in his classroom, and I was interested in monitoring his progress and seeing how the teacher dealt with his problems. This boy had dual sensory impairments (i.e., he had serious hearing and visual impairments) and a history of very serious self-injury (i.e., biting his hand and slapping his face). I had been working with him at home, where we discovered that he often hurt himself to escape from unpleasant situations. Our approach at home (which I describe in more detail in Chapter 9) included getting him to communicate for help when a task was too difficult for him. In this way, he would still be engaged, but we could help him through difficult parts of his work.

As I entered the boy's classroom, I noticed him sitting over in the corner of the room by himself. He had his ear pressed against a radio. Although he had very serious hearing impairments, it was thought that he could hear some sounds. He also seemed to enjoy the vibrations he could feel coming out of the speakers. I continued to observe for a time until his teacher approached him. She held out a laminated card to him with representations of two objects—a toy radio and a toy desk. She prompted him to pick one of the objects, and he touched the radio. The teacher then left him there by the radio. This was repeated about every 15 minutes, and each time the boy picked the radio. When his teacher had a minute, I sat down with her to discuss the plan for his behavior problems and what their goals were for his academics. She was proud to say that they had incorporated this new choice-making option for him and that it had dramatically reduced his self-hitting. If he picked the toy desk, he could do his schoolwork. If he picked the radio, he could listen to music. It soon became clear that the young man was choosing to listen to the radio all day and that no instruction was going on at all. Although this was a sincere effort to give the boy choices throughout the day, it resulted in his almost total lack of skill building at school. Rather than escaping his classwork by hitting himself, he was effectively escaping by always choosing something else (in this case, listening to the radio).

This extreme example illustrates how choice making can be taken too far. Although in this case it served as an emergency strategy to reduce the child's hitting, it also prevented any learning from going on. Unfortunately, because the approach was so "successful," his teacher relied on it as his "program" and felt no urgency to change it. Herein lies the problem with most of the emergency procedures described in this chapter. You can remove all difficult situations, you can spend all of your time with a child, or you can provide everything he or she wants; and these actions may temporarily solve the problem. This is seductive. It is very tempting to rely only on these quick and relatively easy solutions. But, as shown previously, these approaches are only temporary fixes. As soon as the world intrudes with the inevitable challenge, a time arises when the child cannot be given constant attention, or when what your child wants is just not available, we are back to looking for a real and lasting solution. This is especially a problem in school situations because the time a teacher has with a student is limited. If the teacher can make it through to the end of the school year, then for him or her, the problem is solved. The child moves on to another teacher, and the "problem" is averted. Unfortunately, the child has not learned how to deal with these difficulties. Again, the next few chapters cover more lasting solutions.

CREATING PREDICTABLE ROUTINES

As I mentioned in the section titled "Avoiding Difficult Situations," sometimes you can avoid difficulties with children by doing things the same way each time. Bedtime, as seen in Chapter 11, is a good example. Following the same bedtime routine (e.g., first washing up, then getting into pajamas, then reading a book) can be a comforting ritual that over time can help make bedtime easier. It is helpful if these routines can be communicated ahead of time to your child.

Figure 7.1.   Example of picture cues.

For many children, this can be as simple as a reminder (e.g., "Mommy is going to be on the telephone for 5 minutes, and then we can go outside to play," "We need to wash up first, get on your PJs, and then we can read together," "We do not touch other people in the store").

For children who may have a hard time understanding verbal reminders, pictures combined with stories can sometimes be helpful. One version of this process is known as Social Stories.[1] The basic idea is to prepare your child for a situation by talking him or her through what is about to happen (e.g., "We are going to the playground today. You will get to slide down the slide and play on the seesaw"). It is often helpful to point out what will happen if your child is well behaved (e.g., "And, if you are very good and listen to Mommy, we will get some ice cream"). See Figure 7.1 for an example of such picture cues. Occasional prompts to remind your child about what is happening and what is about to happen (e.g., "Remember, if you keep listening to Mommy and play nicely, we will get some ice cream") can help avoid difficulties.

At the risk of repeating myself, I need to again remind you that all of these strategies are primarily short-term solutions to behavior problems. What I discuss in the next two chapters are strategies for long-term and more permanent changes in your child's behavior.

CHAPTER 8

Managing Consequences

Good and evil, reward and punishment, are the only motives to a rational creature: these are the spur and reins whereby all mankind are set on work, and guided.

—John Locke (cited in Axtell, 1968)

"What should I do when my child misbehaves?" This is perhaps the most common question asked by parents, and it is an important one. Previous chapters already have looked at the consequences of your own thoughts (e.g., giving your child cookies for dinner because you felt defeated and you believe that your child will never change), and now it is time to see how the way you and others respond to your child's behavior problems can affect your child. Before beginning, however, I have one personal reflection. Although almost no meaningful research studies have been conducted on what I am about the tell you, my clinical experience tells me that occasional mistakes—responding to a child's behavior problems in a way that might not be helpful—will unlikely produce permanent harm. Parents who have a pessimistic style of thinking about their child and their child's behavior problems can sometimes get caught up in a cycle of constant self-recrimination (e.g., "I shouldn't have let him have the chips in the supermarket when he was whining," "I should give her a bath more often, but it's such a hassle," "I should have kept telling him to put away his toys even though he was ignoring me; now he doesn't listen at all"). Also, as we have seen, some parents can feel that the way that others deal with their child's behavior problems may be causing the problem (e.g., "My ex lets him get away with murder," "I wish my mother wouldn't let him eat dinner in front of the television").

These types of thoughts are rarely productive. They only get in the way of your proceeding along a good path and helping your child behave better. It is also true, however, that even if you or others currently are doing things that might be contributing to the problem, this can be changed—even if your "child" is no longer a child. I have worked with people who have been behaving in certain problematic ways for decades; although some behaviors can be very difficult to change completely, our work shows that we can make meaningful changes in the behaviors and the lives of individuals at any age. So, even if you think you have been handling a problem all wrong but would at least like to try another approach, I can tell you that this is within your capabilities.

In my work, I have also observed on numerous occasions that most children can learn different rules with different people. For example, I spoke with one mother whose in-laws allowed her son to have dessert after meals when he was visiting them. As we discussed this, it became very clear that she was not going to be able to get them to change. "It just drives me up the wall. They know I don't approve and that it's not good for him, but they do it anyway." She admitted that she felt judged by her in-laws and also felt that they were undermining her efforts to help her son. "And then when he's with me, he wants sweets and says, 'Nanna lets me have them.' Then I feel guilty." As we discussed it further, I pointed out that making her feel guilty sometimes worked—she would give in. "Why do you think he says 'Nanna lets me have them?'" "Because she does." I pressed her: "But, why does he say it? Why doesn't he just say 'I want candy?'" "Because he knows I won't give him candy. But I guess he knows that if he says his Nanna does, it will make me feel bad and I will give him sweets." She needed to recognize that her son was quite capable of learning that he could not have sweets at home with her. She should not feel guilty about having a different set of rules. He could, and eventually did, learn to live with these two realities. In addition, she began to let go of the resentment she felt toward her son's grandparents.

To understand how to respond to your child's behavior, it is important to review the power of consequences. When your child behaves in a particular way (e.g., whines for sweets) and the consequence is something positive (e.g., he gets sweets), your child will likely behave that way more often (e.g., whine more in the future). This simple concept is called reinforcement. A behavior that gets reinforced will likely occur more often in the future. Cases throughout this book have illustrated this over and over again. It is important to point out that all of the "messages" that your child is sending with his or her behavior problems (i.e., attention, tangible, sensory, and escape) involve reinforcement. Table 8.1 shows the consequences for each of the "messages."

ATTENTION AS A CONSEQUENCE

If your child misbehaves to get your attention (e.g., tugging on your clothes at the mall when you are trying to look through a store) and you pay attention to your child at that moment, your child was just reinforced and will do similar things to get your attention in the future. Remember, this can include many

Table 8.1. Consequences of the messages sent by a child's misbehavior

Message	Consequences
Attention	Attending to your child in some way (may include interactions—e.g., praising, spending time together, and/or comforting—but for some children may also include yelling or providing explanations)
Tangible	Providing your child with desired things (e.g., toys, foods) or activities; can also be giving in to your child's refusal to end an activity (e.g., not wanting to stop watching a movie) or give up a desired thing (e.g., a toy picked up at a store)
Sensory	Feedback provided by the behavior itself; can include behaviors that may feel good (e.g., face rubbing, twirling in circles), look good (e.g., waving hands in front of eyes), taste good (e.g., eating things off of the floor), or sound good (e.g., making unusual noises)
Escape	Removing undesired requests or activities; can include actions that may appear to be punitive (e.g., sending a child to his room) but may actually be desired (e.g., leaving the dinner table)

different forms of attention including, for some children, yelling or reprimanding them. Sometimes, parents will provide detailed explanations to their child about why the child should not misbehave (e.g., "Remember how we talked about screaming? Screaming is not something you are supposed to do when we are at the park. It makes Mommy upset, and it bothers the other people around us...."). These rationales or explanations can, by themselves, be a form of attention that your child might like. An ABC chart for Teena shows how Teena might be getting reinforced for screaming and hitting her mother by the attention she received when she acted up.

BETSY'S ABC CHART FOR TEENA

Day and time	ANTECEDENTS What was happening just before your child's behavior problem?	BEHAVIOR Write down the behavior(s) as well as the number of times and/or how long they occurred.		CONSEQUENCES How did you or others react to the episode?
Wednesday morning	I was cleaning up after breakfast.	Screaming and hitting	1 minute	I held her to calm her down and explained how she needs to be a big girl and not hit.
Thursday morning	I was helping my son get dressed.	Screaming and hitting.	2 minutes	I put her in my lap and held her arms down. I rocked with her until she calmed down. I told her that big girls don't hit and scream and that Ms. P at school wouldn't like it.

Betsy, Teena's mother, came to us for help with her daughter after numerous efforts by Teena's school to assist Betsy and Teena. Initially, the school made the referral, telling us that Betsy had been very resistant with them and never followed through with the school psychologist's recommendations. They were very concerned about Teena's behavior at school and felt as if Betsy was sabotaging their efforts. When we first met with Betsy, it was pretty clear that getting to the bottom of Teena's screaming and hitting behavior was a major priority because it was happening more and more frequently. We asked Betsy to keep an ABC chart to try to see what might be going on at home. Although Betsy came back for the next session, she had not completed the chart. She was apologetic, saying she had been very busy, but we also discovered over time that her ability to write was limited and, therefore, she may have been embarrassed to try to fill out the chart. So, we sat down with her and recreated two recent incidents. What she told us was that she would try to "calm Teena down" once Teena started to hit and scream and would explain to Teena why she should not behave that way. She felt that comforting Teena was necessary so that Teena would not get more upset. This prompted us to ask Betsy what she was thinking when Teena got upset. "She just hits and screams and looks mad. She can't help it. She's got autism, and that's the way she is. But I can calm her by holding her. Pretty soon she's quiet and happy."

I hope you can see the problem here. In Betsy's eyes, Teena had no control over her behavior. Betsy believed that it was Teena's disorder that was making Teena so upset and that it was her job as Teena's mother to calm her down. Looked at from this perspective, it makes some sense for Betsy to hold Teena and comfort her when she has a tantrum. For Betsy, the goal was to get Teena to stop misbehaving at that moment; however, she did not see how her reactions to Teena's behavior might affect Teena in the future. As you may have guessed, from a reinforcement perspective, Teena was getting massive amounts of very positive attention from her mother when she screamed and hit. So, we suspected that although holding and talking to Teena did eventually stop her from hitting and screaming at that moment, it probably was contributing to why Teena was doing this more and more each day.

Although we pointed out to Betsy that she was reinforcing Teena's misbehavior, what eventually convinced Betsy that how she was reacting to Teena might be encouraging more problems in her daughter was to show her that Teena's behaviors only happened when Betsy was not paying attention to her (e.g., cleaning up after breakfast, getting her son dressed). At other times, Teena would be pretty well behaved. It took a few weeks of noticing this pattern, but eventually Betsy saw that maybe it was not Teena's autism that was causing her to hit and scream but instead was Teena's way of asking for her mother's attention. The simple solution, then, was to switch the way that Betsy responded to Teena. Betsy agreed to hold and hug her daughter only when she was being good and would not do it while she was screaming. As Betsy started the plan, it became even more obvious to her. "Now I see," she told us. "She was kicking and hitting and screaming yesterday, and I was just looking away. I said 'Oh no. You're not getting this. If you're good I'll give you some hugs.' And she's getting it. Now I'm the big one. I'm in control. Before, she was in control of me."

This simple interaction illustrates how your attention can reinforce your child's problem behavior. But it also should highlight how your thoughts can interfere with seeing these patterns. In Betsy's case, believing that Teena's behavior problems were a direct result of Teena's autism made Betsy respond to Teena's tantrums by doing the very thing she should have not been doing— hugging and soothing Teena as a consequence of misbehaving. Once Betsy could see that the tantrums were attempts to get attention, she was able to carry out simple recommendations. These were similar to the recommendations that had been made by Teena's teacher and the school psychologist, only at that time Betsy's thoughts about what was causing Teena's problems were getting in the way. Once we addressed her thoughts, Betsy became a very important part of Teena's later progress both at home and at school.

TANGIBLES AS A CONSEQUENCE

Sometimes, children misbehave to get things that they want. Years ago, I worked with a young man who was only able to say a few words but was quite able to get across certain messages. Jim was over 6 feet tall by the age of 15 and could be very dangerous. If he became upset, he was likely to hit and grab at the school personnel. If they tried to hold him, he would struggle to get free and

TEACHER-COMPLETED ABC CHART FOR JIM

Day and time	**ANTECEDENTS** What was happening just before your child's behavior problem?	**BEHAVIOR** Write down the behavior(s) as well as the number of times and/or how long they occurred.		**CONSEQUENCES** How did you or others react to the episode?
Wednesday, 1:30 p.m.	He grabbed at his magazine. We told him he was supposed to be working and could not have it.	He slapped the teacher and flipped over his desk.	1 minute	We moved him to the back of the room.
Wednesday, 1:45 p.m.	He said "magazine." We told him it was not time for his magazine.	He punched the teacher.	3 times	We took away his work and stood between him and the other students. We gave him the magazine.

sometimes would hit people with his own head. Everyone who worked with Jim was afraid of him and "walked on eggshells." In trying to determine just what might be going on, I had the teachers complete the MAS and an ABC chart. The MAS came out very clearly, with the teachers indicating high scores on all questions related to tangibles. The ABC chart (shown on p. 221) confirmed this information as well.

Only a small sample of Jim's ABC chart is shown, but most of the many pages of ABC charts the teachers completed for Jim showed similar patterns. Many of Jim's problem interactions centered around his favorite magazine or other things he wanted. In Jim's case, he did not care whether anyone paid attention to him, but there were things he wanted; in fact, despite his low verbal ability, he could say the word "magazine." If Jim's teachers did not give him what he asked for, however, he had a way of emphasizing his point. He would even sometimes start to rock back and forth and clench his fists if he did not get what he wanted. It was almost as if his highly aggressive behaviors of hitting and punching were his way of saying, "Perhaps you didn't understand me the first time? I really do want that magazine!" And eventually, as you can see in the ABC chart, he would get his magazine. In other words, the consequence for his behavior problems was to get the item he wanted, which was leading him to continue to be aggressive.

The goal is not to pass judgment on Jim's teachers or on Jim. Should his teachers have just let him have his magazine? Should they have given in to his demands? Is it right to let a student in school have a magazine when he or she should be working? These are all important questions that I address in Chapter 9. For now, it is important to notice two things. First, Jim was getting reinforced for hitting other people by getting the things he wanted. Second, instead of using Jim's magazine to inadvertently reinforce Jim's negative behavior, the magazine could be used as a reinforcer for other things. Just as we had Betsy hug and comfort her daughter when she was being good, Jim's teachers could use the magazine to reinforce Jim's positive behaviors. In other words, the teachers should not be giving Jim the magazine to "calm him down" but instead only when he was behaving well.

There is an important point to raise here. What would be the difference in Jim's behavior if his teachers let him have the magazine while he worked as opposed to letting him get upset first before they eventually gave in? You might experience this dilemma yourself. Often, parents say that their child gets upset in a supermarket to get candy, cereal, or other things that he or she wants. And, sometimes the tantrum can be so violent as to require some emergency response (e.g., leaving the store or giving in). What should you choose to do in this situation? Our rule of thumb is this: If you are not ready to say no in a certain situation (e.g., Jim's teacher and his magazine, a parent's response to a child's request for candy in a store), give in early. What? Give in?

After all that I have said about how conceding to a child's demands might be a problem, why would I recommend giving in under certain circumstances? The reason is straightforward; if you think you will eventually give in, give in early, before the behavior problem has escalated. Let's look at a typical scenario. A mother asks her son to put away his toys at night before bedtime. He squirms around on the floor and wants to continue to play. At the same time, his mother tries to take his hand to help him pick up each toy. He continues to pull away. His mother grabs his hand again, but this time the boy starts to scream. His mother is tired now but is determined to see this through. After a few minutes of screaming, the boy starts to hit his mother and starts throwing the toys around the room. Now the situation is chaotic. The mother is tired and upset, the boy is screaming and flailing around and is sweaty and all red in the face, and the toys are now all over the place. The mother decides that it's late and she needs to do other things, so she lets the boy play with his toys for 10 more minutes while she gets her other child to bed. Her son calms down and continues to play with his toys. What just happened?

Two things were learned in this situation. First, the mother learned to give in. Once things got out of control, one way to handle the chaos was to stop making demands on her son. When the mother did give in, things became more peaceful. The house was quiet again, and she was able to continue with the rest of her nightly routine. The mother was reinforced by the ending of the tantrum and the return of serenity. Second, the son learned to escalate his challenging behavior. He learned that if pulling away from his mother did not work (she still tried to get him to stop playing), then he should scream. If screaming did not stop her, then he should hit her and throw toys. He learned that eventually, with enough escalating behavior, he would get to play with his toys (tangible reinforcer). Researcher Gerald Patterson has named this pattern the coercive family process.[1]

In this scenario, I could recommend that the mother not give in; however, unless she has had a chance to work through the thoughts that might be interfering with her ability to continue through her son's tantrum (e.g., perhaps she is thinking, "I am a terrible mother; I can't even get him to put away his toys" or "This will never end; I'll never have a peaceful night and I will never have a normal life"), she might not be *capable* of persisting. In that case, I might recommend that if she knows this is going to be a problem where she might give in, let her son continue to play with his toys *before his behavior gets worse*. Although this is not a long-term fix for the child's problem, at least he is not learning to increase the severity of his behavior and become more and more disruptive. Let me repeat this: You want to avoid having your child learn to escalate his or her behavior to get what he or she wants. In this case, the mother needs a more optimistic attitude (e.g., "I can do this, and he will eventually listen to me") and the right skills before she can handle the situation properly. This strategic "giving in" should be used sparingly and only when you are preparing to handle a problem situation in a better way. You do not want to put yourself in the position of teaching your child "if at first you don't succeed, cry, cry again!"

SENSORY FEEDBACK AS A CONSEQUENCE

As I mentioned, some behaviors occur simply because they make a person feel good. Right now, as I write, I am listening to background music; I am not doing this to get attention from anyone (I have earphones on), to get anything tangible, or to escape from a difficult situation. I am listening to music because it sounds good and relaxes me. Everyone does things like this. In a similar way, some problem behaviors that are seen in children can occur because of the children's sensory needs. Let's look at Jayden's behaviors to see examples of these types of problems and how complicated they can be.

Angela (Jayden's mother) told us her concerns about how Jayden behaved in groups of children. She said that he would jump up and down, flap his hands, and make a screeching noise. Although he seemed happy as he did this, it tended to make him look very different from the other children, and some kids would

ANGELA'S ABC CHART FOR JAYDEN

Day and time	ANTECEDENTS What was happening just before your child's behavior problem?	BEHAVIOR Write down the behavior(s) as well as the number of times and/or how long they occurred.		CONSEQUENCES How did you or others react to the episode?
Monday, 8:30 a.m.	He was outside at his bus stop waiting for his bus. There were three neighborhood children about his age standing around talking.	Jumping, hand flapping, and screeching	2 times	The other children moved away but tried not to notice. I told him to stop.
Wednesday, 4:15 p.m.	He was in the living room with his sister's friends. They were playing games, and Jayden was standing near them watching.	Jumping, hand flapping, and screeching	3 times	The girls smiled at Jayden, but his sister became embarrassed and asked me if he could play somewhere else.
Saturday, 2:00 p.m.	We were at the mall and we went into a toy store. Jayden immediately went over to the aisle that had his favorite toys.	Jumping, hand flapping, and screeching	3 times	I told him to stop.

try to avoid him as a result. This caused Angela to worry, because she wanted Jayden to be able to make friends and get along with his peers. She also felt that out in public other people would judge him negatively. In completing the MAS, it was very obvious that there was a strong sensory component to Jayden's way of behaving. To confirm that Jayden's behaviors were to meet some sensory need and to see whether there were any "triggers," Angela completed an ABC chart, which is shown on page 224.

The MAS results suggested that Jayden's jumping, hand flapping, and screeching seemed to occur because he liked to do these things (i.e., sensory consequences). The ABC chart gave us additional information. He seemed to do these sensory behaviors when he was happy. He would act this way at times when and in places where he seemed to be having a good time; his smile seemed to indicate he was pleased with what was happening. In discussing this, Angela agreed with this assessment but repeated her concerns about the effects of behaviors on other people. As I alluded to before, sensory behaviors can be complex. The problem here is that Jayden would act this way regardless of the consequences coming from other people. So, if his mother just ignored it, it would not matter. He was not doing it to get attention, and he was not doing it to escape or to get tangibles. The reinforcer was within him (i.e., the positive feelings he would get). Therefore, without any intervention, Jayden would continue to act this way.

The dilemma here is that Angela wanted Jayden to be happy. Because of this, she did not want to take a source of pleasure away from him. At the same time, she felt that Jayden also would be happy having friends but that his problem behaviors were getting in the way. The solution we came up with was a reinforcement-based response. Rather than just telling Jayden to stop, Angela and I designed a social story (which I described briefly in Chapter 7) for Jayden to point out how he should behave with other people (e.g., "When we are around our friends, we do not jump or flap our hands or screech") and what would happen if he avoided acting this way (e.g., "You will get stars on your star chart"). It took a few weeks of working on this in practice situations—Jayden's sister and her friends agreed to help role-play—for Jayden to learn to control his behaviors in public, and Angela sometimes still needs to prompt Jayden to remind him about how he should behave in public (e.g., "Remember how you are supposed to behave at the store?"). Angela did agree that Jayden could do the behaviors at home if he was just with the family; and eventually, Jayden did learn how to tell the difference between these two settings.

I describe later in this chapter how to use structured reinforcement strategies (e.g., star charts), which can be very valuable additions to behavior plans. It is important to point out that often sensory behaviors may need reinforcers that are different from the ones your child might get for other behaviors. For Jayden, Angela used stars to point out when he behaved well out in public and then gave him treats for collecting a number of stars. This was not directly related to the feelings he got from his behaviors. In contrast, this describes using attention for good behaviors when the problem is attention getting and tangibles when the problems are related to tangible reinforcers. However, because it is not possible to change how some behaviors feel (e.g., the effects of hand flapping or repeatedly playing with a piece of lint), it is necessary to rely on outside reinforcers to help encourage other ways of behaving.

ESCAPE AS A CONSEQUENCE

Escape from some unpleasant situation (e.g., not having to clean up your room or brush your teeth) may not seem similar to the other consequences just discussed. In this case, something pleasant (e.g., attention, a thing, or even the positive sensory feelings) is not given to the child for a problem behavior but is a reinforcer nonetheless. Rather than getting something positive, in this case, you are taking away something negative. This kind of reinforcer (called a negative reinforcer) is actually very common. For example, we stop our cars at red lights or stop signs to avoid something negative (e.g., an accident, a ticket). At no time since I was first learning to drive, decades ago, has anyone praised me for stopping at a red light ("Nice driving, Mark!") or have I received some award for this. But we do it anyway because we are reinforced by avoiding the obvious potential negative consequences. In much the same way, children are reinforced for misbehaving to escape or avoid something unpleasant. This was shown previously in the case about Brian; please refer to his ABC chart in Chapter 6.

The reinforcement for Brian's whining, crying, falling to the floor, and kicking and screaming seemed to be escape from an unpleasant situation. By getting upset, Brian successfully escaped from having to put his toys away or change his shirt. The consequences were that his mother put his toys away and stopped asking him to change his shirt. Once we discovered this connection, we could "turn the tables" on Brian. We had his mother, Sarah, begin by making smaller requests such as just putting one toy away. She was to persist until he did this easy task. Then she would let him escape and stopped making requests for a while. What Brian quickly learned was that he could get reinforced with escape. In other words, his mother would stop hassling him if he complied. However, she would very calmly continue to make her request (e.g., "Put the truck in the toy box") until he did what she was asking him to do. Over time, she increased her requests (e.g., "Put those two trucks away") and he learned that escape could only be achieved by following these simple requests.

Again, some children misbehave to escape from unpleasant demands. It could be that a request is too difficult for the child or that it is too boring. Some children, however, try to escape from social attention. This is the opposite of the attention-seeking behavior problems we have discussed; in this case, the message is "leave me alone!" Sometimes, this escape behavior is observed in children with autism spectrum disorders who prefer being alone or, at least, find the presence of too many people uncomfortable. It also can be observed among youth who prefer the company of peers to that of adults. Again, understanding this can help you manage consequences better with behavior problems. If escape from social attention is desired, then you should avoid this consequence for problem behavior (e.g., sending a surly teenager to her room for acting up at dinner, if being left alone is why she acted up in the first place) and instead use it as a reinforcer for good behavior.

By now, I think you can see the important connections between understanding why your child might be misbehaving and how to respond to these problems. I opened this chapter with the question, "What should I do when my child misbehaves?" The answer is, "It depends on *why* your child misbehaves." If your child misbehaves to get attention, then your response to his or her misbehavior should include as little attention as possible. If your child is acting up for tangible reasons, then you should try to avoid giving him or her what he or she seems to want during or right after an episode. Because you have limited control over sensory consequences, how you respond immediately to these types of behaviors may be less important. As I described in that section, prompting a child to act in a less stigmatizing way may be a good approach. Finally, if the behavior seems to be occurring for escape, then you would want to be vigilant about not allowing your child to escape these situations by misbehaving.

USING BEHAVIOR PROBLEMS TO CHOOSE REINFORCERS

As I described how to respond (or how not to respond) to your child's behavior problems, I also mentioned how to use the information about your child's messages to find reinforcers. We typically think of reinforcers as things like food (e.g., candy, ice cream), privileges (e.g., watching a favorite television show, staying up later at night) or even simple praise (e.g., "Very nicely done!"). However, sometimes what your child really likes or wants can be difficult to figure out. When you think about it, however, your child is telling you loud and clear what he or she wants. If your son, for example, spends a great deal of time misbehaving to get your attention, then it is likely that attention will be a very potent reinforcer. If, on the other hand, your child acts up to get a favorite thing or activity, then that can be used to reinforce good behavior. Escape is often the most puzzling for parents. For children who spend a great deal of time trying to escape situations or interactions, I often hear parents say things such as, "He doesn't like anything!" By now, however, you should see that escape itself can be used as a reinforcer. Earlier, I described a study I conducted in which we used "time-out" (or turning away from a child) as a reinforcer for children who had escape behaviors. They would actually work harder to be left alone!

Sensory consequences are a special case, and there still are not good answers for dealing with children who have sensory behavior problems. First, the good news is that serious behaviors such as aggression or severe forms of self-injury rarely happen for their sensory feedback. Often, sensory behaviors are milder problems that can be disruptive (e.g., jumping up and down, hand flapping) but are more of a concern because they can make a child stand out in groups in a negative way. When my colleagues and I talk about reinforcers, then, we tend to discourage using sensory reinforcers to encourage positive behaviors. For example, I would not recommend letting children jump up and down and flap their hands if they are well behaved because allowing this does little to discourage behaviors that may be stigmatizing. Reports from people with conditions such as Asperger syndrome, however, have described how they could engage in more subtle sensory behaviors (e.g., rubbing their fingers together, humming silently to themselves) as a way to calm themselves. I would not discourage using these less obvious and less stigmatizing actions to encourage good behavior. In general, my colleagues and I usually try to incorporate the reinforcer for the problem behavior in any plan to reward a child. These can be combined with more traditional reinforcers to match the plan specifically to your own child's special needs.

PUNISHMENT AND BRIBES

A discussion of consequences requires at least a brief mention of the concepts of *punishment* and *bribes*, both of which can be very controversial topics when dealing with child problem behaviors. Much has been written about punishment, which is another type of consequence but is the opposite of reinforcement. Basically, just as a reinforcer can be anything that encourages a behavior to occur again in the future, a punisher can be anything that discourages a behavior from occurring again. For example, if you were spanked as a child for talking back to your parents, your parents were attempting to use a punisher to get you to be less rude in the future. One of the problems with punishment and the reason that it is controversial is because it is easily abused. Many parents would not question a spank to a child's bottom for trying to run across the street or for some other potentially dangerous behavior. The problem occurs when that one spank does not work and then is repeated frequently, perhaps even becoming more intense. If you find yourself using frequent punishers, it is likely that they are not working—the problem behavior is still occurring—and you need to consider a different approach.

    In our work, my colleagues and I prefer to avoid punishers as a way to improve child behavior. A great deal of research shows that significant improvements in child problem behavior are achievable through more positive approaches. Simply put, it is more desirable to teach your child what to do than just focus on what not to do. Having said that, there are times when mild forms of punishment that do not involve pain or humiliation can be incorporated into a plan (i.e., approaches that avoid, e.g., spanking, slapping, using a belt, or saying "Why are you so stupid," "You're lazy," and so forth). For example, one family with whom I worked had a young boy who kept biting his mother. Assessments indicated that he was using this behavior to escape from doing things he did not want to do (e.g., getting dressed in the morning). In addition to teaching him skills to replace the biting behavior (described in Chapter 9), his mother decided that if he bit her she would take his favorite DVD and put it away in the closet where he could not get it. This form of punishment in combination with teaching him how to ask for help getting dressed completely eliminated his biting. When the child was cooperative when he got dressed, his mother would take the DVD out of the closet and he could watch it that day. These milder forms of punishment should be used sparingly and only in combination with other more positive approaches.

The use of positive approaches sometimes starts a conversation about bribing children. "Why should I have to give her something that she wants to get her to do something she should be doing anyway?" I usually distinguish bribes from reinforcers in this way. A bribe is giving your child something positive (e.g., ice cream) with the anticipation of him or her being good in the future (e.g., "You can have ice cream for dessert tonight if you promise me you will be good on the school bus tomorrow"). For many children, bribing can be a recipe for failure. In this case, once the child has eaten the ice cream, all bets are off. If the child is not good on the school bus, the parent has no recourse other than to punish. Bribing as described here is never recommended. This book has been discussing consequences, and this situation does not conform to our definition of a consequence. A reinforcer would involve giving the child ice cream *after* she was good on the bus.

Even using reinforcers can raise some concerns. "Shouldn't my child eat dinner quietly and with no tantrums without me having to praise her or without giving her a treat?" The forthright former New Yorker in me wants to answer, "Yes, but does she?" Fortunately, the optimistic parent in me sees it this way: Everyone at the table was and is being reinforced for eating nicely and behaving politely. Over the years, you learned proper manners at the dinner table. Perhaps all it took was a little instruction (e.g., "Make sure to put your napkin on your lap," "Elbows off the table," "Please don't raise your voice"), some modeling (e.g., watching how your parents behaved, seeing your siblings being praised for asking to be excused when they were finished), and the approval of other members of your family. Or, maybe there were some bumps in the road (e.g., being yelled at for not eating your vegetables) that you learned to avoid by changing your behavior. Your child, however, probably learns differently (e.g., he or she may not learn well from watching models) and may require different reinforcers than you did (e.g., a nod of approval may not be as important to your child as it was for you). The bottom line is that your child learns differently and needs different types of strategies than you or maybe your other children had to improve his or her behavior. The goal is always to get to the point where artificial programs are no longer needed and when interactions with your child approach your experience of a more natural flow; however, it will take some work and patience to get there.

STRUCTURED WAYS OF REINFORCING YOUR CHILD

It can be very helpful to both you and your child to have a visual aid to remind you about positive consequences. The following example shows how we used one such technique with Jerry, the boy who was noncompliant to requests by his mother in the morning. If you recall, Jerry's mother, Alice, was using a scatter plot to record when Jerry was noncompliant. We also used the information on the scatter plot (along with the MAS and ABC charts) to give us an idea of why Jerry might be misbehaving. Alice liked this format because she said it was easy to complete and, by keeping it on her refrigerator, she was constantly reminded to fill it in. Refer back to the scatter plot for Jerry's noncompliant behaviors (shown in Chapter 6) for a sample of this record keeping, which showed that Jerry was almost always noncompliant during requests to complete his chores in the morning. Jerry did not receive any check marks on the weekends because his mother did not ask him to do chores on these days. The scatter plot data suggested that the tasks that Alice was asking Jerry to do were either too hard or too boring and that he was trying to escape doing them.

We continued to use the scatter plot format once we started a behavior plan to encourage Jerry to be more compliant in the mornings. We asked Jerry's mom to break down her requests for help from Jerry into fewer steps because he had problems with his attention and, sometimes, remembering what he was expected to do next. The scatter plot (shown next) then became a way to remind Jerry of his responsibilities to help out as well as a record of when he did assist his mother with no difficulties. Alice put a sticker or a smiley face on the scatter plot to indicate when Jerry was helpful, and the number of those smiley faces gradually increased.

ALICE'S SCATTER PLOT: WITH JERRY'S BEHAVIOR PLAN

Time of day	Day of the week													
	Monday	Tuesday	Wednesday	Thursday	Friday	Saturday	Sunday	Monday	Tuesday	Wednesday	Thursday	Friday	Saturday	Sunday
7:00 a.m.	X	☺	X	☺	☺			☺	X	☺	☺	☺		
7:30	X	X	☺	X	X			X	☺	☺	☺	☺		
8:00														
8:30														
9:00														

(From Touchette, P., MacDonald, R., & Langer, S. [1985]. A scatter plot for identifying stimulus control of problem behavior. *Journal of Applied Behavior Analysis, 18*[4], 344; adapted by permission.)

At first, Alice required Jerry to earn just one of two possible smiley faces in the morning to get something he wanted that night (e.g., an extra half hour before going to bed, a treat for dessert). Later, Alice expanded her expectation to two smiley faces in the morning for Jerry to get to choose his reinforcer. We made the change because it seemed that once he received his one smiley face sticker, he learned that that was all that was required of him for the morning!

The scatter plot is obviously just one of a number of ways you can organize a visual aid to remind yourself and your child about good behavior. Sometimes, parents even give out fake money for good behavior, which can be exchanged later for favorite things including positive interactions, such as private story time or shopping trips together. However you decide to structure these efforts to reinforce your child, there are a few things to remember:

1. Err on the side of being too lenient in the beginning. Sometimes, it is easy to expect so much that a child never ends up earning a reinforcer. If your child, for example, has never gotten fully dressed in the morning without a tantrum, you might want to give stars or smiley faces for parts of the task (e.g., one star for putting on a shirt, one star for putting on pants). You can always change the rules later—for example, two stars for getting dressed completely with no problems—and children will learn to accept that.

2. Immediate feedback works best. Try to give feedback immediately after your child behaves well (e.g., "Nicely done; you've earned a smiley face!"), even if you have to mark a chart later on. To do this, remember to "parent in the moment" (see Chapter 5) and focus on the interaction so you are sure to "catch your child being good" as soon as possible.

3. Never bribe. Do not give your child something he or she wants with the promise that he or she will behave better later. This only reinforces your child for promising to be good, not for actually being good.

4. Try to view everything from a positive perspective. Saying something such as "I'm happy you didn't hit me" might sound like praise but actually focuses attention on the problem behavior. Instead, phrases such as "You did that well" or "I'm very proud of the way you behaved" put the emphasis on the positive behaviors.

5. If your child misbehaves, remind him or her of a missed reinforcer. But again, this message should be delivered as neutrally as possible. *When in doubt, talk less.* Explanations or rationales should be saved for a time far removed from when your child misbehaves.

6. Find time to go over your child's behavior with him or her at a quiet moment that is separate from the problem situation. This, too, should be a positive experience that emphasizes progress and what could happen if your child is even better behaved. Even if your child has gone from one smiley

face last week to two smiley faces this week, that is progress and should be pointed out.

7. If you think it is warranted, give your child a "bonus." Sometimes your child might handle a situation well that was not anticipated when you set up the rules for your child. In these cases, an extra star or other reinforcer can be used. Use these sparingly so that they are an unexpected pleasant surprise. You want to avoid having your child begin to expect them.

8. Try to give your child opportunities to make choices about what he or she might like as a reinforcer. So, for example, if your child earns a certain number of stars or points, you can offer him or her an array of options from which to choose (e.g., a snack at bedtime, time on the computer, access to a favorite toy). A child's preferences can change from day to day, and this way you know what he or she really wants. If your child is nonverbal, the choices can be presented in picture form.

9. Try to include reinforcers that match the message your child is communicating with his or her behavior problem. This includes "escape time" if you discover that escape is one of the things reinforcing your child's behavior problems.

For older children who will understand it, you may want to draw up a behavioral contract. This is just another way to structure reinforcers and outline expectations. The basics of any contract (in business or at home) is that each person agrees on what he or she wants from the other. For example, you agree on what you want from your child (e.g., you will do your homework without crying) and what your child wants from you (e.g., can play a video game for 30 minutes). Writing up a contract can help remind both parties of expectations. This can be important because it can help to avoid misperceptions and arguments (e.g., "You said I could play the game for an hour!"). Contracts can be revised, usually by mutual consent, to accommodate changing needs. Figure 8.1 shows a sample behavioral contract.

As with scatter plots (or "star charts"), a number of things should be considered if you are planning to use a behavioral contract with your child:

1. Start by making it relatively easy for your child to earn privileges or reinforcers. You want your child to experience success early on in the process.

2. Use very simple language and include timelines (e.g., "We will allow you to play your choice of a video game for 30 minutes *on that day*") to avoid later misperceptions.

3. Avoid setting up negative consequences that become so overwhelming that your child quits trying to earn privileges or reinforcers. For example, if one bad incident results in losing computer privileges for a whole week, then your child has no incentive to behave better the rest of that week.

Date of contract	May 15		
Child agrees:	I will play nicely with my brother after school. I will not hit him or yell at him.	Parent agrees:	We will allow you to play your choice of a video game for 30 minutes on that day.
	If I hit my brother or yell at him, I will not get to play a video game that night.		
Child agrees:	I will come to the dinner table as soon as I am asked, without whining, crying, or complaining.	Parent agrees:	We will let you pick your choice of dessert for that meal.
	If I do not come to the dinner table when asked or if I whine, cry, or complain, I will not get dessert after dinner.		

We agree to the terms of this contract and will review and possibly revise it in _____ weeks.

Child's signature _____

Parent's signature _____

Figure 8.1.   Sample behavioral contract.

4.   Include your child in the process of designing the contract. Make sure that each of you agrees that the terms are fair.

5.   Make copies of the contract, including one to post in a highly trafficked area of your home.

6.   Revise the contract when necessary. Again, include your child in these negotiations whenever possible.

Sometimes, using these types of reinforcing strategies in combination with understanding the messages of the behaviors and how your own thoughts and feelings get in the way can be enough to make a major dent in your child's misbehavior. However, in most plans we also recommend that you try to teach your child a different and better way to communicate the messages he or she is sending with his or her misbehavior. This is the focus of the next chapter.

CHAPTER 9

Replacing Behavior Problems

If some behavior problems are a way for children to tell us something (e.g., "I want your attention," "I don't want to do this"), then what would happen if these children were taught how to ask for what they want but in a better and less disruptive way? In other words, what if we replaced behavior problems with another form of communication? This was the question I tried to answer more than 3 decades ago with my late colleague Ted Carr. We conducted a series of research studies that were designed to see 1) whether we could figure out the messages children were trying to send us with their challenging behaviors and 2) whether their disruptive behaviors would become less of a problem if we taught them better ways to communicate these messages. Our work led to the technique now called functional communication training.[1]

One of the first children with whom I used this approach was a 7-year-old boy named Josh. He had received a diagnosis of autism at the time and had a long history of very severe challenging behavior. This cute little boy with long hair often would bite his hand, slap the side of his face, and cry. His obvious distress concerned his family as well as his teacher, and I was asked to consult with his teacher about how to respond to these outbursts in the classroom. They were interfering with his schoolwork and had been a source of concern since Josh started school. I spent about an hour in Josh's classroom just sitting in the back and observing a typical day. Josh really did not interact with the other children in his class, who also had received a variety of diagnoses related to their developmental problems. Josh was working on a simple puzzle—it only had about 8 pieces—and would put it together and take it apart, over and over. After about 10 minutes of this, Josh's teacher—who had been going from desk to desk working individually with each child—sat down across from Josh. She helped him put the final pieces of the puzzle together and then removed it from his desk. Facing him, she asked, "Josh, what's your name?" He replied in a way that was a little difficult to understand, but I could tell he was trying to say his name. "Good!" his teacher said. "You're sitting nicely and looking at me. Okay, Josh, where do you live?" Almost immediately Josh brought his left hand up to his mouth and his right hand hit the side of his head. "No, Josh. No hitting!" As she said this, the teacher took Josh by his wrists to stop him from biting and hitting himself and led him over to the corner of the room. A small area with a foam mat had been partially partitioned off, and Josh's teacher told him to sit down in the corner. Josh calmed down after a minute or so, and everything settled down again in the classroom.

During Josh's "time-out," I had a chance to speak with his teacher about the plan for Josh's self-injury and why he might be getting so upset. "So, what do you think is going on with Josh?" We talked quietly at the other side of the room, out of earshot of the students in the class. "He seems to do well for long periods," I whispered, "yet he has these outbursts." I had my suspicions about what might be setting off Josh in the classroom (and by now I hope you do too!); but, because I had only watched him for a short time, I wanted to hear his teacher's interpretation. "Well, we think that he's having trouble with his ears. His parents told us that he often gets ear infections, which may be why he hits himself on the side of the face. He just looks so upset when it happens." After a little more information about Josh's medical history, I asked about the plan they were using. "How did you come up with using a time-out with Josh?" His teacher looked a little defensive, and at first I wasn't sure why she looked so uncomfortable. "We discussed this with the school psychologist and the principal and then with his parents. Everyone agreed. We even have a board at school that had to approve using the time-out because it is a restrictive program." Ah, now it began to make sense! She thought I would object to their using the time-out because it was a punisher. Everyone thought that putting Josh in the corner would serve as a punishment to Josh for hitting himself and that he would then do it less often. Later, I better understood that the teacher was being defensive with me because she did not like to use punishments with her students and was not sure if this plan was the right thing to do with Josh. By now it was time for Josh to go back to his seat. His teacher told me that the plan was for a 10-minute time-out but that it could go longer if he was still upset. The teacher led him back to his chair and put the puzzle on his desk. He immediately pulled it apart and started to put it back together.

In the days that followed, I asked Josh's teacher to complete the MAS and an ABC chart for Josh. After 2 weeks, we met again to go over the results of these assessments. I had a chance to look over the information before we met, so I had an idea about what might be triggering Josh's self-injury. "You can see here," I said, "that your answers on the MAS suggest that escape from demands might be involved. This means that Josh may be hitting himself to get out of doing schoolwork." "I don't think that's right," she said. "He doesn't hit himself every time he works. Just sometimes. That's why we think it might be because he is in some pain." "Well, he might be in pain," I agreed, "but it does seem as if this displays itself only at certain times. For example, when I was in the classroom, I never saw him hit himself when he was working with puzzles. And, if you look at the ABC charts that you completed, it seems that he gets upset mostly when you try to work with him." By now, I knew his teacher well enough to recognize the look on her face, and I immediately added, "From what I can see you are doing an extraordinary job of presenting these difficult tasks in a very positive way. I think he either is bored by the tasks—but I doubt it— or they are too difficult for him. Let's take a close look at what you wrote on his ABC charts." By this point, she was looking less defensive, and we went over her charts. A sample of the teacher's ABC chart for Josh follows.

TEACHER-COMPLETED ABC CHART FOR JOSH

Day and time	ANTECEDENTS What was happening just before your child's behavior problem?	BEHAVIOR Write down the behavior(s) as well as the number of times and/or how long they occurred.		CONSEQUENCES How did you or others react to the episode?
Monday, 10:15 a.m.	I was working with Josh on answering his safety questions (e.g., "What's your name?" "What's your address?").	He bit his hand, slapped his face, and started to cry.	1 minute	I put him in the time-out corner for 10 minutes.
Monday, 1:15 p.m.	Josh was with the speech therapist, and she was working on his articulation.	Hand biting, face slapping, and crying	2 minutes	The speech therapist put him in the time-out corner for 10 minutes.
Monday, 1:25 p.m.	Josh's speech therapist was leading him back to his chair after the time-out.	He bit his hand, slapped his face, and started to cry again.	1 minute	The speech therapist put him back in the time-out corner for another 10 minutes.

I continued my conversation with Josh's teacher, saying, "The first thing I noticed was that Josh never hit himself or cried if he was working alone on his puzzles." "Of course," his teacher quickly interrupted. "He would be very well behaved if he could sit all day just working on puzzles. But I can't just let him do that all day. He would never learn anything." "I agree. I wouldn't suggest that. But seeing that it never happens when he is on his own and not being challenged might give us an idea about why he keeps getting so upset. Let's look at the situations in which he does hit himself." We went over the reports from the past 2 weeks, and I pointed out the apparent pattern. "For example, see here—on Monday's report? The first outburst was when you were working with him on the safety questions. I remember when I was watching him before that he had a hard time with this. Also, the second time was during speech therapy. He has a hard time with that as well, doesn't he?" She agreed. "But, here is the telling part." I pointed to the entry. "Notice that he got upset as he was going back to work with the speech therapist. This suggests to me that he didn't want to go back." His teacher was interested. "Are you saying that he would rather be in time-out than at work?" "Yes," I said and waited for her to let this sink in. We went over the entries from other days, too, and, although there were exceptions, we noticed how the patterns were strikingly similar. Josh was clearly hitting himself and crying to escape difficult tasks, and the presumably restrictive time-out program was probably a reinforcer for him because it let him escape.

TEACHER PESSIMISM

Before I describe how we began the plan to replace Josh's behavior problems with communication, it is important to make an observation. Josh's teacher was being very defensive about her role in Josh's program and his success or lack thereof. She felt guilty using the time-out and was trying to protect herself from possible criticism. I mention this because parents are not the only ones who have pessimistic styles of thinking. Josh's teacher seemed to display some of the same perceptions as the mothers and fathers with whom my colleagues and I have worked. For example, when I first discussed Josh's self-hitting, Josh's teacher was quick to blame problems with his ear. In addition, many of her other comments (e.g., "He just looks so upset when it happens.") suggested that she thought his self-hitting was controlled by medical problems. Some parents *and* teachers can believe that these types of problem behaviors are out of a child's control. Again, this type of thought (i.e., that the child has no control over the behavior at all) will clearly interfere with a person's faith in and ultimate success with a plan to change the behavior. Also, Josh's teacher's defensiveness was a sign that she probably believed that I and others were judging her ability to help Josh. Although many of us can imagine feeling judged for the misbehaviors of our own children, imagine feeling judged for the behaviors of a classroom full of children.

My hope is that this perspective on your child's teachers also may help you view them in a more understanding light. It is very common for us as parents and/or professionals to interpret the challenging behavior of teachers— defensiveness or resistance—in a negative way; yet, if we take the time to understand the behavior of teachers (e.g., why Josh's teacher was so defensive about the time-out plan), we may see some order and reason in these responses. Because I could see that Josh's teacher was being self-protective, I learned to always point out the positives that I saw occurring in her classroom. Teachers often can be inundated with critical comments because—as with our children—we tend to pay more attention to problems than to successes. Next, you will see that Josh's teacher showed another pattern common to pessimistic styles of thinking. She would often blame herself or at least take responsibility for problems in the classroom but had a difficult time recognizing when successes were due to her efforts. Making these observations over the years about teachers is what prompted me to incorporate gratitude letters for teachers (see Chapter 5) into Optimistic Parenting. Again, I encourage you to look closely at the behavior of everyone who might pose problems for you in your efforts to help your child and consider that these other important people sometimes struggle with concerns similar to your own.

FUNCTIONAL COMMUNICATION TRAINING

I was waiting in line one day at a large department store; and, because it was a holiday weekend, the delay was longer than usual. People were shifting their weight back and forth impatiently and trying to peer ahead to see what was holding up the line. This was clearly affecting one young child who was pulling on his mother's arm and whining. I have to admit to feeling a little tinge of dread, fearing that we were about to experience a tantrum in this now hot and crowded store. His mother, however, leaned over calmly and said to her son, "Michael, use your words." The young boy then said with some urgency, "I have to go potty," and his mother left the line to go find a bathroom. Here, in a nutshell, is what we call *functional communication training*. Michael was trying to get his mother to take him to the bathroom, and perhaps she understood what he was trying to tell her with his grabbing and whining; yet, instead of reading into what he was doing and taking him to the bathroom, she instead encouraged him to "use his words" and ask her in a better way. This is, for many families, a natural process of encouraging children to get their needs and wants known in a way—with words—that is not annoying. What Michael, the little boy, was learning was that grabbing and whining would not get him what he wanted, but perhaps asking with words would.

In the same way, what my colleagues and I try to do for the children with more significant challenging behavior with whom we work is to 1) find out what they are trying to tell us and 2) teach them better ways of letting us know what they want. Going back to Josh's case, once we agreed that his self-hitting may have been a way of escaping from some of the tasks in his classroom (e.g., answering safety questions such as "Where do you live?" and the work he was doing in his speech therapy sessions), we worked out a plan to teach Josh how to use his words. The first step was to figure out what to get him to say. We all agreed that something along the lines of "I don't want to work"—which would let him escape—was not an acceptable option. I do think that teaching him to say "I don't want to work" when he was faced with unpleasant tasks would have "worked," meaning that once he had learned to say this and then did not have to do the tasks he disliked, he would have hit and bitten himself much less often. However, he also never would have learned how to tell others his address, improve his articulation, or deal with other difficult things in his life. So, instead, I recommended we teach him how to say "help me" when he had a hard time responding to difficult tasks. When you think about it, this is what we all do. For example, the other day my wife was in the kitchen and was having a difficult time opening a jar. She struggled with it a bit, but she did not scream or bite her hand; instead, she called for me in the next room and said, "Can you come here and help me with this?" And, I did. Had I been in the kitchen at the time and seen her struggling, I would not have just taken the jar from her and opened it. She probably would have been pretty annoyed at that. Instead, I would have said something such as, "Do you need help?"—the equivalent to saying, "Use your words." (Marital advice: Never actually say "Use your words" to your spouse in these situations. Trust me.)

For Josh, the words "Help me" seemed like a good, generic way for him to respond to challenges. It assumed that he would still attempt difficult situations but that he might need a little assistance. We started to teach Josh this in one of the situations that commonly made him frustrated. His teacher sat down at his desk across from him and started asking him the safety questions.

Teacher:	"Josh, what's your name?"
Josh:	"Josh."
Teacher:	"Good! Josh, where do you live?" But now, before Josh got upset, his teacher immediately added, "Josh, say, 'Help me.'"
Josh:	"Help me."
Teacher:	"You live at 71 Smith Street. Where do you live?"
Josh:	"71 Smith Street."
Teacher:	"Good."

In this situation, Josh did not hit himself, bite his hand, or cry. Instead, he sort of "escaped." He did not get out of answering the question "Where do you live?" Instead, he asked for and got help in the form of a prompt from his teacher. Asking for help and getting it made this difficult request a little bit easier. Very quickly, Josh's teacher gave him a little less assistance when prompting him to ask for help.

Teacher:	"Josh, what's your name?"
Josh:	"Josh."
Teacher:	"Good! Josh, where do you live?" Now she shortened the help she gave him. "Say help…." She waited a few seconds.
Josh:	"Help me."
Teacher:	"Okay, you live at 71 Smith Street. Where do you live?"
Josh:	"71 Smith Street."
Teacher:	"Good."

Josh's teacher's prompts were further reduced once she saw he could wait a bit without getting upset.

Teacher:	"Josh, what's your name?"
Josh:	"Josh."
Teacher:	"Good! Josh, where do you live?" Now, she shortened the help even further "Say…." She waited a few seconds.
Josh:	"Help me."
Teacher:	"Okay, you live at 71 Smith Street. Where do you live?"
Josh:	"71 Smith Street."
Teacher:	"Good."

Finally, once Josh's teacher asked a difficult question, she would simply look at Josh and wait for his answer.

Teacher:	"Josh, what's your name?"
Josh:	"Josh."
Teacher:	"Good! Josh, where do you live?" She waited a few seconds.
Josh:	"Help me."
Teacher:	"Okay, you live at 71 Smith Street. Where do you live?"
Josh:	"71 Smith Street."
Teacher:	"Good."

This process went fairly quickly with Josh, taking only a few days. Notice that Josh's teacher neither praised Josh nor gave him some treat or a star for saying "Help me"; instead, the reinforcer for saying "help" was…help! We wanted Josh to learn to use his words when he was confronted with a challenging situation so that other people would know what he wanted and could give him the help he needed.

While Josh's teacher was teaching Josh how to ask for help when she asked him safety questions, I also encouraged her to simultaneously set up situations in the classroom that might lead to problems to which Josh did not know how to respond. For example, Josh often would become frustrated when trying to put on his jacket to go outside, which would sometimes set off his self-hitting and crying; therefore, we used each time that Josh needed to leave the classroom to go outside to teach him to ask for help. We tried as much as possible to keep these teaching sessions as close to his usual routine as possible (e.g., only teaching him to ask for help with his coat when it was time to go outside) so that he would make these connections more easily. To make sure Josh had a difficult time putting on his coat each time, we secretly tied one of the coat's arms in a loose knot. This way, we knew Josh would actually need help each time. Please note that we quickly assisted him when he asked for help, which made this much more tolerable. So, each time Josh was to leave the building, his teacher would perform the following teaching steps:

Teacher:	Hands Josh his coat and says, "Josh, put on your coat."
Josh:	Tries to put his arm in his coat but is unable to push it all the way through because of the knot.
Teacher:	Before Josh gets upset, says, "Josh, say 'help me.'"
Josh:	"Help me."
Teacher:	Unties the knot and helps Josh with the coat.

Notice again that Josh's teacher did nothing to reinforce Josh for saying "Help me" other than actually help him. Again, we wanted Josh to learn that saying the words "Help me" got him help but was not an effective way to get anything else. As she had done before with the safety questions, Josh's teacher then very quickly removed her prompts.

Teacher:	Hands Josh his coat and says, "Josh, put on your coat."
Josh:	Tries to put his arm in his coat but is unable to push it all the way through because of the knot.
Teacher:	Before Josh gets upset, says, "Say…."
Josh:	"Help me."
Teacher:	Unties the knot and helps Josh with the coat.

This continued until the only "prompt" for Josh to say "Help me" was the fact that his arm was stuck.

Teacher:	Hands Josh his coat and says, "Josh, put on your coat."
Josh:	Tries to put his arm in his coat but is unable to push it all the way through because of the knot.
Teacher:	Just waits without giving further prompts.
Josh:	"Help me."
Teacher:	Unties the knot and helps Josh with the coat.

Again, Josh made quick progress and learned to say "help me" each time he got his arm stuck in his coat. In addition to putting on his coat, we also set up other mildly frustrating situations in the classroom, all of which could be resolved if Josh said "Help me." For example, we let Josh watch us put his favorite toy in a drawer in the classroom. What we did not let him see was that we rigged the drawer so that it would get stuck. Josh's teacher would work with Josh for a bit and then tell him he could get his toy out of the drawer as a reinforcer. When he went over to the drawer to retrieve the toy, however, he was unable to open the drawer. Again, as she had done in the other situations, Josh's teacher first prompted him to say "Help me" and then quickly reduced the amount of help she gave him to say the words. Soon, in this situation too, Josh learned to say "Help me" without his teacher's prompting, and she would help him get his toy.

In a matter of a few days, Josh was hitting and biting himself much less and was learning to deal with frustrating situations in this new way; however, all was not well. Josh's teacher asked to meet with me on the third day to discuss a problem with this new program. She pointed out that teaching Josh to ask for help was working so well that he was using it in situations other than those in which he had been taught to ask for help. From a behavioral perspective, this is called generalization—Josh was learning to say "Help me" in new frustrating situations without our having to specifically teach him to say it. This is typically a very good sign. However, Josh's teacher was concerned because he was now saying "Help me" in situations in which he really did not need help. For example, whereas before if the teacher had asked, "What's your name?" he would have said "Josh," now if she asked "What's your name?" Josh would say "Help me." This was upsetting to his teacher because it felt to her like a setback.

This was a dilemma. On one hand, we did not want Josh losing skills he had previously possessed (e.g., saying his name); on the other hand, we also wanted him to learn that the words "Help me" were in a sense "magical" and could be used in many different kinds of situations to save him from becoming too frustrated. There is no easy answer to this dilemma. In my judgment, because Josh was using his new words in many situations, I recommended that the teacher not accept "Help me" in situations in which Josh clearly did not need the help. This seemed to satisfy her, and Josh appeared to accept the teacher's nonacceptance and did what she was asking him to do.

The new program worked extremely well, and Josh's behavior that first week was the best it had been the whole time he had attended school. By not letting him escape from difficult situations (his teacher stopped putting him in the time-out corner if he hit or bit himself) and by encouraging him to make these tasks easier by asking for and getting help, Josh found that he no longer needed his challenging behavior but instead could be more successful using his words. This was one of our first successful uses of functional communication training to help significantly reduce severe challenging behavior in a child.

What bears mentioning, however, is Josh's teacher's reaction to the success of this program. As I alluded to before, Josh's teacher had a pessimistic style of thinking about Josh. This does not mean she didn't like him—in fact, she cared for him a great deal—or that she had given up on him—just the opposite—but certain aspects of her thinking resembled some of the thoughts we see in parents. When I met with her at the beginning of the second week of the program, I was ecstatic. Here was our first proof that our theory that challenging behaviors were a form of communication was correct and that teaching a child with behavior problems to communicate in a more effective way could be a very positive technique for reducing significant behavior problems. My good frame of mind was soon dashed, however. "I was looking at Josh's data for this week, and they look terrific! By Friday there were almost no outbursts. This is great!" His teacher looked at me, and I could see that she didn't share my enthusiasm. "Yes, he had a good week. He was in a good mood last week." A good mood?

After all of the work we had both put into Josh's plan and all of her special teaching efforts, she was unable to accept credit for his success. She could not see the connection between her teaching him to say "Help me" and his dramatically improved behavior. Again, this all too frequent reaction—one that puzzles many professionals—is the result of a pessimistic style of thinking and was not Josh's teacher's way of somehow trivializing the plan. When bad things happened, she would internalize those things and blame herself. When good things happened (e.g., Josh's good mood), she attributed the successes to external circumstances. In fact, she quickly switched her concern from Josh's previous self-hitting, biting, and crying to his problems with toileting. "His real problem is that he sometimes has accidents in the class. This is going to be a major problem for him and will probably keep him out of general education classrooms." Again, Josh's teacher did not take the time to enjoy the success—even if it was just a good mood—but instead immediately focused on another one of Josh's problems. In addition, she catastrophized Josh's toileting problems, making a few accidents in a month out to be more than they actually were.

My strategy for working with Josh's teacher included taking her concerns seriously. We discussed ways of helping Josh have fewer toileting accidents, and these improved significantly. However, I also made a point of highlighting her contributions to Josh's improvement to her principal and asked the principal to make a visit to the class to see what progress was being made. My role at that point was to help this teacher get the recognition she deserved and remain as positive and future-focused as possible. Some of my colleagues' and my research underway now is designed to see whether we can create an "optimistic teaching" approach to assist teachers such as Josh's in ways similar to what we do with Optimistic Parenting.

Josh's case highlights many of the steps my colleagues and I use to replace behavior problems with communication using the technique of functional communication training. Table 9.1 outlines how we go through this process. Note that previous chapter discussions already described in some detail how to assess the function of the behavior or find the messages behind your child's behavior problems.

Step 1: Find the Messages Behind the Problem Behaviors

Chapter 6 described how to look at situations to see what your child might be telling you with his or her challenging behavior. I always encourage parents and professionals to try more than one of these techniques for looking at problem behaviors. This way, you have more information about what might be going on. Usually, if a child seems to be acting up to communicate one of the social messages (e.g., "I want your attention," "I want that toy," "I want to be left alone"), then we move to the next steps. However, if the message is not social (e.g., "This feels good"), then I might encourage parents to use the strategies described in

Table 9.1. Steps for using functional communication training

Steps	Description
1. Find the messages behind the problem behaviors.	Use the techniques described in Chapter 6 to determine what your child is trying to communicate through problem behavior. Try to use more than one technique (e.g., the Motivation Assessment Scale and the ABC chart).
2. Select the way you want your child to communicate.	Select how you want your child to communicate in a new way depending on your child's level of skills (e.g., telling you with words, pointing to pictures).
3. Select and create the situations you will use to teach this new communication skill.	Identify situations in your child's world that are triggers for problem behavior (e.g., difficult tasks), and use these situations as the places for teaching this new skill.
4. Teach your child how to communicate in a new way.	Encourage your child to "use his or her words" during situations in which you would like him or her to communicate in a different way. Provide as little help as possible to encourage independence.
5. Reduce the amount of help you give your child to communicate.	Try to give less help over time as long as your child remains well behaved.
6. Teach new messages.	When possible, teach new versions of the communication (e.g., saying "Help me" or "I don't understand") that may be helpful in different situations.
7. Change things about your child's world.	When appropriate, changes in your child's world—for example, offering more choices at meals or being less protective—should be considered.

Chapter 8, "Managing Consequences," to try to encourage the child to do other more helpful behaviors and to create incentives for your child not to act in ways that only result in sensory feedback (e.g., playing with saliva, hand flapping).

Step 2: Select the Way You Want Your Child to Communicate

Usually, this step is easy. If your child already can use words to let you know what he or she wants, then you would use words. In Josh's case, although his verbal abilities were limited, he still could let us know what he wanted with simple words or phrases. Words have the advantage of being understood by the most people. Some children, however, have limited or no verbal skills. I have worked with some children for whom problem behaviors are their only way of letting us know what they need. If your child has limited or no verbal skills, choosing how you want him or her to communicate can be more difficult. My rule of thumb is to choose the method that is the easiest for your child to use—at least at first. One example may help to illustrate this potential problem.

I worked with one little girl, Natasha, who had no understandable words and would usually let us know what she wanted by grabbing at things. Unfortunately, she also spent a great deal of time screaming at home and in her classroom, which was obviously highly disruptive. I met with Natasha's mother and teacher to go over the results of the assessments, and they strongly suggested that the message she was trying to communicate with her misbehavior was for tangibles. As we went over the options, we all agreed that any plan for Natasha should include teaching her how to better ask for the things she wanted; however, one area of disagreement was in how she was to tell us. Her speech therapist at school was trying to teach Natasha how to say words (including "yes" and "no") and was strongly advocating for having Natasha ask for things with words. She had very sound reasons for this as a future goal and wanted all communication plans to be similar. There was a problem with this plan, however. One of the things that my colleagues and I have found over the years is that if it is too difficult to communicate using words, children will go back to doing what is easiest—in this case, probably grabbing and crying. Robert Horner and his colleagues at the University of Oregon demonstrated this in a number of studies showing that children will resort to whichever mode of communication (behavior problem or some better way to ask) works best.[2] My concern with Natasha's program was that she might become frustrated if we tried to get her to say what she wanted. Saying words was difficult for her, and my guess was that she would give up trying and go back to acting up.

As we discussed these issues, I offered a compromise. What if we first taught her just to point to a picture of what she wanted and, once that was successful, start to encourage her to say the word along with pointing to it? This way, Natasha could get what she wanted quickly and easily, and we would hopefully see her be better behaved. It took a little convincing, but eventually everyone agreed to give it a try. It helped to know that most research suggests that using some of these alternative communication strategies such as pointing to pictures or using sign language does not interfere with efforts to help children talk and, in fact, might make it easier.[3] Fortunately, our efforts with Natasha paid off quickly. She learned how to point to pictures of what she wanted, which dramatically reduced the amount of time she was grabbing at things and crying. And, this new way of "talking" opened up a whole new world for Natasha. Her teacher kept adding pictures to her communication device (including one for using the bathroom), and Natasha seemed to really enjoy being able to make her needs known.

Not all of our efforts to teach other ways of communicating have been as successful as this. Another lesson I learned early on was that in addition to making the new form of communication easy to do, everyone must be able to understand it. If, for example, a child uses sign language to communicate but does not do it clearly or tries to use it with people who do not understand sign language, problems will result. This is not unique to sign language. Any modes of communication taught to your child must be easily understood by other people. This is why we sometimes start with pictures for children who have difficulty communicating in other ways. Pointing to a picture of a bathroom or a glass of water makes it pretty clear what the child wants. Again, keep these issues in mind as you are making decisions about how you want your child to tell other people his or her needs.

Step 3: Select and Create the Situations You Will Use to Teach This New Communication Skill

Once you know what you want your child to say (e.g., "Help me") and how you want your child to say it (e.g., by talking to you), the next step is to think through where you want to teach your child this new skill. The main idea is to create opportunities for communication. For example, when we worked with Josh, we made it difficult for him to put on his coat (tying a knot in the arm) and to open a drawer that had a favorite toy (by rigging it to be stuck closed). The important part of this step is to match the opportunity with why your child is misbehaving. Table 9.2 provides a few sample opportunities for communication that can be used for teaching a new communication skill.

The goal for each of these activities is to set up a situation that usually triggers problem behavior in your child. However, as I describe in the next step, you do not really want your child to get upset or act out; instead, you want to quickly encourage your child to communicate in this new way, which will end the uncomfortable situation. Therefore, if your child is misbehaving to get attention, use one of the sample opportunities—for example, playing with your child and then turning your attention to another child or someone else in the

Table 9.2.   Sample opportunities for teaching communication

Message	Opportunity
Attention	Play with your child in the living room, and then go to the next room for a minute.
	Play with your child, and then turn your attention to another child or someone else in the room.
	Start a telephone call during which it is okay if you are interrupted.
	Read a story together that will end with you leaving your child (e.g., at bedtime).
	Have a brother, sister, or other child play with your child in the living room. Then, have the other child go to the next room for a minute.
	Have a brother, sister, or other child play with your child. Then, have the other child turn his or her attention to another child or someone else in the room.
Tangible	Place a favorite toy, object, or food in your child's sight but in a place that he or she cannot get it on his or her own.
	Allow your child to play with a favorite toy or object for a short period of time, and then signal that it is time to stop.
	Allow your child to have a small piece of a favorite food or small amount of a favorite drink.
	Allow your child to engage in a favorite activity for a short period of time, and then signal that it is time to stop.
Escape	Ask your child to do a less preferred task around the house.
	Ask your child to engage in a nonpreferred activity.

room—as the place and time to teach the new communication. Similarly, if the message your child is trying to communicate is for tangibles, then you might allow your child to play with a favorite toy or object for a short period of time and then signal to him or her that it's time to stop. You can see that this might be a usual time when your child would resist. One strategy in this situation might be to teach your child to ask for more time (e.g., "Can I play for 5 more minutes?"). However, if this is your goal, be sure to be clear that you mean 5 minutes—not 10 or more. Sometimes, a timer can help make this clear for some children; however, if your child starts to scream or misbehave, you would make sure that the fun activity ends. Period. The lessons? Ask nicely and good things can happen (e.g., more play time). Misbehave and you get no extra time.

Similarly, if escape is your child's message, then the teaching situation would be a typical situation in which your child would misbehave to escape. Again, in Josh's case, we identified a number of situations around his classroom that frustrated him and used those situations as opportunities to teach him to ask for help. Sometimes, it is appropriate to teach children to ask for help—for example, if your child has difficulty getting dressed or washing up. Other times, teaching your child to ask for a break can be more appropriate. Asking for a break is used a great deal at school and in work programs for adults. A difficult situation can be made less difficult if the time it takes to finish can be broken up into smaller increments. For example, if you are asking your child to clean up his or her room, which can take a while, it would be fine to teach your child to ask to do part, take a short break, and then finish. Obviously, the break should be short and your child needs to return to the task until it is completed.

Step 4: Teach Your Child How to Communicate in a New Way

With all of these examples, it is important to note that the children are being taught in the actual situations that have become a problem. In my experience, this is not typically how parents try to instruct their child to be better behaved. Sometimes, parents have a tendency to preach rather than to teach. "You know you shouldn't hit Mommy!" "What did I tell you about yelling in the store? You know you're not supposed to do that." "We are going to grandma's house. Are you going to be good?" Although I do not want to downplay giving your child feedback on bad behavior, the focus is on teaching new and better ways to behave. The best way to do that is to instruct your child in better ways to respond to these difficult situations by recreating the situations and giving feedback as I am describing. If you find yourself preaching—verbally reminding your child how to behave after the fact or telling your child to be good in the future—then you should keep these concerns in mind. Teach, don't preach.

Having preached to you on the importance of teaching (ironic isn't it!), teaching and not preaching can be difficult. For some children, it can be easy just to model what they need to say or otherwise communicate (e.g., "Can you come here?"). For others, it can be more complicated. If you find yourself needing more assistance, a number of helpful resources are listed in Appendix B at the back of this book.

Step 5: Reduce the Amount of Help You Give Your Child to Communicate

Let's look back at how we taught Josh to say "Help me" because there are lessons in that situation for how to teach children who may need more assistance. Josh's teacher and I selected putting on his coat as a good situation to teach Josh to ask for help because this often frustrated him. If you remember back to earlier in the chapter, Josh's teacher began the instruction by asking Josh to put on his coat; then, as soon as Josh looked as if he was having a difficult time but before he became upset she would tell him to ask for help—"Josh, say 'help me.'"

Once Josh could do this easily and his teacher could send him on his way without a tantrum, she then gave him a little less help with what he should say when he needed help; instead of saying, "Josh, say 'help me'" to Josh, she limited her prompt to a simple "Say...." Her voice went up in anticipation of a response from him, and then she waited. This can be hard for teachers and parents to do. We all want to jump right in and help our children, but waiting and saying nothing can actually be a very powerful teaching technique. In fact, when I teach groups of parents how to teach their children better ways of communicating, I will repeat Josh's scene and say to the group, "Say..." and wait. Invariably, about a quarter of the audience fills in the blanks by saying "Help me!" Did I tell them to say it? No. But simply leaving this open makes people feel just a little bit uncomfortable, and their natural instinct is to complete the sentence. So, sometimes less is more; prompt less and see what your child does.

Finally, Josh's teacher stopped indicating that she wanted Josh to say something by no longer including the phrase "Say..." and waiting to see what Josh would do. Here, his teacher just used the situation itself (i.e., I can't get my arm in the coat) to trigger his new communication. My observation has been that when your child can start to use the new form of communication independently, you will really start to see improvements in his or her behaviors.

Step 6: Teach New Messages

Once you feel comfortable with your child's progress, it may be helpful to consider other messages to teach your child. For example, in Josh's case, we also eventually taught him how to say "I don't understand" when he was asked a question and did not know the answer. Although saying "Help me" also might work in getting people to assist him with difficult questions, it seemed more natural for him to say "I don't understand" when someone spoke to him and he did not know what to do.

It also is often the case that children will misbehave for multiple reasons (e.g., to get attention when left alone and to get things that are not available). In these cases, we would first work on the most disruptive situation (e.g., screaming in the car). Then, once we were successful, we would move on to teach other forms of communication as well. For the second situation, we follow all of the same steps as with the first situation.

Step 7: Change Things About Your Child's World

I have spent a considerable amount of time throughout this book recommending that you avoid changing your world to avoid problem behavior in your child. For example, you would not want to put a child's car seat in the front passenger's seat, which is dangerous, because your child gets upset in the back or stop going out to the store with your child because of your concern that he or she will be disruptive. There are times, however, when what your child is trying to communicate can lead to helpful changes in your child's world. For example, screaming in a supermarket may indicate that your child is hungry and tired. In this case, in addition to teaching your child better ways to communicate, you may want to plan ahead by giving your child a snack and starting off with shorter shopping trips.

MORE HELP

The information I provided in this chapter as well as in the previous three chapters should be helpful to many families when it comes to helping their children improve their problem behaviors. Some special situations, however, may require more information and assistance. Transitions (e.g., going from the house to the car, going from the television to the dinner table) are one type of situation that may require special attention. In addition, sleep problems often cannot be properly addressed without knowing more details about the kind of problem your child is experiencing. Because of this, I have added two separate chapters in the last section of the book—"Special Topics"—that might prove helpful to you if your child experiences one or more of these difficulties.

If, after going through this entire book and trying the suggestions, you need more help, I have added a list of additional resources at the end of this book that may assist you with more examples and details. I would also encourage you, however, to seek out support and services from others. Your child's school might be a very good source for this kind of information. If you have not yet considered it, I would encourage you to create a support network that can provide you with emotional support (especially along the lines of the Optimistic Parenting support group I described in Chapter 5) as well as additional ideas. I also would encourage you to find a good counselor or therapist who can help you with your own struggles as well as with your struggles with your child. More and more professionals are recognizing the need to incorporate CBT (such as the Optimistic Parenting described here) for many parents of children with behavior problems along with good behavioral parenting techniques. Finding a professional with whom to work might be a challenge, but other parents may be able to direct you to good resources. One hint: I always tell people who are looking for any type of counselor that they should use their intuition. If you are uncomfortable with the first person you see, move on. It is difficult to be successful with someone who you might not trust or who may just have a personality that does not mesh with yours. This is common, and you should not feel uncomfortable about looking for another person who is a better match.

Whatever you decide to do, do it well and with a hopeful approach. Important positive change is possible for you and your family if you persist. I wish you a successful and pleasant voyage!

SECTION III

Special Topics

CHAPTER 10

Transitions

If you want to make enemies, try to change something.

—Woodrow T. Wilson (1856–1924, U.S. president)

At the top of the list of difficulties that many families face when living with a child who is challenging is problems with transitions. Handling the disruption that can occur when trying to get a child to leave one setting or activity and move to another can be particularly upsetting. Although transitions can be difficult for any child, children with autism spectrum disorders or those with symptoms of OCD are particularly at risk for resisting change. This chapter touches on a variety of approaches for improving transitions. It builds on the skills used in the previous chapters to help you implement effective techniques for reducing child resistance while simultaneously encouraging the practice of Optimistic Parenting techniques to reduce your own frustration. The story of one mother's difficulty with her child's resistance to change follows:

Inez is a young mother of a little girl with a diagnosis of PDD-NOS. Five-year-old Viviana liked to play by herself and showed little interest in other children. Inez told us, "She can sit and play with one of her blankets for hours at a time." Her blankets were now small pieces of cloth that had been shredded into pieces that Viviana liked to pick up and watch fall to the ground. "Viviana will watch the fuzz drop from her hand, and she will stare at it with her head turned to the side. Sometimes, she will smile and flap her hands in front of her eyes, and that's how you can tell she's happy." Viviana was a relatively easy child to live with as long as you did not interrupt her when she was playing. Of course, she could not spend her days watching fuzz fall to the floor, and her mother was desperate for help to get her to engage in other important activities such as getting dressed, washing up, eating, and going out to her school bus. It was during these times, when Viviana was asked to change from one activity to another, that she would get upset. Inez told us that Viviana would at first try to ignore her mother's requests but then start to scream as well as try to kick and hit her. "I usually wait until the last minute to ask her to do something so she has a lot of time to play, but I still have to get her going, you know? I mean, I can't just let her play with her blankets all day. But then she seems so unhappy, I don't know what to do!"

My colleagues and I began our process of trying to help Viviana and Inez by obtaining information about why Viviana might be getting so upset. Although it seemed pretty obvious to all of us that Viviana's meltdowns were the result of her trying to escape from the demands being placed on her (e.g., "Time to come to dinner," "We have to go out to the bus stop"), we asked Inez to fill out the MAS and an ABC chart just to make sure we were not missing anything. This information from Inez confirmed our suspicions, and so we set out to help Inez with Viviana's behavior problems.

In addition to completing the MAS and an ABC chart for Viviana, we also believed that it was important for us to understand Inez's thoughts about Viviana's tantrums so that we could help Inez with the plans we would be asking her to use. Inez's self-talk journal proved very helpful for all of us. A typical entry appears next and shows how Inez looked at these problem situations.

INEZ'S JOURNAL: INITIAL ENTRY

SITUATION What happened (success or difficulty)?	THOUGHTS What did you think or say to yourself when this happened?	FEELINGS What emotions did you experience and how did you react physically when this happened?
Viviana was in the living room playing with her blankets. It was time to get washed up for bed, and I asked her to come into the bathroom. She ignored me, so I took her arm to get her up and she started to scream. She kicked me a few times and was trying to get away from me. (difficulty)	I thought that this is always a problem and that it is never going to end. What will happen to her if I'm not around? Why does she have this problem (PDD-NOS)?	I wanted to cry and escape. I was angry at her; then I felt guilty because I had gotten angry.

Typically, people will make a series of recommendations to a parent at this point about how to set up the situation differently to prevent the child's outbursts; however, my colleagues and I knew that unless we also dealt with

Inez's thoughts and feelings, she would be less likely to be successful. We began by looking for the "themes" of Inez's thoughts about her daughter and her daughter's problems and recognized several of the more common ones (see Chapter 3). Then, we engaged Inez in the disputation process to see whether her thoughts were accurate and coached her in using some distraction techniques (see Chapter 4).

Inez's self-talk showed us several major themes surrounding her concerns:

1. My child's disability or condition is causing or contributing to this problem ("Why does she have this problem [PDD-NOS]?").

2. This type of situation is always a problem for my child ("I thought that this is always a problem").

3. This will never get better or may become worse ("...it was never going to end").

4. I will never have time for just me ("I wanted to cry and escape").

Although other themes were present as well, these were the ones that came up over and over in Inez's interactions with Viviana. My colleagues and I then went through the disputation process with Inez to see which of these thoughts were realistic and which might be overblown (see the following example). We also tried to help Inez determine whether her thoughts were helpful to her, even if they were accurate.

INEZ'S JOURNAL: DISPUTATION PROCESS

SITUATION What happened (success or difficulty)?	THOUGHTS What did you think or say to yourself when this happened?	FEELINGS What emotions did you experience and how did you react physically when this happened?	DISPUTATION Were your thoughts accurate and useful?
Viviana was in the living room playing with her blankets. It was time to get washed up for bed, and I asked her to come into the bathroom. She ignored me, so I took her arm to get her up and she started to scream. She kicked me a few times and was trying to get away from me. (difficulty)	I thought that this is always a problem and that it was never going to end. What will happen to her if I'm not around? Why does she have this problem (PDD-NOS)?	I wanted to cry and escape. I was angry at her; then I felt guilty because I had gotten angry.	It is always a problem, but I guess it is not helpful to think this way. And, thinking that it was never going to end or that it was all due to her problem is also not helpful. It's not wrong to feel angry as long as I don't act on it by hitting her or something like that.

As you can see from Inez's responses to the disputation process, the issues with Viviana really were "always a problem." Unlike some other children, Viviana *did* get upset every time she was asked to stop playing. However, although this was an accurate thought, it wasn't a helpful one. The thought that Viviana's behavior was always a problem caused Inez to dread each of these situations and approach them tentatively. If you remember, Inez told us that she did her best to avoid interfering with Viviana's playtime (i.e., "I usually wait to the last minute to ask her to do something so she has a lot of time to play. But I still have to get her going, you know?"). What we discovered was that Inez was avoiding getting her daughter to do things in anticipation of Vivana's reaction. For example, although Inez wanted Viviana to put on her own shoes, she had stopped asking her some time ago; now she would just get Viviana's shoes and put them on Viviana herself so that she did not to have interrupt her playing. This, you will recall, is part of what I call the concession process (i.e., giving in to the needs and demands of your child at the expense of your needs and the needs of the rest of your family) and was causing Inez to ask less and less of her daughter. We also went over Inez's feelings of guilt about getting angry and helped her understand that feeling angry—but not acting on that anger—was very common and not something to be concerned about.

Once we had addressed Inez's thought processes, we began to design a plan for Viviana. We started by asking Inez to describe what she had liked to do best when she was a little girl. "Oh, I loved to sing and dance. My little sister and I would put on music and make believe we were famous. We made up routines and everything!" This brought a big smile to her face, and she told us she hadn't thought about those times in years. Next, we asked her to think about something she had to do as a little girl that she did not like doing. Immediately, she said, "Housework! My mother was working, and we had to vacuum and dust and clean the bathroom. I hated to clean the bathroom. Ugh!" We pointed out that for Viviana, playing with her blankets was like what singing and dancing with her sister was for Inez. "For Viviana, this is her favorite thing to do. Imagine, now, if you were having fun with your sister and had just started a new routine and your mother said you had to clean the bathroom. What would you do in that situation?" "Oh. My mother always told us when we had to do the chores. So we knew when we could be 'stars' together and how long we had." Here was our *in*. We pointed out that Viviana never knew how much time she had to play with her blankets. At some point in time, usually with no warning, she was asked to stop doing her favorite thing and do something unpleasant. In Viviana's world, this was all unpredictable.

We followed up on these observations. "Did you ever play music when you did your chores?" She smiled. "Yes. And sometimes the vacuum or the toilet brush was my microphone." We pointed out that Inez was able to make cleaning the bathroom and other chores more bearable by pairing something pleasant (music and singing) with these unpleasant chores. So, we asked, "How could we make Viviana's transition from play to work more like what you did when you were younger?"

Using these personal examples, we worked together to create a plan. First, we needed to make the transitions from Viviana's playtime to other activities predictable. That way, over time, Viviana could start to anticipate when she was going to have to stop a favorite activity and start a less-preferred activity, which would make that time easier to handle. Second, we wanted to make the unpleasant situation (e.g., getting dressed, washing up, going to the bus stop) more pleasant. Predictability and making positive transitions are the basic components of improving transitions. Before describing Viviana's new plan, however, it will be helpful to finish describing our work with Inez and her thoughts about these situations. The following example of Inez's self-talk journal entries with the distraction technique we taught her shows how we worked through these obstacles.

INEZ'S JOURNAL: DISTRACTION TECHNIQUE

SITUATION What happened (success or difficulty)?	THOUGHTS What did you think or say to yourself when this happened?	FEELINGS What emotions did you experience and how did you react physically when this happened?	DISPUTATION Were your thoughts accurate and useful?	DISTRACTION What did you do to shift your attention?
Viviana was in the living room playing with her blankets. It was time to get washed up for bed, and I asked her to come into the bathroom. She ignored me, so I took her arm to get her up and she started to scream. She kicked me a few times and was trying to get away from me. (difficulty)	I thought that this is always a problem and that it is never going to end. What will happen to her if I'm not around? Why does she have this problem (PDD-NOS)?	I wanted to cry and escape. I was angry at her; then I felt guilty because I had gotten angry.	It is always a problem, but I guess it is not helpful to think this way. And, thinking that it was never going to end or that it was all due to her problem is also not helpful. It's not wrong to feel angry as long as I don't act on it by hitting her or something like that.	Each time before I needed to ask her to do something I went over the plan in my mind. This way, I knew what I needed to do and how I should react if she acts up.

Once we had gone through the disputation process with Inez, we had her practice a distraction technique. Instead of approaching these situations with thoughts of impending doom—feelings that possibly could have been picked up on by her daughter, making the transition that much more unpleasant—we taught Inez how to think through what she was going to do next and how she would react if it became a problem. The goal here was to make her feel more in control of these situations. So, instead of thinking, "Oh, no, here we go again," we decided that Inez would distract herself by thinking, "I know what to do. First I will…" Even before the plan began to be effective, Viviana told us that going into each of these situations reminding herself about what she needed to do made her feel better and more empowered to carry out the plan or deal with problems if they arose.

To return to our strategy for dealing with Viviana's difficulty with leaving her playtime, we incorporated the two main aspects of every transition plan— predictability and making positive transitions. Helping Viviana make the transition from playing with her blankets to some other activity was a little challenging. Viviana had no words, and it wasn't clear how much of what Inez told her she could understand; therefore, telling her "Two minutes before it's time to wash up" might not be understood. It quickly became clear that using words alone to warn Viviana would not be a good signal of what was to come. Because of Viviana's limited verbal ability, we worked out that Inez would use a timer and a picture of the next activity. The timer could be set for a few minutes, and then a bell would ring. The plan was that when the bell rang the first time, Inez would 1) take all of Viviana's blankets except for one, 2) show her a picture of what they were going to do next (e.g., a picture of Inez and Viviana washing up in the bathroom), and 3) re-set the timer in front of her for two minutes saying, "We are going to wash up in the bathroom in two minutes." Again, we were not sure whether Viviana could understand what was being said; however, even if she could not, we decided that she might be able to pick up the message over time. Once the timer rang (after 2 minutes), Inez was to show Viviana the picture again, tell her it was now time to wash up, and lead her over to the bathroom. Instead of leaving the last blanket where it was, however, Inez was to pick it up and take it with them to the bathroom.

This last step—taking the remaining blanket to the next activity—was part of the making positive transitions aspect of our plan. Just as Inez had liked to play music when cleaning the bathroom as a girl, we wanted to add some positive quality to Viviana's other activities. In this case, Inez brought Viviana's blanket to the next chore or task; once Viviana finished the next activity, she could have more time with her blanket. By carrying it with her, Inez was using the blanket as a transition object—something that is positive and comforting that, in this case, makes going to the next activity more pleasurable. Getting the blanket at the end of the task also gave Viviana something to look forward to once she finished her task. So, instead of going from a great time (i.e., playing with her blanket) to a bad time (i.e., washing her face), we could make Viviana's transition a bit more positive.

Inez told us that the first few days of this plan were difficult. Viviana still acted out when it was time to leave her playtime, and the timer and the picture did not seem to help. We anticipated that the new transition plan would not be successful right away and had prepared Inez for this. Again, this is where the distraction technique was useful, reminding Inez that she had a plan and she was able to carry this out. After the first few days, however, Viviana seemed to understand what was going on and several situations were becoming easier. In about a week, the number of tantrums decreased by more than half; and, after 2 weeks, Viviana was fairly well-behaved during these transitions. Inez said that Viviana seemed to accept that she had to stop playing but that if she cooperated with her mother she could get back to playing sooner. Inez was so encouraged by this that she made up a picture book of transition activities and was able to communicate with Viviana what was going to happen next. Occasionally, Viviana pointed to pictures in the book, indicating things she actually did want to do, and the book became a new communication tool they could use at home.

PREDICTABILITY

Again, the two components of good transition plans include predictability and making positive transitions. For many children, predictability can be very comforting. Knowing what is going to happen next can allow the child to prepare mentally and emotionally for changes in routines. For some children, increasing predictability can be as easy as saying, "Dinner in 10 minutes!" Even in these cases, however, we sometimes find that parents do not use predictability as a regular tool. For example, in our research with sleep problems, one of our common observations is that many families do not have a regular bedtime for their children.[1] The bedtime reminder is usually something like, "Oh my goodness. Look what time it is. Go to bed." This abrupt change from having a good time to sending a child off to bed can be disruptive and too much for some children to handle. Again, some children need more structure and behave better when they can anticipate what will happen next.

There are a number of ways to increase predictability for children. In Viviana's case, the ringing timer—first for the "2-minute warning" and then for the time to actually move—was one successful tool for warning her about what was going to happen. Some parents and teachers have used handmade clocks with hands they could move themselves to show their child when one activity was about to end and the next one about to begin.

Using pictures, especially in the form of picture schedules, is also a very useful tool for children who may not be able to keep track of upcoming activities on their own. This is essentially what Inez created following her initial efforts to get Viviana away from her blankets. Over time, Inez created a picture schedule that showed dinnertime, playtime, washing up, bedtime, and so forth. Inez would carry it around and periodically remind Viviana of what activity she was doing currently and what she was to do next. Now that digital cameras are becoming cheaper and more accessible, it is easy to create real pictures of your child engaged in each activity. Although Viviana learned how to use her picture schedule without any problems, other children may require more training. If this is the case for your child, a number of good resources are available for how to teach your child to use these types of aids.[2]

Sometimes, you cannot predict what will happen next; this, too, may cause disruption for your child. In one family, for example, the daughter would scream if her parents didn't follow their usual route home from the store. Unfortunately, her parents occasionally needed to go to another destination along a different road or construction along their usual route required a detour. In these cases, the parents would brace themselves for a prolonged tantrum. We helped them by using a picture schedule that included a road map to show their daughter which way they were driving. If they needed to change the schedule—for example, not go right home after the store—they went over the change in schedule using picture cues and also showed her how they would be driving a different way. As with Inez's efforts with Viviana, this took some time for the daughter to understand, but once she did her parents were able to increase the amount of change their daughter could handle by making it predictable.

For children who are capable of handling it, we sometimes build in some of the skills I described in Chapter 9, "Replacing Behavior Problems." The goal here is to teach a child to ask for a little more time to engage in his or her preferred activity. This is a tricky technique to do successfully, so I would encourage you to approach this carefully. For example, some parents who read to their children at night before bed have found that their children are already very talented at doing this—"Just one more story!"—and know how difficult it is to limit this. You do want to encourage your child to have some control over these situations because that can make the transitions even more positive. The ground rules, however, need to be clear. If you are going to allow one more story, 5 more minutes of playing or television or computer time, or one more cookie, then there must be a very clear understanding about what you will and will not allow. Children can learn the "one more" rule if you can be firm and *only* allow one more. Basically, what I am asking you to do is to be rigid in your flexibility. In this way, you again make clear that how you will respond is predictable, which is the goal.

MAKING POSITIVE TRANSITIONS

In addition to predictability, it is important to create a situation in which the transition away from a favorite activity has some benefits for your child. Again, if from your child's perspective he or she is having a good time and then suddenly is being dragged off unexpectedly (e.g., getting washed, getting dressed, being interrupted), then you should not be surprised at his or her resistance. In each effort to improve transitions, we try to build in positive aspects for each of the following parts of transition:

1. The warning that a change is coming soon

2. The actual transition activity—for example, putting toys away, turning off the television, dealing with a change in routine

3. Arriving at the new activity

4. Being well behaved throughout the transition

Going back to the example from Inez and Viviana, we attempted to incorporate positive aspects into each of these four parts of the transition. When Inez approached Viviana with the activity change picture and the timer, she tried to be as upbeat and positive as she could. Viviana liked to be tickled, so each time Inez started the warning, she would take a few seconds to tickle and play with her daughter, basically communicating that what was happening was fun. Then, as they were making a transition to the next activity, Inez again would try to make it fun for Viviana and also allowed Viviana to bring along one of her blankets. Whenever possible, Inez tried to make the arrival at the next activity as positive as she could. For example, if it was time to wash up, once they got to the bathroom Viviana was allowed to take a few seconds to turn on and off the water in the sink, which she liked to do. If the transition was to go to the kitchen for lunch, Inez had a piece of Viviana's favorite food (e.g., chips) already on the table for Viviana to eat. And finally, if Viviana went with her mother without screaming, Inez allowed Viviana to go right back to playing with her blankets—giving her all of the blankets back to her—as soon as the activity was done. Again, positive components were added to each aspect of the transition.

I described in Chapter 9 how providing choices can be one way to make a situation more positive for a child. Children like to have some control over situations—just as adults do—and this should be considered whenever possible. The case of one mother and her daughter provides an example of using choices in transition situations. Jaynie, a single mother with a daughter, Rebecca, who had an autism spectrum disorder, told me this story about her difficulties getting Rebecca onto the school bus in the morning. Jaynie would ask Rebecca each morning, "Are you ready to go to the bus stop?" Right away, this question breaks the cardinal rule of parenting—never ask a question if you do not want "no" for an answer! Rebecca would routinely say "no," which would start the struggle. It was not clear to Jaynie just why Rebecca did not like getting on the bus. Was it because she did not want to leave home or her mother? Was it school she didn't like or the bus ride itself? None of this made sense at first, but it was essential that Rebecca get on the bus. So, Jaynie decided to give Rebecca some choices. Instead of saying, "Are you ready to go to the bus stop?" she would say, "What do you want to take to the bus stop? Your blue backpack or your pink backpack?" Because Rebecca liked to have some control over this decision, it immediately focused her attention on preparing her choice of backpack for the day rather than on the bus stop. Once they arrived at the bus stop, Jaynie would ask Rebecca, "Do you want to sit in the front or the back of the bus?" Once again, the choice was not whether she wanted to ride the bus but instead *how* she wanted to ride the bus. There still was a choice, but now it did not include whether to go to school.

Another method for making a situation more acceptable is to do what is called a mood induction. I described using music to change one's mood in Chapter 6 when I was highlighting research with children with severe behavior problems. Essentially, it involves preparing yourself or someone else for what might be a challenging situation by starting off with some activity that puts you in a good mood. Most of us do this already. For example, it might be the few minutes in the morning spent reading the newspaper and having a cup of coffee before you start to make lunches and wake up your children. For people who work in offices, mood induction might involve checking e-mail before starting up the day. At most conferences where I give talks, the organizers usually give the attendees coffee and something to eat to put them in a relaxed and positive mood before they have to sit through hours of my droning voice.

In much the same way, you can use a mood induction to transform a transition into a positive activity. Playing upbeat music is one easy way to accomplish this for many people. For example, we suggested to Inez that she play music to put herself in a good mood and that maybe that mood would rub off on Viviana. A favorite food or drink also can be a good way to start off what might be an unpleasant activity. A small snack before bedtime, for example, can curb your child's nighttime hunger and also be a positive start to an otherwise unpleasant routine (i.e., getting ready for bed).

Problems with transitions can take many different forms, and it is difficult to provide you with examples that will fit your situation perfectly. It is important to remember, however, to follow the basic steps I described for assessing your individual situation and developing strategies for yourself and for your child. These steps include the following:

1. Assess why your child might be having a difficult time with transitions (refer to Chapter 6).

2. Assess your own thoughts and feelings as they relate to this problem, and practice the strategies described to help you through the difficult times (refer to Chapters 3 and 4).

3. Incorporate aspects of predictability into your child's plan.

4. Incorporate making positive transitions into each part of the transition activity (i.e., the warning, the actual transition activity, arriving at the new activity, and consequences for successful making successful transitions).

SUMMARY

As we have seen with all types of behavior problems, the first step in helping any child is to first understand the situation from his or her perspective. In the case of transitions, often the difficulty lies in trying to get a child to give up a pleasant activity. You can improve the chances of success in these situations by making it clear when time is up for the current activity (predictability) and building in an incentive to go to the next activity (making positive transitions). The next chapter on sleep problems shows that sometimes bedtime issues are just a special case of a problem with transitions. But, as with all child difficulties, first it is important to try to understand the sleep issues that your child might have and how your thoughts and feelings might be helping or hurting your efforts to assist your child.

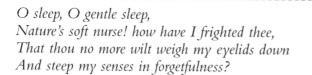

CHAPTER 11

Sleep Problems

O sleep, O gentle sleep,
Nature's soft nurse! how have I frighted thee,
That thou no more wilt weigh my eyelids down
And steep my senses in forgetfulness?

—William Shakespeare, *King Henry IV, Part II*

The life of a parent with a challenging child can be particularly stressful. Unfortunately, this stress is significantly increased if the child—and therefore the parent—does not sleep well. Problems with bedtime, night waking, or sleeping at the wrong times are just a few of the difficulties surrounding sleep that can negatively affect a child and his or her family. This chapter provides you with an introduction to common sleep problems and simple strategies you can use to improve not only the sleep of your child but your own sleep as well. Again, techniques of Optimistic Parenting are incorporated to help you follow through on these techniques.

WHAT IS SLEEP?

Before I describe how to help you and your child sleep better, it is useful first to describe what sleep is and how it affects you. Sleep, which usually occurs at night, is actually a change in the way your brain behaves. It does not shut down, otherwise your heart would stop beating and you would stop breathing as well. Instead, the brain goes through a number of different cycles of rapid eye movement (REM) sleep, which is when you dream, and non-REM, or dreamless, sleep. Despite many years of research on these basic experiences, sleep experts still do not fully understand all of the functions of sleep. It is known that sleep is as necessary as food, water, and oxygen and that if you stop sleeping completely, eventually you will die. It also is known that sleep is involved with how people learn, their memory, and even aspects of their physical health. This is why sleep is so important to both you and your child.

It is a common belief that everyone needs 8 hours of sleep, but the amount of sleep required to be healthy and alert differs by person and also by age. Usually, sleep professionals determine whether you are getting enough sleep by how you act during the day. Basically, if you sleep only 6 hours each evening but you wake up generally rested and are not overly tired during the day, then you probably are getting enough sleep at night. However, if you find that you are tired or otherwise affected by the amount of sleep you get, then experts would consider you to have a sleep problem. So, if you sleep 10 hours per night but are tired throughout the day, you may have a sleep problem.

Similarly, the amount of sleep people need changes as they age. Once an infant is born and out of the mother's womb, it can take several months to adapt to the new world of light and noise. Sleep professionals typically do not consider when an infant sleeps to be a problem until he or she is about 6 months of age. After that time, an infant is expected to be able to sleep through the night without disruption. Infants need on average about 14–15 hours of sleep (including naps) (National Sleep Foundation, 2011). As children grow older, they sleep a little less each year. The National Sleep Foundation (2011) provides additional information on sleep requirements for various age groups.

SLEEP PROBLEMS

If your child is sleeping significantly more or less than average and seems tired or cranky during the day, this could be a sign of a number of different problems with sleep. Also, if your child has behavior problems around sleep—for example, tantrums at bedtime, frequent disruptive night waking after 6 months of age— this could be an indication of a problem with bedtime habits or other sleep-related problems. To help you figure out what type of sleep problem your child might have, I have created a series of questions that help examine the separate categories of sleep difficulties. This is a necessary first step before making suggestions for help. Please note that some problems children experience around sleep can require medical intervention (e.g., breathing-related problems) or may call for a more in-depth sleep assessment. I will point these out as I discuss each sleep issue. After I cover these questions, I describe a number of different approaches to improving the sleep of your child, which you should be able to carry out on your own.

The following questions are adapted from the Albany Sleep Problems Scale (ASPS), a copy of which is included in Appendix A in the back of this book. It covers all of the more common difficulties children and adults experience with sleep and is a good first screening tool to see what might be a problem for your child. It is important to note that these questions also are appropriate for adults and may help you, your spouse, or a friend identify your own sleep difficulties.

1. Does your child have a fairly regular bedtime and time that he or she awakens? The brain's biological clock works best with regularity. This is especially true for children who are prone to sleep problems. If bedtime or the time your child wakes changes too much, this by itself can disrupt a child's sleep schedule and make it difficult for him or her to fall asleep at night or stay asleep throughout the night. (See the section "Good Sleep Habits.")

2. Does your child have a bedtime routine that is the same each evening? In the chapter on problems with transitions (Chapter 10), I pointed out the importance of predictability. In addition to a regular bedtime, the series of events that lead up to sleep (e.g., washing up, changing into pajamas, reading) is important for signaling to the brain that sleep is approaching. For children who have a hard time falling asleep at night, a regular bedtime routine is essential. (See the section "Good Sleep Habits.")

3. Does your child work or play in bed right up to the time he or she goes to sleep? Different places signal different things. Sitting at the kitchen table, for example, can by itself make you feel hungry. In the same way, the bed should signal sleep for a child; however, if it is also a place to play or, for older children, a place to do homework, the bed can actually be a difficult place to fall asleep. (See the section "Good Sleep Habits.")

4. Does your child sleep poorly in his or her own bed but better away from it? This question relates to the previous one and tells us whether your child is having trouble with sleep because of poor associations with his or her bed. Your child's bed may be a place where he or she worries about school or gets excited because it is where he or she plays video games; these other associations can make it difficult to fall and stay asleep. (See the section "Good Sleep Habits.")

5. Does this person smoke, drink alcohol, or consume caffeine in any form? The ASPS, from which these questions are adapted, addresses all issues that can interfere with sleep. Although I hope your child does not smoke or drink alcohol, you may, and both of these habits can disrupt your sleep.

In addition, consuming drinks or food with caffeine too close to bedtime also can cause sleep problems. I address these issues in more detail in the treatment section. (See the section "Good Sleep Habits.")

6. Does your child engage in vigorous activity in the hours before bedtime? Parents sometimes believe that roughhousing or exercising can tire their child out before bedtime. These activities, however, actually have a reverse effect and can make it more difficult for your child to fall asleep. (See the section "Good Sleep Habits.")

7. Does your child resist going to bed? This is a general screening question that lets us know that bedtime is a problem. It does not tell us *why* your child has a problem with bedtime—this is the role of some of the other questions—but it alerts us to this issue. (See the section "Bedtime Problems.")

8. Does your child take more than an hour to fall asleep but does not resist? This is a different type of problem than resisting bedtime, and sometimes parents might not even be aware that their child has this problem. Usually, a person—child or adult—should require only 15–20 minutes to fall asleep at night. Much longer than that is a sign of a problem with sleep. (See the section "Bedtime Problems.")

9. Does your child awaken during the night but remain quiet and in bed? Like the previous question, this may be something parents do not know about their child, and they may need to check up on this from time to time. The reason why the answer to this question is important is because it may require a different type of intervention than that needed by a child who wakes up and becomes disruptive. (See the section "Night Waking Problems.")

10. Does your child awaken during the night, and is he or she disruptive (e.g., tantrums, oppositional)? This is another regular screening question that helps us identify the specific problems your child may be experiencing. (See the section "Night Waking Problems.")

11. Does your child take naps during the day? Although napping is typical for young children, a nap for an older child or adult that lasts too long (i.e., more than 20–30 minutes) or that occurs too late in the day can interfere with the ability to fall asleep later that night.

12. Does your child often feel exhausted during the day because of lack of sleep? Being tired during the day—to the point of sometimes falling asleep in quiet situations—is a sign of not getting enough sleep. My colleagues and I assess "sleepiness" to determine just how much of an impact sleep disruption is having on your child.

13. Has your child ever had an accident or near accident (e.g., falling down stairs) because of sleepiness from not being able to sleep the night before?

Again, this is another sign of sleepiness, and we use this information to determine the extent of your child's problem.

14.   Does your child ever take prescription drugs or over-the-counter medications to help him or her sleep? We frequently see children with sleep problems whose parents give them medications such as Benadryl (an antihistamine that causes drowsiness) to help them fall asleep at night. (See the section "Sleep Medications.")

15.   Have you found that the sleep medication doesn't work as well with your child as it did when he or she first started taking it? This question helps us understand the effects that long-term medication use has on your child's sleep. The brain can become adapted to any medication and may require more and more over time to achieve the initial effect. (See the section "Sleep Medications.")

16.   If your child takes sleep medication, do you find that your child can't sleep on nights without it? Again, this question relates to your child's experience with sleep medications, and answering yes may be a sign that some change is needed. (See the section "Sleep Medications.")

17.   Does your child fall asleep early in the evening and awaken too early in the morning? Some children have problems with *when* they sleep. Their sleep habits may not match those of the rest of the family or school schedules and by themselves can create difficulties. (See the section "Bedtime Problems.")

18.   Does your child have difficulty falling asleep until a very late hour and have difficulty awakening early in the morning? This is another question related to sleeping at the wrong times. (See the section "Bedtime Problems.")

19.   Does your child wake up in the middle of the night upset? This is one of the questions we ask about night waking. As you will see, children wake up at night for a variety of reasons. (See the section "Night Waking Problems.")

20.   Is your child relatively easy to comfort after waking at night upset? The disruption that occurs with night waking due to simple sleep pattern problems or nightmares usually can be handled with comforting from a parent; however, other problems such as sleep terrors can be detected through how difficult it is to comfort a child during these episodes. (See the section "Night Waking Problems.")

21.   Does your child have episodes when he or she is sleeping during which he or she screams loudly for several minutes but is not fully awake? Again, this can be a sign of sleep terrors, a disruption of sleep that needs to be handled in a way that may differ from how you handle a nightmare or a simple night waking. (See the section "Night Waking Problems.")

22.   Is your child difficult to comfort during these episodes? If a child resists comforting during these types of awakenings, this suggests again that the episodes may be sleep terrors. (See the section "Night Waking Problems.")

23. Does your child experience sleep attacks (falling asleep almost immediately and without warning) during the day? These types of episodes can be the sign of a more serious type of sleep problem (e.g., narcolepsy, hypersomnia). If you answered *yes* to this question, you may want to get additional information[1] and perhaps consult your pediatrician or a sleep professional.

24. Does your child experience excessive daytime sleepiness that is not accounted for by an inadequate amount of sleep? Starting at this point, the next series of questions is designed to determine whether your child's sleep problems are related to another problem, particularly difficulties with breathing at night or problems with limb movement disorders. Here, we look to see if sleepiness is a problem even if your child seems to be getting enough sleep time.

25. Does your child snore when asleep? Snoring is a sign of obstructed breathing while sleeping. If your child snores while asleep and has problems with sleepiness during the day, you should consult with your pediatrician or a sleep professional.

26. Does your child sometimes stop breathing for a few seconds during sleep? Interrupted breathing such that the child can be observed to stop breathing for a few seconds is a sign of apnea or other breathing problems. These breathing difficulties at night can result in excessive tiredness during the day, and you should consult your pediatrician or a sleep professional for a formal assessment.

27. Does your child have trouble breathing? Allergies, asthma, or other medical problems can cause interrupted breathing both during the day and at night. If your child experiences these problems and is tired during the day or difficult to awaken in the morning, you should consult with your pediatrician.

28. Is your child overweight? Being overweight can lead to difficulty breathing at night. Even if you have not observed your child having trouble breathing while asleep, if he or she is difficult to wake up in the morning, it may be helpful to report this to your child's pediatrician.

29. Does your child often walk in his or her sleep? Sleepwalking is not, by itself, a problem for a child unless he or she is in danger of getting hurt. However, excessive sleepwalking can be a sign of a child not getting enough sleep (even if you do not see problems during the day) and may be helped with the same approach we use for sleep terrors. (See the section "Night Waking Problems.")

30. Does your child talk while asleep? In the same way that sleepwalking is not a serious problem, neither is sleeptalking. However, again, it can be a sign of inadequate sleep, and you may wish to consider the treatment we use for sleep terrors if this seems excessive (i.e., multiple times each week). (See the section "Night Waking Problems.")

31. Are your child's sheets and blankets in extreme disarray in the morning when he or she wakes up? Very active children can be very active sleepers. In some cases, however, children can have a limb movement disorder, which causes them to move a great deal during sleep and also awaken briefly. If you suspect this is a problem, it should be brought to your pediatrician's attention.

32. Does your child wake up at night because of kicking legs? This is another question designed to assess whether your child may be awakened frequently at night as the result of limb movement disorder.

33. While lying down, does your child ever experience unpleasant sensations in his or her legs? This is a sign of restless leg syndrome and can cause some children and adults to have a difficult time falling asleep. Again, medical evaluation is recommended if you suspect this may be a cause of your child's problem.

34. Does your child rock back and forth or bang a body part (e.g., head) to fall asleep? Some children need "soothing" to help them fall asleep. This can take more typical forms such as cuddling with a stuffed animal but in some cases may involve rocking or light banging of a part of the body such as the head. Usually, this is not harmful and should not be a major concern; however, for those cases in which the self-soothing behavior is causing physical injury, a treatment for bedtime problems might be useful. (See the section "Bedtime Problems.")

35. Does your child wet the bed? Bedwetting is not technically a sleep problem but may be of concern. Other resources are available that can help you with your child's toileting problems.[2]

36. Does your child grind his or her teeth at night? Teeth grinding is also not a sleep disorder but can be of concern because of resultant dental problems or because it may be related to anxiety. The first step would be to contact your child's dentist for an evaluation.

37. Does your child sleep well when it doesn't matter, such as on weekends, but sleep poorly when he or she *must* sleep well, such as when a busy day at school is ahead?

38. Does your child often have feelings of apprehension, anxiety, or dread when he or she is getting ready for bed?

39. Does your child worry in bed?

40. Does your child often have depressing thoughts, or do tomorrow's worries or plans buzz through his or her mind when he or she wants to go to sleep?

41. Does your child have feelings of frustration when he or she can't sleep?

42. Has your child experienced a relatively recent change in eating habits? Questions 37–42 are related to anxiety and/or depression and their

influence on your child's sleep. If your child is anxious about school, for example, this can cause difficulties falling asleep or staying asleep. You can first try interventions designed to help with the bedtime or night waking problem. If this is unsuccessful, you may want to explore these difficulties using additional resources.[3]

43. Does your child have behavior problems at times other than bedtime or upon awakening? We typically ask this question of parents who bring their child to us primarily because of sleep problems. One of the reasons is that sleep problems can make some daytime problems worse, and we need to be sure we address all concerns.

44. When did your child's primary difficulty with sleep begin?

45. What was happening in your child's life at that time or a few months before? The answers to Questions 44 and 45 help us discover whether the sleep problem can be traced to some particular event (e.g., moving to a new classroom or getting a new teacher) or other possible causes (e.g., a recent illness).

46. Is your child under a physician's care for any medical condition? Sometimes, a medical condition (e.g., allergies, stomach problems) can disturb sleep. In addition, sometimes the medications prescribed for other problems (e.g., stimulants prescribed for ADHD) can affect your child's sleep. If you suspect that a medical problem or a drug your child is taking may be disturbing your child's sleep, inform your child's pediatrician for help in dealing with this problem.

SLEEP ASSESSMENT

In addition to the answers to the previously listed questions, we often collect additional information, usually on the extent of the child's sleep problems. We typically recommend that parents complete a sleep diary for their child for at least 2 weeks to give us an idea about how long and when their child sleeps. We look at the amount of time a child sleeps to see whether it falls within the range of what is typical; in addition, we sometimes use this information for a particular intervention called sleep restriction. An example of a sleep diary is included next to show how it is completed and the type of information we look for in these diaries. Appendix A contains a blank sleep diary that you can use with your own child. The diary that follows was completed for 11-year-old Amani, a child with cognitive impairments and significant sleep problems. Amani would have tantrums at bedtime and would also experience night waking, at which time he would become disruptive as well. His mother was distraught by his sleep problems because it interrupted the sleep of her other children and that of her and her husband.

SLEEP DIARY FOR AMANI

Time axis (P.M. → A.M.): Midnight · 10:00 · 8:00 · 6:00 · 4:00 · 2:00 · Noon · 10:00 · 8:00 · 6:00 · 4:00 · 2:00 · Midnight

Day	Date
Tues.	7/22
Wed.	7/23
Thurs.	7/24
Fri.	7/25
Sat.	7/26
Sun.	7/27
Mon.	7/28
Tues.	7/29
Wed.	7/30
Thurs.	7/31
Fri.	8/1
Sat.	8/2
Sun.	8/3
Mon.	8/4
Tues.	8/5

There are several important things to look for in these diaries. First, notice that the amount of time Amani sleeps per day varies from as few as 4 hours to as many as 11 hours (indicated by the shaded areas). On average, Amani slept about $8\frac{1}{2}$ hours per day, which was a good average for a child his age, but the large day-to-day changes were a problem. Notice also that Amani sometimes took long naps during the day, which may have contributed to his difficulty falling asleep some nights. In addition, note that the time he was put to bed (indicated by the downward-pointing arrows) was different almost every night, and the time he was awakened (indicated by the upward-pointing arrows) was different as well. As we will see, this too could have contributed to his sleep problems.

This information proved very helpful in our efforts to help Amani sleep better, and I describe the techniques we used to help him next. However, it is important to point out how his mother responded to these problems. As an infant, Amani had many medical problems and needed surgeries to repair some heart defects. Because he was so sick as an infant, Amani's mother assumed that his sleeping problems were medically related. Over the years, once Amani's medical problems improved, Amani's mother still thought that his sleep problems were related to his medical problems and, because of that, felt unsure about his ability to change how he slept. As a result of these types of pessimistic thoughts, Amani's mother let Amani fall asleep anywhere he was (usually in front of the television) and did not have a set bedtime for him. When Amani's mother came to us for help, Amani was on his summer break from school; therefore, his mother let him sleep in whenever he wanted and nap later in the day to catch up on his sleep. Both the sleeping in and the naps likely contributed to his continued disturbed sleep. We needed to work with Amani's mother to point out that his sleep problems were neither unusual nor unique to someone with Amani's problems. We informed Amani's mother that we should be able to help Amani sleep better and assured her that she was quite capable of putting in place a successful plan. This helped us implement some of the important changes to Amani's sleep schedule.

GOOD SLEEP HABITS

Before trying out formal sleep plans, my colleagues and I generally recommend going through a checklist of things that can improve sleep. Just following these good sleep habits (more formally referred to as sleep hygiene) can be effective in improving the sleep of the majority of children. Go through the list in Table 11.1 to see how many of these habits, or lack thereof, might be affecting your child and how you might want to add some of these changes to your daily schedule. Again, remember that these steps can assist *you* as well, and you might want to keep an eye on how they can improve your sleep. The following sections provide more details.

Table 11.1. Good sleep habits

1. Establish a regular bedtime and a regular time to awaken. Do not let your child stay up or sleep in on a regular basis.
2. Create a regular bedtime routine that lasts 30 minutes, keeping the timing and order of the activities consistent. Do not extend the time for the bedtime routine.
3. Restrict activities in bed to those that help induce sleep (e.g., reading a bedtime story, listening to music). Do not let your child watch television or play games just before bedtime.
4. Make sure your child gets regular exercise during the day. Do not let your child exercise or engage in physical activity in the hours just before bedtime.
5. Reduce noise or light in the bedroom, and keep the bedroom at a consistent temperature. Do not make too much noise around bedtime, and do not leave lights on in the bedroom.
6. Substitute caffeinated beverages and foods with caffeine-free alternatives. Do not let your child consume food or drink containing caffeine for 6 hours before bedtime.

Establish a Regular Bedtime and a Regular Time to Awaken

For children who have difficulty falling asleep or staying asleep, a regular schedule for going to bed and waking up in the morning is essential. The problem we run into with this recommendation is getting families to stick to the schedule even on days when they do not have to awaken their child in the morning (e.g., on weekends or holidays). It is very enticing to have your son or daughter sleep a little later because that means a little more time for you. Unfortunately, doing so means your child's already sensitive sleep schedule will now be out of balance, and it can be a challenge to get your child back on a regular routine. On the bright side, this doesn't mean you have to wake your child at the same time as for school (e.g., 6:30 a.m. on a Saturday). We usually recommend trying to adopt a modified weekend schedule (e.g., awaking your child at 8:00 a.m. instead of letting your child sleep until 10:00 a.m.) and trying to keep a regular bedtime. That way, when Sunday night rolls around, you are not faced with a child who is not tired and cannot fall asleep at a good bedtime and then is cranky Monday morning.

For Amani, we selected 11:00 p.m. as a good bedtime because he would often fall asleep on his own by that time. Also, when school started again that fall, he would need to wake up at 6:30 a.m. to get to the bus on time; therefore, we selected 7:30 a.m. as a good time to awaken Amani during the summer because that would give him his average $8\frac{1}{2}$ hours of sleep. Later in this chapter, I explain how we modified this schedule to help Amani fall asleep without tantrums and stay asleep through the night.

Create a Regular Bedtime Routine that Lasts 30 Minutes

Just as a regular sleep schedule is important, it is equally important to have a good predictable bedtime routine. For Amani, this meant that at about 10:30 p.m. (30 minutes before his new bedtime) his mother would start the routine to help him get ready for bed (putting on pajamas, brushing teeth, reading together). Amani's mother was instructed not to include any activities that could prove to be disruptive (e.g., picking out clothes for the next day). In addition, it was important to remind her not to let Amani significantly increase the time past his 11:00 p.m. bedtime by asking for one more story or using some other stalling tactic.

Restrict Activities in Bed to Those that Help Induce Sleep

As I mentioned earlier, the bed can be a signal for sleep or it can signal other things (e.g., playing, worries about school). The goal is to make sure that as much as possible the things your child does in bed all contribute to and lead up to falling asleep. Therefore, no homework, playing, or other activities should occur in bed.

Make Sure Your Child Gets Regular Exercise During the Day

This suggestion seems counterintuitive for some families who try to tire out their child before bed. Parents sometimes think that exercise or roughhousing right before it is time to fall asleep will make their child easier to put to bed. But this trick can backfire and actually make it more difficult for your child to settle down to sleep. Part of the problem has to do with the body's internal body temperature, which increases and decreases throughout the day. In the early hours of the morning, body temperature starts to rise, triggering us to become more alert and finally to wake up. In the early evening hours, body temperature starts to drop (we become cooler), which makes us sleepy. Therefore, any type of vigorous activity can artificially increase your temperature, thereby making you more alert. You can use this phenomenon to your advantage, however, by having your child exercise in the late afternoon. This will increase his or her body temperature, which will then fall more dramatically around bedtime (it takes a few hours to drop), helping to improve your child's ability to fall asleep.

Reduce Noise or Light in the Bedroom, and
Keep the Bedroom at a Consistent Temperature

When my colleagues and I conduct research on sleep problems, our practice is to record the bedtime routine. Inevitably, when we review the videorecording we can often hear everything that is going on in the next room (e.g., television, people laughing). It is important to be aware of this and limit the amount of noise in the house around bedtime. Lights, too, should be limited, although a nightlight is fine.

Substitute Caffeinated Beverages
and Foods with Caffeine-Free Alternatives

Caffeine is another concern and should be limited during the day and not consumed at all in the hours before bedtime. Some people are not sensitive to caffeine and can drink a cup of coffee and still fall asleep. However, others are very sensitive and, unfortunately, caffeine can stay in one's system for hours. I usually recommend no caffeinated foods or drinks within 6 hours of bedtime.

SLEEP MEDICATIONS

The most common recommendation for sleep problems made by pediatricians is to use some form of medication. Typically, parents are directed to use over-the-counter medications such as Benadryl (an antihistamine that causes drowsiness), melatonin, or prescription medications such as clonidine to aid with sleep onset. Most sleep professionals, however, would only recommend medication as a short-term solution or for a specific problem associated with sleep, such as a limb movement disorder or narcolepsy (i.e., sudden sleep attacks). Medication is not recommended as a long-term solution for the majority of sleep problems observed in children with and without disabilities. In fact, a group of sleep professionals advise using caution with medications for child sleep problems because of a lack of information about their safety and about how effective the medications are in the long term.[4] The science of sleep medicine for children does not support using these drugs for children.

Behavioral interventions are the treatment of choice for difficulties such as bedtime disturbances, night waking, or sleeping at the wrong times (circadian rhythm disorders). Typically, the first step in treating sleep problems is to assess daily habits that might interfere with sleep—caffeine use, bedtime routines, and sleep–wake times—which can often resolve many sleep problems. When problems surrounding sleep cannot be resolved with these interventions, behavioral interventions are recommended.

BEDTIME PROBLEMS

Sleep experts commonly recommend two different plans—each with its pluses and minuses—for improving your child's ability to fall asleep each evening without disruption. We typically select one of the two plans based on the lifestyle and attitudes of the family with whom we are working. Before describing how we determine which one to use, I will first describe each of the approaches.

Graduated Extinction

Graduated extinction involves spending increasingly longer amounts of time ignoring the cries and protests of a child at bedtime. The goal of this treatment is to fade the amount of time you attend to your child around bedtime. At the same time, it gives you the opportunity to check on your child. This method appears to work by forcing the child to learn to fall asleep on his or her own. The advantages of graduated extinction are that it only needs to be carried out if and when the child is disruptive and it gives a parent the opportunity to check on the child. This last advantage helps some parents who are unsure about their child's well-being during the disruptive episodes. The disadvantages of graduated extinction include having to endure long bouts of crying and tantrums, a temporary increase in disruption caused by the plan, and the fact that the plan is not useful if the child has difficulty falling asleep but is not disruptive.

Sleep Restriction

Sleep restriction involves reducing the amount of time the child sleeps. Once the child is sleeping less, bedtime becomes easier because the child is tired and will more readily fall asleep. Also, night waking tends to decrease as well. For children who sleep at the wrong times, this is also a way to help "reset" your child's biological clock and help him or her sleep at times that better conform to the family schedule. Once the child is falling asleep well, then bedtime is faded back to a better time. Sleep restriction can involve moving bedtime to later in the evening or waking the child up earlier in the morning. The goal of sleep restriction is to make the child drowsy to decrease the likelihood of bedtime disturbances. It seems that the child's increased tiredness may make it easier for him or her to practice falling asleep without parents present. The advantages of sleep restriction include that it allows families to avoid most of the crying and tantrums and that it can be used for children who have trouble falling asleep but are not disruptive. The disadvantages of sleep restriction include that it requires families members to stay up later with the child and that it can be difficult to keep the child awake for the later bedtime.

Which Plan Should You Choose?

Before my colleagues and I suggest any plan for sleep problems, we try to assess how the family will be able to carry out the steps needed to be successful. I typically ask a series of questions that relate to the potential success of using graduated extinction, sleep restriction, or scheduled awakening (a third treatment that we sometimes use for night waking problems). These questions make up the Sleep Intervention Questionnaire (SIQ).[5] This questionnaire is located in Appendix A at the back of this book.

How to Do Graduated Extinction

If you have decided to use graduated extinction for your child's bedtime problems, follow these steps.

1. Create or maintain a regular bedtime routine that takes approximately 30 minutes.

2. Set an agreed-on bedtime that will not change over the course of the plan.

3. Decide on the amount of time you will wait before going in to check on your child. A typical time would be between 3 and 5 minutes the first night.

4. Select the night to begin the plan. Assume that no one will have a good night's sleep on the night you start. Because of this, Friday night might be a good choice.

5. On the first night, follow the bedtime routine and put your child to bed at his or her regular bedtime. Leave the room, and then wait the agreed-on time (e.g., 3 minutes) before checking on your child.

6. If, after waiting the full time, your child is still crying, you can go into the room, tell him or her to go to bed, and then leave. You should not pick up your child, give him or her food or a drink, or engage in extensive conversation.

7. Wait the same amount of time (e.g., 3 minutes) before going back into the room again. Continue this pattern until your child is asleep. If you feel comfortable, start to wait longer between visits.

8. On each subsequent night, extend the time an additional 2–3 minutes between visits. Continue using the same procedure as in Step 6 when returning to the child's room.

A final caution about graduated extinction: If you feel that you will stop the plan if your child gets too upset, we recommend that you try using sleep restriction instead.

How to Do Sleep Restriction

If you have decided to use sleep restriction for your child's bedtime problems, follow these steps.

1. Create or maintain a regular bedtime routine that is shorter than usual (about 10–15 minutes) because your child will eventually be very tired.

2. Select a bedtime when your child is likely to fall asleep with little difficulty—within about 15 minutes. To determine this bedtime, use the sleep diary to find a time when your child tends to fall asleep if left alone (e.g., 11:00 p.m.), then add 30 minutes to this time (e.g., new bedtime = 11:30 p.m.).

3. Set an alarm to awaken your child at a time that, when combined with the new bedtime, will allow your child to get about 90% of the average amount of sleep he or she currently gets.

4. If your child falls asleep within 15 minutes of being put to bed at this new bedtime and without resistance for two successive nights, move the bedtime up by 15 minutes (e.g., from 11:30 p.m. to 11:15 p.m.).

5. Keep your child awake before the new bedtime even if he or she seems to want to fall asleep.

6. If your child does not fall asleep within about 15 minutes of being put to bed, have him or her leave his or her bedroom and extend the bedtime for 1 more hour.

7. Continue to move up the bedtime (e.g., from 11:15 p.m. to 11:00 p.m.) until the desired bedtime is reached.

We used sleep restriction for Amani's bedtime problems as well as his disruptive night waking. We noticed that on a typical night he would tend to fall asleep by about 10:00 p.m. Based on that information (from his sleep diary), we selected 10:30 p.m. as his new bedtime and 6:30 a.m. as the time to wake him up. This meant he would sleep only about 8 hours rather than his average of $8\frac{1}{2}$ hours. On the first night, Amani had trouble falling asleep at his bedtime, and his mother practiced her distraction technique (saying to herself that this would soon be better) to get through the bad night. On the second night, Amani was tired because he had been awakened early that morning and was not allowed to nap, and he fell asleep quickly following his bedtime routine. He also did not have a nighttime disruption. This schedule was continued for 2 weeks, and then his bedtime was moved to 10:00 p.m. Because this schedule (a 10:00 p.m. bedtime and a 6:30 a.m. waking) worked for school, Amani's mother decided to keep these times. Amani was now much easier to put to bed and only occasionally woke up again at night. Over the following months, a few setbacks (e.g., illness, going on vacation) disrupted the schedule, but Amani's mother reminded herself that restarting the plan would be successful—and it was.

Cautions

Parents often make a few common mistakes when trying to implement these bedtime techniques. You should try to avoid the following to ensure a successful plan:

- Lying down with your child until he or she falls asleep
- Letting your child take more or longer naps during the day
- Extended discussions with your child over the rationale for the plan at bedtime
- Interruptions due to illness or other changes (e.g., sleeping away from home)
- Giving in to delay tactics (e.g., asking for another story or something more to drink)
- Guilt over the child's distress—especially when using graduated extinction

Again, if you feel the need for more detailed instructions, there are additional resources that should be helpful.[6]

NIGHT WAKING PROBLEMS

Nighttime problems that occur after your child initially falls asleep can take several forms: disruptive night waking, nondisruptive night waking, nightmares, sleep terrors, sleepwalking, or sleeptalking. We tend to rely on three approaches to help with these problems: graduated extinction, sleep restriction, or scheduled awakening. Again, each one of these approaches has its pluses and minuses, and we recommend choosing one approach based on your answers to the SIQ (see the previous "Bedtime Problems" section). Graduated extinction is carried out in the same way as at bedtime but in this case would be in response to disruptive behavior after your child awakens at night. Because sleep restriction can both help a child at bedtime and reduce or eliminate certain night-waking problems, it is implemented exactly as described previously. For cases in which graduated extinction and sleep restriction may not be desired or helpful (e.g., graduated extinction for nondisruptive night waking, nightmares, or sleep terrors), we usually recommend scheduled awakening. Scheduled awakening can help reduce or eliminate disruptive and nondisruptive night waking as well as sleep terrors. For other types of nighttime sleep disturbances, you should seek additional help from your pediatrician or other resources.

Scheduled Awakening

Scheduled awakening involves waking your child a short period of time prior to the time he or she usually awakens or has a sleep terror. The goal of this approach is to have your child fall back asleep from this brief awakening without your involvement. When it works, the child sleeps through the rest of the night without waking up again. Then, over time, you can stop this scheduled awakening. The reason why scheduled awakening is effective is not currently understood but may involve "reprogramming" the sleep cycle to a more regular sleep–wake schedule. It also may give your child experience falling asleep alone while drowsy. The advantages of this approach include that it avoids most crying and tantrums and that it can be used for nondisruptive night waking and sleep terrors. The disadvantages include that it requires parents to wake up or stay up later themselves and that it only works for night waking problems that occur at about the same time each evening.

How to Do Scheduled Awakening

If you have decided to use scheduled awakening for your child's nighttime problems, then follow these steps.

1. Use the sleep diary to determine the time or times that your child typically awakens during the night.

2. On the night that you begin the plan, wake up your child approximately 30 minutes before his or her typical awakening time. For example, if your child usually has a night waking or sleep terror at 12:30 a.m., then wake up your child at 12:00 a.m. If your child seems to awaken very easily, move the time up 15 minutes the next night and on all subsequent nights (e.g., 11:45 p.m.).

3. If there is a broad range in the times your child awakens (e.g., at some time between 12:00 a.m. and 1:30 a.m.), awaken your child about 30 minutes prior to the earliest time (e.g., in this case, 11:30 p.m.).

4. Do not fully awaken your child. Gently touch and/or talk to your child until he or she opens his or her eyes, then let him or her fall back to sleep.

5. Repeat this plan each night until your child goes a full seven nights without a night waking or sleep terror event. Once your child has achieved this level of success, skip the scheduled awakening one night during the next week. If your child has awakenings, then go back to waking your child every night. Slowly reduce the number of nights with scheduled awakenings until your child no longer wakes during the night.

For any of the discussed sleep interventions, you may find an initial increase in episodes of sleepwalking, sleeptalking, or sleep terrors. These are non–dream-related problems that sometimes occur when someone is not getting enough sleep. Sleep terrors are especially troublesome for families because the child experiencing this problem is so upset (e.g., screaming, sweaty) but is really not awake. Attempting to awaken a child from a sleep terror is difficult but not dangerous as some think. The good news is that the child will have no memory of this in the morning. Try to be patient with these changes, and try to take note of how often they happen. Our experience is that they decrease as a child's sleep improves.

This chapter covers the basic and most common of the sleep problems experienced by children. There are more than 80 diagnosable sleep disorders, many of which are very rare. If you find that the descriptions of sleep problems here do not match the problems your child is experiencing, you should seek additional help. Sophisticated assessments (sometimes requiring an overnight stay in a sleep laboratory) can help pinpoint more complex issues with sleep; however, our experience is that the vast majority of sleep concerns raised by families who have a challenging child can be handled at home with some of these basic approaches. It is worth mentioning one last time that there is reason for optimism with all of your child's difficulties, including those with sleep. Be patient and confident that things will improve and that you can achieve a meaningful and satisfying family life.

Epilogue

Despite my promise not to include my family in this book, it is fitting to sum up its major theme by relaying one last personal anecdote. About two decades ago, my wife and I were watching television with our son, and it was getting close to bedtime. As I described before, my son's sleep problems were a constant source of stress in the house and as a result bedtime was never eagerly anticipated. However, this night was different. Without either of us saying a word, my son yawned, raised his arms over his head, and calmly told us, "I'm tired, I think I'll go to sleep." We were speechless. After years of nightly battles and resistance, no better words were ever spoken. He kissed us goodnight and strutted off to bed.

My wife and I looked at each other incredulously and hugged. This was what we had wished for each night for years. A child who did not fight to go to bed but did so willingly and happily. Parents who have children who do this routinely never could understand our joy and elation over this one small victory, but we knew. This meant hope. We knew that tomorrow night might be a completely different scenario (and it was). But, for one night, we could see progress. We could see that all of our efforts and patience were paying off, and it made the next night's problems just a little bit easier to handle. There was a light at the end of this tunnel and, although it may never be exactly what we hoped for, things would get better.

My wish for you is that through the information and exercises in this book, you too get a glimpse at a brighter future for your family. Your child's problem behaviors can improve, and you are capable of making that change a reality. It is possible and will happen. When it does, embrace those moments for the little gifts they are. Hope is a palpable feeling that pushes you forward through life's inevitable obstacles. And don't forget to appreciate those times and be grateful, for these are the keys to true happiness!

Endnotes

INTRODUCTION

1. Durand, Hieneman, Clarke, & Zona (2009).

CHAPTER 1

1. Durand (2001).

CHAPTER 3

1. Seligman (1998).
2. Seligman & Maier (1967).
3. Kamen & Seligman (1987); Shepperd, Carroll, & Sweeny (2008).
4. Gigerenzer (2007).
5. Durand (1998).

CHAPTER 4

1. Baxter et al. (1992).
2. Salary.com (2005).
3. Suls, Martin, & Wheeler (2002).
4. Kipling (1910).
5. For example, see Janney & Snell (2006).

CHAPTER 5

1. Seltzer, Greenberg, Hong, Smith, Almeida, Coe, et al. (2010).
2. Durand & Barlow (2010).

3. Nagel (1972).
4. Zak, Stanton, & Ahmadi (2007).
5. Diener, Emmons, Larsen, & Griffin (1985).
6. Ibid.
7. Davidson, Kabat-Zinn, Schumacher, Rosenkranz, Muller, Santorelli, et al. (2003); Hofmann, Sawyer, Witt, & Oh (2010).
8. Brown & Ryan (2003).
9. Kabat-Zinn (1994).
10. Hayes, Follette, & Linehan (2004).
11. Eifert & Forsyth (2005).
12. Emmons & McCullough (2004).
13. Emmons & McCullough (2003); Seligman, Steen, Park, & Peterson (2005).
14. Seligman, Steen, Park, & Peterson (2005).
15. Ibid.
16. Csikszentmihalyi (1990).

CHAPTER 6

1. Touchette, MacDonald, & Langer (1985).
2. Durand, Crimmins, Caulfield, & Taylor (1989).
3. Durand (1990).
4. Gottman, Coan, Carrere, & Swanson (1998).
5. Durand & Mapstone (1998).
6. Durand & Crimmins (1992); Monaco & Associates (2010).

CHAPTER 7

1. Gray & Garand (1993).

CHAPTER 8

1. Patterson, DeBaryshe, & Ramsey (1989).

CHAPTER 9

1. Durand (1990); Durand & Carr (1992).
2. Horner & Day (1991); Horner, Sprague, Obrien, & Heathfield (1990).
3. Carr (1979).

CHAPTER 10

1. Durand & Mindell (1990).
2. Cohen & Sloan (2007); McClannahan & Krantz (2010).

CHAPTER 11

1. Durand (1998).
2. Wheeler (2004).
3. Durand (1998).
4. Mindell et al. (2006).
5. Durand (2008).
6. Durand (1998).

References

Aristotle (350 B.C.E.). *Nicomachean Ethics* (Book 9, Chapter 7).

Axtell, J.L., (Ed). (1968). *The educational writings of John Locke: A critical edition with introduction and notes.* New York: Cambridge University Press.

Baxter, L., Jr., Schwartz, J., Bergman, K., Szuba, M., Guze, B., Mazziotta, J., et al. (1992). Caudate glucose metabolic rate changes with both drug and behavior therapy for obsessive-compulsive disorder. *Archives of General Psychiatry, 49*(9), 681.

Braude, J.M. (1962). *Lifetime speaker's encyclopedia.* Englewood Cliffs, NJ: Prentice Hall.

Brown, K.W., & Ryan, R.M. (2003). The benefits of being present: Mindfulness and its role in psychological well-being. *Journal of Personality and Social Psychology, 84*(4), 822–848.

Carr, E. (1979). Teaching autistic children to use sign language: Some research issues. *Journal of Autism and Developmental Disorders, 9*(4), 345–359.

Cohen, M., & Sloan, D. (2007). *Visual supports for people with autism: A guide for parents and professionals.* Bethesda, MD: Woodbine House.

Csikszentmihalyi, M. (1990). *Flow: The psychology of optimal performance.* New York: Cambridge University Press.

Davidson, R., Kabat-Zinn, J., Schumacher, J., Rosenkranz, M., Muller, D., Santorelli, S., et al. (2003). Alterations in brain and immune function produced by mindfulness meditation. *Psychosomatic Medicine, 65*(4), 564.

Diener, E., Emmons, R.A., Larsen, R.J., & Griffin, S. (1985). The satisfaction with life scale. *Journal of Personality Assessment, 49*(1), 71–75.

Durand, V.M. (1990). *Severe behavior problems: A functional communication training approach.* New York: Guilford Press.

Durand, V.M. (1998). *Sleep better! A guide to improving sleep for children with special needs.* Baltimore: Paul H. Brookes Publishing Co.

Durand, V.M. (2001). Future directions for children and adolescents with mental retardation. *Behavior Therapy, 32*, 633–650.

Durand, V.M. (2008). *When children don't sleep well: Interventions for paediatric sleep disorders, therapist guide.* London: Oxford University Press.

Durand, V.M., & Barlow, D.H. (2010). *Essentials of abnormal psychology* (5th ed.). Belmont, CA: Wadsworth/Cengage Learning.

Durand, V.M., & Carr, E.G. (1992). An analysis of maintenance following functional communication training. *Journal of Applied Behavior Analysis, 25*, 777–794.

Durand, V.M., & Crimmins, D.B. (1992). *The Motivation Assessment Scale (MAS) administration guide.* Topeka, KS: Monaco and Associates.

Durand, V.M., Crimmins, D.B., Caulfield, M., & Taylor, J. (1989). Reinforcer assessment I: Using problem behavior to select reinforcers. *Journal of the Association for Persons with Severe Handicaps, 14,* 113–126.

Durand, V.M., Hieneman, M., Clarke, S., & Zona, M. (2009). Optimistic parenting: Hope and help for parents with challenging children. In W. Sailor, G. Dunlap, G. Sugai, & R.H. Horner (Eds.), *Handbook of positive behavior support* (pp. 233–256). New York: Springer.

Durand, V.M., & Mapstone, E. (1998). The influence of "mood-inducing" music on challenging behavior. *American Journal on Mental Retardation, 102,* 367–378.

Durand, V.M., & Mindell, J.A. (1990). Behavioral treatment of multiple childhood sleep disorders: Effects on child and family. *Behavior Modification, 14,* 37–49.

Eifert, G.H., & Forsyth, J.P. (2005). *Acceptance and commitment therapy for anxiety disorders: A practitioner's treatment guide to using mindfulness, acceptance, and values-based behavior change strategies.* Oakland, CA: New Harbinger.

Emmons, R.A., & McCullough, M.E. (2003). Counting blessings versus burdens: An experimental investigation of gratitude and subjective well-being in daily life. *Journal of Personality and Social Psychology, 84*(2), 377–389.

Emmons, R., & McCullough, M. (2004). *The psychology of gratitude.* New York: Oxford University Press.

Gigerenzer, G. (2007). *Gut feelings: The intelligence of the unconscious.* New York: The Viking Press.

Gottman, J., Coan, J., Carrere, S., & Swanson, C. (1998). Predicting marital happiness and stability from newlywed interactions. *Journal of Marriage and the Family, 60*(1), 5–22.

Gray, C., & Garand, J. (1993). Social stories: Improving responses of students with autism with accurate social information. *Focus on Autism and Other Developmental Disabilities, 8*(1), 1–10.

Hayes, S.C., Follette, V.M., & Linehan, M. (2004). *Mindfulness and acceptance: Expanding the cognitive-behavioral tradition.* New York: The Guilford Press.

Hofmann, S.G., Sawyer, A.T., Witt, A.A., & Oh, D. (2010). The effect of mindfulness-based therapy on anxiety and depression: A meta-analytic review. *Journal of Consulting and Clinical Psychology, 78*(2), 169–183.

Horner, R.H., & Day, H.M. (1991). The effects of response efficiency on functionally equivalent competing behaviors. *Journal of Applied Behavior Analysis, 24*(4), 719–732.

Horner, R.H., Sprague, J.R., Obrien, M., & Heathfield, L.T. (1990). The role of response efficiency in the reduction of problem behaviors through functional equivalence training: A case-study. *Journal of the Association for Persons with Severe Handicaps, 15*(2), 91–97.

Janney, R., & Snell, M. (2006). *Social relationships and peer support* (2nd ed.). Baltimore: Paul H. Brookes Publishing Co.

Kabat-Zinn, J. (1994). *Wherever you go, there you are: Mindfulness meditation in everyday life.* New York: Hyperion Books.

Kamen, L., & Seligman, M. (1987). Explanatory style and health. *Current Psychological Research & Reviews, 6*(3), 207–218.

Kipling, R. (1910). If–. In R. Kipling, *Rewards and fairies.* Garden City, NY: Doubleday, Page & Company.

McClannahan, L., & Krantz, P. (2010). *Activity schedules for children with autism* (2nd ed.). Bethesda, MD: Woodbine House.

Mindell, J.A., Emslie, G., Blumer, J., Genel, M., Glaze, D., Ivanenko, A., et al. (2006). Pharmacologic management of insomnia in children and adolescents: Consensus statement. *Pediatrics, 117*(6), 1223–1232.

Monaco & Associates. (2010). *The Motivation Assessment Scale.* Retrieved June 30, 2010, from http://www.monacoassociates.com/mas.php?source=general

Nagel, T. (1972). Aristotle on eudaimonia. *Phronesis, 17*(3), 252–259.

National Sleep Foundation. (2011). *How much sleep do we really need?* Retrieved January 28, 2011, from http://www.sleepfoundation.org/article/how-sleep-works/how-much-sleep-do-we-really-need

Patterson, G., DeBaryshe, B., & Ramsey, E. (1989). A developmental perspective on antisocial behavior. *American Psychologist, 44*(2), 329–335.

Pirsig, R. (1974). *Zen and the art of motorcycle maintenance: An inquiry into values.* New York: Bantam.

Salary.com. (2005). *Americans waste more than 2 hours a day at work.* Retrieved May 24, 2010, from http://www.salary.com/sitesearch/layoutscripts/sisl_display.asp?filename=&path=/destinationsearch/

Seligman, M. (1998). *Learned optimism.* New York: Pocket Books.

Seligman, M.E.P., & Maier, S.F. (1967). Failure to escape traumatic shock. *Journal of Experimental Psychology, 74,* 1–9.

Seligman, M., Steen, T., Park, N., & Peterson, C. (2005). Positive psychology progress: Empirical validation of interventions. *American Psychologist, 60*(5), 410–421.

Seltzer, M.M., Greenberg, J.S., Hong, J., Smith, L.E., Almeida, D.M., Coe, C., et al. (2010). Maternal cortisol levels and behavior problems in adolescents and adults with ASD. *Journal of Autism and Developmental Disorders, 40*(4), 457–469.

Shepperd, J., Carroll, P., & Sweeny, K. (2008). A functional approach to explaining fluctuations in future outlooks: From self-enhancement to self-criticism. In E.C. Chang (Ed.), *Self-criticism and self-enhancement: Theory, research and clinical implications* (pp. 161–180). Washington, DC: American Psychological Association.

Suls, J., Martin, R., & Wheeler, L. (2002). Social comparison: Why, with whom, and with what effect? *Current Directions in Psychological Science, 11*(5), 159–163.

Touchette, P., MacDonald, R., & Langer, S. (1985). A scatter plot for identifying stimulus control of problem behavior. *Journal of Applied Behavior Analysis, 18*(4), 343–351.

Wheeler, M. (2004). *Toilet training for individuals with autism & related disorders: A comprehensive guide for parents & teachers.* Arlington, TX: Future Horizons Inc.

Varela, J.S. (1977). Social technology. *American Psychologist, 32,* 914–923.

Zak, P.J., Stanton, A.A., & Ahmadi, S. (2007). Oxytocin increases generosity in humans. *PLoS ONE, 2*(11), e1128.

Blank Forms

SELF-TALK JOURNAL
(THOUGHTS AND FEELINGS)

SITUATION What happened (success or difficulty)?	THOUGHTS What did you think or say to yourself when this happened?	FEELINGS What emotions did you experience and how did you react physically when this happened?

SELF-TALK JOURNAL
(CONSEQUENCES)

SITUATION What happened (success or difficulty)?	THOUGHTS What did you think or say to yourself when this happened?	FEELINGS What emotions did you experience and how did you react physically when this happened?	CONSEQUENCES What happened as a result of your thoughts and feelings?

SELF-TALK JOURNAL
(DISPUTATION)

SITUATION What happened (success or difficulty)?	THOUGHTS What did you think or say to yourself when this happened?	FEELINGS What emotions did you experience and how did you react physically when this happened?	CONSEQUENCES What happened as a result of your thoughts and feelings?	DISPUTATION Were your thoughts accurate and useful?

SELF-TALK JOURNAL
(DISTRACTION)

SITUATION What happened (success or difficulty)?	THOUGHTS What did you think or say to yourself when this happened?	FEELINGS What emotions did you experience and how did you react physically when this happened?	DISPUTATION Were your thoughts accurate and useful?	DISTRACTION What did you do to shift your attention?

SELF-TALK JOURNAL
(SUBSTITUTION)

SITUATION What happened (success or difficulty)?	THOUGHTS What did you think or say to yourself when this happened?	FEELINGS What emotions did you experience and how did you react physically when this happened?	DISPUTATION Were your thoughts accurate and useful?	SUBSTITUTION What is a more positive way to think about this?

ABC CHART

Day and time	**ANTECEDENTS** What was happening just before your child's behavior problem?	**BEHAVIOR** Write down the behavior(s) as well as the number of times and/or how long they occurred.		**CONSEQUENCES** How did you or others react to the episode?

Scatter Plot

Day and time	Day of the week													
	Monday	Tuesday	Wednesday	Thursday	Friday	Saturday	Sunday	Monday	Tuesday	Wednesday	Thursday	Friday	Saturday	Sunday
7:00 a.m.														
7:30														
8:00														
8:30														
9:00														
9:30														
10:00														
10:30														
11:00														
11:30														
12:00 p.m.														
12:30														
1:00														
1:30														
2:00														
2:30														
3:00														
3:30														
4:00														
4:30														
5:00														
5:30														
6:00														
6:30														
7:00														
7:30														
8:00														
8:30														
9:00														

From Touchette, P., MacDonald, R., & Langer, S. (1985). A scatter plot for identifying stimulus control of problem behavior. *Journal of Applied Behavior Analysis, 18*(4), 344; adapted by permission. Further reproduction prohibited without permission from the orignal publisher.

In *Optimistic Parenting: Hope and Help for You and Your Challenging Child* by V. Mark Durand (2011, Paul H. Brookes Publishing Co.)

BEHAVIORAL CONTRACT

Date of contract _____			
Child agrees:		Parent agrees:	
Child agrees:		Parent agrees:	

We agree to the terms of this contract and will review and possibly revise it in _____ weeks.

Child's signature _____

Parent's signature _____

Satisfaction with Life Scale

Below are five statements with which you may agree or disagree. Using the 1–7 scale below, indicate your agreement with each item by placing the appropriate number on the line following that item. Please be open and honest in your responding.

The 7-point scale is as follows:

1 = strongly disagree
2 = disagree
3 = slightly disagree
4 = neither agree nor disagree
5 = slightly agree
6 = agree
7 = strongly agree

1. In most ways, my life is close to my ideal. _____

2. The conditions of my life are excellent. _____

3. I am satisfied with my life. _____

4. So far, I have gotten the important things I want in life. _____

5. If I could live my life over, I would change almost nothing. _____

Scoring

Add up the scores for all of your answers and compare them with the totals below.

Total Score
31–35 = Extremely satisfied
26–30 = Satisfied
21–25 = Slightly satisfied
　　20 = Neutral
15–19 = Slightly dissatisfied
10–14 = Dissatisfied
　5–9 = Extremely dissatisfied

From Diener, E., Emmons, R., Larsen, R., & Griffin, S. (1985). The satisfaction with life scale. *Journal of Personality Assessment, 49*(1), 71–75.

In *Optimistic Parenting: Hope and Help for You and Your Challenging Child* by V. Mark Durand (2011, Paul H. Brookes Publishing Co.)

Mindful Attention Awareness Scale

Day-to-Day Experiences

Instructions: Below is a collection of statements about your everyday experience. Using the 1-6 scale below, please indicate how frequently or infrequently you currently have each experience. Please answer according to what really reflects your experience rather than what you think your experience should be. Please treat each item separately from every other item.

1	2	3	4	5	6
Almost Always	Very Frequently	Somewhat Frequently	Somewhat Infrequently	Very Infrequently	Never

I could be experiencing some emotion and not be conscious of it until sometime later.	1	2	3	4	5	6
I break or spill things because of carelessness, not paying attention, or thinking of something else.	1	2	3	4	5	6
I find it difficult to stay focused on what's happening in the present.	1	2	3	4	5	6
I tend to walk quickly to get to where I'm going without paying attention to what I experience along the way.	1	2	3	4	5	6
I tend not to notice feelings of physical tension or discomfort until they really grab my attention.	1	2	3	4	5	6
I forget a person's name almost as soon as I've been told it for the first time.	1	2	3	4	5	6
It seems I am "running on automatic," without much awareness of what I'm doing.	1	2	3	4	5	6
I rush through activities without being really attentive to them.	1	2	3	4	5	6
I get so focused on the goal I want to achieve that I lose touch with what I'm doing right now to get there.	1	2	3	4	5	6
I do jobs or tasks automatically, without being aware of what I'm doing.	1	2	3	4	5	6
I find myself listening to someone with one ear, doing something else at the same time.	1	2	3	4	5	6
I drive places on "automatic pilot" and then wonder why I went there.	1	2	3	4	5	6
I find myself preoccupied with the future or the past.	1	2	3	4	5	6
I find myself doing things without paying attention.	1	2	3	4	5	6
I snack without being aware that I'm eating.	1	2	3	4	5	6

Scoring Information

To score the scale, simply compute the mean of the 15 items. Higher scores reflect higher levels of dispositional mindfulness.

THOUGHTS QUIZ

Instructions: Reflect back on a recent problem situation; then, for each of the statements below, indicate whether you were thinking this or a very similar thought at the time of the difficult situation. Circle *Yes* or *No.*

	Thoughts	Strongly Disagree				Strongly Agree
1.	I have little or no control over this situation.	1	2	3	4	5
2.	I am not sure how best to handle this situation.	1	2	3	4	5
3.	In this situation, others are judging me negatively as a parent.	1	2	3	4	5
4.	In this situation, others are judging my child negatively.	1	2	3	4	5
5.	My child is not able to control this behavior.	1	2	3	4	5
6.	My child's disability or condition is causing or contributing to this problem.	1	2	3	4	5
7.	This type of situation is always a problem for my child.	1	2	3	4	5
8.	This will never get better or may become worse.	1	2	3	4	5
9.	I will never have time for just me.	1	2	3	4	5
10.	My child is doing this on purpose.	1	2	3	4	5
11.	This situation is [spouse's, partner's, family member's, or other's] fault for not handling this like I suggested.	1	2	3	4	5
12.	It is my fault that this is a problem.	1	2	3	4	5
13.	Why am I always responsible for my child's behavior?	1	2	3	4	5

Scoring

For each thought that you scored a *4* or *5*, consider those themes when examining your thoughts in both difficult and successful situations with your child.

Albany Sleep Problems Scale (ASPS)

Name:	Date of birth:
Diagnoses:	Sex:
Name of respondent:	Date administered:

Instructions: Circle one number that best represents the frequency of the behavior (0 = never; 1 = less than once per week; 2 = one to two times per week; 3 = three to six times per week; 4 = nightly).

1.	Does the person have a fairly regular bedtime and time that he or she awakens?	0	1	2	3	4
2.	Does the person have a bedtime routine that is the same each evening?	0	1	2	3	4
3.	Does this person work or play in bed often right up to the time he or she goes to sleep?	0	1	2	3	4
4.	Does this person sleep poorly in his or her own bed but better away from it?	Yes			No	
5.	Does this person smoke, drink alcohol, or consume caffeine in any form?	0	1	2	3	4
6.	Does this person engage in vigorous activity in the hours before bedtime?	0	1	2	3	4
7.	Does the person resist going to bed?	0	1	2	3	4
8.	Does the person take more than an hour to fall asleep but does not resist?	0	1	2	3	4
9.	Does the person awaken during the night but remain quiet and in bed?	0	1	2	3	4
10.	Does the person awaken during the night, and is he or she disruptive (e.g., tantrums, oppositional behavior)?	0	1	2	3	4
11.	Does the person take naps during the day?	0	1	2	3	4
12.	Does this person often feel exhausted during the day because of lack of sleep?	0	1	2	3	4
13.	Has this person ever had an accident or near accident because of sleepiness from not being able to sleep the night before?	Yes			No	
14.	Does this person ever take prescription drugs or over-the-counter medications to help him or her sleep?	0	1	2	3	4
15.	Has this person found that sleep medication doesn't work as well as it did when he or she first started taking it?	Yes			No/NA	
16.	If he or she takes sleep medication, does this person find that he or she can't sleep on nights without it?	Yes			No/NA	
17.	Does the person fall asleep early in the evening and awaken too early in the morning?	0	1	2	3	4
18.	Does the person have difficulty falling asleep until a very late hour and difficulty awakening early in the morning?	0	1	2	3	4
19.	Does this person wake up in the middle of the night upset?	0	1	2	3	4
20.	Is the person relatively easy to comfort from these episodes?	Yes			No/NA	

(continued)

(continued)

21.	Does the person have episodes during sleep where he or she screams loudly for several minutes but is not fully awake?	0	1	2	3	4
22.	Is the person difficult to comfort during these episodes?	Yes		No/NA		
23.	Does the person experience sleep attacks (falling asleep almost immediately and without warning) during the day?	0	1	2	3	4
24.	Does the person experience excessive daytime sleepiness that is not accounted for by an inadequate amount of sleep?	0	1	2	3	4
25.	Does this person snore when asleep?	0	1	2	3	4
26.	Does this person sometimes stop breathing for a few seconds during sleep?	0	1	2	3	4
27.	Does this person have trouble breathing?	0	1	2	3	4
28.	Is this person overweight?	Yes		No		
29.	Has this person often walked when asleep?	0	1	2	3	4
30.	Does this person talk while asleep?	0	1	2	3	4
31.	Are this person's sheets and blankets in extreme disarray in the morning when he or she wakes up?	0	1	2	3	4
32.	Does this person wake up at night because of kicking legs?	0	1	2	3	4
33.	While lying down, does this person ever experience unpleasant sensations in the legs?	Yes		No		
34.	Does this person rock back and forth or bang a body part (e.g., head) to fall asleep?	0	1	2	3	4
35.	Does this person wet the bed?	0	1	2	3	4
36.	Does this person grind his or her teeth at night?	0	1	2	3	4
37.	Does this person sleep well when it doesn't matter, such as on weekends, but sleep poorly when he or she "must" sleep well, such as when a busy day at school is ahead?	Yes		No		
38.	Does this person often have feelings of apprehension, anxiety, or dread when he or she is getting ready for bed?	0	1	2	3	4
39.	Does this person worry in bed?	0	1	2	3	4
40.	Does this person often have depressing thoughts, or do tomorrow's worries or plans buzz through his or her mind when he or she wants to go to sleep?	0	1	2	3	4
41.	Does this person have feelings of frustration when he or she can't sleep?	0	1	2	3	4
42.	Has this person experienced a relatively recent change in eating habits?	Yes		No		
43.	Does the person have behavior problems at times other than bedtime or upon awakening?	Yes		No		
44.	When did this person's primary difficulty with sleep begin?					

In *Optimistic Parenting: Hope and Help for You and Your Challenging Child* by V. Mark Durand (2011, Paul H. Brookes Publishing Co.)

45.	What was happening in this person's life at that time or a few months before?		
46.	Is this person under a physician's care for any medical condition? (If yes, indicate condition below.)	Yes	No
Other comments:			

In *Optimistic Parenting: Hope and Help for You and Your Challenging Child* by V. Mark Durand (2011, Paul H. Brookes Publishing Co.)

SLEEP DIARY

Day	Date	Midnight	2:00	4:00	6:00	8:00	10:00	Noon	2:00	4:00	6:00	8:00	10:00	Midnight
				A.M.						P.M.				
Mon.														
Tues.														
Wed.														
Thurs.														
Fri.														
Sat.														
Sun.														
Mon.														
Tues.														
Wed.														
Thurs.														
Fri.														
Sat.														
Sun.														

Sleep Intervention Questionnaire (SIQ)

Disruption Tolerance

1. Does your child misbehave at bedtime or when waking up at night in a way that is too serious or upsetting to ignore?

   Yes   No

2. Would it be difficult or impossible for you to listen to your child being upset for long periods of time (more than a few minutes)?

   Yes   No

3. Do you find it too difficult to put your child back in bed once he or she gets up?

   Yes   No

Scoring: If you answer *yes* to one or more of these questions, you may not be a good candidate for using *graduated extinction* as an intervention for your child's sleep problems.

Schedule Tolerance

4. Are you or another member of your family willing to stay up later at night to put a sleep plan into action?

   Yes   No

5. Are you or another member of your family willing to get up earlier in the morning to put a sleep plan into action?

   Yes   No

Scoring: If you answer *no* to one or more of these questions, you may not be good candidates for *scheduled awakenings* or *sleep restriction* as interventions for your child's sleep problems.

Attitudinal Barriers

6. Do you feel emotionally unable to deal directly with your child's sleep problem?

   Yes   No

7. Do you feel guilty making your child go to bed (or go back to bed) when he or she does not want to?

   Yes   No

8. Do you think it would be emotionally damaging to your child if you tried to change the way he or she slept?

   Yes   No

Scoring: If you answer *yes* to one or more of these questions, you may benefit from cognitive-behavioral intervention to explore your attitudes about your ability to improve sleep.

Permission to reprint the Sleep Intervention Questionnaire on page 137 from "When children don't sleep well: Interventions for paediatric sleep disorders, therapist guide" by Durand VM (2008) by permission of Oxford University Press, Inc. Further reproduction prohibited without permission from the original publisher.

In *Optimistic Parenting: Hope and Help for You and Your Challenging Child* by V. Mark Durand
(2011, Paul H. Brookes Publishing Co.)

Additional Resources

SECTION I: HOPE

Chapter 1: Optimistic Parenting

Durand, V.M., & Hieneman, M. (2008). *Helping parents with challenging children: Positive family intervention, Facilitator's guide.* New York: Oxford University Press.

Durand, V.M., & Hieneman, M. (2008). *Helping parents with challenging children: Positive family intervention, Workbook.* New York: Oxford University Press.

Chapter 2: Confident Parenting

Seligman, M. (2006). *Learned optimism: How to change your mind and your life.* New York: Pocket Books.

Chapter 3: Insight into Your Thoughts and Feelings

Gigerenzer, G. (2007). *Gut feelings: The intelligence of the unconscious.* New York: Viking.

Seligman, M. (2006). *Learned optimism: How to change your mind and your life.* New York: Pocket Books.

Chapter 4: Changing the Way You Think

Janney, R., & Snell, M. (2006). *Social relationships and peer support* (2nd ed.). Baltimore: Paul H. Brookes Publishing Co.

Seligman, M. (2006). *Learned optimism: How to change your mind and your life.* New York: Pocket Books.

Chapter 5: How to Become a Happier Parent

Csikszentmihalyi, M. (1990). *Flow: The psychology of optimal performance.* New York: Cambridge University Press.

Emmons, R., & McCullough, M. (2004). *The psychology of gratitude.* New York: Oxford University Press.

Kabat-Zinn, J. (1994). *Wherever you go, there you are: Mindfulness meditation in everyday life.* New York: Hyperion Books.

Seligman, M.E.P. (2002). *Authentic happiness: Using the new positive psychology to realize your potential for lasting fulfillment.* New York: Free Press.

SECTION II: HELP

Chapter 6: A Close Look at Your Child's Behavior

Durand, V.M. (1990). *Severe behavior problems: A functional communication training approach.* New York: Guilford Press.

Durand, V.M., & Crimmins, D.B. (1992). *The Motivation Assessment Scale (MAS) administration guide.* Topeka, KS: Monaco and Associates.

Chapter 7: Emergency Strategies

Hieneman, M., Childs, K., & Sergay, J. (2006). *Parenting with positive behavior support: A practical guide to resolving your child's difficult behavior.* Baltimore: Paul H. Brookes Publishing Co.

Chapter 8: Managing Consequences

Hieneman, M., Childs, K., & Sergay, J. (2006). *Parenting with positive behavior support: A practical guide to resolving your child's difficult behavior.* Baltimore: Paul H. Brookes Publishing Co.

Chapter 9:
Replacing Behavior Problems

Carr, E.G., Levin, L., McConnachie, G., Carlson, J.I., Kemp, D.C., & Smith, C.E. (1994). *Communication-based intervention for problem behavior: A user's guide for producing positive change.* Baltimore: Paul H Brookes Publishing Co.

Durand, V.M. (1990). *Severe behavior problems: A functional communication training approach.* New York: Guilford Press.

Sigafoos, J., Arthur-Kelly, M., & Butterfield, N. (2006). *Enhancing everyday communication for children with disabilities.* Baltimore: Paul H. Brookes Publishing Co.

SECTION III: SPECIAL TOPICS

Chapter 10: Transitions

Cohen, M., & Sloan, D. (2007). *Visual supports for people with autism: A guide for parents and professionals.* Bethesda, MD: Woodbine House.

McClannahan, L., & Krantz, P. (2010). *Activity schedules for children with autism* (2nd ed.). Bethesda, MD: Woodbine House.

Chapter 11: Sleep Problems

Durand, V.M. (1998). *Sleep better! A guide to improving sleep for children with special needs.* Baltimore: Paul H. Brookes Publishing Co.

Durand, V.M. (2008). *When children don't sleep well: Interventions for pediatric sleep disorders, Therapist guide.* New York: Oxford University Press.

Durand, V.M. (2008). *When children don't sleep well: Interventions for pediatric sleep disorders, Workbook.* New York: Oxford University Press.

Index

Page numbers followed by *t* and *f* indicate tables and figures, respectively.